INDIAN METROPOLIS

JAMES B. LAGRAND

# Indian Metropolis

*Native Americans
in Chicago,
1945–75*

UNIVERSITY OF ILLINOIS PRESS

URBANA AND CHICAGO

Library of Congress Cataloging-in-Publication Data
LaGrand, James B., 1968–
Indian metropolis : Native Americans in Chicago, 1945–75
/ James B. LaGrand.
p.   cm.
Includes bibliographical references and index.
ISBN 0-252-02772-8 (cloth : alk. paper)
1. Indians of North America—Urban residence—Illinois—
Chicago. 2. Chicago (Ill.)—Social conditions—20th century.
I. Title.
E98.U72L34    2002
305.897'077311'09045—dc21        2002003959

*For Betsy*

# Contents

*Illustrations follow page 44*

# Acknowledgments

A number of people have given generously of their time and efforts in assisting the writing of this book.

I would like above all to thank the members of the Indian community in Chicago who kindly agreed to be interviewed and who shared their knowledge and memories with me. In the course of my research, I spent many days at several community organizations. Samson Kehana and Ronald Bowan at the American Indian Center and Fr. Peter John Powell at St. Augustine's Center for the American Indian were very helpful and forthcoming.

I have had the pleasure of working with a number of librarians and archivists who expressed interest in this study and assisted in tracking down materials. David Beck at NAES College, Archie Moteley at the Chicago Historical Society, Harvey Markowitz at the D'Arcy McNickle Center for the American Indian, Scott Forsythe at the Great Lakes branch of the National Archives in Chicago, Ann Cummings at the National Archives in Washington, D.C., Nancy Lurie at the Milwaukee Public Museum, Stan Larson at the University of Utah's J. Williard Marriott Library, and James Harwood at the National Anthropological Archives all went above and beyond the call of duty.

I was also blessed in the course of my research in Chicago to enjoy the selfless hospitality of the Franz family. Jean, John, and the late Henry Franz asked questions about my work, took messages, introduced me to some of Chicago's finest food, and in general made conducting research enjoyable. I remain ever-grateful to them. The VanderMeer family and Claire VandePolder were also gracious hosts during sometimes-extended research trips.

Messiah College granted me a scholarship grant and reduced teaching load, which helped in completing this book.

Several people have provided helpful readings of all or parts of this book. John Bodnar and Michael McGerr at Indiana University helped me as I worked to bring twentieth-century American Indian history and U.S. social and political history into one coherent narrative. In thanking R. David Edmunds, I echo many students and colleagues who have found him to be a loyal friend and conscientious critic. This book has benefited from his counsel and careful readings in countless ways. Those studying twentieth-century American Indian history enjoy some of the most helpful and generous colleagues in the historical profession. Peter Iverson, Donald Parman, Donald Fixico, and Frederick Hoxie all took an interest in this project—even in its earliest, most inchoate stages—and consistently offered encouragement, advice, and critical readings. John LaGrand gave the manuscript a thorough reading at its completion, and Liz Dulany guided the book through the production process.

Despite the vast amount of intellectual assistance I have received while working on this book, it would not have been possible without my family's support. Jacob and Margaret, in arriving near the book's completion, encouraged me to finish it. Finally, words are not sufficient to express my gratitude to my wife, Betsy. She walked beside me along the road, picked me up when I fell, and rejoiced with me at the end of the journey.

# *Abbreviations*

| | |
|---|---|
| MC | Manuscript Collections |
| ML | J. Williard Marriott Library, University of Utah, Salt Lake City |
| MPM | Milwaukee Public Museum |
| MRLC | Municipal Reference Library of Chicago |
| NA-GLR | National Archives–Great Lakes Region, Chicago |
| NA-WDC | National Archives–Washington, D.C. |
| NAA | National Anthropological Archives, Smithsonian Institution, Washington, D.C. |
| NAC | Native American Committee, Chicago |
| NAES | Native American Educational Services College, Chicago |
| NCAI | National Congress of American Indians |
| NCIO | National Council on Indian Opportunity |
| NIYC | National Indian Youth Council |
| NL | Newberry Library, Chicago |
| NR | Narrative Reports, Field Placement and Relocation Office Employment Assistance Records, Record Group 75, National Archives |
| OEO | Office of Equal Opportunity |
| PSR | Placement and Statistical Reports, Field Placement and Relocation Office Employment Assistance Records, Record Group 75, National Archives |
| REA | Reports on Employment Assistance, Chicago Field Employment Assistance Office, Record Group 75, National Archives |
| RG | Record Group |
| SC | Special Collections |
| SHSW | State Historical Society of Wisconsin, Madison |
| SI | Smithsonian Institution, Washington, D.C. |
| UIDA | Urban Indian Development Association |
| URC | Urban Records Collection, Community Archives, Native American Services College, Chicago |
| UU | University of Utah, Salt Lake City |
| WCMC | Welfare Council of Metropolitan Chicago |
| YTO | Young Tribal Organization |

INDIAN METROPOLIS

# Introduction:
# Who Are Urban Indians?

Early summer in Chicago's Uptown neighborhood is powwow season. At local parks scattered around this area about eight miles north of the Loop some of the city's American Indian residents and others from as far away as Oklahoma, Montana, and Arizona gather to dance, eat, visit, and catch up on news from other parts of Indian Country. The "powwow circuit" is a regular and important part of many Indian people's lives, and before the larger and more celebrated gatherings of late summer draw people to the West, Chicago takes its turn hosting both Indians from many different tribes and interested non-Indians.

Responding to the frequent presence of whites and other non-Indians at powwows, emcees often serve an educational function by sprinkling their monologues with bits of Indian history and culture. At a powwow held over a cool June weekend in Chicago, a Blackfoot man served as emcee. He not only directed dancers and kept the crowd entertained with jokes but also talked at various times about what it meant to dance, sing, pray, and think "in the Indian way." Of course, none of the Indian people in attendance needed to be told that Sioux dances differed from those of the Winnebagos or to be informed of many other differences in tribal cultural traditions. Likewise, the Blackfoot man himself recognized the differences between his own tribesmen and Native Americans from other tribes. Yet his statements about how Indian people—from whatever tribe—conduct themselves at powwows or live their lives in general obviously meant something to his Indian listeners, his non-Indian listeners, and himself. He hoped in part to convince whites who were listening of the beauty and wisdom of the "Indian way of life." The ideas represented by the word *Indian* took on positive and inviting connotations.[1]

About that same time, and on the other side of Chicago, a young Choctaw man commented on Indian political activism. In part because many of his friends and family members live in Minneapolis, he was familiar with the American Indian Movement (AIM), which had formed there in the summer of 1968 and developed into what many view as the most important radical political group for Native Americans in the late 1960s and early 1970s. In the Choctaw man's current home, Chicago, however, AIM had not built as much strength. As a result, few Indian people in Chicago had become involved with the group in any sort of formal capacity. Responding to what he considered a naïve question about whether, given the chance, he would have joined AIM, he stated matter-of-factly, "Sure, I'm still an Indian, aren't I?" For him, being militant in some way and "being Indian" went hand in hand. He thought it obvious that an Indian man of his age would at least strongly consider joining AIM. After all, membership was the way in which many of his generation defined themselves as Indians, especially in the midst of a predominantly non-Indian society. To suggest that he might not be interested in militant causes was to challenge his identity as an Indian. The young Choctaw man apparently used the term *Indian* to mark distance from the broader, non-Indian society in which he lived—and perhaps from his non-Indian interviewer.[2]

These anecdotes appear to express very different meanings of "Indianness" or what it means to be an Indian. One is open and embracing, and the other is restrictive and contentious. Both, however, are contingent on urban life and the experience of living side by side with non-Indians in a modern American metropolis. Beyond their superficial differences, these accounts demonstrate the important and symbiotic relationship between Indian urbanization and concepts of Indian identity. They point to important connections between urban life and what "being Indian" has meant to Native Americans since the 1950s. The shift from a strictly tribal identity to one focused on a larger, more diverse group of Indians (often called "pan-Indianism" or "pan-tribalism") and political activism are only two among many.

This suggestion borrows from and builds on a theme that is popular in many studies in American Indian history. Since the 1980s, numerous scholars have discussed how Indian people have thought about and constructed identities in response to experiences with foreign people and institutions. Examples of such experiences include first contacts with Europeans, the introduction of the horse and rifle, the influence of trading patterns and a market economy, and the development of reservations. Many Indian people initially viewed these developments as novel and even strange, but eventually they adopted them in some form as a part of their culture and identity. In recognizing and studying these processes of cultural change, a generation of historians has overthrown the older scholarly model that often portrayed Indians and their cultures as static and frozen in time. Most historians who study American Indians now acknowledge important changes in the lives of their subjects, and they are examining how these changes have shaped Indian notions of identity.[3]

The greatest part of the attention to changing notions of Indian identity has focused on the colonial era and nineteenth century. In addition, it is apparent that in the twentieth century cattle ranching shaped the self-identity of Indians who took it up on reservations and in other rural areas.[4] But what of those Indians in the twentieth century who have not lived on reservations or in rural areas? The question remains, What sorts of experiences have shaped them and their notions of identity?

This is no idle question, given the demography of American Indians in the twentieth century. Although popular culture portrays warriors roaming the Plains in search of buffalo or enemy war parties and would have us believe that Indians are both frozen in the past and exclusively rural, the reality is otherwise. Since the late 1970s, more than half of all American Indians have lived in urban areas. Moreover, their transformation from a completely rural people to one with a large urban component occurred with remarkable quickness. In 1940, roughly one-half of all whites and blacks were urban-dwellers, whereas fewer than one-tenth of Indians lived in cities. By 1980, 71 percent of whites lived in cities, as did 85 percent of blacks. The percentage of American Indians who lived in urban areas, however, increased even faster—it jumped from about one-tenth to more than one-half in just forty years. In 1980, 53 percent of all Indian people lived in cities. Almost every racial and ethnic group in the United States has become more urbanized since World War II, but none as quickly and dramatically as American Indians.[5]

This study looks at American Indians in Chicago from 1945 to 1975, during part of this period of remarkable demographic growth. According to census reports, Chicago's American Indian population grew from 274 in 1940 to 775 in 1950, then to 3,394 in 1960, and to 6,575 in 1970—more than a twentyfold increase.[6] This book tells the story of how and why people like the Blackfoot powwow emcee, the militant young Choctaw, and thousands of other Indian people came to Chicago. It examines what factors influenced their migration, why some stayed in their new urban home while others soon returned to the reservation, and what sort of Indian community was built in Chicago. It also addresses how their lives and those of other Indians changed as a result of migration. Because numbers and statistics alone reveal relatively little about the human side of the urbanization process, I will attempt to determine what the phenomenon meant for those who migrated, for those who stayed on reservations, for cities like Chicago, and for the nation.

---

Both the broad and narrow context of this study have received relatively little attention. Vine Deloria, Jr., Frederick E. Hoxie, Donald L. Parman, and others have noted the need for more studies of twentieth-century Indian history in all its facets, and, if anything, histories of urban Indians in the twentieth century are even scarcer.[7] The sizable number of Native Americans who have made their homes in cities since the 1950s have not received the kind of scholarly historical attention that their nineteenth-century, reservation-dwelling, forebears have.[8] To some extent, academic disciplinary differences help explain this phenomenon. Geographers, anthropologists, sociologists, and other social scientists—many of them interested in discussing and explaining contemporary events—have been more alert than historians to Indian urbanization. During the late 1960s and early 1970s, anthropologists and sociologists at various universities in the West studied urban Indians. Researchers at UCLA, Washington State University, Brigham Young University, and the University of Colorado undertook projects on Native Americans in Los Angeles, San Francisco, Seattle, and Denver. The pathbreaking papers and journal articles that resulted provided a wealth of data and raw material; many publications included tables of social-scientific data. From a historian's perspective, however, the studies that emerged from various social sciences were somewhat dissatisfying. They frequently focused on contemporary events and only sketchily examined how urban Indians came to their contemporary situations. Furthermore, several common perspectives soon emerged in this literature that were stimulating and useful for furthering discussion but failed to capture urban Indians and their experiences in all the complexity they deserved.[9]

One group of anthropologists and sociologists viewed urban Indians as downtrodden proletarians in a "world" or "national" system. Emphasizing the dire economic problems that many Indian people have faced, this interpretation saw what anthropologist Joseph Jorgensen calls "the metropolis" or the world capitalist system inexorably and completely crushing all Indian people it encountered. An emphasis on large-scale forces and structures resulted in the conviction that individual Indians had played little or no part in determining what happened to them. Anthropologist Jeanne Guillemin even expressed disdain for other scholarly models that devoted what she thought to be excessive attention to the thoughts and actions of individual Indian people. Clearly, this approach left little room for individual agency, because large-scale economic forces were bound to overwhelm urban Indians. Furthermore, the position tended to be ahistorical and saw little difference in Indians' experiences with a supposedly uniform monolith of world capitalism, whether in the 1860s, 1920s, or 1960s.[10]

A second group of scholars of the 1960s and 1970s resembled the first group, but on a smaller scale. They considered urban Indians as anachronisms who inevitably assimilated to the ways of white America. Whereas Jorgensen maintained that the world political economy overpowered Indian people, those in the second group argued, either implicitly or explicitly, that the cities where Indian people lived overpowered them culturally, forcing them to conform to local value systems. Some of the especially enthusiastic adherents of this perspective asserted that Indians moved to cities for final validation of a long-running process of acculturation. Other aspects of urban migration and urban experiences that fell outside the boundaries of the assimilation process went largely unstudied in this approach. Instead, scholars in this camp made widespread use of social-science methodologies to determine precisely, they contended, the levels of acculturation or assimilation that various groups of urban Indians had reached. Ultimately, the assumption that Native Americans of all tribes and from all different backgrounds would eventually acculturate and assimilate in a steady, linear fashion was behind much of this research.[11]

A third group viewed urban Indians primarily through the organizations they formed in cities such as Chicago, Phoenix, and Los Angeles. For this group, urban Indians played an organizational role. Such an approach was attractive, in part because of its convenience. Scholars have sometimes found it difficult to study urban Indian communities. Accounts abound of scholarly inability to make contacts among, and gain the confidence of, Indian people. The community centers or organizations that have developed in most urban centers of American Indian population, however, provide scholars with opportunities for making contacts and observing activities. If an organization has documents concerning its history, so much the better.

Several scholars have followed this approach and provided careful, useful information about urban Indian institutions. Some investigated the phenomenon of institution-building on a broad scale and have constructed a detailed hierarchy of the urban Indian groups that appeared to develop chronologically. This third approach to the study of urban Indians, however, has caused some to misjudge the degree to which urban Indian institutions represent the population as a whole. In many cases, only a small minority of urban Indians had contact with such groups, a fact some scholars candidly acknowledge but others avoid. Joan Weibel-Orlando, in a study of the Indian community in Los Angeles during the twentieth century, recognizes that no more than one in five of all Indians in the Los Angeles area participated in established organizations. Nevertheless, she focuses on them, in part to counter and offset the work of scholars intent on proving assimilation and loss of identity by Indian people. Weibel-Orlando's goal is to "demonstrate the work of ethnic community maintenance, not its dissolution." She is admirably forthright about the choices she made in deciding on subjects and themes and includes several interesting and revealing descriptions of various Indian organizations. Yet even this, the best example of the institutional or organizational approach for studying urban Indians, does not provide a full picture of their lives.[12]

Finally, a fourth group of scholars has written about urban Indians in the 1970s and starkly contrasted "traditional" Indian life with contemporary industrial life, discussing urban Indians primarily as foils to modern Americans. Widespread disgust over perceived narcissism and materialism in the general culture, as well as general opposition to how Indian people have been treated in the United States, yield a stark, sometimes moralistic, dichotomy between "Indian culture" and "mainstream American culture." Sol Tax, a professor of anthropology at the University of Chicago and a long-time friend to many Indians in Chicago, followed that approach and contrasted Indians' "sharing cultures" with urban America's "large, economically oriented, individualized, impersonal, urbanizing society," placing the two groups at opposite ends of a continuum. Despite paying valid attention to the unique aspects of various Native American cultures, this fourth approach fails to consider the Indian people who live in cities—or elsewhere—on their own terms. Instead, Indians play the role of "peaceful conscientious resisters and exemplars" to a mass of urban white Americans.[13] This updated version of the "noble savage" idea, which depicts urban Indians more as foils to white Americans than as legitimate historical actors in their own right, too often resembles the "simplistic melodrama" type of historical script that Frederick Hoxie and other historians have criticized.[14]

Although social-science models for studying urban Indians have proved somewhat unsatisfactory, historians at times have not done much better. Those who have studied American Indians living during the latter half of the twentieth century most often have focused on two major policies of the federal government's Bureau of Indian Affairs (BIA) during that period: termination and relocation. Monographs by Larry W. Burt, Donald L. Fixico, and Laurence M. Hauptman feature these policies to one degree or another, and others have discussed them in articles and dissertations.[15] Repeatedly, scholars have seen the two policies as inseparable twin manifestations of a century-old emphasis on Indian assimilation. There are some good reasons to follow this approach. Federal Indian policy had significant effects on Indian people for decades and has gone through periods when it aimed at consistent goals, especially assimilation.[16] It is necessary, however, to understand the urban migration of Indian people as something more than an outgrowth of BIA policies. The movement of thousands of Indian people to urban areas in the latter half of the twentieth century is most often considered to be a predictable outcome of policy.

A number of articles published during the 1980s and 1990s began to criticize the exclusively policy-focused nature of twentieth-century American Indian history, arguing that it presented an incomplete picture and failed to do justice to the myriad experiences of Indian people.[17] That valuable and instructive literature has helped set the stage for histories of those Indian people who live in cities—work that goes beyond an exclusive focus on policy. This statement should be made with modesty and caution, however, for it is surely not the first time such a sentiment has been expressed. The task of trying to avoid policy history has proven to be a popular but difficult undertaking that is boasted about more often than accomplished.

Many studies have begun by boldly opposing policy history but have stumbled into it eventually. They have taken different routes toward this common end point. Some have successfully avoided making Indian policy their central concern yet have used government sources to move the story forward. Congressional reports and Senate committees, in such instances, drive the narrative. If not policy history per se, it is certainly policy-driven history.

Other studies appear concerned primarily with the way in which policymakers have been seen and focus on their shortcomings in order to counteract an earlier, lenient approach to government officials. In the process, the studies have confused an emphasis on policy with a positive assessment of Indian policy. Yet bitter attacks on Indian policy are no less closely focused on policy than are fawning portraits.

Finally, some scholars—again asserting their boldness and independence from what they view as old-fashioned policy history—have avoided focusing entirely on white politicians and policymakers. Although they have successfully paid more attention to Indian figures, they view them as political actors only. The Indians play the roles of testifiers before Congress and "legal warriors" who move the forum for Indian-white conflict from the battlefield to the courts.

Twentieth-century Indian history and the history of Indian urbanization during the latter part of the twentieth century deserve more than social science–driven models or accounts of the government policies directed at Indian people. They deserve a full and complete history. Yet in critiquing policy history, I do not mean to advocate looking at an Indian community only "from the inside." This study is not purely ethnography or even ethnohistory as those terms are usually defined. Rather, it is positioned between historical studies that view twentieth-century Indian people as products of government policy and anthropological studies that sometimes neglect to examine the effects of important social, political, and economic trends on Indian people. Indians who lived in Chicago during the latter half of the twentieth century—and many other Indian people during this time as well—did not live in an environment absent of outside influences. Rather, they were profoundly influenced by their urban environment in many ways, as they were by their home reservations and age-old tribal customs and practices. This study attempts to account for the many different structures and forces that impinged on their lives. Federal policies fall into this category, as do social, political, economic, and cultural matters. Everything—from laborers to stories— flowed back and forth between Chicago and reservation communities and affected both.[18]

This study, then, endeavors to be a social history of Indian people in Chicago. It uses the techniques and perspectives of social history, which have come only recently and infrequently to twentieth-century American Indian history. It follows other social histories in making use of a variety of sources—both quantitative sources such as census reports and qualitative sources such as Indian newsletters and oral histories.[19]

This type of social-history approach—which gives careful attention to both urban Indians in the twentieth century and the broader environments in which they lived—is still relatively uncommon in the scholarly literature. In general, Indians who live in cities play cameo roles in discussions of Indian policy. According to these brief asides, many Indians were forced into cities during the 1950s. There, they invariably suffered from alcoholism, homelessness, and unemployment. Their story is short and simple—they lived miserably ever after. According to one such account, "Many of those who left for jobs in the cities ended up in slums, victimized, and unemployed."[20] The simple, uniform nature of this basic narrative is repeated frequently and is remarkable, either on its own terms or compared with other historical literature. Thousands of American Indians have lived in cities for decades, yet their experiences have often been lumped into one basic account. At best, they have been sorted into a handful of rigid categories. The complexity of urban Indian life, and the different types of lives Indians built for themselves, has been little explored. It seems implausible that a vast, multifaceted demographic phenomenon could be so quickly and neatly summarized.

An examination of historical scholarship beyond American Indian history also suggests that urban Indians have been shortchanged. Perhaps the most obvious examples are in the scholarly literature on other migrants and immigrants to American cities. No one, for example, would discuss nineteenth-century immigrants from Italy or Ireland and assert that an unknown number had moved from the countryside to American cities and were, judging from a handful of accounts, doing poorly there. Scholars have examined European emigration to America with great care. They have used both qualitative and quantitative sources to provide detailed, precise information on migration networks, families, labor and economic mobility, churches, social organizations, housing and residential patterns, politics, and many other topics. In the process, many immigration historians have noted important connections between economics and society. They have shown, for example, that industrialization frequently influenced not only the work life of European immigrants but also their family life.[21]

Much of the work in immigration history has come from a social-history perspective and thus speaks to this study of American Indians in Chicago in a number of ways. One concerns how Europeans reacted to and experienced the pull of jobs in U.S. cities. At one time, immigration historians emphasized the role of labor agents (called *padrones* among Italians) and viewed their claims and pleas as the primary reasons that Europeans immigrated to America. Since the 1970s, however, historians have tempered that emphasis through recognition that those who immigrated often had personal motivations for doing so, economic and otherwise, which mixed in varying proportions with the actions of labor agents. Similarly, to see BIA officials as the sole reasons that Indian people relocated and took jobs in urban areas is inaccurate. Like earlier immigrants to American cities, Indians possessed their own motivations, and those sometimes coincided and sometimes clashed with BIA policies.

A second way in which immigration and ethnic history informs and benefits American Indian urban history is through its descriptions of the formation of ethnic groups. Repeatedly, historians have demonstrated how the regional identities (for example, Sicilian) that were strongest in the homeland and early in the place of immigration slowly transformed into national identities (for example, Italians or Italian Americans). In a similar fashion, many Sioux, Chippewa, and members of other tribes—including the Blackfoot man presiding over the powwow—began to think of themselves as Indians in specific contexts and situations during the twentieth century.

Scholarship abounds on the experiences of immigrants in American cities, and studies are often detailed, discussing the experiences of one ethnic group in one city. Chicago's significant American Indian population, however, has never received full treatment, although a wealth of literature exists on almost every other ethnic or racial group in that city. Monographs have been written on the city's Irish, Italians, Poles, Germans, Swedes, Norwegians, Mexicans, and Puerto Ricans, among others.[22] These case studies have brought the many concerns of immigration history to bear on particular situations. In addition, several monographs exist on African Americans in Chicago and their migration there. One of the first was St. Clair Drake and Horace R. Cayton's *Black Metropolis.* That classic sociological study, first published in 1945, examines the South Side ghetto or "Black Belt" and how it developed. Other studies have focused on labor and economics, politics, or race relations and racial violence.[23] Many of these case studies, although examining small-scale matters, have also contributed to knowledge of larger issues. James R. Grossman, for example, has suggested that blacks who migrated to Chicago during the early part of the twentieth century changed their definition of full citizenship and independence from rural homesteading to urban industrial employment.[24]

American Indian history could profitably follow the lead of case studies in African American and immigration history. The authors of such works have recognized that abstract discussion of urbanization or migration becomes vague and unproductive. In addition to providing accuracy and specificity, case studies of Indian urbanization might permit the comparative study of migration and urbanization patterns by drawing specifically on immigration and African American history and noting similarities as well as differences among various migration streams.[25] Every urban area to which Native Americans migrated during the twentieth century had its own particular economic, political, and social structures. Future study may help account for those differences. Besides Chicago, numerous other cities have had significant American Indian populations that warrant monograph-length case studies.[26]

---

In the pages that follow, the thousands of American Indians who lived in Chicago during the latter half of the twentieth century will be discussed, and the connections they have made between their urban life and their Indian identity will be explored. Although historians of twentieth-century American Indians have not studied notions of identity to the extent that their colleagues in colonial history have, some work has begun. William T. Hagan, a historian, has noted several influences on twentieth-century Indian identity, including intermarriage, blood quantum, pan-Indianism, termination, the actions of unrecognized tribes, political activism, and changing public opinion.[27] It will be seen that Indian urbanization provides an umbrella concept that encompasses many of those elements; consequently, it plays an important role in shaping twentieth-century Indian experiences.

During the three decades between 1945 and 1975, Chicago became an Indian metropolis as its Native American population increased from roughly five hundred to ten thousand. Chicago Indians' ideas about identity changed profoundly during this period. A pan-Indian movement composed of members of many tribes developed in Chicago during the latter half of the twentieth century. Members of tribes that had sometimes considered each other foes began to focus on shared experiences and challenges. They also began to think of themselves as sharing a common Indian identity. An Oneida man in Chicago provided one of many examples of this phenomenon. After recounting age-old tribal rivalries, he succinctly explained his experiences with members of other tribes: "When we get to the city we begin to think of ourselves more as Indians. Here, we all stick together."[28] As Chicago developed into an Indian metropolis during the latter half of the twentieth century, its Native American residents became metropolitan Indians, changed by city life in important ways.

## Notes

1. Fieldwork notes, 10 June 1995.
2. Author interview with Josephine Willie and son (Choctaw), Chicago, 14 June 1995.

3. R. David Edmunds, "On Being Indian: Cultural Change in Historical Perspective," unpublished ms. in author's possession; Loretta Fowler, *Arapahoe Politics, 1851–1978: Symbols in Crises of Authority* (Lincoln: University of Nebraska Press, 1982); Loretta Fowler, *Shared Symbols, Contested Meanings: Gros Ventre Culture and History, 1778–1984* (Ithaca: Cornell University Press, 1987); Michael D. Green, *The Politics of Indian Removal: Creek Government and Society in Crisis* (Lincoln: University of Nebraska Press, 1982); Frederick E. Hoxie, "From Prison to Homeland: The Cheyenne River Indian Reservation before World War I," *South Dakota History* 9 (Winter 1979): 1–24; Frederick E. Hoxie, *Parading through History: The Making of the Crow Nation in America, 1805–1935* (New York: Cambridge University Press, 1995); Peter Iverson, *"We Are Still Here": American Indians in the Twentieth Century* (Arlington Heights: Harlan Davidson, 1998); Daniel H. Usner, Jr., *Indians, Settlers, and Slaves in a Frontier Exchange Economy: The Lower Mississippi Valley before 1783* (Chapel Hill: University of North Carolina Press, 1992); Richard White, *Roots of Dependency: Subsistence, Environment, and Social Change among the Choctaws, Pawnees, and Navajos* (Lincoln: University of Nebraska Press, 1983); Richard White, *The Middle Ground: Indians, Empires, and Republics in the Great Lakes Region, 1650–1815* (New York: Cambridge University Press, 1991).

4. Peter Iverson, *When Indians Became Cowboys: Native Peoples and Cattle Ranching in the American West* (Norman: University of Oklahoma Press, 1994).

5. Russell Thornton, "Patterns and Processes of American Indians in Cities and Towns: The National Scene," in *Urban Indians: Proceedings of the Third Annual Conference on Problems and Issues Concerning American Indians Today* (Chicago: Newberry Library, 1981), 26; Nancy Shoemaker, *American Indian Population Recovery in the Twentieth Century* (Albuquerque: University of New Mexico Press, 1999), 77.

6. Elaine M. Neils, *Reservation to City: Indian Migration and Federal Relocation* (Chicago: University of Chicago Department of Geography, 1971). Statistics for the exact size of Chicago's twentieth-century American Indian population are notoriously inaccurate and should be considered approximate estimates.

7. Expressions of this need can be seen in Vine Deloria, Jr., "The Twentieth Century," in *Red Men and Hat Wearers: Viewpoints in Indian History*, ed. Daniel Tyler (Boulder: Pruett Publishing, 1976), 155; Hoxie, *Parading through History*, 1; Donald L. Parman, "Indians of the Modern West," in *The Twentieth-Century West: Historical Interpretations*, ed. Gerald D. Nash and Richard W. Etulain (Albuquerque: University of New Mexico Press, 1989), 165.

8. This scholarly neglect may be ending. Among more recent work, see Terry Straus and Grant P. Arndt, eds., *Native Chicago* (Chicago: Native Chicago, 1998); Susan Lobo and Kurt Peters, eds., *American Indians and the Urban Experience* (Lanham, Md.: Rowman and Littlefield, 2000); and Donald L. Fixico, *The Urban Indian Experience in America* (Albuquerque: University of New Mexico Press, 2000).

9. Päivi Hoikkala also notes the shortcomings of social-science studies of Indian urbanization. See Hoikkala, "Feminists or Reformers? American Indian Women and Community in Phoenix, 1965–1980," in *American Indians and the Urban Experience*, ed. Lobo and Peters, 127–45.

10. Joseph G. Jorgensen, "Indians and the Metropolis," in *The American Indian in Urban Society*, ed. Jack O. Waddell and O. Michael Watson (Boston: Little, Brown, 1971), 67–111; Hugh Brody, *Indians on Skid Row* (Ottawa: Department of Indian Affairs and Northern Development, 1971); Jeanne E. Guillemin, *Urban Renegades: The Cultural Strategy of American Indians* (New York: Columbia University Press, 1975).

11. Harry W. Martin, "Correlates of Adjustment among American Indians in an Urban Environment," *Human Organization* 23 (Winter 1964): 290–95; Theodore D. Graves and Minor Van Arsdale, "Values, Expectations, and Relocation: The Navaho Migrant in Denver," *Human Organization* 25 (Winter 1966): 300–307; John A. Price, "The Migration and Adaptation of American Indians to Los Angeles," *Human Organization* 27 (Summer 1968): 169–75; Lynn C. White and Bruce A. Chadwick, "Urban Residence, Assimilation, and Identity of the Spokane Indian," in *Native Americans Today: Sociological Perspectives*, ed. Howard M. Bahr, Bruce A. Chadwick, and Robert C. Day (New York: Harper and Row, 1972), 239–49.

12. Merwyn S. Garbarino, "The Chicago American Indian Center: Two Decades," in *American Indian Urbanization*, ed. Jack O. Waddell and O. Michael Watson (West Lafayette: Institute for the Study of Social Change, 1973), 74–89; John A. Price, "U.S. and Canadian Urban Ethnic Institutions," *Urban Anthropology* 4 (1975): 35–52; John A. Price, "The Development of Urban Ethnic Institutions by U.S. and Canadian Indians," *Ethnic Groups* 1 (1976): 107–31; Janusz Mucha, "From Prairie to the City: Transformation of Chicago's American Indian Community," *Urban Anthropology* 12 (Fall 1983): 337–71; Edward D. Liebow, "Urban Indian Institutions in Phoenix: Transformation from Headquarters City to Community," *Journal of Ethnic Studies* 18 (Winter 1991): 1–27; Joan Weibel-Orlando, *Indian Country, L.A.: Maintaining Ethnic Community in Complex Society* (Urbana: University of Illinois Press, 1991), quote from 69; Joan Weibel-Orlando, "And the Drumbeat Still Goes On . . . Urban Indian Institutional Survival into the New Millennium," in *American Indians and the Urban Experience*, ed. Lobo and Peters, 95–113.

13. Sol Tax, "The Impact of Urbanization on American Indians," *Annals of the American Academy of Political and Social Sciences* 436 (March 1978): 121–35; Guillemin, *Urban Renegades*. Although taking the perspective of the artist rather than the social scientist, a number of American Indian authors have also emphasized the harshness and alienating difficulties of urban life for Indian people. See N. Scott Momaday, *House Made of Dawn* (New York: Harper and Row, 1968), and Leslie Marman Silko, *Ceremony* (New York: New American Library, 1977).

14. Hoxie, *Parading through History*, 3; George Miles, "To Hear an Old Voice: Rediscovering Native Americans in American History," in *Under an*

*Open Sky: Rethinking America's Western Past*, ed. William Cronon, George Miles, and Jay Gitlin (New York: Norton, 1992), 55.

15. Examples of scholarship on twentieth-century American Indian history that focuses on Indian policy include Larry W. Burt, "Roots of the Native American Urban Experience: Relocation Policy in the 1950s," *American Indian Quarterly* 10 (Spring 1986): 85–99; Larry W. Burt, *Tribalism in Crisis: Federal Indian Policy, 1953–1961* (Albuquerque: University of New Mexico Press, 1982); Donald L. Fixico, *Termination and Relocation: Federal Indian Policy, 1945–1960* (Albuquerque: University of New Mexico Press, 1986); Larry J. Hasse, "Termination and Assimilation: Federal Indian Policy, 1943 to 1961," Ph.D. diss., Washington State University, 1974; Laurence M. Hauptman, *The Iroquois Struggle for Survival: World War II to Red Power* (Syracuse: Syracuse University Press, 1986); Clayton R. Koppes, "From New Deal to Termination: Liberalism and Indian Policy, 1933–1953," *Pacific Historical Review* 46 (Nov. 1977): 543–66; Kathryn L. MacKay, "Warrior into Welder: A History of Federal Employment Programs for American Indians, 1878–1972," Ph.D. diss., University of Utah, 1987; Kenneth R. Philp, "Termination: A Legacy of the Indian New Deal," *Western Historical Quarterly* 14 (April 1983): 165–80; Kenneth R. Philp, "Dillon S. Myer and the Advent of Termination: 1950–1953," *Western Historical Quarterly* 19 (Jan. 1988): 37–59; Kenneth R. Philp, *Termination Revisited: American Indians on the Trail to Self-Determination, 1933–1953* (Lincoln: University of Nebraska Press, 1999); and Francis Paul Prucha, "American Indian Policy in the Twentieth Century," *Western Historical Quarterly* 15 (Jan. 1984): 5–18.

16. Thomas Biolsi, *Organizing the Lakota: The Political Economy of the New Deal on the Pine Ridge and Rosebud Reservations* (Tucson: University of Arizona Press, 1992), makes a case for the significant influence of the BIA on the Sioux during the early twentieth century.

17. Peter Iverson, "Building toward Self-Determination: Plains and Southwestern Indians in the 1940s and 1950s," *Western Historical Quarterly* 16 (April 1985): 164; Kenneth R. Philp, "Stride toward Freedom: The Relocation of Indians to Cities, 1952–1960," *Western Historical Quarterly* 16 (April 1985): 175; Nancy Shoemaker, "Urban Indians and Ethnic Choices: American Indian Organizations in Minneapolis, 1920–1950," *Western Historical Quarterly* 19 (Nov. 1988): 431; Blue Clark, "Bury My Lungs in Smog: Assessing Urban Indian Studies," in *Native Views of Indian-White Historical Relations*, ed. Donald L. Fixico (Chicago: Newberry Library, 1989), 162; R. David Edmunds, "Native Americans, New Voices: American Indian History, 1895–1995," *American Historical Review* 100 (June 1995): 735. In writing about a later period of American Indian history, Paul Chatt Smith and Robert Allen Warrior have also critiqued the scholarly tradition that has focused on the deficiencies of federal Indian policy and, consequently, "too often saw Indian people as mere victims and pawns." Paul Chatt Smith and Robert Allen Warrior, *Like a Hurricane: The Indian Movement from Alcatraz to Wounded Knee* (New York: Free Press, 1996), vii–viii.

18. NAES Religion and Philosophy Class (Summer 1986), "Narrative Tra-

ditions of the Chicago American Indian Community," in *Indians of the Chicago Area*, ed. Terry Straus (Chicago: NAES College, 1990), 169–81.

19. For an example of a social history perspective used in American Indian history, see Melissa L. Meyer, *The White Earth Tragedy: Ethnicity and Dispossession at a Minnesota Anishinaabeg Reservation, 1889–1920* (Lincoln: University of Nebraska Press, 1994). On the use of quantitative history in American Indian history, see Frederick E. Hoxie, Richard A. Sattler, and Nancy Shoemaker, *Reports of the American Indian Family History Project* (Chicago: Newberry Library, 1992). On oral history in American Indian history, see Joseph H. Cash and Herbert T. Hoover, eds., *To Be an Indian: An Oral History*, rev. ed. (St. Paul: Minnesota Historical Society Press, 1995), including the new introduction by Donald L. Fixico; K. Tsianina Lomawaima, *They Called It Prairie Light: The Story of Chilocco Indian School* (Lincoln: University of Nebraska Press, 1994); and James B. LaGrand, "Whose Voices Count? Oral Sources and Twentieth-Century American Indian History," *American Indian Culture and Research Journal* 21 (Winter 1997): 73–105. On source material for studies of urban Indians, see also Clark, "Bury My Lungs in Smog," 157–65.

20. Review of Fixico's *Termination and Relocation* in *Journal of Arizona History* 29 (Spring 1988): 107.

21. Some prominent and influential works in immigration and ethnic history include John Bodnar, *The Transplanted: A History of Immigrants in Urban America* (Bloomington: Indiana University Press, 1985); Herbert G. Gutman, *Work, Culture, and Society in Industrializing America: Essays in American Working-Class and Social History* (New York: Knopf, 1976); Mark Wyman, *Round-Trip to America: The Immigrants Return to Europe, 1880–1930* (Ithaca: Cornell University Press, 1993); Virginia Yans-McLaughlin, *Family and Community: Italian Immigrants in Buffalo, 1880–1930* (Ithaca: Cornell University Press, 1977); and Olivier Zunz, *The Changing Face of Inequality: Urbanization, Industrial Development, and Immigrants in Detroit, 1880–1920* (Chicago: University of Chicago Press, 1982).

22. John M. Allswang, *House for All Peoples: Chicago's Ethnic Groups and Their Politics, 1890–1936* (Lexington: University Press of Kentucky, 1970); Philip J. Anderson and Dag Blanck, eds., *Swedish-American Life in Chicago: Cultural and Urban Aspects of an Immigrant People, 1850–1930* (Urbana: University of Illinois Press, 1992); Adria Bernardi, *Houses with Names: The Italian Immigrants of Highwood, Illinois* (Urbana: University of Illinois Press, 1990); Melvin G. Holli and Peter d'A. Jones, eds., *The Ethnic Frontier: Essays in the History of Group Survival in Chicago and the Midwest* (Grand Rapids: Eerdmans, 1977); Hartmut Keil and John B. Jentz, eds., *German Workers in Industrial Chicago, 1850–1910: A Comparative Perspective* (DeKalb: Northern Illinois University Press, 1983); Odd S. Lovoll, *A Century of Urban Life: The Norwegians in Chicago before 1930* (Chicago: Norwegian-American Historical Association, 1988); Lawrence McCaffrey, *The Irish in Chicago* (Urbana: University of Illinois Press, 1987); Humbert S. Nelli, *Italians in Chicago, 1880–1930: A Study in Ethnic Mobility* (New York: Oxford University Press, 1970);

Dominic A. Pacyga, *Polish Immigrants and Industrial Chicago: Workers on the South Side, 1880–1922* (Columbus: Ohio State University Press, 1991); Felix M. Padilla, *Puerto Rican Chicago* (Notre Dame: University of Notre Dame Press, 1987); Leslie V. Tischauser, *The Burden of Ethnicity: The German Question in Chicago, 1914–1941* (New York: Garland, 1990).

23. St. Clair Drake and Horace Cayton, *Black Metropolis: A Study of Negro Life in a Northern City* (New York: Harcourt, Brace and Company, 1945); James R. Grossman, *Land of Hope: Chicago, Black Southerners, and the Great Migration* (Chicago: University of Chicago Press, 1989); Arnold R. Hirsch, *Making the Second Ghetto: Race and Housing in Chicago, 1940–1960* (New York: Cambridge University Press, 1983); Nicholas Lemann, *The Promised Land: The Great Black Migration and How It Changed America* (New York: Knopf, 1991); Allan H. Spear, *Black Chicago: The Making of a Negro Ghetto, 1880–1920* (Chicago: University of Chicago Press, 1967); William M. Tuttle, *Race Riot: Chicago in the Red Summer of 1919* (New York: Atheneum, 1970).

24. Grossman, *Land of Hope.*

25. Frederick E. Hoxie explores the potential of looking at American Indian history in a comparative context in *Parading through History*, 1–16, 344–75.

26. Future case studies would add to a list that includes Weibel-Orlando, *Indian Country, L.A.*, and Edmund Jefferson Danziger, *Survival and Regeneration: Detroit's American Indian Community* (Detroit: Wayne State University Press, 1991). Susan Lobo has made a persuasive call for more case studies of Indian urbanization. See "Is Urban a Person or a Place? Characteristics of Urban Indian Country," in *American Indians and the Urban Experience*, ed. Lobo and Peters, 73.

27. William T. Hagan, "Full Blood, Mixed Blood, Generic, and Ersatz," *Arizona and the West* 27 (Winter 1985): 309–26.

28. Merwyn Garbarino, "Life in the City: Chicago," in *The American Indian in Urban Society*, ed. Waddell and Watson, 174.

# 1  Land, Labor, and War

Born in 1929 on the Rosebud Reservation, Rudy Arcoren was among the third generation of Sioux to watch his native homeland—and his share of it—steadily diminish. When Rudy's grandfather, John Arcoren, turned thirty-two in 1889, the Rosebud Reservation was created. John and others of his generation watched federal officials carve the two-million-acre area in south central South Dakota from the traditional Sioux homeland. Soon after, when the Sioux at Rosebud began to hold land individually or "in severalty," John and his wife Josephine were assigned an allotment of 160 acres. No longer was land to be owned communally as it had in the past. John Arcoren and many of his fellow Sioux were unable to produce much on the arid, barren parcels of land they had been allotted. When certain Indian allottees were declared "competent" to lease or sell parts of their allotments to white farmers and ranchers in 1906, many Rosebud Sioux decided to do so.[1]

While the shift from communal to individual ownership of land continued as a result of the federal government's allotment policy, the Rosebud Reservation was shrinking in other ways as well. The generation that followed John Arcoren's saw some parts of the reservation pass directly into white hands without going through the allotment process. As John's son, Luther Arcoren, grew to adulthood, large tracts of unallotted land at Rosebud were declared "surplus" and immediately opened to white homesteaders. That occurred three times during Luther's early twenties—in 1904, 1907, and 1910. Parts of three of the four counties originally contained within the reservation's boundaries were forever lost to Luther Arcoren, his new wife Susie White Bird, his eleven siblings, and the roughly five thousand other Sioux who lived at Rosebud during the early twentieth century.[2]

And so it was that long before Luther and Susie Arcoren's son Rudy was born, only one of the four counties originally contained within Rosebud remained untouched by non-Indian land buyers. The Rosebud estate had diminished drastically, and the effects on its residents were becoming clear. In 1927, two years before Rudy was born, a group of reformers and policymakers finished a tour of Indian reservations. After their experience, they ominously predicted that a "generation of landless, almost penniless, unadjusted Indians [was] coming on."[3]

The Sioux and members of other tribes also suffered from disease during this time. Infant mortality rates among Indian people at the turn of the twentieth century ranged from 10 percent to 50 percent on some especially disease-ridden reservations.[4] Four of Luther and Susie Arcoren's eight children died in childhood. Before Rudy was born, his parents had watched three daughters die before the children reached the age of two. By contrast, Rudy's safe birth in 1929 and healthy development into boyhood during the 1930s gave his parents reason to rejoice. Rudy grew up in a community—like many Indian communities—that cherished ceremonies emphasizing generosity, a wide-ranging and close family, and a sense of spiritual connection.

Yet despite his physical well-being and the many comforts of home, Rudy learned that there would be few opportunities for economic advancement at Rosebud Reservation. By the time he reached adulthood after World War II, his allotment was too small and too widely dispersed to be of much value. Along with thousands of other Sioux, Rudy could no longer raise crops or cattle profitably on his meager portion of land. Many had to work for white farmers or ranchers, who for decades had been buying or leasing land from the Sioux. Finally, in the spring of 1952, twenty-three-year-old Rudy Arcoren became one of the first American Indians to take part in the federal government's new relocation program. He moved from South Dakota's Rosebud Reservation to Chicago with his wife and two children.[5]

The story of the three generations of Arcorens—marked by land dispossession, economic marginalization, and a reservation community suffering from poverty and disease—was not unique to the Rosebud Sioux. Other Indian people endured similar conditions. For Rudy Arcoren and for many other Indian people born three and four generations after allotment started the process of Indian land dispossession, these economic hardships influenced the decision to leave their reservations and move to urban areas. Eventually, thousands of Indian people from dozens of other tribes in all parts of the country joined the Arcorens in Chicago. Most Indian people who emigrated there during the middle of the twentieth century came from the Upper Midwest and Northern Plains. There were Chippewas, Winnebagos, Menominees, and Oneidas from Minnesota, Wisconsin, and Michigan, and from North and South Dakota and parts of Nebraska and Montana there were Sioux, Crow, Cheyenne, and members of the Three Affiliated Tribes (Hidatsa, Mandan, and Arikara).

Although the first significant movement of Indian people to Chicago began with individuals like Rudy Arcoren who arrived in the early 1950s, the roots of Indian urbanization lie in the preceding decades and in the experiences of the ancestors of those urban migrants. Like so many others, Native Americans' migration experiences have been marked by a continuing interplay between their old and new homes.[6] A full understanding of Indian urbanization and migration to Chicago during the latter half of the twentieth century requires an examination of both Chicago and of Indian reservations before this time—especially those in the Upper Midwest and on the Northern Plains.

———

Indian lands have always attracted white settlers, and by the 1870s and 1880s the federal government had forced most tribes onto reservations composed of only a fraction of their previous hunting grounds and living areas. The lives of Indian people would never be the same again. Previous patterns of life, when groups moved frequently over large expanses of land, became impossible. Of tribes that would later be represented in Chicago, the first to be forced onto reservations were bands of Chippewas in Wisconsin and Minnesota. By the 1850s and 1860s their lands were reduced, and their freedom of movement outside the new reservations was restricted. The Chippewas who lived near trade routes on the southern shores of Lake Superior were the first to have their lives changed by white settlers, traders, and government agents. Soon thereafter, those who lived in the forested areas of north central Wisconsin and Minnesota also developed more frequent contacts with non-Indians.[7] To the West, where most Sioux and other Indians of the Northern Plains also were forced onto reservations, results were similar.

The General Allotment Act of 1887 (the "Dawes Act") affected Indians even more profoundly than the introduction of reservations. Allotment, which divided Indian land into individual parcels, forever changed Native American social, political, and economic life. In time, it also contributed to the migration of Indian people from reservations.

There were two reasons for allotment. First, white reformers during the late nineteenth and early twentieth centuries were attempting to eradicate native cultures and assimilate Native Americans. Members of the Lake Mohonk Conference and other reform groups confidently predicted that if Indian people imitated white culture and mores, including the individual ownership of land, they would succeed in modern America. Second, large railroad, lumber, mineral, and oil interests of the early twentieth century looked longingly at Indian land. They frequently acquired this valuable land by ignoring government policy or manipulating it to suit their purposes.[8]

Whatever motives influenced federal officials, allotment for Indian people always meant the loss of land. Fifty years after the General Allotment Act, the Indian land base had diminished from 138 million to 52 million acres—well over half of tribally held land. Some tribes fared even worse; the Crow lost more than three-quarters of their land base during these years. Despite the stark results of allotment from tribe to tribe, the way in which land dispossession occurred often differed, and it took many twists and turns, even on the same reservation. The malign effects of the Dawes Act only gradually became apparent during the years after it was signed into law in 1887. Thus, the loss of land that began with allotment did not immediately cause Indian migration. Instead, it ushered in a period of adjustment as Indian people attempted to face new challenges. In time, however, some of these adjustments prepared them for urban residency and sometimes made life in the city more feasible or attractive.[9]

The process of Indian land dispossession generally took place in three phases: the allotment, the leasing, and finally the selling of the land. From 1887 to 1900, the federal government assigned 32,800 allotments totaling 3.3 million acres. Most of these, however, were in the Pacific Northwest, far from Chicago and its nearby reservations. Not until the turn of the century did the Sioux on the Northern Plains, the Chippewa in the Upper Midwest, and the other tribes that later would send many members to Chicago begin to suffer the full effects of allotment. From 1900 to 1921 the federal government assigned 85,860 allotments for 14.3 million acres, many of them to the Chippewas in Minnesota and the Sioux in North and South Dakota. Allotment size differed by region and by tribe. On the Northern Plains and in many other regions, heads of families usually received 160 acres, and single men received eighty. The BIA, however, provided less land to Indians who lived on land thought to be more productive. Oneidas, for instance, received only forty-five acres per family.[10]

The Dawes Act stipulated that allotments would be held in trust by the federal government for twenty-five years. These lands, said to be in "trust-patent" status, initially could not be leased or sold. Federal reformers supported the policy because they believed that Indian owners needed time to learn how to earn a living by farming or ranching on their allotments. Indian land in the Upper Midwest, on the Northern Plains, and in most other areas of the country, however, was leased and even sold long before 1912. Starting at the turn of the century, several laws permitted the BIA to make direct transfer of allotments to Indians in "fee simple" or outright ownership. Moreover, the BIA established "competency commissions" in 1915 to determine when Indian landowners could graduate from trust to fee-patent status. The commissions, however, occasionally forced fee patents on reluctant or even unconsenting and illiterate Indians in order to make land available for settlement. With a new, less restrictive fee-patent status, millions of acres of Indian land were more easily leased or sold to neighboring farmers or ranchers at bargain rates early in the twentieth century.

Leases represented the first step by which many Indians lost control of their land. Rentals discouraged them from using it, and those who wanted to end lease arrangements after the leases ran out frequently met with frustration. Allottees who leased were unable to take the initiative against influential local whites who successfully appealed to the BIA to continue the arrangements. The BIA's sympathy for white businesspeople, farmers, and ranchers, and its liberalized leasing policy begun in 1894, resulted in a rash of leases during the late nineteenth century. From 1887 to 1893, the BIA approved an average of just one lease a year; between 1895 and 1900, however, the bureau approved an average of 2,500 leases annually.[11]

The poor quality of the land that was often allotted to Indians and a sense of powerlessness under pressure from the BIA and white land interests contributed to dissolution of the Indian land base. In 1928 a study group reported that many Indians were "living on lands from which a trained and experienced white man could scarcely wrest a reasonable living."[12] Moreover, many allotments required intense irrigation. It is little wonder that some Indians decided to lease or sell their allotments.

There were some, however, who enjoyed a brief sense of pride after receiving an allotment. Unfortunately, such exhilaration was short-lived. A Sioux man from the Crow Creek Reservation in central South Dakota remembered that the land became his "own affair" immediately after he received his allotment, and he could "have his voice." He recalled, however, that after a short period he had no chance to retain the land or improve it. White ranchers, who had reached initial agreements with both BIA officials and Indian landowners to rent or lease land, usually went directly to the BIA superintendent with subsequent questions and concerns. Indians were often excluded from any discussion regarding the land they owned. By 1928 almost half the land at Crow Creek had been lost to non-Indians.[13]

Even greater loss of Indian land resulted from early-twentieth-century shifts away from complete federal control of Indian policy to greater participation by local BIA officials. In 1921 the federal government again liberalized leasing regulations and granted more authority to area superintendents, who proved more susceptible than officials in Washington to pressure and manipulation from neighboring whites and local business interests. The two groups, sometimes working in tandem, often skirted the law to further speed the leasing and selling of Indian land, a process begun even before the shift of administrative authority to the local level. In Minnesota during the 1890s, local members of Congress had Washington officials allot parcels of land on the White Earth Reservation—land containing valuable timber—to Chippewas who had agreed to sell the allotments to timber companies. A similar loss of pasture land occurred on the Fort Peck Reservation in Montana in 1926.[14]

World War I further contributed to the loss of Indian land. Woodrow Wilson's administration urged all Americans, including Indians, to make sacrifices in the name of wartime emergency and under the threat of punishment. During the three years of U.S. involvement in the war—1917 to 1919—the federal government issued more fee patents than it had in the previous ten years. Most were on the Northern Plains, and additional millions of Sioux acres were opened for eventual white control. Leases increased as well. Cattle and sugar beet companies convinced the federal government that they were contributing to the war effort and were able to lease Indian land quickly and easily. At the Crow Agency, government officials turned a blind eye while two sugar companies avoided dealing with tribal leaders yet managed to lease twenty thousand acres of precious irrigated reservation land within weeks of U.S. entry into the war. During the war years, white ranchers in South Dakota grazed cattle on the Pine Ridge Reservation without the permission of the Sioux and without BIA opposition.[15]

Although the Indian land base dwindled during the early twentieth century, some Native Americans still tried to farm or raise cattle. Most who pursued such plans, however, were repeatedly thwarted by the BIA's lack of realism and foresight. Federal officials asserted that the allotment process would quickly turn American Indians into yeoman farmers. Yet in many areas, the parcels of land that Indians owned were too small, arid, or infertile to produce adequate yields. Few Indian stockmen on the arid

Northern Plains during the early twentieth century owned the three or four hundred acres necessary to graze a small herd adequately. Some allotments were on land too dry for any type of agriculture. Much of the Crow Creek Reservation in South Dakota, for example, lacked the rainfall necessary for farming. Whites and Indians alike had repeatedly tried and failed to establish farms or ranches there.[16] Even when they enjoyed some rare success in stock raising or farming, Indians found themselves isolated from distant markets and in stiff competition with large farming and ranching units. The hardest work, the best weather conditions, and the most steadfast resistance to land buyers could seldom make 160 acres of reservation land produce a living. Under such conditions, the decision of many Indians to lease or sell parts of their allotments becomes easily understandable.

Money gained from land sales and leases seldom meant that Indian people would be able to feed and clothe themselves adequately other than in the short term. Many took up wage labor and moved frequently to find it. The pattern of movement in search of labor had begun. A generation or two later it would lead many Indians to cities. John Arcoren and his generation, who first experienced allotment, and the generation of his grandson Rudy and other third-generation allottees, who migrated to urban areas in the early 1950s, both turned to wage work, but they differed in some ways. John relied on hunting and gathering for subsistence, whereas Rudy took a job in a Chicago factory to make his living. Yet the differences between them should not be exaggerated. A consistent pattern of mobility and wage labor extended from John Arcoren to his grandson Rudy, from the late nineteenth to the mid-twentieth centuries.[17]

———————

From earliest times until the late nineteenth century, Indian people relied on seasonal economic opportunities. Using what was available to them during each season, Indians on the Northern Plains and in the Upper Midwest fed and clothed themselves, their families, and their kinsmen. In the nineteenth century, the Yankton Sioux who lived on trust-patented lands in southeastern South Dakota typically raised vegetables in the spring, summer, and early fall. Then, late in the fall they moved with their relatives to settlements on the banks of the Missouri River, where they fished and hunted during the winter. Chippewas in northwestern Minnesota lived on the White Earth Reservation and similarly fished in its lakes, hunted in its forests, and used its western half for agricultural purposes. Until about 1890, White Earth's prairie-forest transition zone enabled the reservation to become a "region of refuge" for the Chippewas who lived there. The Winnebagos of central Wisconsin also practiced a seasonal round. Many picked wild blueberries in the summer and cranberries in the fall for white buyers. Later they moved to camp sites on the banks of the Mississippi River near La Crosse to trap and hunt during the winter.

In the early twentieth century, however, subsistence agriculture and hunting and gathering strategies began to fail the Indians of the Northern Plains and Upper Midwest. As more Yankton Sioux received fee patents and started to lose their allotments, their cyclical pattern of subsistence agriculture and hunting and gathering was short-circuited. They no longer had enough land for self-sufficient farming or raising livestock. After 1900 the White Earth Chippewas also saw their homeland diminish to the point that the economic strategies they practiced previously no longer worked. The Winnebagos of Wisconsin also were forced to adjust as whites bought more blueberry fields and cranberry bogs during the early twentieth century. Allotment and the loss of land to non-Indians often meant that areas once incorporated into the seasonal round became off-limits, marked off by fences and signs warning against "trespassing" on land recently acquired by whites.[18]

As subsistence agriculture became more difficult and even unfeasible for Indian people throughout the Northern Plains and Upper Midwest, many turned to wage labor. Types of wage labor, however, differed from tribe to tribe and reservation to reservation. A minority thrived in their new economic lives as wage laborers. The Menominees had their own sawmill in Neopit, Wisconsin, which employed numerous tribesmen in a variety of jobs, as foresters, lumberjacks, truck drivers, stackers, saw operators, planers, and warehouse workers. Menominees, however, were usually shut out of the most prestigious and well-paying jobs. Local whites filled most positions in engineering, accounting, and sales. Still, the mill usually provided jobs for 350 to 550 Menominees, depending on the season, and made the tribe the second most prosperous in the country in the early twentieth century. Wage labor also made Menominees mobile. From felling trees in the middle of Wisconsin's densest forests, to sawing and planing boards at the tribal sawmill in Neopit, to selling lumber in towns throughout Wisconsin, the Menominees involved in the timber industry moved frequently during the course of their jobs.[19]

Most tribes did not have tribally owned enterprises or businesses, however, and did not fare as well as the Menominees. Yet one important similarity bound many together: Wherever Indians participated in wage labor, a life of mobility resulted. In much of the Upper Midwest they worked on white-owned farms and in their orchards during the early twentieth century. As a result, they were on the move, governed by the sequence of harvest. After blueberry and cranberry picking could no longer support them, for example, Winnebagos worked for wages in strawberry fields and cranberry bogs owned by whites. They also found wage work by picking cherries, corn, and peas for white farmers as well as digging potatoes. Many Potawatomis in northeastern Wisconsin picked cherries in mid-summer and later traveled in large groups to potato fields, where they earned around eight cents for each bushel they dug. Various bands of Chippewas also picked berries and vegetables for whites at harvest time.[20]

The Sioux and other Indian people on the Northern Plains also performed wage labor, often as farm or ranch hands. In the early twentieth century, the BIA encouraged Sioux at Rosebud and Pine Ridge to engage in wage labor, and the Indians continued to do so in later years on their own. Edward E. Goodvoice, a Sioux born at Rosebud in 1930, remembers moving around for wage work: "When you're on a reservation, you hear of . . . potato farmers hiring down in Nebraska. And right away, they would have a sign up, and [Indians] all go to sign up. Or by word of mouth, they would say they're hiring railroad section hands in the next town. And then Indians would set up tents right along the railroad tracks and work on section gangs."[21]

The adaptation of Indian people from the Northern Plains and Upper Midwest to wage labor seems to have been less an earth-shattering change than an adjustment of old seasonal economic practices. Instead of moving from fishing site to berry patch, they followed the wages offered to pick crops for white farmers. For many, a cash economy replaced one of subsistence and barter. Yet one of the greatest problems of the seasonal pattern remained. Even in areas of the greatest economic diversity, Indian wage laborers could at best hope to work from spring through fall. In some areas, only summer promised the opportunity for work. Almost everywhere, wage labor was unavailable during the long winter months, a period that severely taxed people's resources. Moreover, as agriculture became more mechanized by the 1950s, the need for Indian labor diminished, and some became open to the possibility of mobility of a new type.[22]

Wage labor on farms and orchards soon led some Indians to look for work in small towns near reservations. Like the seasonal round and migration to farms and fields to pick crops, migration to nearby towns was usually temporary. It was part of a pattern that included periods of time spent back on the reservation and, occasionally, in other towns. By the 1920s, a few Oneida, Potawatomi, and Stockbridge Indians began exploring the possibility of performing wage work in nearby factories during the winter. The pattern of seasonal work in small towns would continue and slowly expand in Wisconsin.[23]

Elsewhere, the presence of Indian schools influenced urban migration. Soon after the Phoenix, Arizona, Indian School was established in 1891, for example, it attracted the attention of that city's business class. Working with the BIA, school administrators helped develop an "outing system" in which Indian youth left school for a few months and worked for white families. Girls served as domestics and boys as laborers. School officials claimed that the outing system provided Indian youth with good work habits and also contributed to Phoenix's economy.[24]

Increasing numbers of Indians began to migrate toward towns during the early twentieth century, but they usually lived on the outskirts, sometimes in small, self-contained Indian settlements. Consequently, many still had very little contact with non-Indians. Laguna Pueblo railroad workers who spent time in Richmond, California, did not move into the city's working-class or middle-class neighborhoods. Instead, they lived in converted boxcars in isolated railyards. While in California, they remained closely tied to Pueblo communities back in New Mexico.[25]

About three thousand Sioux, mostly from Pine Ridge, lived in nearby Rapid City, South Dakota, during the early twentieth century. A small number made Rapid City their permanent residence and found homes in working-class or middle-class neighborhoods. Most, though, viewed the town as only a home for the winter and would return to the reservation after a brief stay. While in Rapid City, these seasonal visitors were relegated to the "least desirable living quarters of the city," according to one observer. Many lived on the outskirts of town in a cluster of tents on land owned by a lumber company. For that meager housing, they paid three dollars a month in 1950. Others rented small shacks or cabins. As on reservations, disease and poverty abounded in small-town Indian campgrounds.[26]

Crow and Blackfeet in Montana had similar experiences in Great Falls, Helena, and Butte during this period. The slum conditions in which they lived, often on the outskirts of these towns, offered few physical or material improvements over reservations. They were only slightly more likely to have indoor plumbing than reservation residents and less likely to have electricity. Still, many Crow and Blackfeet claimed that they were attracted by even the small improvements and conveniences that towns offered. Employment opportunities also drew Crow and Blackfeet to nearby towns. Only about half of those who lived on reservations were employed during October 1954, a peak employment period in Montana.

In contrast, about three-quarters of the Indians who lived in Montana towns had work during that same period. Although few managed to attain skilled positions, many worked in semiskilled jobs.

Allotment resulted in the loss of land, and that also encouraged Crow and Blackfeet to migrate to nearby towns. Almost none of the Indians who lived in town reported receiving income from allotments, whereas about half of reservation residents did. One man, asked why he stayed on the reservation, responded, "Land, land, land." As others began to lose land, however, they saw fewer advantages to reservation life and began to move to town. Although some said they would prefer to stay on their reservations, a lack of economic opportunity or the effects of allotment and land dispossession made doing so impossible.[27]

In the early twentieth century, many Indian people who migrated either permanently or seasonally to towns in Wisconsin, South Dakota, Montana, and elsewhere did so on their own. A few, however, participated in programs organized by the federal government, which sometimes worked in conjunction with private labor placement organizations. These programs would become prototypes for a larger relocation program that the BIA would undertake in the 1950s. Through the Dawes Act and allotment, the federal government in the nineteenth century had attempted to turn warriors into farmers. In the twentieth, the government would increasingly try to turn them into urban wageworkers.[28]

During the 1920s, the BIA responded to labor shortages in the West by encouraging Indians to follow the jobs. In 1929 the bureau received an appropriation of $7,000 from Congress to hire Indians to pick beets in Colorado. The next year, it received $50,000 to establish off-reservation placement centers in Minneapolis, Salt Lake City, Kansas City, Missouri, Phoenix, Los Angeles, Riverside, and Berkeley. Several of these placement centers were located near Indian schools and served as pipelines for their graduates. Los Angeles, which was linked to nearby Sherman Institute, and Phoenix, which was connected to the Phoenix Indian School, offered employment opportunities for Indian school graduates. Arizona's cotton industry needed laborers to work in the fields, on irrigation projects, and on roads and railway tracks connecting Arizona fields and factories. In 1923 the BIA sent an agent to Arizona to establish a program that would bring Indian laborers from throughout the state to Phoenix for this purpose.

After the start of the Great Depression, however, the federal government disbanded most programs that had encouraged Indian urban migration. During the 1930s, the BIA encouraged Indians to stay on reservations because cities were experiencing labor surpluses. The BIA's main tool for encouraging reservation residency was the Indian Division of the Civilian Conservation Corps (CCC-ID). Although pressure from organized labor ensured that wages would be low, many Indians relied on the program during the depression and worked on projects on or near their reservations. In 1933, 40 percent of the male heads of household at Rosebud and 60 percent at Pine Ridge were employed by the CCC-ID.[29]

Indians in the early twentieth century had begun to be incorporated into the national economy, but it was by tentative steps and temporary engagement. Their entry was not irrevocable, and most engagement was seasonal or pickup labor at the lowest pay levels. As Melissa Meyer, a historian, describes the economic situation many Indian people faced, "Most Indians entered the mainstream of American society from a landless and impoverished position."[30]

---

Regardless of residency or employment, Indians in the early twentieth century began to live closer to whites—one of the many changes Indian families and communities experienced during this time. Non-Indians continued to move into rural regions once dominated by reservation communities, and prejudice against Indians often surfaced as the white population increased. Some small towns near reservations in the Upper Midwest and on the Northern Plains were notorious for discriminating against Indians. A Winnebago man remembers that when he was growing up in the 1920s, deputies in west central Wisconsin would occasionally shoot at Indians: "You would see a lot of Indians in the twenties, used to be limping around because they were shot through the leg. They let you run first because they knew you were going to run and when you were running they shot you in the leg. . . . So everybody our age got that stuff straight in their hind end."[31]

On the Northern Plains, relations between whites and Indians were often no better. An Oglala Sioux man born about the same time as Rudy Arcoren suffered slights and discrimination when his family moved to Alliance, Nebraska, when he was ten. Alliance, roughly one hundred miles south of Pine Ridge, had a "ladder of racism," the Sioux remembers. Whites were on top, Mexicans below them, blacks below them, and Indians were at the very bottom. Blacks and Mexicans in Alliance, he recalls, would pick on Indians to demonstrate their marginally superior position in the town's racial and social hierarchy. In Rapid City, South Dakota, another center of Sioux migration about sixty miles northwest of Pine Ridge, many middle-class whites would not allow Indians in restaurants, hotels, stores, schools, and hospitals. Indian people generally kept to themselves or sometimes associated with poorer, less reputable members of the town's white population. Such treatment at the hands of whites bothered many Indian people, including a Sioux woman who later moved to Chicago, in part because of the prejudice of rural South Dakota: "There are signs on the door: 'Indians and dogs, not allowed;' 'Indian trade not wanted.' . . . I had always grew up with the idea that we were as good as anybody else. But when I got out there, I found being Indian made you different and being dark, we couldn't hide it. You were treated differently in the stores and schools."[32]

With increasing contact with non-Indians came the emergence of a new cultural figure: the Indian cultural broker who skillfully straddled both worlds, facilitating interaction. Sometimes, however, interaction also brought cultural and political factionalism among Indians. That phenomenon—along with the loss of land and introduction of wage labor—helped shape many Indian communities and eventually helped lead to twentieth-century Indian urbanization. Loss of land and being relegated to the bottom ranks in the wage labor economy occasionally created rifts in Indian families, bands, and tribes. In addition, non-Indian individuals and organizations exerted political, cultural, and religious pressure. In some cases, these phenomena would split groups of Indian people into two or more factions. Factions could emerge from differing opinions about allotment, economic enterprise, the BIA and native leaders, religious practice, or consumer goods.

Such factionalism arose during the late nineteenth century in parts of the Upper Midwest and Northern Plains, but it peaked during the 1930s with the "Indian New Deal" of John Collier. Collier, the new commissioner of Indian affairs under President Franklin Roosevelt, burst into office promising to overturn the assimilationist policy of the late nineteenth century. In particular, he set about trying to strengthen Indian self-determination and build tribal land ownership through his Indian Reorganization Act (IRA) of 1934, which provided credit for reservation communities that voted to incorporate under the act.

Not all Indian people, however, embraced Collier's offers of aid. Some reservation communities, including the Rosebud and Pine Ridge Sioux, split into two opposing factions over the IRA. Traditionalist "old-dealers" who found Collier manipulative and controlling opposed his program, while "new-dealers" saw Collier as offering a promising future and worked with him to form new tribal governments in which they took power. Collier's IRA, then, resulted in some Indian communities debating the meaning of an authentic Indian cultural identity. It also led to economic conflict. New-dealers in political office would sometimes use the IRA credit system to direct loans toward members of their faction and away from their opponents.[33]

Factionalism occasionally went beyond community debate and economic favoritism to reach violent levels. Several Northern Plains reservations suffered from breakdowns in law and order during the 1930s and 1940s, and murders, knifings, and suspicious car accidents became more common. At the Lower Brule Sioux Reservation in South Dakota, well-connected Sioux men occasionally beat up political opponents without reprisal. This factionalism and the resulting law enforcement failures began to influence mobility and migration patterns in the 1930s and 1940s. Although many tribes continued to experience remarkable cultural continuity into the mid-twentieth century, some Indian people responded to political or cultural rifts by making a fresh start in a new location. When asked why they had left their reservations for nearby towns, several Crow and Blackfeet replied that there was better law and order in the city than on the reservation.[34]

While Indian reservations changed in dramatic fashion early in the twentieth century—frequently overwhelmed by white settlers and corporations and beset by poverty, disease, and factionalism—they changed in more subtle ways as well. These less apparent changes, too, had an important effect on Indian people, including those who would in time decide to migrate to urban areas. The composition of Indian families among many tribes gradually began to change during the late nineteenth and early twentieth centuries. Although some tribes had intimate contact with Europeans and Euro-Americans for decades, many held to well-established practices regarding family and children, even into the twentieth century. They often only married within the tribe and sometimes only within a specific band or clan. The birth of a child was a momentous occasion, drawing in not only birth parents but also other family and clan members as well as religious and political leaders. Parents traditionally determined the names of unborn children through dreams, as well as information on how to raise the children. Grandmothers often carried infants in cradle boards. Grandparents and other family members presented songs to mark accomplishments or stages in life.

Although many of these cherished social and cultural practices continued into the early twentieth century, Indian families changed broadly in two ways: Family size increased, and marriage patterns adjusted to accommodate new economic situations. Intermarriage with non-Indians contributed greatly to the growth in the Native American population as well as to changing patterns of Indian residency. Around 1910, intermarriage among some tribes in the Upper Midwest and on the Northern

Plains became much more frequent. Scholars have shown that increasing intermarriage with members of other tribes and with non-Indians during the early twentieth century produced greater cultural and economic opportunities for Indian people. The establishment and popularity of intermarriage, then, contributed to later urban migration by some Indian people.[35]

Tribes such as the Crow had a general twentieth-century demographic increase peak during the 1930s. The Crow baby boom of that decade produced many tribespeople who would reach maturity in the early 1950s, about the time the reservation economy would have difficulty supporting them and the relocation program would be initiated.[36] The increase in young Crow and Indian people from other tribes also contributed to a greater number of single people and to some households that were single-headed. Throughout the late nineteenth and early twentieth centuries, Indian men were more likely to be single than Indian women. Still, the marital status of Indian women was changing as it became more and more common for them to remain single into young adulthood. One-fifth of Indian women over the age of fifteen in 1900 were single; by 1930 that group had grown to one-fourth of all Indian women. Chippewa women typified this trend, Sioux women were less likely to be single, and Winnebago women more likely. Whatever their tribal background, single Indian women were more likely to be geographically mobile than were married women.[37] Increasing numbers of single Indian women, along with a general increase in the Native American population, would positively influence later urban migration.

The popularity of wage labor for an increasingly wider spectrum of Indian people was a strong factor in promoting urbanization. During the late nineteenth century, as the Indian land base dwindled, many young and single Indians took up wage labor jobs to survive. Married adults during this period, however, seldom adopted that economic practice. At the White Earth Reservation in Minnesota, for example, relatively few Chippewa men participated in wage labor before 1900. Most of the few who did were unmarried and planned to work only a few years before they did marry and become farmers. During the late nineteenth century, few Chippewa men married while they still worked as wage laborers. After 1900, however, wage labor became a more common way of life for Chippewa men, and more did marry while working as wage laborers, abandoning what they saw as the elusive goal of owning a self-sufficient farm. They had committed themselves to wage labor on a more permanent scale. That pattern—what might be called the "normalization of wage labor"—would continue to be important among

White Earth Chippewas and other Indian communities throughout the twentieth century.[38]

---

Loss of land, development of wage labor patterns, and changing demographics all contributed to Indian urbanization. The World War II experience, however, dwarfed them all in importance. It profoundly influenced the American nation as a whole, separating friends, families, and neighborhoods and causing the greatest internal migration in American history. Remarkably, the war affected Indian people even more dramatically than it did most other Americans. During the war years, American Indians gained knowledge of different parts of the United States and the world. Twenty-five thousand served in the U.S. military during the war—one-third of all able-bodied Indian men from the ages of eighteen to fifty—which was a larger proportion than any other racial or ethnic group. Forty thousand more Indian men and women worked in defense plants, where they dramatically increased their incomes.

The effect of the participation of such a large percentage of the Indian population in the war effort would be hard to exaggerate. Between the beginning and end of the war, the average Indian income jumped from $400 to $1,200 per year. Experiences on the battlefront and on the home front ended the isolation in which many Indians had lived. As historian Alison Bernstein notes, by the end of the war, "Indians were part of the American political process, their economic, social and cultural status irrevocably altered by the conflict."[39] By 1945 the expectations of many Indian people, whether economic, political, or social, were much higher than before the war. Some would attempt to fulfill these expectations in cities like Chicago.[40]

Experiences gained during the war years gave many Indian people increased confidence and hope of success. Indian soldiers played a more prominent role in World War II than their numbers would suggest. The most famous were the Navajo code-talkers, 420 men who volunteered to help create a code the Axis would be unable to break. Combining the complex and little-studied Navajo language with a set of code words for technical terms and names, places, and weapons used in military communications, the code was critical to many maneuvers and operations in the Pacific theater. Code-talkers impressed non-Indian soldiers through their dedication and courage. Many volunteered for dangerous missions, especially if their units had suffered heavy casualties and assistance was needed. One Navajo whom the Japanese captured was tortured for more than a year but did not reveal the secret code that helped the United States win the war in the Pacific.

Other Indian soldiers demonstrated great bravery and fighting skill as well. Unlike black G.I.s, virtually all Indian personnel served in integrated units. In some divisions, though, Indians were more numerous and thus their accomplishments more visible. Twenty percent of the 45th Infantry Division from Fort Sill, Oklahoma, was Indian. In these and other units, Indians remarked that they seldom if ever experienced discrimination. Whatever prejudice there was on the battlefields of Europe or the South Pacific never approached that of towns such as Alliance or Rapid City back home.

In addition to meeting people of different racial, ethnic, and geographic backgrounds, many Indian soldiers were affected by the countries and people they encountered. As a Navajo stationed temporarily in Australia noted in a letter, "It's quite interesting to know how some people live in some parts of the world." Sometimes encounters with foreigners pleasantly surprised Indian soldiers and underscored the discrimination and lack of political and social opportunities back home. Indian soldiers on furlough in Europe could buy alcohol in bars and stores, a purchase still illegal for them in Arizona and New Mexico. In general, most felt they were treated better overseas. An Iroquois fighting for the Canadian Army in the European theater was impressed by how well the English treated him, even under trying circumstances. "They are really swell, working-class people," he wrote, "and in their distress they show a spirit which we never find in Canada."[41]

Back in the United States, many Indians who had not enlisted found the labor market much more open during the war. The degree to which white farmers and ranchers had for years depended upon Indian labor became clear during wartime as fewer Indians were available to work in agriculture. Even before the United States entered the war, the Arizona Farm Bureau Federation was alarmed when few Indian laborers showed up to harvest cotton in the summer of 1941. In response, the group asked the BIA to delay sending a work relief payment to Arizona Indians and use it instead as leverage to force the workers to harvest local crops.[42]

After the war began the demand for labor increased, as did Indians' employment options. The federal government saw great need for various natural resources, including Arizona cotton, during the war. In 1942 Paul V. McNutt, chair of the War Manpower Commission, asked BIA superintendents for assistance in finding Arizona Indians to pick this crop "considered by the Military Services as a most essential agricultural product for the war effort." Even private citizens involved themselves in the sudden interest in Indian labor. A Massachusetts woman, drawing on patriotism and myths of Indian laziness, wrote to Secretary of the Interior Harold Ickes in 1944 to suggest that he "release the idle manpower of the Indians on Reservations for work on Desert Plants and their contribution to the war effort." The Navajos and other southwestern tribes, she claimed, could use cactus and yucca to make rope for the Armed Forces and thereby "contribute to the much needed manpower."[43]

There was, in fact, very little untapped manpower on Indian reservations during the war. A telegram sent in September 1942 from Washington, D.C., to BIA superintendents in various western states indicates the extent to which Indian people quickly took advantage of the wartime labor shortage. To a request for inexperienced Indians to work in the mines of New Mexico, Arizona, Montana, and Idaho, area BIA superintendents gave remarkably similar responses. "Acute shortage exists here," the Pima Agency in Arizona stated. The answer of the Sells Agency, also in Arizona, was similar: "No men available at present." The Mescalero Agency in New Mexico repeated the theme: "Manpower on this reservation practically exhausted now." The Fort Lapwai Agency in Idaho replied that most able-bodied Indians there were either in the Armed Forces or had defense work. Indians at the Flathead Agency in Montana were hard at work in mining and lumber industries or in the military and defense work. An official at the Navajos' Window Rock Agency in Arizona responded that they had "reached point where necessary to comb reservation in order to meet labor demands." And, finally, the Whitewater Agency in Arizona took the opportunity to respond to rumors spread by government officials as well as ordinary citizens. "There is false impression," the superintendent wrote curtly, "as to available labor on reservation."[44]

Clearly, many American Indians benefited from the labor shortage during the war. Some even found employment in distant defense factories and mines. The effects of the wartime labor shortage, however, reached beyond such high-profile jobs. As Indian people left reservations for work directly connected to the war effort, other jobs became available on and near reservations, and Indians relatively new to wage work, including women, frequently filled them. Those who took jobs in tribal enterprises or in agricultural work on local farms during the war often earned less than those who worked in defense factories. Yet their lives, their experiences with labor and migration, and their expectations for the future all changed dramatically as a result of the war.

Even during wartime with its special labor needs, more Indians worked in seasonal agricultural jobs than in the defense industry. A 1942 survey of thirty-five reservations found that Indians on all but one continued to look for seasonal work in sugar beet, cranberry, potato, cotton, and wheat fields. Although 225 Pimas worked in defense factories in California and Washington state in 1942, more than twice that number remained in Arizona to pick cotton. Tribes further removed from West Coast war activity were even more likely to continue working in agriculture. Seven hundred Chippewa, for example, left Turtle Mountain early in the war for agricultural work, whereas only twenty-five found work in industry and none in defense jobs. Similarly, the Rosebud Sioux followed their old labor patterns and continued to work in the beet fields, only in larger numbers.

Such employment provided better working conditions and higher pay during the war than before, however. A government official who examined the situation in the summer of 1942 declared, "Almost overnight an acute labor shortage [had] developed" after the harsh drought and depression of the 1930s. He observed that in this new, more labor-friendly environment, competition for workers was fierce, and "sugar beet companies recruiting workers for independent farmers regard the Sioux Indians of South Dakota as a promising labor supply."[45]

Even with greater governmental involvement in the economy, Indian people often responded to the wartime labor shortage by continuing to rely on well-established job networks. Both private and government employers tried to insist that Indians follow prescribed bureaucratic channels and rules during wartime and seek employment in an orderly and rational fashion. Many federal officials spent the war years trying to squeeze all the productivity possible out of the national work force. Most Indian laborers, however, flaunted these demands and continued to look to kinsmen and acquaintances to find work. At the Pine Ridge Reservation in South Dakota, the BIA superintendent wrote with some frustration that "in most cases the Indians secure their own jobs." Many Sioux there had "adjusted themselves over a long period of years" to seasonal agricultural work and were in the practice of going to the same areas season after season. "Most families," the superintendent wrote, "have certain localities in which they have been in the habit of working and they return to the same place from year to year." At North Dakota's Turtle Mountain Reservation as well, officials commented on the Chippewas' adjustment to agricultural labor by the 1940s and on their skill and self-reliance in following the crops season by season. Although the BIA was supposed to guide Indian people in their labor, especially during wartime, the Turtle Mountain superintendent admitted that trying to do so was a lost cause. "They receive no advice or information from the agency," he wrote. "They were gone before the agency knew they were going." Among the Blackfeet in Montana, the reservation office served as the central meeting place where residents who had returned for visits after working elsewhere could share information about what they had seen.[46] Despite the BIA's best efforts, Indians continued to look to their own people in making decisions about moving and jobs. Although bureau employees criticized the practice of relying on "unverified rumors circulating on the reservation" for information, Indian people nationwide continued age-old patterns in their search for employment—before, during, and after the war.[47]

The war and the resulting chain reaction in wage labor also opened jobs to Indian women. Among some tribes, women for the first time became responsible for planting and harvesting crops after men left to fight or find work. Other women—as many as twelve thousand by 1943—acquired defense jobs. As the war continued, Indian women's labor, along with that of all Americans, continued to be sought and highly valued. Never before had the government or private employers been so interested in their skills and abilities. The young Sioux women who visited the Sisseton Agency office in South Dakota in 1943 were presented with a "fine opportunity to assist in the War Effort." Posters in reservation offices announced, "You are urged to join the ranks of the GREAT COMPANY OF AMBITIOUS YOUNG WOMEN who are striving to help their Government win the WAR." The War Manpower Commission offered women free training in light defense jobs that could eventually pay as much as $120 a month.[48]

Although the war increased the demand for labor, it was not an equal opportunity employer. The economic benefits that Indians received from World War II were not as great as those other groups of Americans gained. Even among Indians themselves, benefits were not shared equally. Tribes located near the burgeoning defense plants of West Coast cities frequently benefited more than did tribes living on the Northern Plains and in the Upper Midwest. Western tribes were close to many defense plants and the jobs they offered during the war. Furthermore, these tribes had long enjoyed access to many trade-oriented Indian schools in the Far West and Southwest. No schools on the Northern Plains or in the Upper Midwest rivaled the reputations of Los Angeles's Sherman Institute or the Phoenix Indian School. During the war, these Indian schools and others in the West—such as Chemewa in Oregon, Chilocco in Oklahoma, and Haskell in Kansas—served as employment agencies for defense plants.[49]

Indian students and graduates prospered during the war due to their technical training. A superintendent at a California agency in 1942 noted, "In Portland, Seattle, and the other West Coast cities, the need for skilled workers is so great that industry picks up people in training before they have completed their courses." Aircraft companies in Tulsa and Oklahoma City also fostered connections to Indian schools and hired many Chilocco and Haskell graduates.[50]

By contrast, Indians further removed from centers of wartime employment and without extensive formal training often had to remain on or near their reservations for the duration. Sioux and Chippewa men frequently commented that they did not have enough money to make the trek West, find a job and a place to live, and still be able to make it to the first paycheck. The Lac Courte Oreilles Chippewas in northwestern Wisconsin were among those who could not afford to seek jobs aggressively, even during the war. At the Turtle Mountain Chippewa Reservation in North Dakota, a BIA agent explained the small number of off-reservation war workers by noting, "Employment is very distant from this supply of labor." At North Dakota's Fort Berthold Reservation, an agent wrote, "Very few Indians seek outside employment."[51]

It is clear that tribes experienced the war's economic effects differently. Southwestern tribes such as the Navajo often fared best, winning defense industry jobs at ammunition depots and elsewhere. The Sioux occupied a lower rung in the wartime socioeconomic ladder, often continuing to pick beets and potatoes for slightly higher wages yet having some success in industrial and construction jobs. Chippewas in Wisconsin seemed to benefit the least from the transformation of the national economy during the war. They continued to pick cherries, cranberries, and blueberries on a seasonal basis for low wages. Moreover, working conditions during the war were sometimes as hazardous as before. Groups of Chippewas who picked cherries at an orchard in Sturgeon, Wisconsin, often returned with dysentery caused by the unsanitary living and working conditions there.[52]

The Indian people who would later migrate to Chicago and other urban centers would continue to be influenced by wartime experiences, whether good or bad. Chippewas in particular became accustomed by the mid-twentieth century to a life of mobility and material deprivation. Groups that fared better economically during the war had positive experiences with the outside world that would also influence postwar decisions about migration and employment.

Work in wartime defense industries provided Indians with their first experiences with labor unions. Responses varied widely. Abe Showaway from Oregon wrote to Commissioner of Indian Affairs John Collier in 1944 to complain about the closed shop he found at many factories and other places of work. He emphasized the role Indians were playing on the battlefield and on the home front in "contributing in some way to the winning of the war." "As one of [those] Red men" who contributed to the war effort through a construction job, Showaway asked Collier to enable him and other Indian workers to find employment without having to join unions, which, he believed, did not represent Indian people. He argued that his union's initiation and monthly fees were unjust and explained what he thought to be most Indians' natural labor pattern: "An Indian usually quits his employment when fishing season comes around and then when the berry season comes around he quits again. . . . In other words, while he may temporarily labor, he is not a laborer within the strict sense of the word, and should not have to pay this tribute to labor unions."[53]

Other Indians, however, were more receptive toward labor unions and the general employment situation in mid-twentieth-century America. The Blackfeet tribal council during the war formed a "defense committee" to help tribal members apply for defense jobs and to loan them money to pay initial union dues. In Portland, some unions successfully recruited Indian workers and, recognizing the particular problems they faced, decided to defer dues until the workers had received their first paychecks.[54]

More important, World War II and the social conditions it produced incorporated many Indian people into a broader world in a number of different ways. Some took new jobs and joined unions. Others enjoyed buying new clothing and automobiles for the first time in their lives. Those who lived alongside non-Indians began to befriend and sometimes even marry them. At the end of the war, however, the economic and social changes in Indian life that World War II had fostered seemed to fade. The labor shortage ended, and many Indians who had grown accustomed to, even dependent upon, wage labor again suffered economically. One white employer in Rapid City illustrated the often short-lived nature of Indians' wartime gains. "I have no labor problem," he boasted just a year after the war ended. "I can hire all the Indians I want for 45 cents an hour."[55]

Indians' wartime experiences, whether on the battlefront or the home front, raised their expectations for the period after the war. Many hoped for political, social, and economic improvements. Historian Gerald Nash has commented that Indian soldiers who had seen the world "could not be expected to accept a passive role as non-voting wards of the United States government upon their return." The veterans who returned to their reservations had been changed by the war in ways great or small. A Flandreau Sioux Marine remembered that when he and other veterans returned home they immediately began to try to diminish the BIA's role in day-to-day tribal life. This "communist form of government," he said, "told you what to buy, where to buy, what to sell, when to sell, and things like this." The veteran, who "fought to keep America free," was adamant about exercising "the freedom that the Constitution guarantees" after he returned to his home reservation.[56] Yet many other Indians who went through the war, whether stateside or overseas, began the move to urban centers during the 1950s and 1960s. They would try to fulfill their postwar plans in Chicago and other cities in the West and Midwest.

---

Many of the same economic conditions that Indian people suffered under during the late nineteenth and early twentieth centuries still remained when Indians began to move to urban areas. In some ways, the lives of John Arcoren, born in 1857, Luther Arcoren, born in 1885, and Rudy Arcoren, born in 1929, were quite similar. The three generations of Arcorens all experienced a lack of jobs and satisfactory living conditions during all or part of their lives. Those factors did not drive John or Luther away from the Rosebud Reservation, but they did play a part in convincing Rudy to leave for Chicago in 1952. What had changed? The most straightforward explanation is the federal government's relocation program, of which Rudy took advantage during its first year of operation. That is only part of the answer, however. Other factors having nothing to do with government policy were also important in Indian urbanization. During the early twentieth century, Indians' economic circumstances continued to worsen as the non-Indian economic world exerted more and more control. Migration and the labor patterns developed by Indians who had lost their allotted land also influenced later urbanization. In their struggle to survive, many Indian people in the Upper Midwest and on the Northern Plains changed the ways in which they tried to support themselves and their families. They adjusted their seasonal patterns of subsistence agriculture to include wage labor. By the time Rudy Arcoren and thousands of other American Indians began moving to cities in large numbers during the 1950s, many had worked numerous wage-labor jobs, both close to and far from their reservations. Many

Indians were well accustomed to lives of mobility and were on the brink of embarking on something new.

*Notes*

1. Rosebud Agency census, rolls 428–45, M595, Record Group 75, National Archives–Washington, D.C. [hereafter RG 75, NA-WDC].

2. Rosebud Agency census, rolls 428–45, M595, RG 75, NA-WDC; Thomas Biolsi, *Organizing the Lakota: The Political Economy of the New Deal on the Pine Ridge and Rosebud Reservations* (Tucson: University of Arizona Press, 1992), 6; Frank Pommersheim, *Broken Ground and Flowing Waters: An Introductory Text with Materials on Rosebud Sioux Tribal Government* (Rosebud, S.D.: Sinte Gleska College Press, 1979), 43–48.

3. Lewis Meriam et al., *The Problem of Indian Administration* (Baltimore: Johns Hopkins University Press, 1928), 40.

4. Frederick E. Hoxie, Richard A. Sattler, and Nancy Shoemaker, *Reports of the American Indian Family History Project* (Chicago: Newberry Library, 1992), 4:61.

5. Rosebud Agency census, rolls 428–45, M595, RG 75, NA-WDC; List of persons provided relocation services to Chicago, box 11, Narrative Reports, Field Placement and Relocation Office Employment Assistance Records, Record Group 75, National Archives–Washington, D.C. [hereafter NR, FPROEAR, RG 75, NA-WDC].

6. See, for example, John Bodnar, Roger Simon, and Michael P. Weber, *Lives of Their Own: Blacks, Italians, and Poles in Pittsburgh, 1900–1960* (Urbana: University of Illinois Press, 1982); James R. Grossman, *Land of Hope: Chicago, Black Southerners, and the Great Migration* (Chicago: University of Chicago Press, 1989).

7. Robert A. Ritzenthaler, "Southwestern Chippewa," in Bruce G. Trigger, ed., *Handbook of North American Indians*, vol. 15: *Northeast* (Washington: Smithsonian Institution Press, 1978), 745; Patricia A. Shifferd, "A Study in Economic Change: The Chippewa of Northern Wisconsin, 1854–1900," *Western Canadian Journal of Anthropology* 6, no. 4 (1976): 19–20.

8. Donald L. Parman emphasizes the importance of white reformers in shaping allotment policy in *Indians and the American West in the Twentieth Century* (Bloomington: Indiana University Press, 1994), 1–58. Melissa L. Meyer emphasizes the expansion of market capitalism and the power of large corporations over the actions of the reformers and government agents in "'We Can Not Get a Living as We Used To': Dispossession and the White Earth Anishinaabeg, 1889–1920," *American Historical Review* 96 (April 1991): 68–94, and Meyer, *The White Earth Tragedy: Ethnicity and Dispossession at a Minnesota Anishinaabeg Reservation, 1889–1920* (Lincoln: University of Nebraska Press, 1994). Frederick E. Hoxie combines both these explanations in *A Final Promise: The Campaign to Assimilate the Indians, 1880–1920* (Lincoln: University of Nebraska Press, 1984).

9. Janet A. McDonnell, *The Dispossession of the American Indian, 1887–1934* (Bloomington: Indiana University Press, 1991), 121; Frederick E. Hoxie, *Parading through History: The Making of the Crow Nation in America, 1805–1935* (New York: Cambridge University Press, 1995), 269; Hoxie, *A Final Promise.*

10. McDonnell, *Dispossession of the American Indian,* 8; "The Oneida Indians of Wisconsin: Milwaukee Public Museum Bulletin no. 19 no. 1," Nov. 1950, Robert E. Ritzenthaler Field Notes, Milwaukee Public Museum [hereafter Ritzenthaler Field Notes, MPM].

11. McDonnell, *Dispossession of the American Indian,* 43, 96–97.

12. Meriam et al., *The Problem of Indian Administration,* 5.

13. Interview with Dan Clark (Sioux), Summer 1968, American Indian Oral History Research Project [hereafter AIOHRP], pt. 1, no. 19, MS 7.

14. McDonnell, *Dispossession of the American Indian,* 48, 58; Meyer, "'We Can Not Get a Living as We Used To,'" 383.

15. McDonnell, *Dispossession of the American Indian,* 33, 47, 65–66, 108; Hoxie, *Parading through History,* 281.

16. McDonnell, *Dispossession of the American Indian,* 28.

17. Roger L. Nichols also notes the continuity of twentieth-century Indian migration in "Something Old, Something New: Indians since World War II," in *The American Indian Experience: A Profile,* ed. Philip Weeks (Arlington Heights: Forum Press, 1988), 292–312.

18. Herbert T. Hoover, "Yankton Sioux Experience in the 'Great Indian Depression,' 1900–1930," in *The American West: Essays in Honor of W. Eugene Hollon,* ed. Ronald Lora (Toledo: University of Toledo Press, 1980), 65–66; Meyer, "We Can Not Get a Living as We Used To," 368–94; Nancy O. Lurie, "Winnebago," in Bruce G. Trigger, ed., *Handbook of North American Indians,* vol. 15: *Northeast* (Washington: Smithsonian Institution Press, 1978), 704; Robert E. Bieder, *Native American Communities in Wisconsin, 1600–1960: A Study of Tradition and Change* (Madison: University of Wisconsin Press, 1995), 206.

19. "The Menominee Indian Sawmill: A Successful Community Project," Ritzenthaler Field Notes, box 1, folder 45, MPM; Louise S. Spindler, "Menominee," in Bruce G. Trigger, ed., *Handbook of North American Indians,* vol. 15: *Northeast* (Washington: Smithsonian Institution Press, 1978), 708–24; Brian C. Hosmer, *American Indians in the Marketplace: Persistence and Innovation among the Menominees and Metlakatlans, 1870–1920* (Lawrence: University Press of Kansas, 1999), 19–108; Bieder, *Native American Communities in Wisconsin,* 161.

20. Lurie, "Winnebago," 704–5; Bieder, *Native American Communities in Wisconsin,* 206; "The Potawatomis Indians of Wisconsin: Milwaukee Public Museum Bulletin no. 19 no. 3," Ritzenthaler Field Notes, box 1, folder 45, MPM; John Gillan, "Acquired Drives in Culture Contact," *American Anthropologist* 44 (Oct.–Dec. 1942): 545–54; Ritzenthaler Journal no. 1, Ritzenthaler Field Notes, box 2, folder 14, MPM; Ritzenthaler, "Southwestern Chippewa," 743–59; Meyer, "'We Can Not Get a Living as We Used To,'" 368–94.

21. McDonnell, *Dispossession of the American Indian*, 61; Biolsi, *Organizing the Lakota*, 24–27; author interview with Edward E. Goodvoice (Sioux), Chicago, 14 June 1995.

22. Lurie, "Winnebago," 705.

23. Robert E. Ritzenthaler and Mary Sellers, "Indians in an Urban Situation," *Wisconsin Archeologist* 36 (Dec. 1955): 147–61. This temporary migration to find labor was practiced by members of several other tribes as well, including the Navajos. See Colleen O'Neill, "The 'Making' of the Navajo Worker: Navajo Households, the Bureau of Indian Affairs, and Off-Reservation Wage Work, 1948–1960," *New Mexico Historical Review* 74 (Oct. 1999): 375–405.

24. Robert A. Trennert, "Phoenix and the Indians: 1867–1930," in *Phoenix in the Twentieth Century: Essays in Community History*, ed. G. Wesley Johnson (Norman: University of Oklahoma Press, 1993), 53–68.

25. Kurt Peters, "Santa Fe Indian Camp, House 21, Richmond, California: Persistence of Identity among Laguna Pueblo Railroad Laborers, 1945–1982," *American Indian Culture and Research Journal* 19 (Summer 1995): 33–70.

26. E. Russell Carter, "Rapid City, South Dakota," *The American Indian* 6 (Summer 1953): 29–38.

27. George Engstrom and Sister Providencia, "City and Reservation Indians," *Social Order* 5 (Feb. 1955): 59–68.

28. Meriam et al., *The Problem of Indian Administration*, 39; Kathryn L. MacKay, "Warrior into Welder: A History of Federal Employment Programs for American Indians, 1878–1972." Ph.D. diss., University of Utah, 1987.

29. MacKay, "Warrior into Welder," 95–120; Trennert, "Phoenix and the Indians," 65–67; Donald L. Parman, "The Indian and the Civilian Conservation Corps," *Pacific Historical Review* 40 (Feb. 1971): 39–56; Biolsi, *Organizing the Lakota*, 113–14; Edmund Jefferson Danziger, Jr., *The Chippewas of Lake Superior* (Norman: University of Oklahoma Press, 1979), 138–40.

30. Meyer, "'We Can Not Get a Living as We Used To,'" 393.

31. Interview with Willard LaMere (Winnebago), Chicago, 1 Feb. 1984, Chicago American Indian Oral History Pilot Project, no. 009, Newberry Library, Chicago and Native American Educational Services College, Chicago [hereafter CAIOHP, NL and NAES].

32. Mark Monroe, *An Indian in White America* (Philadelphia: Temple University Press, 1994), 20; Carter, "Rapid City, South Dakota," 35; interview with Phyllis Fastwolf (Sioux-Oneida), Chicago, 8 May 1983, no. 006, CAIOHP, NL and NAES.

33. Bieder, *Native American Communities in Wisconsin*, 125; Meyer, "'We Can Not Get a Living as We Used To,'" 385; Hoover, "Yankton Sioux Experience," 53–71; Biolsi, *Organizing the Lakota*; Kenneth R. Philp, "Termination: A Legacy of the Indian New Deal," *Western History Quarterly* 14 (April 1983): 174–75.

34. Philp, "Termination," 172–73; interview with Lenora DeWitt (Sioux), 25 Aug. 1971, AIOHRP, pt. 1, no. 39, MS 786; Engstrom and Providencia, "City and Reservation Indians," 65.

35. Hoxie, Sattler, and Shoemaker, *Reports*, 2:66–72.

36. Hoxie, *Parading through History*, 298–99.

37. Marlita A. Reddy, ed., *Statistical Record of Native North Americans* (Detroit: Gale Research, 1993), 201–2.

38. Hoxie, Sattler, and Shoemaker, *Reports*, 2:54–57.

39. Gerald D. Nash, *The American West Transformed: The Impact of the Second World War* (Bloomington: Indiana University Press, 1985), 128–47; Alison R. Bernstein, *American Indians and World War II: Toward a New Era in Indian Affairs* (Norman: University of Oklahoma Press, 1991), 21. For a very different view that emphasizes the destructive and damaging effects of World War II on Indian people, see Carol Miller, "Native Sons and the Good War: Retelling the Myth of American Indian Assimilation," in *The War in American Culture: Society and Consciousness during World War II*, ed. Lewis A. Erenberg and Susan E. Hirsch (Chicago: University of Chicago Press, 1996), 217–37.

40. For a survey that takes Americans' heightened economic and social expectations during this time as its theme, see James T. Patterson, *Grand Expectations: The United States, 1945–1974* (New York: Oxford University Press, 1996).

41. Nash, *The American West Transformed*, 132; Laurence M. Hauptman, *The Iroquois Struggle for Survival: World War II to Red Power* (Syracuse: Syracuse University Press, 1986), 3.

42. Arizona Farm Bureau Federation to BIA, 29 Aug. 1941, box 1, Financial Program, Field Placement and Relocation Office Employment Assistance Records, Record Group 75, National Archives–Washington, D.C. [hereafter FP, FPROEAR, RG 75, NA-WDC].

43. Paul V. McNutt to William Zimmerman, 10 Oct. 1942, and Edna Claire Davis to Harold Ickes, 8 March 1944, box 1, FP, FPROEAR, RG 75, NA-WDC.

44. Pima, Sells, Mescalero, Fort Lapwai, Flathead, Window Rock, and Whitewater Agencies to BIA, n.d. (late 1942?), box 1, FP, FPROEAR, RG 75, NA-WDC.

45. Survey, box 1, FP, FPROEAR, RG 75, NA-WDC; Gordon Macgregor and John Useem, "Proposals for Assisting Indian Labor in War Industry and Agricultural Work Preliminary Report Based on the Employment Survey of Rosebud, Yankton, and Pine Ridge Reservations and Nearby Communities in the Summer of 1942," box 3, FP, FPROEAR, RG 75, NA-WDC.

46. Feb. 1942 reports from the Pine Ridge, Turtle Mountain, and Blackfeet agencies, box 1, FP, FPROEAR, RG 75, NA-WDC.

47. Macgregor and Useem, "Proposals."

48. Sisseton Agency report, 18 Jan. 1943, box 1, FP, FPROEAR, RG 75, NA-WDC; Grace Mary Gouveia, "'We Also Serve': American Indian Women's Role in World War II," *Michigan Historical Review* 20 (Fall 1994): 153–82; Bernstein, *American Indians and World War II*, 73; MacKay, "Warrior into Welder," 126–56; Tom Holm, "Fighting a White Man's War: The Extent and Legacy of American Indian Participation in World War II," *Journal of Ethnic Studies* 9 (Summer 1981): 69–81.

49. Margaret Connell Szasz, *Education and the American Indian: The Road to Self-Determination* (Albuquerque: University of New Mexico Press, 1974), 106, 100–101.

50. Sacramento Indian Agency report, 4 Jan. 1942, box 1, FP, FPROEAR, RG 75, NA-WDC; Bernstein, *American Indians and World War II*, 71–2.

51. Bernstein, *American Indians and World War II*, 75; Robert E. Ritzenthaler, "The Impact of War on an Indian Community," *American Anthropologist* 45 (April–June 1943): 325; Fort Berthold Agency report, 10 March 1943, box 1, FP, FPROEAR, RG 75, NA-WDC.

52. Great Lakes Agency reports on permanent and seasonal employment, 15 July 1944, box 2, FP, FPROEAR, RG 75, NA-WDC.

53. Abe Showaway to John Collier, 20 March 1944, box 1, FP, FPROEAR, RG 75, NA-WDC.

54. Blackfeet Agency report, 6 March 1942, and John Rockwell to John Collier, 4 Jan. 1942, both in box 1, FP, FPROEAR, RG 75, NA-WDC.

55. Nash, *The American West Transformed*, 146; Carter, "Rapid City, South Dakota," 32.

56. Nash, *The American West Transformed*, 133; interview with Keith Wakeman (Sioux), summer 1971, AIOHRP, pt. 1, no. 32, MS 825.

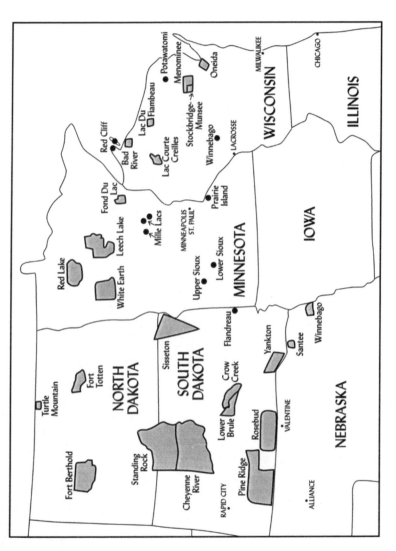

Reservations in Wisconsin, Minnesota, North Dakota, and South Dakota.

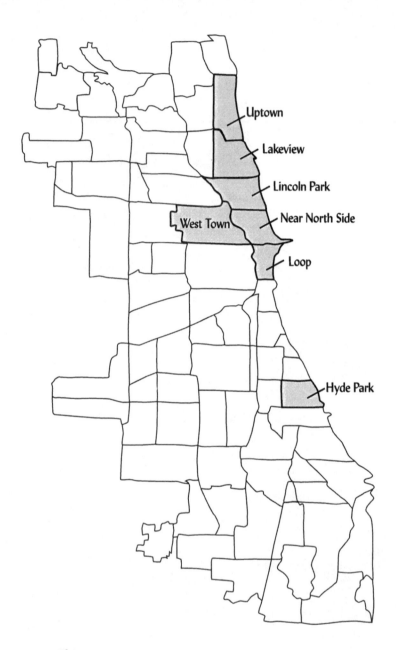

Chicago

Indian women wait their turn to dance at the ninth annual American Indian Center powwow in September 1962. (Chicago Historical Society)

A promotional poster commissioned by the Bureau of Indian Affairs advertises the benefits that awaited Indians who participated in the relocation program, including satisfying religious, family, and educational environments. (National Archives Record Group 75, 075-N-L-[2])

Many young single Indian men and women who came to Chicago because of the relocation program during the 1950s lived at the YMCA on the city's Near North Side during their first few weeks. (National Archives Record Group 75, 31-5)

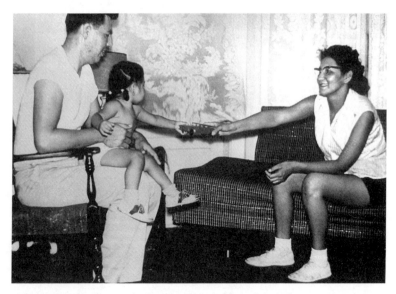

Indian parents play with their young child in their Chicago apartment.
(National Archives Record Group 75, 30-9, no. 15)

Indian family walks by a local grocery store near their apartment.
(National Archives Record Group 75, 32-17)

An Indian man who relocated to Chicago at work at a machine shop. (National Archives Record Group 75, 33-14, no. 5)

An Indian woman participating in the Bureau of Indian Affairs' vocational training program learns her trade in a Chicago salon. (National Archives Record Group 75, 33-20, no. 11)

An Indian mother and her non-Indian neighbor take their children for a stroll.
(National Archives Record Group 75, 075-N-34)

An Indian family gathers around the television set in their new Chicago apartment. (National Archives Record Group 75, 075-N-31)

## 2  Relocation and Its Attractions

By 1945 the lives of Indian people had changed remarkably in just half a century. Land dispossession had eliminated farming and ranching as feasible economic strategies for thousands. Thousands more, in search of wages, had begun to migrate from reservations. Finally, experiences obtained during World War II had a profound effect on those who went overseas and those who remained on the homefront.

Indian policy changed as well in the years after World War II. Between 1945 and 1952 the Indian policy pursued during the 1930s under President Roosevelt and Commissioner of Indian Affairs John Collier fell into greater disfavor. Cultural pluralism and incentives to stay on reservations, characteristic of Indian policy of the 1930s, were eliminated. In their place, new policies emerged that were more intent on the integration and assimilation of Indian people into the American mainstream. Two programs dominated Indian policy during the 1950s: termination and relocation.

Termination as policy was put in place through two pieces of legislation: House Concurrent Resolution 108, which ended federal responsibility for several tribes, and Public Law 280, which transferred criminal jurisdiction on some reservations from tribal councils to state governments. Both pieces of termination legislation were passed into law in 1953.

The "voluntary relocation program" through which thousands of American Indians moved from their reservation homes to cities—including Chicago—did not result from any specific piece of legislation. Nevertheless, the program, officially inaugurated in 1952, was at least as important as termination policy in its long-term effects on Indian peo-

45

ple. Along with land dispossession, the growing influence of wage labor, and wartime experiences, the relocation program contributed to the urbanization of American Indian people during the latter half of the twentieth century. This and other factors pulled them toward Chicago at the same time they were being pushed away from reservations.

———————

Although termination and relocation started within a two-year period during the early 1950s, they were based on events and trends in both Indian policy and national politics that stretched back to before World War II. In some sense, mid-twentieth-century Indian policy resembled that of the late nineteenth century. In 1887 the federal government had tried to force Indians to become yeoman farmers, and it opened Indian land for non-Indians through the Dawes Act. By the 1950s, the nation's economic structure had changed, and policymakers turned to different methods to assimilate American Indians. The fact that America had become an indisputably urban nation influenced Indian officials and some members of Congress in their support for relocation and termination. Indians, too, it was thought, should become urban.

In addition to a long-standing wish to assimilate Indian people, termination and relocation emerged out of the postwar political environment. The arguments for termination and relocation and for full and equal citizenship for American Indians after World War II were persuasive and powerful because they were often shared by both liberals and conservatives. Indian policy was one of many areas that brought liberals and conservatives, Democrats and Republicans, into frequent cold war consensus.

Conservatives were attracted to policies of termination and relocation by the anticipated reduction in government regulation and interference. Moreover, the anticommunism of the 1950s caused many to look with suspicion on "communal" reservations and any policies that appeared to endorse this characteristic. Western conservatives in particular wanted to see Indian lands in the West opened to development and to be part of the postwar boom in the West.

Liberals, too, were pleased by some of what they saw in termination and relocation policies. After the transition from Roosevelt's New Deal to Truman's Fair Deal, liberals and the federal government in general began to place less emphasis on redistribution of wealth and more on economic growth. Furthermore, the Truman years saw the beginnings of a civil rights movement that emphasized individual rights based on equality under the law and retreated from rights based on special group status in the wake of Nazi Germany's use of group status for deadly purposes. Increasing numbers of politicians and others during the 1950s saw integration into the national community and a breakdown of barriers that isolated groups of people as ideas whose time had come. Thus, House Concurrent Resolution 108, which in 1953 made "Indians within the territorial limits of the United States subject to the same laws and entitled to the same privileges and responsibilities as are applicable to other citizens of the United States" and which granted them "all of the rights and prerogatives pertaining to American citizenship," appealed to many politicians and federal officials.[1]

It had not taken long for John Collier's Indian New Deal to begin to unravel. As early as 1937, Sen. Burton K. Wheeler of Montana had repudiated his sponsorship of the Wheeler-Howard Act, the centerpiece of the Indian New Deal. Wheeler's reasoning—that its community emphasis bore too close a resemblance to the collectivist and totalitarian movements then sweeping the world—would be picked up by others during the 1940s and 1950s. Such critics subjected Collier's ideas to a withering and widespread attack after World War II.[2]

Indian people's experiences during World War II also convinced many government officials and non-Indians in general that the government was no longer needed in the "Indian business" and that native people could make it on their own. Many Indians themselves adopted those beliefs after the war. Some veterans returned to reservations in the late 1940s intent on winning general types of civil rights in keeping with their status as American citizens and war heroes. They asked for the loosening of federal regulations restricting their ability to borrow money for land purchases and wanted an end to the prohibition of liquor sales on and off reservations. Others, however, were less interested in individual freedoms but instead wanted more federal responsibility and involvement on reservations. For example, in 1956 an Omaha tribal chair praised the way the BIA had sponsored economic ventures on reservations during World War II. He then asked bureau officials, "Why can't the government do this in peace time the same as in war?"[3] But those who looked for more federal aid for reservations after the war waited in vain. During the war, the nation was desperate for all labor, including that of Indian people. Afterward, there was little need for the overwhelmingly unskilled labor force represented by Indian people. Washington had little interest in undertaking new programs on reservations.

After the end of the war, the federal government became less active and in many areas, including Indian affairs, attempted to slow the rate of centralization seen during the war years. In 1946, during the tenures of Commissioner of Indian Affairs William A. Brophy and Assistant Commissioner William Zimmerman, Jr., the BIA reorganized under pressure from Congress to decentralize Indian affairs.[4] The Hoover Commission, which attempted to streamline the executive branch of government, in 1948 continued this trend. Urging the reduction of all federal bureaucracies, it specifically addressed the BIA and recommended that the federal government transfer responsibility for Indian affairs to the states. The commission, which included John R. Nichols, who the next year would become commissioner of Indian affairs, asserted, "Assimilation must be the dominant goal of public policy. . . . The only questions are: What kind of assimilation, and how fast?"[5] To add to the swelling chorus, President Harry S. Truman in 1948 urged, "We need to make much further progress in our efforts to bring all the Indians to full participation in our national life."[6]

Dillon S. Myer, who succeeded Nichols as Indian commissioner in 1950, also believed in a decentralized system of Indian affairs in which the BIA's role would diminish and that of states and nongovernmental organizations expand. A career bureaucrat, Myer had previously worked as a county extension agent during the 1920s, served on the staff of the Agricultural Adjustment Administration during the New Deal, and directed the War Relocation Authority during World War II. After the war ended, he resettled evacuated Japanese-Americans and served briefly with the Federal Housing Administration. A year into his term as commissioner of Indian affairs, Myer seized the opportunity to outline his plans for Indian policy in a December 1951 speech before the National Council of Churches. He specifically chose that audience because its members represented the new nongovernment groups he hoped would carry more of the load in the future.[7]

According to Myer, Indians' needs were almost always better and more efficiently served by either the private sector or state governments than by the federal government. He announced that those who worked among Indians were entering a new era in which "organizations such as those represented here today can and should be playing a broader and more dynamic role in Indian affairs than ever before." After paying lip service to the "special relationship of the Indians to the Federal Government," Myer proposed that the time had come to weaken or dissolve this very relationship, thereby decreasing BIA paternalism toward Indian people and reversing historical processes that had set "Indians apart from other American citizens." Myer specifically addressed members of church groups when he asked for help in assuring that "no vacuum is left when the Indian Service withdraws its supervision and services from any particular Indian group." In suggesting ways in which members of church groups, including his listeners, might help relocated Indians assimilate to urban communities, Myer said that Indian children would need "assistance and guidance in being introduced into such organizations as the Girl Scouts and Boy Scouts." Whether religious and civic groups were working with Indian children or adults, Myer hoped that such organizations would help them become integrated and assimilated. "The job, in a word," he concluded, "is one of furnishing these people with positive incentives for taking up a new life in ordinary American communities."[8]

In years to come, Myer and his co-workers at the bureau would repeatedly return to this dichotomy. "Ordinary" or "normal" American communities where relocated Indians might assimilate were seen as beneficial. Reservation communities, often foreign and mysterious to non-Indians, at best were viewed as examples of the kind of paternalism Myer referred to as the "glass case policy," which would freeze Indians in place for the enjoyment of white tourists. Myer and other white policymakers considered reservations at the worst to be destructive.[9] Charles Miller, chief of the BIA's Placement and Relocation Division, was, if anything, even clearer than Myer about the decentralization of Indian affairs and relinquishing responsibility to nongovernmental agencies. "The sooner we can get out," he said, "the better it will be for the Indians and for the country." Another official contributed to the drumbeat for integration and assimilation by praising relocation for breaking down the "vicious pattern of isolation perpetuated by the reservation."[10]

Termination enjoyed political support outside the bureau as well, strengthening the concept politically and making it even more dangerous to Indians who feared it. Sen. Arthur V. Watkins (R-Utah), in his powerful post as chair of the Senate Subcommittee on Indian Affairs, was the foremost congressional supporter for termination and relocation. Watkins had grown up in rural Utah, shaped by the Mormon church and the Republican party. In the churches he attended and at Brigham Young University, Watkins learned the Mormon teachings about Indians—that they were a fallen race in need of the civilization that Mormons could provide. As he became more prominent in Utah civic life as a young lawyer, Watkins also worked as a journalist, and he injected editorial comments into the stories he wrote. Indians in Utah, he advocated, should be treated as all other U.S. citizens, and the BIA should be dismantled. After winning election to the U.S. Senate in 1946 with the help of powerful Mormon backers, Watkins attempted to bring these opinions to bear on public policy. He soon became even more stridently opposed to the BIA and argued against bureau control and reservation life and for termination and relocation. He dramatically predicted that his generation was finally on the verge of solving the "Indian problem" once and for all. "Following in the footsteps of the Emancipation Proclamation of ninety-four years ago," Watkins proclaimed, "I see the following words emblazoned in letters of fire above the heads of the Indians—THESE PEOPLE SHALL BE FREE!"[11]

In addition to the experiences of World War II and postwar calls for the integration and assimilation of Indians, a natural event also contributed to the beginning of the relocation. In the winter of 1947–48, fierce blizzards struck the Southwest. The BIA responded by helping the Navajos and Hopis who had suffered from the storms move to Los Angeles, Denver, or Salt Lake City. In these cities, however, most were able to find only temporary work, often on farms or for the railroad.[12]

Two years later, in 1950, the BIA negotiated with the Railroad Retirement Board and with federal and state employment services in North and South Dakota, Montana, and Arizona in an attempt to find employment for Indians. Both the BIA and the other agencies hoped to assist not only Navajos and Hopis but also other tribes in finding employment.[13] The approach was consistent with Hoover Commission recommendations that the federal government share responsibility with local government and the private sector in Indian policy. Some BIA officials believed the trend toward less federal and more state and nongovernmental responsibility for Indian employment would continue. John Cooper, BIA area director for North and South Dakota, emphasized the role of the South Dakota State Employment Service over that of the BIA because he thought he had a responsibility to "plan for the time when services of the Bureau of Indian Affairs will be withdrawn." He also wished to ensure that local Indians would establish the "habit of contacting the local Employment Service Office for assistance in securing employment and in discussing their job needs."[14] The trend eventually became a part of what has been called the "cooperative commonwealth" of the Eisenhower administration, where the federal government, local government, and business sector attempted to work together in a self-restrained, disinterested fashion to stimulate national economic growth.[15]

Through 1951, however, the BIA under Dillon Myer devoted relatively limited resources to searching for employment for Indians. Although federal officials made some attempts to assist tribes on the Plains and in the Midwest and Southwest, only a fraction of the reservations nationwide were affected. Jobs that were found resembled those Indians had held for years—seasonal and low-paying. Federal officials acknowledged that as many as 90 percent of these jobs were temporary. Furthermore, the new jobs were often located near reservations in small towns and rural areas. Many did not require Indians to move from their reservations to work, a goal increasingly important to many federal officials. Small- to medium-sized towns near reservations continued to present the same challenges and disadvantages to Indian people after World War II as they had before. After visiting Rapid City, South Dakota, in 1949, the Chippewa-Cree BIA official D'Arcy McNickle urged Indians to stay away. Discouraged by the city's labor surplus and housing shortage, he warned that "Indians going into the city are inviting disaster to themselves." A few years later, another observer described the sections of Rapid City where Indians usually lived as shanty-towns and junkyards.[16]

As federal officials and others involved in this early relocation program began to recognize some of its shortcomings, the program began to be changed. First, the BIA focused on finding permanent industrial jobs for Indians. Second, it focused on larger cities, usually far from reservation communities. These "normal American communities," as BIA officials often referred to them, appeared to be a complete and perfect contrast to the atypical, isolated reservations frequently criticized as "rural slums" or even "concentration camps." The more distant cities formed the beginnings of a relocation program that would send thousands of Indians to urban centers across the nation over the next two decades.

During 1951 and 1952, the BIA hired forty people—half of them Native Americans—to work for the relocation program. Some were responsible for coordinating relocation over vast areas, such as the Dakotas or all of Wisconsin; others were stationed on individual reservations; and still others served in the first four urban field relocation offices (called "FROs" by bureau officials), which opened in late 1951. At this time, offices in Los Angeles, Denver, and Salt Lake City—which had earlier served Navajos and Hopis forced from their homes—were retooled to serve Indians of all tribes. In addition, the BIA set up a fourth relocation office in Chicago at 608 South Dearborn Street near the southern edge of the Loop. Among the first four BIA-run offices, Chicago's was the only one that had not previously been involved in the Navajo and Hopi relocation program. The office opened in November 1951 with a small staff and began accepting Indian relocatees in January 1952. A month later, Kurt Dreifuss came over from the Chicago Welfare Department's Division of Rehabilitation to direct the office, a position he would hold for six years.[17]

Dreifuss was fairly typical of the BIA employees involved in relocation. Many were highly educated and came from positions in social work. Nearly all were optimistic about their ability to improve Indian policy and the lives of Indian people, an optimism that would appear over time as naïve or paternalistic to some. One BIA employee, Alida Bowler, who directed Los Angeles's relocation office in the early 1950s, had earned a master's degree in psychology in 1911 and during the 1920s worked for the Children's Bureau, a refugee program, a commission on prohibition enforcement, and John Collier's American Indian Defense Association. In the 1930s, as the BIA's first woman superintendent at the Carson Agency in Nevada, Bowler devoted herself to the protection of the Pyramid Lake Indians' land and water rights. After working in the private sector for a few years, she was back with the bureau in the late 1940s and finished her career by working on relocation in the 1950s. Dealing with Indian people, who were often uninterested in or opposed to bureau policy, often presented new challenges to employees such as Bowler.[18]

Bowler, Dreifuss, and other BIA employees hoped to build on the successes of earlier relocation and employment programs and learn from previous mistakes. In the early months of the new program, the bureau explained its choice of cities for the first relocation offices and others that would soon follow in the San Francisco Bay area, St. Louis, Joliet, Waukegan, Cincinnati, Cleveland, and Dallas. It announced, "Towns were chosen for these Relocation Offices generally on the basis of two major considerations—a widely diversified industrial economy, with year-round employment in many different kinds of jobs, and secondly, a rapidly and steadily growing population, for it seems that here the Indian is able to fit in most successfully."[19]

During the planning stages of the relocation program, the BIA decided what sorts of services would be offered to Indians interested in relocating to Chicago, Los Angeles, Denver, or Salt Lake City. The most time-consuming decision involved financial aid. During World War II, many Indians had been forced to refuse job offers from urban factories and defense plants because they lacked enough money to travel to work sites or secure adequate housing. These jobs usually paid weekly or bimonthly, and many frustrated Indians knew they did not have enough money to keep themselves fed and clothed in an expensive city for even a week or two. As a result, BIA officials decided to give relocatees a stake—enough money to get a start in a new urban environment. Yet because Congress wanted to "free" Indians from federal control and integrate them into the national political economy, the bureau was intent on not making the initial aid too lucrative or extending it for too long.

The bureau decided to cover only basic transportation and subsistence expenses. Initially, it gave relocatees to Chicago four cents a mile if they drove themselves or the cost of bus or train fare up to $50. After relocatees arrived in Chicago, the BIA provided $25 per week for heads of families and $10 for each additional family member for two weeks. Later, the BIA increased the length of subsistence payments to three weeks and then four and also increased the amount given for subsistence. With these increases also came reimbursement for the cost of shipping household goods and grants so relocated Indians could buy medical insurance, household goods, furniture, and tools and clothes for work.[20]

Employees at Chicago's relocation office often tried to fine-tune the amount that relocatees received. They felt it had to be enough to help those truly in need but not so much that some might continue to rely on the BIA. Mary Nan Gamble, who worked alongside Kurt Dreifuss, wanted the amount to be enough for food, board, and bus fare to work but little enough to "preclude any possible purchase of cigarettes, newspapers, phone calls, postage stamps, any recreation, etc."[21]

The BIA would send some of the money to a relocatee's reservation before the move so a bus or train ticket could be purchased. The rest stayed in Chicago until the individual or group arrived in town. A bureau employee often met Chicago relocatees at the train or bus station and took them to the office on South Dearborn Street. There, the BIA worker would hand out a bit more start-up money and give instructions about what it should be used for and when the relocatee might return for more. At this point, employees in the relocation office also secured housing and employment for newly arrived Indians and provided general advice about Chicago. BIA officials also found schools for Indian children and informed families about churches and shops in their new neighborhoods. A Sioux man who was employed in the BIA's relocation program during this time remembers counseling urban newcomers about "who they should associate with and where they can go to church and shopping centers; the better areas of town; what to do as hobbies."[22]

In Chicago and other relocation centers, the BIA followed recommendations of the Hoover Commission and, in accord with the political spirit of the time, continued to work with nongovernmental organizations. Members of the Travelers Aid Society sometimes filled in for BIA employees in meeting newcomers at train and bus stations and in helping them acclimate. In some cities where the BIA had no relocation office but still placed some Indians, the Travelers Aid Society bore the entire work load. In Milwaukee, for instance, society members held and distributed BIA checks and helped Indians find jobs and apartments.[23]

At the beginning of the relocation program in 1952, BIA employees in Chicago as well as those stationed on reservations across the country were very concerned about making a good start and building momentum. They were intent upon achieving early success in order to sell the program to other Indians, employers who might provide jobs to relocated Indians, the American public, and federal government officials. In January, Mary Nan Gamble wrote, "I think it is highly important that the pilot crew of Indians in any plant be good representatives of the best type of employee we can offer." BIA workers kept close tabs on pilot groups from each area or reservation and above all tried to prevent "wash outs," relocatees who returned to their reservations, at taxpayer expense, after a brief stay in the city. Too many of these, the BIA worried, would cast doubt on the relocation program as a whole.[24] Moreover, they also occasionally complained that recent recruits were unsatisfactory—too difficult to acclimate and match with jobs.

The BIA initially intended for the relocation program to benefit both Indians and the nation at large. In 1950, before the program's official beginning, a BIA memo pointed out that "any program which will bring these people into or increase their effectiveness in the fields of labor, industry, business, government will not only benefit these people but the nation as well." Yet experiences in the field sometimes refuted that notion. BIA employees stationed on reservations and in urban relocation centers occasionally disagreed about the relocation program and its implementation. Some internal squabbles revolved around whether it was more important to benefit the nation's taxpayers or the Indians. Bureau officials on reservations felt pressure to keep a steady stream of migrants going to cities, and rumors of official or unofficial quotas for relocation officers spread both within and outside of the BIA. Gordon Jones, a Sioux who served as a relocation official on several reservations throughout the Northern Plains, maintained that the program would have been more successful had the central BIA office not been so concerned about numbers. Under pressure on one occasion to send more people from his reservation, Jones joked to his superior that he could easily locate the required number of relocatees if he were permitted to recruit at the city jail.[25]

A few years after the relocation program began, a long-running and sometimes acrimonious battle for public opinion was launched. Conservatives and liberals, friends and foes of the assimilation-minded BIA, squared off in the pages of national magazines to argue the merits of relocation. What is striking in hindsight is the degree to which both sides—who saw each other as uninformed and even misguided—stereotyped Indian people for their own purposes. A perceptive report released in December 1956 by the Association on American Indian Affairs (AAIA), a reform organization that included both Indians and non-Indians, recognized this. One side, it observed, saw the Indian as "Horatio Alger from the reservation," and the other as "the Paleolithic innocent set adrift in the atomic age."[26]

Former U.S. senator O. K. Armstrong, representing the first group as seen by the AAIA, weighed in first with a laudatory report on relocation. Armstrong described seeing nothing but misery on a tour of reservations (which he called "country slums"). He also spent a few days in Chicago, including at the BIA relocation office there, while working on the article. After the visit, he depicted the "miraculous" ability of relocation to turn around aimless Indian lives and quoted a BIA official who called the program "a rainbow of hope." In addition to emphasizing the ways in which the relocation program benefited Indian people, Armstrong also reminded readers of the financial benefit relocation would give the nation. In looking at five families who had participated in the program, he found they had paid more in taxes after a year than they had cost the federal government and taxpayers in relocation costs.[27]

Two months later, a piece published in *Look Magazine* also made the case for relocation, albeit indirectly, by emphasizing the hopelessness of reservation life. The BIA was clearly pleased with the publicity and freely provided information and data to other friendly authors in the hope that information about the relocation program would be disseminated to the public. A few days after the article in *Look* was published, an employee of the South Dakota State Employment Service involved in relocation wrote to Charles Miller of the BIA and congratulated him on the two articles and the positive spin on relocation they produced. "I thought your article in the *Reader's Digest* in January was excellent," he wrote, "and you no doubt already have *Look Magazine* in your hip pocket."[28]

Although they convinced some readers of the BIA's goodwill, the articles angered others who considered themselves to be the true "friends of the Indian." Dorothy VandeMark was a white Chicago resident who had long been interested in Indian affairs, and in pursuing this interest had become a friend and great admirer of John Collier. The relocation program as well as the BIA's termination policies infuriated VandeMark. Reading what she considered BIA propaganda concerning these programs angered her further. She dismissed Armstrong as a shill for the BIA and felt compelled to respond to and refute his piece. The resulting article was published in *Harper's Magazine* in March 1956. Although VandeMark pointed out exaggerations in Armstrong's piece, hers was no less skewed and one-sided. In her wish to halt relocation and termination, she portrayed Indians as tragic figures doomed to failure in the white world. In a letter to Collier earlier in 1956, VandeMark expressed particular sympathy for Indian relocatees, describing some as being "like mad people or like a wild thing that has been caught."[29]

Like many BIA critics at the time, VandeMark saw relocation and termination as working in tandem. Termination would make reservation life more and more difficult, and relocation would provide the final shove to push Indians off reservations. The ultimate purpose of both policies, VandeMark argued, was to transfer even more Indian land into the hands of whites, the most recent development in what she called "an old and dishonorable game." VandeMark thought that talk about relocation representing an "opportunity" for Indians was a sham. Strictly speaking, she claimed, Indians had no true options and were coerced into leaving their reservations. VandeMark had visited Indian reservations before writing the piece, and she was also influenced by how she saw the relocation program working in Chicago. As she became involved in the city's Indian community, she encountered more and more relocatees whom she thought unprepared for urban life and ill-served by the BIA that had sent them there.[30]

On the West Coast, Ruth Mulvey Harmer was developing opinions about the relocation program similar to VandeMark's. Harmer, a resident of Los Angeles, the second major relocation site during the 1950s, also was dismayed by what she saw. She published her criticisms of the BIA and its relocation program in the March 1956 issue of *Atlantic Monthly*. Like VandeMark, Harmer disputed the voluntary nature of the "voluntary relocation program," as it was known at the time, calling it "one of the most extraordinary forced migrations in history." She noted Indians' problems with housing, health issues, and the police in Los Angeles and wrote that the majority of relocatees soon returned to their reservations. Ignoring the problems of reservation life, she described a family transformed immediately from being "at peace" on a reservation to being trapped in an urban slum, "adrift in a new and hostile environment." Harmer, together with VandeMark, called for the abolition of relocation and termination and the introduction of federal programs that would allow Indian reservations to develop economically.[31]

As much as the *Reader's Digest* and *Look* articles pleased BIA officials, VandeMark's and Harmer's angered them. They shot back letters to *Harper's* and the *Atlantic* to refute the pieces. Moreover, Secretary of the Interior Douglas McKay emphatically replied, "It is NOT the policy of the present administration to see a solution of the Indian problem in the dispersal of Indian communities." Despite the BIA's speedy and pointed rebuttals to critical accounts, however, VandeMark's and Harmer's articles had a lingering effect. They helped convince the BIA to increase the relocation program's annual budget threefold in June 1956 from just over $1 million to almost $3.5 million. The criticisms also convinced some Indians and non-Indians that BIA policies were unwise or even treacherous. Many Americans had little knowledge of Indian people or Indian policy, and VandeMark's and Harmer's articles often were the first things the public read about BIA policy. Afterward, many politicians and Indian leaders used the articles in further criticism of the BIA. Even years later, wrinkled copies of the articles were being waved in the air and read at meetings where Indian policy was debated.[32]

Despite periodic criticism from VandeMark, Harmer, and others who felt the same way, the BIA continued to present a consistent message, rooted in the program's initial goals of integration and assimilation, to relocatees and would-be relocatees. The bureau's chief concern was that relocation be permanent, but pursuing that goal was often frustrating. Commissioner of Indian Affairs Glenn L. Emmons in 1955 stated that among the requirements that relocatees had to meet was to "show some evidence that they want to live permanently away from the home area." Officials in the local Chicago office also emphasized the permanency of relocation. One claimed that "one applicant successfully, happily, and reasonably permanently relocated is worth a dozen who take a tour at the public's expense and go home in a week or a month." In order to ensure that relocations were permanent, the BIA urged Indians to think long and hard about their decision before leaving and not relocate impulsively. "Relocation means PLANNING—careful planning by the whole family," emphasized a BIA memo in October 1956. Despite its constant and sometimes intrusive involvement in Indian people's lives during the relocation process, the BIA tried to encourage Indians to take some responsibility for themselves. As one brochure told those in the process of relocating, "This relocation plan is your plan." For those on the verge of returning to the reservation and adding to the numbers of nonpermanent relocations, the BIA had straightforward advice: "WORK HARD—work hard on the job—take overtime if you can get it. Work hard keeping house— If you get mad and discouraged and lonesome, clean up the house or apartment—work out your energy in keeping the place spotless, and it will pay off." The BIA also encouraged relocated Indians to integrate themselves into urban society as soon as possible by joining churches, sewing circles, and PTA groups. Repeatedly, BIA officials urged, "Know your town."[33]

In its more ambitious moments the BIA envisioned relocation and termination as permanently and totally improving Indian affairs and the lives of Indians. Although it acknowledged that some would stay on reservations, the bureau wanted as many as possible to relocate. It saw the program functioning as a powerful wave that would sweep Indians from reservations across the country to Chicago, Los Angeles, Denver, and Salt Lake City. Bureaucrats envisioned relocation as operating in the same way among all Indian people, as a monolithic force.

Formal policies and the ways in which people respond to them are two entirely different matters, however, and Indian people responded to termination and relocation in their own ways. They faced a formidable challenge in doing so, however. How could they maintain and defend the cultural separateness of their cultures and reservations at a time when doing so enjoyed little support nationwide? Moreover—and more important for many Indians—how could they stem the flood of support for termination, which seemed to be the obvious conclusion of integration and assimilation? Eighty men and women from a wide range of tribal backgrounds met at a Denver hotel in November 1944, in part to address these questions and in general to lobby the federal government on behalf of American Indians. The organization they formed, the National Congress of American Indians (NCAI), would become the foremost Indian political organization in the postwar period and would lead the charge against termination.

Initially, the NCAI focused on the twin goals of preserving Indian cultural values and protecting Indians' individual rights as U.S. citizens. The first goal led to such things as attempts to protect land claims, while the second led to the demand for Indian suffrage in Arizona and New Mexico. Many NCAI leaders—such as N. B. Johnson, Helen Peterson, and Ruth Muskrat Bronson—wanted to reconcile voluntary integration with continued tribal survival, in effect arguing for Indians' dual identity within American society. Bronson once explained that she did not completely reject integration and assimilation, but Indians wanted "to move in their own way and at their own pace as a unit."[34] To some extent, the NCAI's ambivalence about integration and assimilation, as expressed in federal Indian policy and elsewhere, resembled that of many Indian people, whether on reservations or in small towns and large cities across the nation in the mid-twentieth century.

As terminationists in Congress and the BIA pushed their program on Indians in the 1950s, the NCAI grew less optimistic about prospects for integration and assimilation. This new and dangerous environment, they argued, did not allow for a voluntary type of integration. Pointing to the American tradition that valued the consent of the governed, NCAI members maintained that avid proponents of termination were acting undemocratically. They also grew frustrated as many politicians refused to acknowledge the important distinction, as NCAI saw it, between coercive termination and a more gradual and effective type of termination. By 1954 the membership of NCAI was almost unanimous in opposition to termination as it was being practiced, and some foretold later debates. D'Arcy McNickle noted that "the battle for civil rights may not yet be won, but the battle for the right to be culturally different has not even started." Similarly, Bronson argued that "in a full democracy there must be room for freedom, room that is, for people to be different from their neighbors."[35]

In response to the government's hard line on termination, the NCAI wrote what it called a "Declaration of Indian Rights" in 1954. Directly confronting the arguments of those who would dissolve reservations because they seemed to represent cultural separatism, the organization stated, "Reservations do not imprison us. They are ancestral homelands, retained by us for our personal use and enjoyment. We feel we must assert our right to maintain ownership in our own way, and to terminate it only by our consent." Other Indian organizations in the 1950s also tried to explain and defend Native Americans' unique position in American society. The Midwestern Intertribal Council, for example, focused on exercising "the two sets of rights which all Indians have: Indian rights and equal rights."[36] Such public statements represented what many Indian people said to one another in an environment filled with talk about termination and relocation. Many agreed that cultural traditions needed to be protected and that calls for integration and assimilation should be viewed with a wary eye.

During the early 1950s, Indians also began to respond to the BIA's relocation program, often with evidence of conflicting feelings. A few resolutely distrusted relocation and never gave it a second thought. Others embraced it immediately as the answer to their problems and left for Chicago or Los Angeles or Denver without much hesitation. The great majority, however, were torn between reservations, cherished as ancestral homelands, and the glittering appeals of urban life, which sometimes appeared too good to be true in second- and thirdhand reports. Indian people who interacted with the relocation program often spent a good deal of time weighing its pros and cons. They were far from pawns for BIA workers to move as they pleased.

Although often poor and sometimes hauntingly desolate, the reservations on the Northern Plains and in the Upper Midwest provided homes for those who resided there. Discussions in Washington and in national publications about reservations being "rural slums" seemed overblown to Indian people. They derived many pleasures from their reservations, the deepest of which was the nearby presence of kinsmen and friends—people with whom one ate, talked, socialized, hunted, and fished. Because of such communal pleasures, those who left for cities often did so reluctantly and with a nagging sense of loss.[37]

At the same time, reservation areas suffered from deep-rooted economic and social problems. By the 1950s, decades of land dispossession and low-paying wage labor had made the economic problems appear permanent. Like their early-twentieth-century forbears, many Indians in the 1950s had adopted economic and migration patterns that made wage labor a normal part of their lives. Frequently, however, the best they could hope for was seasonal wage work, often fruit and berry picking. Furthermore, as blacks in the Deep South saw their agricultural jobs being threatened by new mechanical cottonpickers, the Indians of the Upper Midwest and Northern Plains also suffered from advancements in agricultural machinery. The vast potato fields of Nebraska and Colorado, traditionally employing hundreds of Indians at harvest time, now relied on machines. Only 40 percent of the men and 20 percent of the women among the nearby Oneida enjoyed permanent work in 1958.[38] In North and South Dakota, white-owned ranching operations continued to expand, which left Indian efforts even less competitive. In 1950 the average reservation resident earned $950. Tribes such as the Yankton Sioux in South Dakota fared even worse, earning an average of $730. Comparable figures in 1950 for whites averaged almost $4,000, and blacks on average earned more than $2,000.[39]

By the 1950s Chicago possessed a far more diversified economy than most other cities nationwide and certainly more so than the rural areas of the Upper Midwest and Northern Plains. Since the nineteenth century it had been a national center for several industries, including steel and meatpacking. This economic clout was one of the most powerful forces that pulled Indian people from their reservations, even if reluctantly. Indeed, American Indians were far from alone in being drawn to Chicago after the war. Whites from the Upper South and blacks from the Deep South also migrated there, attracted by economic opportunities and other advantages. The millions of Americans on the move during the mid-twentieth century profoundly reshaped northern and western cities, and the nation as a whole, politically, culturally, and economically.[40]

American Indians migrating to Chicago during the 1950s and 1960s, however, would not enter the same economy as had European immigrants or even some black migrants decades before. First, the overwhelming majority arrived with few or no skills and were unfit for many jobs the city had to offer. Moreover, the nature of Chicago's economy was changing. Heavy industry was slowly losing its foothold, and mechanization was eliminating jobs. A new service economy was emerging. Thus, part of the BIA's logic in bringing Indians to cities such as Chicago under the relocation plan was flawed, as many critics have since pointed out. In retrospect, Kurt Dreifuss's claim that Chicago's "industrial might" made it a natural place for Indians during the 1950s rings somewhat hollow.[41] In most cases, however, Chicago offered Indian people more opportunities than they had in their former homes on isolated and impoverished reservations. Some critics have rightly noted that Indians in the relocation program often started on the bottom rung of the socioeconomic ladder in cities such as Chicago, and they often remained there.[42] Yet many who lived on reservations during these years were entirely off the ladder. Their standard of living was worse—often incomparably worse— than that of any other group of Americans. In that context, regular work, no matter how little it paid, was sometimes enough to convince Indians to come to Chicago. During periods of labor shortage in the mid-1950s, the economic pull exercised by cities such as Chicago was even greater. By 1955 even the *Wall Street Journal* had noted the phenomenon, commenting that "companies in other cities in the Far West, Midwest, and Southwest are reaching out for the Red Man to help solve labor shortage problems."[43]

---

Even earlier, the limited but still significant economic opportunities in Chicago had influenced Indian people. Benjamin Bearskin in 1947 left his Winnebago reservation in Wisconsin, where work was "running out for Indians," for Chicago and its promise of "fifty paychecks a year." Likewise, a Papago woman who in 1952 came to Chicago from Arizona as a young girl with her parents and four siblings recalled that her father was a farm laborer when work was available back home and often had to travel to Nebraska and Kansas to combine wheat. In some years he would be gone for as much as six months at a time while working in the wheat fields. When he heard about the relocation program, she remembered, "he jumped at it."[44] For some, however, economic possibilities or advantages were not enough to convince them to move. As time passed, though, the small Chicago American Indian community grew and became a magnet for those who lived on reservations and pondered the pros and cons of the relocation program. As well as the prospect of employment, moving to Chicago could mean joining others of their tribe or Indian people of other tribes.

The Indian community that grew up during the 1950s did not, of course, represent the first settlement of Indians in Chicago. Even before there was a city named Chicago there was a military installation named

Fort Dearborn, and various Indian tribes lived in and traveled through the region around it. After the Treaty of Chicago in 1833, however, most were removed westward. Furthermore, Chicago changed dramatically throughout the nineteenth century, growing from a frontier village to a major urban center. During Chicago's industrial age in the late nineteenth and early twentieth centuries, American Indians there numbered at most a hundred or so at any one time. Among them was Carlos Montezuma, the famous Yavapai medical doctor, speaker, and writer on Indian policy.

Peripatetic throughout his life, Montezuma as a child lived with his guardian as he moved from Galesburg, Illinois, to Chicago, then back to Galesburg, to Brooklyn, and then to Urbana, Illinois. After graduating from the University of Illinois in 1883, Montezuma attended Chicago Medical College. After receiving his M.D., he spent a few years working in the Indian Service and in 1896 opened a private medical practice in Chicago. His office remained at 100 State Street from 1896 until 1922, when he left for Arizona, ill with tuberculosis and wishing to return home to die. Although much of his time in Chicago was spent on his medical practice, Montezuma was also involved with Indians, but primarily at a policy level. He devoted time to raising support for the Carlisle Indian Industrial School, established by his friend Richard H. Pratt in Carlisle, Pennsylvania. There, and at other Indian boarding schools around the turn of the century, Indian children lived for months, removed from their families as school officials attempted to assimilate them. Montezuma also developed a profound opposition to the BIA, which he constantly attacked for opposing the true self-interest of Indians and perpetuating the rule of paternalist white officials. He hoped that the BIA would be eliminated in his lifetime and even began a journal in 1916, the sole purpose of which, he wrote, was "freedom for the Indians through the abolishment of the Indian Bureau." In support of these passionately held causes, he undertook frequent and lengthy speaking tours to the Southwest and elsewhere. Montezuma occasionally hosted prominent Indians who traveled through Chicago, but he seemed to have had little interaction with other Indians who lived in Chicago during this period.[45]

Yet Chicago's young and small Indian community was becoming more politically active in the early twentieth century. The Grand Council Fire of American Indians, an organization composed of both Indians and predominantly upper-middle-class whites interested in Indian affairs, began in Chicago in 1923 and ten years later was renamed the Indian Council Fire. During the 1920s and 1930s, four city judges were members of the group. In its early years, the organization focused on a variety of activities, including influencing Indian policy and legislation, informing whites about Indians' historical contributions to American life, and providing some social services to Indian people. During the administration of Chicago mayor William Hale ("Big Bill") Thompson in the late 1920s, the Indian Council Fire challenged the city to include more accurate American Indian history in school textbooks. Over time, however, the Indian Council Fire phased out most of its lobbying and social work and focused most of its energies on highlighting the achievements of prominent American Indian individuals, honoring them annually since 1933 by the National Indian Achievement Award.[46]

Both the Council Fire and *Amerindian*, its publication begun in 1952 and edited by Council Fire secretary Marion Gridley, espoused an assimilationist philosophy and emphasized the importance of higher education for Indians. The Council Fire appealed to those who modeled themselves after Carlos Montezuma—or at least his focus on gradual, voluntary assimilation—but the organization seemed out of touch and somewhat condescending to many of the less-educated Indians who began to trickle into Chicago during the 1940s. Like other groups, the Indian Council Fire was sometimes romantic and backward-looking. The president, for example, was called "Chief of Chiefs"; the vice president, "Chief of Lodge"; the secretary, "Keeper of Lore"; the treasurer, "Chief Wampum Keeper"; and the five directors were "Chief Arrow Maker," "Chief Rain Maker," "Chief of Fire," "Chief Pipe Bearer," and "Chief Medicine Man."[47]

Scott Peters, a Chippewa, served as chief of chiefs from 1925 to 1934 and played an important role in Chicago's Indian community during those years. Born in 1877 on a Chippewa reservation in Michigan, he attended Carlisle Indian Industrial School as a boy and then moved to the Chicago area, where he worked as a tailor. He lived in Waukegan and other northern suburbs of Chicago for twenty years. After leaving the tailoring business, he went to work for the BIA during the 1930s as an guidance and placement officer. During this time, he made numerous recruiting trips throughout the Upper Midwest and Northern Plains, looking especially for graduates of Indian schools such as Carlisle, Flambeau, and Haskell who were interested in moving to Chicago, Milwaukee, Detroit, or other cities. A Winnebago, Willard LaMere, who benefited from Peters's work later spoke highly of him as a "one-man relocation team." After he found people who were interested in migrating, Peters would visit factories and other workplaces to secure jobs for them. One such migrant later praised Peters as being "really instrumental" in finding him a job at Chicago's Stewart-Warner factory and observed that there were "a lot of Indians working there." Peters also helped bring several young single Indian women to Chicago and found them jobs as domestics. Ironically, Peters died in 1952, the year a more intensive and organized government-sponsored relocation plan began.[48]

News of Peters's work and the success of some of those who participated in it continued to bring other Indians to Chicago during the 1930s. With the outbreak of World War II, however, this migration increased. Chippewas and Winnebagos from nearby Wisconsin dominated the group. By 1940, the census counted 274 Indians living in Chicago, although that number should be seen as an approximation; demographers have argued for both higher and lower numbers. Some who arrived during the early 1940s worked at jobs related to the war effort. One Sioux man who served in the military during World War II visited Chicago on leave and later settled there. Some who found jobs in steel plants that had defense contracts bought houses in the southwestern part of the city. Others employed by the BIA came to Chicago in 1942 when the agency's central office moved there temporarily from Washington. A few stayed on after the war ended and the office had returned to the District of Columbia. More Indians, however, worked in occupations not directly related to the war effort. They were nurses, teachers, cab drivers, seamstresses, and house cleaners.[49]

Those who resided in Chicago before the relocation program took advantage of the employment opportunities the city offered. A Winnebago woman recalled that the first time she performed wage work was in 1940. While she lived in East Chicago, an industrial suburb in Indiana, she sewed pants for the army. A Sioux woman who came to Chicago in 1940 commented that during World War II, "The jobs were getting plentiful. You could see there was a war coming on. . . . So when I could see they were paying a little bit more money at another plant, I would go work there. And then I got acquainted with different people. They would tell me, 'Well, they're paying more over here.' Well, I would go there."[50]

During the pre-relocation period as well as after, Indians in Chicago relied on each other for many different things. A Sioux woman remembers with pride the way Indians looked out for each other during the 1940s. They shared already cramped apartments in rooming houses in addition to news about jobs and other important information about city life. Always they searched for familiar faces amid a sea of whites and blacks. "We would know when a new one came in," she recalls.[51] Once a new Indian arrived in Chicago, an older resident would usually try to use employment connections to help the newcomer acquire a job. The electrical equipment manufacturer Stewart-Warner and the publishing firm R. R. Donnelley were among companies that employed the Indians. Indians also assisted each other by providing opportunities to assemble for social, cultural, or religious occasions. Although the wartime housing shortage made things difficult, the small Indian community tried to congregate socially by living near each other. A few lived on the city's West Side around West Madison and Garfield Park, a few on the South Side around Lake Park and Forty-seventh Street, and a few on the Near North Side around Fullerton and Diversey.[52] It often was difficult to find other Indians. One man remembers that he walked around for several days by himself before he encountered another Indian.[53]

The most anticipated social occasions came when groups gathered for powwows, dances, or meetings. A small group—including Willard LaMere (Winnebago), Scott Thundercloud (Ottawa), and Benjamin Bearskin (Winnebago-Sioux)—along with Russell Minea, a non-Indian, removed itself from the assimilationist and often paternalist Indian Council Fire and started the North American Indian Council (soon to be renamed the North American Indian Mission) in 1946. When that group folded soon thereafter, Benjamin Bearskin helped start the Inter-Tribal Council, which focused on social activities. Hotels, YMCAs, or sometimes city parks would either loan or rent their facilities to groups of Indians for an evening. The social events were important to the small Indian community. They provided occasions when those who had lived in Chicago for several years could share information about the city with newcomers. Indian women, for instance, would reveal where to shop, how to use public transportation, and how to enroll children in local schools. The small community of Indian people who resided in Chicago before the relocation program of the 1950s served as a nucleus of information and assisted migrants who later would arrive. The "old-timers" had gained valuable experience, and they were willing to share it.[54]

---

One further thing pulled Indians to Chicago during the early 1950s and after—a carefully planned and widespread advertising campaign mounted by the BIA. Bureau officials realized that a strategy focused solely on money and material advantages would not be very effective in convincing Indians to leave their homes for Chicago and other relocation sites. Instead, they presented a message that combined Chicago's material and its social benefits. They noted that Indian people already lived in Chicago and presented pictures of friends, family, and fellow tribe members there to convince residents of reservations that city life would be rewarding.

The campaign attempted to entice Indians to participate and to refute relocation program critics. In May 1952, when BIA area directors met to plan for the coming year, they believed they were in an information and propaganda battle and made plans accordingly, frequently using military terminology. Some suggested more frequent use of community meetings to explain relocation. "A regular and consistent exposition of the facts through a combination of the written and spoken word," one claimed, "will keep us on the offensive." BIA employees at the meeting viewed a consistent and persuasive "selling job" as the preferable position and strategy but made contingency plans as well in case opponents of the relocation program appeared to be gaining too much ground. "If we have to adopt the defensive," one said, "then we should bring up our heavy guns."[55]

During the early 1950s, Indian people on reservations throughout the Upper Midwest and Northern Plains found posters and brochures advertising the relocation program almost everywhere—tacked to bulletin boards in BIA offices and local stores, stuffed into agency bulletins and newsletters, and carried home by children returning from bureau-run schools. Places where Indians gathered frequently were adorned with elaborate displays that included large posters covered with snapshots of the Chicago lakefront, Los Angeles defense factories, and other urban scenes.[56]

In 1953 the BIA developed a slide show to illustrate features of Chicago life that Indian people found attractive. The program was suggested by Brice Lay, the BIA's relocation officer in charge of North and South Dakota, who asked Kurt Dreifuss at the Chicago relocation office to develop a program that would specifically address Indian people and their needs. Lay argued that in addition to noting Chicago's economic advantages, an effective slide program would also show Indians in Chicago, people those back on the reservations might recognize. "Many of our people here feel group and kinship ties very closely," Lay instructed Dreifuss. "They behave in a way which is acceptable to the group they are identified with." Following Lay's suggestions, a group of BIA workers spent two and a half weeks in Chicago in February 1953, taking pictures of relocatees. After sixty-one slides had been chosen and printed, the BIA sent a set of them and an accompanying script to all large reservations in North and South Dakota, including Pine Ridge, Rosebud, Fort Berthold, Turtle Mountain, and Standing Rock. Indian students at Chilocco and other schools also experienced the program as part of visits by BIA officials.[57]

Some slides and commentary emphasized the immense size, scope, and power of Chicago, a message similar to that any civic booster would use to impress a rural person. The Merchandise Mart, for example, was described as the "largest commercial building in the world." Moreover, the stage at the Civic Opera was thirteen stories high, the stockyards covered more than one square mile, and as many as 350,000 people came to free concerts at Grant Park.

To provide a striking contrast to life in economically depressed reservation communities, several Indian people were pictured on the job in Chicago stockyards, factories, and retail stores. There were even job opportunities in Chicago, the BIA noted, for those who had little chance of gaining employment back home. Young women were pictured stocking shelves in stores and answering telephones in office buildings, and Indian people with handicaps and disabilities were also seen enjoying employment in Chicago. A Navajo man who had lost three fingers, for example, was shown at his work in a body shop. Slides of apartments that had steam heat, refrigerators, and washing machines also pointed out the differences between reservation and urban housing conditions.

Chicago presented, according to the slide program, endless opportunities for Indian people to shop and acquire consumer goods. Two Winnebago girls were shown peering into a shopping center from the sidewalk as the commentator announced, "If you like to window shop, Chicago has the stores for it." A Chippewa woman was shown shopping at "one of Chicago's many super markets," where her husband worked as a clerk. Viewers even learned of employee discounts for those who worked in department stores. Two Winnebago sisters who worked at Butler Brothers, for example, were able to take 40 percent off the price of all goods they bought there.

The social as well as economic benefits of Chicago living were shown by photographs of Indian people enjoying aspects of urban life. Such pictures encouraged those considering relocation but who feared the isolation and loneliness it could bring. Friends and siblings were seen working together, side by side, on a Chicago assembly line or typing in the same office. It appeared that Indian people could earn better wages while still retaining and cherishing traditional social bonds.

According to the presentation, Indian families from different tribes lived in the same apartment buildings, rooming houses, and neighborhoods. In one picture, five recently relocated families—two of them Sioux and the others Choctaw, Pima, and Seminole—leave the West Side apartment building where they all live. The Evangeline Residence, a rooming house that housed only young, single women, including several relocated Indians, was described as having "extremely liberal" rules, information young viewers could contrast with their experiences at notoriously strict boarding schools. Indian people were also shown attending church together, which indicated that those active in their church back on the reservation could continue to be so in the city. One Indian boy was pictured with other officers of a sodality at his Catholic school. For the many reservation residents who saw some advantages to city life but had no interest in assimilation or in interacting with predominantly non-Indians, pictures of a viable Indian community, participating in activities together in Chicago, were extremely attractive.

Finally, the BIA's program emphasized the many recreational opportunities of Chicago. Because young Indians frequently had great interest in sports, they were told they could continue to pursue those interests in Chicago. Ten successive slides pictured Indians playing basketball in various city leagues. Other slides depicted powwows and other social gatherings where Indians congregated. The show concluded with pictures of Lake Michigan, which was said to belong "to everybody" and have beaches "free for everybody to use."[58]

Sometimes, however, the BIA's propaganda efforts backfired. Those who remained on the reservation and those suspicious of the relocation program and its motives could enjoy a laugh at the agency's expense. Some individuals pictured in promotional material were recognized as having given up on city life and being back on their reservations.[59]

---

Migration proceeded despite periodic failures and problems. Thousands of Indian people were attracted to Chicago, whether because of the appeal of jobs, a small Indian community that welcomed them, BIA advertising, or countless other reasons. Although BIA policy and a favorable image of life in Chicago were important, patterns of individual migration often differed. Indians came from different reservation communities, and their various experiences before urbanization would greatly influence the ways in which they would come to Chicago and what happened to them there.

## Notes

1. Assessments of termination and relocation policies are found in Larry W. Burt, "Roots of the Native American Urban Experience: Relocation Policy in the 1950s," *American Indian Quarterly* 10 (Spring 1986): 85–99; Larry W. Burt, *Tribalism in Crisis: Federal Indian Policy, 1953–1961* (Albuquerque: University of New Mexico Press, 1982); Donald L. Fixico, *Termination and Relocation: Federal Indian Policy, 1945–1960* (Albuquerque: University of New Mexico Press, 1986); Larry J. Hasse, "Termination and Assimilation: Federal Indian Policy, 1943 to 1961," Ph.D. diss., Washington State University, 1974; Clayton R. Koppes, "From New Deal to Termination: Liberalism and Indian

Policy, 1933–1953," *Pacific Historical Review* 46 (Nov. 1977): 543–66; Kenneth R. Philp, "Dillon S. Myer and the Advent of Termination: 1950–1953," *Western Historical Quarterly* 19 (Jan. 1988): 37–59; Kenneth R. Philp, "Termination: A Legacy of the Indian New Deal," *Western Historical Quarterly* 14 (April 1983): 165–80; Kenneth R. Philp, *Termination Revisited: American Indians on the Trail to Self-Determination, 1933–1953* (Lincoln: University of Nebraska Press, 1999); and John R. Wunder, *"Retained by the People": A History of American Indians and the Bill of Rights* (New York: Oxford University Press, 1994), 97–111. The quotation is from U.S. Congress, House, *Termination of Federal Supervision, Concurrent Resolution 108*, 83d Cong., 1st sess., 1 Aug. 1953 (Washington: Government Printing Office, 1953).

2. Koppes, "From New Deal to Termination," 555.

3. Philp, "Dillon S. Myer," 45; Burt, "Roots of the Native American Urban Experience," 93 (quotation).

4. S. Lyman Tyler, "William A. Brophy (1945–48)," in *The Commissioners of Indian Affairs, 1824–1977*, ed. Robert M. Kvasnicka and Herbert J. Viola (Lincoln: University of Nebraska Press, 1979), 285; Hasse, "Termination and Assimilation," 100–101.

5. William J. Dennehy, "John Ralph Nichols (1949–50)," in *The Commissioners of Indian Affairs, 1824–1977*, ed. Robert M. Kvasnicka and Herbert J. Viola (Lincoln: University of Nebraska Press, 1979), 289–92; Francis Paul Prucha, *The Great Father: The United States Government and the American Indians* (Lincoln: University of Nebraska Press, 1984), 1029 (first quotation); Philp, "Termination," 166–68; Kenneth R. Philp, "Stride toward Freedom: The Relocation of Indians to Cities, 1952–1960," *Western Historical Quarterly* 16 (April 1985): 176 (second quotation).

6. Hasse, "Termination and Assimilation," 100.

7. Philp, "Dillon S. Myer," 38; Philp, *Termination Revisited*, 89–107; Patricia K. Ourada, "Dillon Seymour Myer (1950–1953)," in *The Commissioners of Indian Affairs, 1824–1977*, ed. Robert M. Kvasnicka and Herbert J. Viola (Lincoln: University of Nebraska Press, 1979), 293–99.

8. "The Needs of the American Indian" [address by Dillon Myer], 12 Dec. 1951, Welfare Council of Metropolitan Chicago Files, 146–1, Manuscript Collections, Chicago Historical Society.

9. Philp, *Termination Revisited*, 90; Grant P. Arndt, "Relocation's Imagined Landscape and the Rise of Chicago's Native American Community," in *Native Chicago*, ed. Terry Straus and Grant P. Arndt (Chicago: Native Chicago, 1998), 114–15.

10. "Indians Make Good as City Migrants," *New York Times*, 18 May 1953, 23; "Indians Move Here at U.S. Urging," *Chicago Sun-Times*, 22 March 1956, 78.

11. R. Warren Metcalf, "Arthur V. Watkins and the Indians of Utah: A Study of Federal Termination Policy," Ph.D. diss., Arizona State University, 1995, 27–55 (first quotation); Arthur V. Watkins, "Termination of Federal Supervision: The Removal of Restrictions over Indian Property and Person," *Annals*

*of the American Academy of Political and Social Sciences* 311 (May 1957): 51 (second quotation).

12. Philp, "Stride toward Freedom," 177–78; Fixico, *Termination and Relocation*, 134–35; Margaret Connell Szasz, *Education and the American Indian: The Road to Self-Determination* (Albuquerque: University of New Mexico Press, 1974), 116–17.

13. Joe Miller to Harold Huxley, 9 Oct. 1951, box 1, Financial Program, Field Placement and Relocation Office Employment Assistance Records, Record Group 75, National Archives–Washington, D.C. [hereafter FP, FPROEAR, RG 75, NA-WDC]; BIA information circular, Feb.–Mar. 1952, Robert Rietz Collection, Community Archives, Native American Educational Services College, Chicago [hereafter Rietz Collection, CA, NAES].

14. John Cooper to Charles Miller, 16 March 1953, box 1, FP, FPROEAR, RG 75, NA-WDC.

15. Philp, "Stride toward Freedom," 179–80; Robert Griffith, "Dwight D. Eisenhower and the Corporate Commonwealth," *American Historical Review* 87 (Feb. 1982): 87–122.

16. BIA information circular, Feb.–Mar. 1952, Rietz Collection, CA, NAES; D'Arcy McNickle to John Provinse, 18 Nov. 1949, box 1, FP, FPROEAR, RG 75, NA-WDC; LaVerne Madigan, *The American Indian Relocation Program* (New York: Association on American Indian Affairs, 1956), 10.

17. Chicago FRO Report, Jan. 1952, box 1, Reports on Employment Assistance, 1951–1958, Chicago Field Employment Assistance Office, Record Group 75, National Archives–Great Lakes Region, Chicago [hereafter REA, CFEAO, RG 75, NA-GLR].

18. Donald L. Parman, "Lewis Meriam's Letters during the Survey of Indian Affairs, 1926–1927 (Part 2)," *Arizona and the West* 24 (Winter 1982): 342.

19. Brice Lay to Aberdeen Area Superintendents, 12 Oct. 1956, box 4, NR, FPROEAR, RG 75, NA-WDC.

20. Warren Spaulding to Selene Gifford, 13 Oct. 1950, box 1, Placement and Statistical Reports, 1948–54, Field Placement and Relocation Office Employment Assistance Records, Record Group 75, National Archives–Washington, D.C. [hereafter PSR, FPROEAR, RG 75, NA-WDC]; "Relocation Expense Report," Chicago FRO Report, Feb. 1952, box 1, REA, CFEAO, RG 75, NA-GLR.

21. Mary Nan Gamble to Selene Gifford, 28 Jan. 1952, box 1, FP, FPROEAR, RG 75, NA-WDC.

22. Interview with Gordon Jones (Sioux), 2 June 1971, American Indian Oral History Research Project [hereafter AIOHRP], pt. 1, no. 34, MS 684.

23. Aileen Pinkerton, "Report of the Milwaukee Relocation Committee," April 1953, Rietz Collection, CA, NAES.

24. Mary Nan Gamble to Selene Gifford, 28 Jan. 1952, box 1, FP, FPROEAR, RG 75, NA-WDC; Billings Area Report, March 1952, box 1, PSR, FPROEAR, RG 75, NA-WDC.

25. "Indian Placement Program," 3 Jan. 1950, Rietz Collection, CA, NAES;

interview with Gordon Jones (Sioux), 2 June 1971, AIOHRP, pt. 1, no. 34, MS 684.

26. Madigan, *The American Indian Relocation Program*, 14–15.

27. O. K. Armstrong and Marjorie Armstrong, "The Indians Are Going to Town," *Reader's Digest* 66 (Jan. 1955): 39–43.

28. "The Sioux Indians: Their Plight Is Our Worst Disgrace," *Look*, 19 April 1955, 32–37; Lynus Stoneback to Charles Miller, 21 April 1955, box 1, FP, FPROEAR, RG 75, NA-WDC.

29. Dorothy VandeMark to John Collier, 14 Jan. 1956, reel 42, Collier Papers, Archives and Manuscripts Division, Sterling Memorial Library, Yale University, New Haven, Conn.

30. Dorothy VandeMark, "The Raid on the Reservations," *Harper's Magazine* 212 (March 1956): 48–53.

31. Ruth Mulvey Harmer, "Uprooting the Indians," *Atlantic Monthly* 197 (Mar. 1956): 54–57. A year later, *Atlantic Monthly* published another article critical of the BIA and its relocation and termination programs. See Edith R. Mirrielees, "The Cloud of Mistrust," *Atlantic Monthly* 199 (Feb. 1957): 55–59.

32. "Interior Secretary Issues Official Reply to Policy Critics," *Amerindian* (Jan.–Feb. 1956): 1; Madigan, *The American Indian Relocation Program*, 9; Burt, "Roots of the Native American Urban Experience," 92.

33. Glenn L. Emmons, "U.S. Aim: Give the Indians a Chance," *Nation's Business* 43 (July 1955): 42 (first quotation); Alida Bowler, "A Brief Study of Relocation Activities and Results in California," 1 Apr. 1952–31 Mar. 1953, Rietz Collection, CA, NAES (second quotation); "So You're Going Away!" [BIA pamphlet], Nov. 1953, Rietz Collection, CA, NAES (fourth quotation); Brice Lay to Aberdeen Area Superintendents, 12 Oct. 1956, box 4, NR, FPROEAR, RG 75, NA-WDC (third, fifth, and sixth quotations).

34. Gretchen G. Harvey, "Cherokee and American: Ruth Muskrat Bronson, 1897–1982," Ph.D. diss., Arizona State University, 1996, 194.

35. Thomas W. Cowger, "'The Crossroads of Destiny': The NCAI's Landmark Struggle to Thwart Coercive Termination," *American Indian Culture and Research Journal* 20 (1996): 132 (first quotation); Harvey, "Cherokee and American," 116–17 (second quotation).

36. Thomas W. Cowger, *The National Congress of American Indians: The Founding Years* (Lincoln: University of Nebraska Press, 1999), 134 (first quotation); Gretchen G. Harvey, "Cherokee and American: Ruth Muskrat Bronson, 1897–1982," Ph.D. diss., Arizona State University, 1996, 116–98; Bernstein, *American Indians and World War II*, 112–58; *Indian Affairs* (Sept. 1957): 5 (second quotation).

37. Joan Ablon, "American Indian Relocation: Problems of Dependency and Management in the City," *Phylon* 26 (Winter 1965): 362–71; Frederick E. Hoxie, "From Prison to Homeland: The Cheyenne River Indian Reservation before World War I," *South Dakota History* 9 (Winter 1979): 1–24; Peter Iverson, *When Indians Became Cowboys: Native Peoples and Cat-

*tle Ranching in the American West* (Norman: University of Oklahoma Press, 1994), 205–7.

38. *The Pine Ridge,* 1 Sept. 1954, Rietz Collection, CA, NAES; "Report on the Labor Force and the Employment Conditions of the Oneida Indians," Oct. 1958, folder 2, box 2, Illinois–Wisconsin Friends Committee for American Indians Papers, State Historical Society of Wisconsin Archives, Madison.

39. Alan L. Sorkin, "The Economic and Social Status of the American Indian, 1940–1970," *Journal of Negro Education* 45 (Fall 1976): 433; Philp, "Stride toward Freedom," 182.

40. Nicholas Lemann, *The Promised Land: The Great Black Migration and How It Changed America* (New York: Knopf, 1991); James N. Gregory, *American Exodus: The Dust Bowl Migration and Okie Culture in California* (New York: Oxford University Press, 1989).

41. "Transition Hard for Indians Here," *Chicago Sun-Times,* 20 May 1957, Clip File: "Ethnic Groups-Chicago-Indians, American," Harold Washington Public Library, Chicago.

42. Burt, "Roots of the Native American Relocation Experience," 89–90.

43. "Indians and Industry," *Wall Street Journal,* 28 Dec. 1955, 1.

44. "Transition Hard For Indians Here"; interview with Marlene Strouse (Papago), Chicago, 18 July 1983, Chicago American Indian Oral History Pilot Project, no. 011, Newberry Library, Chicago, and Native American Educational Services College, Chicago [hereafter CAIOHP, NL and NAES].

45. Peter Iverson, *Carlos Montezuma and the Changing World of American Indians* (Albuquerque: University of New Mexico Press, 1982), 106.

46. Rosalyn R. LaPier, "'We Are Not Savages, but a Civilized Race': American Indian Activism and the Development of Chicago's First American Indian Organizations, 1919–1934," M.A. thesis, DePaul University, 2000; David R. M. Beck, "Native American Education in Chicago: Teach Them Truth," *Education and Urban Society* 32 (Feb. 2000): 243.

47. Undated notes by Willard LaMere, box 1, Indian Council Fire Papers, Special Collections, Newberry Library [hereafter ICF Papers, SC, NL]; Indian Council Fire press release, 7 May 1944, box 2, ICF Papers, SC, NL; *The Warrior* (March 1971); *Amerindian* (Sept.–Oct. 1955): 1; ICF Bylaws, 1 May 1955, box 1, ICF Papers, SC, NL; David R. M. Beck, "The Chicago American Indian Community," in *Native Chicago,* ed. Terry Straus and Grant P. Arndt (Chicago: Native Chicago, 1998), 172.

48. Marion Gridley, *Indians of Today* (Chicago: N.p., 1936), 98; *National Congress of American Indians Bulletin* (May–June 1952), Rietz Collection, CA, NAES; interview with Willard LaMere (Winnebago), Chicago, 1 Feb. 1984, CAIOHP, no. 009, NL and NAES (quotations); Edmund Jefferson Danziger, *Survival and Regeneration: Detroit's American Indian Community* (Detroit: Wayne State University Press, 1991), 36; LaPier, "'We Are Not Savages, but a Civilized Race.'"

49. Author interview with Susan K. Power (Sioux), Chicago, 19 June 1995;

Janusz Mucha, "From Prairie to the City: Transformation of Chicago's American Indian Community," *Urban Anthropology* 12 (Fall 1983): 341.

50. Interview with Rose Maney (Winnebago), Chicago, 2 May 1984, CAIOHP, no. 002, NL and NAES; interview with Ada Powers (Sioux), Chicago, 19 April 1984, CAIOHP, no. 012, NL and NAES.

51. Author interview with Susan K. Power (Sioux).

52. George D. Scott, John Kennardh White, and Estelle Fuchs, *Indians and Their Education in Chicago* (Washington, D.C.: Educational Resources Information Center, 1969), 3; Merwyn S. Garbarino, "Indians in Chicago," in *Urban Indians: Proceedings of the Third Annual Conference on Problems and Issues Concerning American Indians Today* (Chicago: Newberry Library, 1981), 56; Merwyn S. Garbarino, "The Chicago American Indian Center: Two Decades," in *American Indian Urbanization*, ed. Jack O. Waddell and O. Michael Watson (West Lafayette: Institute for the Study of Social Change, 1973), 75; Mucha, "From Prairie to the City," 341.

53. Author interview with Daniel Battise (Alabama-Coushatta), Chicago, 15 June 1995.

54. Willard LaMere, "History of Indians in Chicago" [transcript of lecture], 9 Oct. 1979, NAES; author interview with Diane Maney (Winnebago), Chicago, 20 June 1995; Grant Arndt, "'Contrary to Our Way of Thinking': The Struggle for an American Indian Center in Chicago, 1946–1953," *American Indian Culture and Research Journal* 22, no. 4 (1998): 118–19.

55. "Summary of Area Directors' Conference," 12–16 May 1952, Rietz Collection, CA, NAES.

56. Aberdeen Area Report, Jan. 1952, box 1, PSR, FPROEAR, RG 75, NA-WDC; Brice Lay to Aberdeen Area Superintendents, 12 Mar. 1957, box 4, NR, FPROEAR, RG 75, NA-WDC; *New York Times*, 16 Dec. 1956, 75; Madigan, *The American Indian Relocation Program*, 10; Arndt, "Relocation's Imagined Landscape," 117.

57. Brice Lay to Kurt Dreifuss, Dec. 1952, Rietz Collection, CA, NAES; "Monthly Progress Report, February 1953," Rietz Collection, CA, NAES; *Indian School Journal*, 26 Feb. 1955, 1.

58. Robert Rietz and Joseph Gauthier to John Cooper, 21 Feb. 1953, Rietz Collection, CA, NAES.

59. Wade B. Arends, Jr., "A Socio-Cultural Study of the Relocated American Indians in Chicago," M.A. thesis, University of Chicago, 1958, 48.

# 3   Coming to Chicago

In April 1952 Rudy Arcoren, his wife, their two young children, and Rudy's bachelor cousin John left their home on the Rosebud Sioux reservation in the midst of a still bitter South Dakota winter. After several months of sporadic work, Rudy, twenty-three, and John, twenty-four, had made their decision. Before dawn one morning the group filed onto an old and run-down bus that traveled ten miles south to Valentine, Nebraska, the nearest railroad station to the reservation. There, the five Arcorens waited on the platform for the Chicago and Northwestern train to pull in. They boarded, and by the end of the day they were standing in Chicago's Union Station. Their life in Chicago had begun.[1]

The Arcoren family was far from alone in participating in the early relocation program. Along with John, eleven other single Rosebud Sioux came to Chicago in 1952. In addition to Rudy's family, six other Rosebud Sioux families relocated. In all, 35 persons from Rosebud and 703 Indians from reservations across the country moved to Chicago under the relocation program in 1952, its first year of operation. Thousands more came during the years following.[2]

The Indian people who migrated to Chicago in the 1950s were from various backgrounds and came at different times in their lives and for different reasons. Some, like Rudy Arcoren, were married, and some, like his cousin John, were single. Some came with family or friends, others came alone. Some were middle-aged and some still adolescents. The urbanization of Indian people was not a single, unitary experience. Nor was the migration to even one particular city—Chicago—the same for all. Rather, numerous types of migrations were influenced by reservation

74

experiences, kinsmen, BIA officials, economic situations, and other factors. The ways in which American Indians migrated to Chicago sheds light on their premigration experiences and their plans and hopes for life in the city.

<hr>

The structure of relocation to Chicago during the 1950s reveals information about the families, tribes, and reservations of relocatees and the shape of Chicago's slowly developing Indian community. Almost thirty thousand American Indians participated in the BIA's relocation program between 1952 and 1959 (table 1). They went to Chicago, Los Angeles, Denver, Salt Lake City, the San Francisco Bay area, St. Louis, Joliet, Waukegan, Cincinnati, Cleveland, and Dallas. In 1959 the BIA stopped keeping careful count of relocatees, in part to avoid further criticism of the program. Chicago alone received almost five thousand relocatees and the greater Chicago area six thousand, accounting for about 20 percent of Indian relocatees to all locations during this eight-year period (table 2).

These numbers, for Chicago and nationwide, represent only a fraction of the total number of Indian people who moved to urban areas. It is likely that between one-half and two-thirds of the Indians who migrated to urban areas after World War II did so on their own, without BIA assistance.[3] Yet information about the minority who came to Chicago through the BIA's relocation program between the bureau's fiscal year 1952 and 1959 is valuable for the details it provides about the Indian

*Table 1.* Participants in Relocation Program to All Cities by Year and Family Status, 1952–59

| | Singles | | Families | | All | |
|---|---|---|---|---|---|---|
| | Units | Persons | Units | Persons | Units | Persons |
| 1952 | 227 (51%) | 227 (26%) | 215 (49%) | 641 (74%) | 442 | 868 |
| 1953 | 377 (54%) | 377 (26%) | 320 (46%) | 1,093 (74%) | 697 | 1,470 |
| 1954 | 752 (62%) | 752 (29%) | 470 (38%) | 1,801 (71%) | 1,222 | 2,553 |
| 1955 | 804 (54%) | 804 (23%) | 696 (46%) | 2,655 (77%) | 1,500 | 3,459 |
| 1956 | 1,078 (52%) | 1,078 (21%) | 1,005 (48%) | 4,041 (79%) | 2,083 | 5,119 |
| 1957 | 1,580 (55%) | 1,580 (23%) | 1,302 (45%) | 5,384 (77%) | 2,882 | 6,964 |
| 1958 | 1,397 (59%) | 1,397 (24%) | 976 (41%) | 4,331 (76%) | 2,373 | 5,728 |
| 1959 | 1,043 (63%) | 1,043 (29%) | 612 (37%) | 2,517 (71%) | 1,655 | 3,560 |
| | 7,258 (56%) | 7,258 (24%) | 5,596 (44%) | 22,463 (76%) | 12,854 | 29,721 |

*Sources:* Adapted from "Report on Branch of Relocation Services," Oct. 1957, box 8, NR, FPROEAR, RG 75, NA-WDC; "BIA Voluntary Relocation Services Program," Jan. 1962, box 14, Lyman Papers, ML, UU.

*Table 2.* Participants in Relocation Program to Chicago by Year and
Family Status, 1952–59

| | Singles | | Families | | All | |
|---|---|---|---|---|---|---|
| | Units | Persons | Units | Persons | Units | Persons |
| 1952 | 267 (70%) | 267 (38%) | 113 (30%) | 436 (62%) | 380 | 703 |
| 1953 | 239 (63%) | 239 (31%) | 140 (37%) | 525 (69%) | 379 | 764 |
| 1954 | 236 (70%) | 236 (38%) | 102 (30%) | 385 (62%) | 338 | 621 |
| 1955 | 224 (62%) | 224 (29%) | 136 (38%) | 547 (71%) | 360 | 771 |
| 1956 | 263 (62%) | 263 (30%) | 152 (37%) | 616 (70%) | 415 | 879 |
| 1957 | 205 (74%) | 205 (43%) | 172 (26%) | 273 (57%) | 277 | 478 |
| 1958 | 98 (58%) | 98 (24%) | 70 (42%) | 313 (76%) | 168 | 411 |
| 1959 | 115 (71%) | 115 (38%) | 46 (29%) | 191 (62%) | 161 | 306 |
| | 1,647 (66%) | 1,647 (33%) | 831 (33%) | 3,286 (67%) | 2,491 | 4,933 |

*Source:* Adapted from list of persons provided relocation services to Chicago, box 11, NR,
FPROEAR, RG 75, NA-WDC.

migration stream. Indeed, the lists of official relocatees during the 1950s
constitute the only sources of detailed information about its composition. Data on informal migration, unfortunately, do not exist. Surprisingly, though, data on official relocation have not thus far been used in
studies of Indian urbanization and here will perhaps sketch out in far
more detail at least part of the significant Indian urbanization stream
during the 1950s.

The Indian people who relocated to Chicago between 1952 and 1959
did not, of course, constitute a representative or average sample of Indians nationwide. Chicago's Indian migrant stream, like that of most other urban centers of Indian population, was emphatically regional. Almost
70 percent of the relocatees during the 1950s came from the Upper Midwest (Michigan, Wisconsin, and Minnesota) and the Northern Plains
(North Dakota, South Dakota, Nebraska, and Montana [table 3]).[4] Blue
Clark, a historian, has also noted the regional nature of Indian urbanization, with New York City serving as a center for the East, Chicago for
the Midwest, and Los Angeles and other California cities for the West.[5]
One consequence of this regional aspect of Indian urbanization was that
western cities attracted more graduates of Indian schools than Chicago,
because most schools were located in the West. After graduation, students
were more likely to make a short move to Los Angeles or Oklahoma City
than a long journey to Chicago.

During the first two years of the relocation program, Chicago topped
the other three urban centers. In 1952 it was the most popular relocation
site, drawing roughly 40 percent of all relocatees. In 1953 Chicago was
still receiving one-third of all relocatees, but by 1954 Los Angeles had

*Table 3.* Regional Background of Persons Participating in Relocation Program to Chicago, 1952–59

|  | 1952–55 | | 1956–59 | | Totals | |
|---|---|---|---|---|---|---|
| Upper Midwest (Mich., Wis., Minn.) | 1,149 | (40%) | 673 | (32%) | 1,822 | (37%) |
| Northern Plains (N.D., S.D., Nebr., Mont.) | 973 | (34%) | 539 | (26%) | 1,512 | (31%) |
| Oklahoma | 400 | (14%) | 261 | (13%) | 661 | (13%) |
| Southwest (Ariz., N.M., Utah) | 274 | (10%) | 334 | (16%) | 608 | (12%) |
| Other Regions | 63 | (2%) | 267 | (13%) | 330 | (7%) |
|  | 2,859 | (100%) | 2,074 | (100%) | 4,933 | (100%) |

*Source:* Adapted from list of persons provided relocation services to Chicago, Box 11, NR, FPROEAR, RG 75, NA-WDC.

overtaken it. The two cities' locations and proximity to reservations in part explains this trend. By 1955 greater Los Angeles received about half of the relocatees, in part because almost one-fourth of the nation's four hundred thousand Indians lived nearby in Arizona, New Mexico, and Utah. During the 1950s, Chicago received just over six hundred relocatees from the Southwest, only 12 percent of all relocatees for the period (table 3).[6]

The relocation program's quick start in Chicago and its more gradual development in other cities suggest a relationship between earlier migration patterns and the relocation of the 1950s. Many Indian people in the Upper Midwest and on the Northern Plains continued the patterns of mobility their parents and grandparents had established in the late nineteenth century. Indeed, in 1952 and 1953 as many Indian people from the Upper Midwest migrated to Milwaukee, Minneapolis–St. Paul, and other cities in Wisconsin and Minnesota without BIA aid as migrated to Chicago with it. Clearly, some Native Americans who sought employment and planned to move to an urban area for work on their own took advantage of the relocation program to Chicago in its early days. Brice Lay, who coordinated the program in North and South Dakota, noted that numerous early relocatees from those states had off-reservation living experience that likely prepared them to meet the challenges of urban life. "We have assisted many Indian people who were more or less ready to leave," he wrote in 1954.[7]

Given the strong regional nature of Indian migration, it is not surprising that the Chippewas and Sioux made up the bulk of Chicago's relocatees during the 1950s. These were the largest tribes in the Upper Midwest and on the Northern Plains, respectively. One-third of all Indian people who relocated to Chicago were Chippewas, and one-fifth were Sioux. Together, the two tribes contributed about half of all the reloca-

*Table 4.* Tribal Affiliation of Persons Participating in Relocation Program to Chicago, 1952–59

|  | 1952–55 | 1956–59 | Totals |
|---|---|---|---|
| Chippewa | 1,033 (36%) | 593 (29%) | 1,626 (33%) |
| Sioux | 505 (18%) | 429 (21%) | 934 (19%) |
| Cherokee | 147 (5%) | 129 (6%) | 276 (6%) |
| Navajo | 68 (2%) | 198 (10%) | 266 (5%) |
| Choctaw | 174 (6%) | 56 (3%) | 230 (5%) |
| Winnebago | 96 (3%) | 102 (5%) | 198 (4%) |
| Three Affiliated Tribes | 113 (4%) | 29 (1%) | 142 (3%) |
| Others | 723 (25%) | 538 (26%) | 1,261 (26%) |
|  | 2,859 (99%) | 2,074 (101%) | 4,933 (100%) |

*Source:* Adapted from list of persons provided relocation services to Chicago, box 11, NR, FPROEAR, RG 75, NA-WDC.

tees to Chicago during the 1950s. Navajo, Cherokee, Choctaw, Winnebago, and the Three Affiliated Tribes—the Arikara, Mandan, and Hidatsa—from the Fort Berthold Reservation were also well represented (table 4).

Two women who arrived in Chicago during the first four years of the program illustrate one of the city's attractions. Phyllis Fastwolf, a Sioux from South Dakota, relocated with her husband in 1955 and had a choice of relocation sites. "The most important reason [for choosing Chicago] was that my home was near," she explained. "I was thinking that was the closest I could get to coming back." Margaret Redcloud, a Chippewa from Minnesota, relocated with her husband in 1953. She also remembers choosing a city and how tugs from home influenced the decision: "We had a choice of going to San Francisco [or Cleveland] or Chicago. And, well, we decided on Chicago because it was closest to our home. And when we did move here, we got to go back up there every Fourth of July, somehow. Poor as we were—when we got started we always managed to get back home."[8]

Alike in some ways, the Chippewas and Sioux sometimes differed in the ways in which they thought about the program and about migration to Chicago. The differences emerged from their experiences with migration and wage labor long before the relocation program had begun. Although many Sioux would travel back and forth between Chicago and their reservation, distance often mitigated against doing that, as did any experience they had with wage labor. The Chippewas, however, in general treated Chicago as a temporary home. They could travel shorter distances to reach the city and by the middle of the twentieth century were accustomed to lives of almost constant mobility. For the Chippewas especially, Chicago was often a continuation of a previous seasonal, cyclical pattern of migration for either subsistence food collection or wage work. During the 1950s, BIA officials and critics of the bureau occasionally questioned the relocation program's high "return rate," an important example of the way in which the program often failed to live up to its stated goals. Yet seen in context, these complaints miss the point. It is no more surprising that the Chippewas did not stay in Chicago permanently than that they did not stay forever on a Wisconsin farm a hundred miles from their home reservation, picking strawberries.[9]

Chippewa reservations appear to have been more influenced by relocation than were large Sioux reservations, because larger proportions of their populations participated. Both the Pine Ridge and Rosebud Sioux reservations sent roughly three hundred people to Chicago on relocation during the 1950s (table 5). Yet that represented only about 3 percent of Pine Ridge's total population of roughly ten thousand and about 4 percent of Rosebud's 8,200-strong reservation. In contrast, various smaller Chippewa reservations—including Bad River, Red Cliff, Lac Courte Oreilles, and Lac du Flambeau, which ranged in size from 700 to 1,700—sent 9 to 13 percent of their populations to Chicago during the 1950s (table 6).[10] Considering that significant numbers were also migrating temporarily or permanently to other cities—including Minneapolis–St. Paul and Milwaukee—during this time, it is clear that twentieth-century urbanization had a profound effect on numerous Chippewa reservations and quickly drew many of their residents.

The ways in which people migrate often reveal much about their motivations. During the late nineteenth and early twentieth centuries, when millions of Europeans migrated to the United States, movement often occurred in two phases. Families wishing to avoid a decline in social and economic status and planning to remain in the United States

*Table 5.* Sioux Participants in Relocation Program to Chicago by Reservation and Family Status, 1952–59

|  | Singles | | Families | | All | |
|---|---|---|---|---|---|---|
|  | Units | Persons | Units | Persons | Units | Persons |
| Standing Rock | 19 (63%) | 19 (31%) | 11 (37%) | 43 (69%) | 30 | 62 |
| Sisseton | 37 (62%) | 37 (27%) | 23 (38%) | 101 (73%) | 60 | 138 |
| Rosebud | 58 (48%) | 58 (17%) | 63 (52%) | 277 (83%) | 121 | 335 |
| Pine Ridge | 59 (50%) | 59 (20%) | 59 (50%) | 236 (80%) | 118 | 295 |
| Other Sioux | 34 (65%) | 34 (33%) | 18 (35%) | 70 (67%) | 52 | 104 |
|  | 207 (54%) | 207 (22%) | 174 (46%) | 727 (78%) | 384 | 934 |

*Source:* Adapted from list of persons provided relocation services to Chicago, box 11, NR, FPROEAR, RG 75, NA-WDC.

*Table 6.* Chippewa Participants in Relocation Program to Chicago by Reservation and Family Status, 1952–59

|  | Singles | | Families | | All | |
|---|---|---|---|---|---|---|
|  | Units | Persons | Units | Persons | Units | Person |
| White Earth | 35 (80%) | 35 (48%) | 9 (20%) | 38 (52%) | 44 | 73 |
| Red Cliff | 31 (76%) | 31 (46%) | 10 (24%) | 37 (54%) | 41 | 68 |
| Leech Lake | 45 (75%) | 45 (42%) | 15 (25%) | 62 (58%) | 60 | 107 |
| Bad River | 67 (74%) | 67 (40%) | 24 (26%) | 102 (60%) | 91 | 169 |
| Cass Lake | 37 (73%) | 37 (45%) | 14 (27%) | 45 (55%) | 51 | 82 |
| Red Lake | 55 (67%) | 55 (35%) | 27 (33%) | 101 (65%) | 82 | 156 |
| Lac Courte Oreilles | 48 (62%) | 48 (30%) | 29 (38%) | 113 (70%) | 77 | 161 |
| Lac du Flambeau | 24 (53%) | 24 (25%) | 21 (47%) | 73 (75%) | 45 | 97 |
| Turtle Mountain | 38 (48%) | 38 (18%) | 41 (52%) | 168 (82%) | 79 | 206 |
| Other Chippewas | 188 (71%) | 188 (37%) | 76 (29%) | 319 (63%) | 264 | 507 |
|  | 568 (68%) | 568 (35%) | 266 (32%) | 1,058 (65%) | 834 | 1,626 |

*Source:* Adapted from list of persons provided relocation services to Chicago, Box 11, NR, FPROEAF RG 75, NA-WDC.

were usually the first to come. Next, single migrants began to dominate European migration. They frequently planned to migrate only temporarily, hoping to make enough money in the New World to return home and finance economic activity there.[11]

American Indian migration also was marked by a similar pattern of singles and families moving from reservations to Chicago and other cities. Differences existed among various tribes and cities in this area. Nationwide during the 1950s, about 56 percent of "units" (the BIA's term for family groups) and one-quarter of the persons relocating were either single or came alone (table 1). Some cities drew more families than the national average and some more singles. Chicago was among the most singles-oriented cities of the field relocation sites: 66 percent of its units and one-third of those who relocated there during the 1950s were singles (table 2).

Among the tribes well represented in Chicago during the 1950s, the Chippewas accounted for the greatest percentage of young single people. Chippewa relocatees were even more likely to be single during the first four years of the relocation program. Fully 70 percent of units or groups and 38 percent of persons relocating during this time were single. From 1956 to 1959 the trend would moderate; a more typical 64 percent of units and 29 percent of persons relocating were single. As a result, an average of 68 percent of units and 35 percent of persons were single during the 1950s. Some Chippewa reservations exaggerated the tribal norm and sent strikingly few families on relocation. At Minnesota's White Earth and Leech Lake reservations and Wisconsin's Red Cliff and Bad River reservations, about three-quarters of all units that relocated were singles throughout the 1950s. At Lac du Flambeau in Wisconsin and especially Turtle Mountain in North Dakota, the number of singles and families was more evenly split (table 6). There the situation more closely resembled that among the Sioux, whose migration stream to Chicago was more family-based. As many family units as single people from the Pine Ridge Sioux reservation in South Dakota, for example, relocated to Chicago during the 1950s (table 5).[12]

Many young women were among Chicago's single relocatees. Fully one-quarter of all single relocatees were female, even more in the early 1950s when they composed about 30 percent of all single relocatees (table 7). That, too, differed by tribe. Single female relocatees ranged from 13 percent among the Navajo, to 16 percent among the Sioux, to 31 percent among the Chippewas. At some Chippewa reservations, including Red Lake and Red Cliff, about 40 percent of all single relocatees were women (table 8).[13]

The migration of single young Chippewa women to Chicago during the mid-twentieth century suggests parallels with other migration streams. Among the Irish during the nineteenth century, for example, young women, especially those who were landless, were impelled to move when land in Ireland began to be transferred to only one or two children. An immi-

*Table 7.* Single Participants in Relocation Program to Chicago by Sex, 1952–59

|  | 1952–55 | 1956–59 | Totals |
|---|---|---|---|
| Single men | 686 (71%) | 537 (79%) | 1,223 (74%) |
| Single women | 280 (29%) | 144 (21%) | 424 (26%) |
|  | 966 (100%) | 681 (100%) | 1,647 (100%) |

*Source:* Adapted from list of persons provided relocation services to Chicago, box 11, NR, FPROEAR, RG 75, NA-WDC.

*Table 8.* Single Chippewa Participants in Relocation Program to Chicago by Sex, 1952–59

|  | 1952–55 | 1956–59 | Totals |
|---|---|---|---|
| Single Chippewa men | 265 (67%) | 125 (73%) | 390 (69%) |
| Single Chippewa women | 132 (33%) | 46 (27%) | 178 (31%) |
|  | 397 (100%) | 171 (100%) | 568 (100%) |

*Source:* Adapted from list of persons provided relocation services to Chicago, Box 11, NR, FPROEAR, RG 75, NA-WDC.

gration network soon developed as single women joined aunts, siblings, or cousins in America. Once there, they often acquired domestic jobs. The fact that many who migrated were single and female contrasted Irish immigration with the more familial, and largely male, immigration streams from other European countries.[14] In ways similar to earlier migrant groups, the single young Indian women who relocated to Chicago often traveled together, lived together in rooming houses such as the Evangeline Residence, and worked together in offices and factories.

Single young Chippewa women and those from other tribes had many reasons for migrating to Chicago, among them—as always—the availability of jobs. Reservation employment conditions, poor in general, were usually even worse for young Indian women. Although World War II produced a small employment boomlet in some areas, it dried up quickly soon after the war's end. In one Wisconsin county, for example, only twenty-six Chippewa women were employed in 1950, a marginal increase over the prewar period. Moreover, some women who had received clerical training from government or boarding schools had nowhere to use such skills on reservations. Even before the relocation program officially began, the superintendent of the Red Lake Reservation predicted its appeal for young women. An observer at the Fort Berthold Reservation in 1954 also noted that "local jobs for women have been so scarce and so poorly paid" that he thought few single women there would be able to earn and save enough to be able to try the relocation program.[15]

Job opportunities in Chicago, however, led many single Indian women to do everything possible to move there. From the beginning of the relocation program in 1952, they read job advertisements in reservation newsletters and bulletins. One "large Chicago company," for instance, wanted "seventy-five women, preferably unmarried and childless, between the ages of eighteen and thirty-five" to work as "file clerks, order fillers, baggers and boxers, service clerks and typists."[16] The fact that many Chicago employers clearly wanted to hire Indian women came as a pleasant surprise to reservation born and bred people. What is more, employers were often more interested in female workers—usually for the burgeoning service sector of the economy—than male workers. The company that placed the advertisement, for example, was interested in hiring only twenty-five males in contrast to seventy-five females.

Some separated or divorced female relocatees took urban jobs not out of preference but of necessity. They also faced the challenge of caring for children while relocating to a strange city and trying to find a job. A Mandan who relocated to Denver in 1953, for example, had a new baby and two teenaged girls at a Catholic mission school; she also faced many obstacles in trying to acquire a job. She wished both to be near the older girls' school and to find someone to look after her baby while she worked.[17]

Single relocatees to Chicago and elsewhere tended to be significantly younger than married relocatees. The large number of young single migrants, together with other demographic trends, resulted in an urban Indian population that was younger than the reservation population. By 1970 one-third of adult urban Indians were in their twenties in contrast to fewer than one-fourth of adult rural Indians.[18]

Chippewa relocatees, especially those who came as singles, were consistently younger than Sioux relocatees. Of Chippewa singles, 38 percent were under twenty-two, compared with only 20 percent of Sioux singles. The average age of Chippewa single relocatees was about twenty-six, and that of Sioux single relocatees was about twenty-nine. The great number of young and single Chippewa relocatees was especially evident among women. Single Chippewa women were by far the youngest of all groups that relocated to Chicago; fully 65 percent were under twenty-two. Their average age was 22.3, compared to 24.8 for single Sioux women, 28.2 for single Chippewa men, and 30 for single Sioux men (table 9). Year after year, groups of adolescent females left reservations in Minnesota and Wisconsin for the city. In 1952, for example, six single women aged eighteen to twenty-two left Minnesota's White Earth Reservation, and five aged eighteen and nineteen left the state's Cass Lake Reservation for Chicago. In 1954 four eighteen-year-old single women left Wisconsin's Red Cliff Reservation.[19]

*able 9*. Ages of Participants in Relocation Program to Chicago by Family Status, ribe, and Sex, 1952–59

|  | Average Age (Years) | Percentage under 19 | Percentage under 22 | Percentage under 30 | Number |
| --- | --- | --- | --- | --- | --- |
| oux family heads | 32.2 | — | 7 | 40 | 174 |
| l family heads | 30.9 | 1 | 8 | 51 | 831 |
| hippewa family heads | 30.6 | 1 | 8 | 57 | 266 |
| ngle Sioux men | 30.0 | 3 | 14 | 54 | 173 |
| ngle Sioux | 29.1 | 6 | 20 | 57 | 207 |
| ngle Chippewa men | 28.2 | 11 | 26 | 64 | 390 |
| ngle men | 27.7 | 8 | 26 | 65 | 1,223 |
| l singles | 26.5 | 12 | 34 | 70 | 1,647 |
| ngle Chippewas | 26.4 | 19 | 38 | 71 | 568 |
| ngle women | 23.1 | 24 | 58 | 83 | 424 |
| ngle Chippewa women | 22.3 | 37 | 65 | 85 | 178 |

*Source:* Adapted from list of persons provided relocation services to Chicago, Box 11, NR, FPROEAR, : 75, NA-WDC.

Relatives, BIA officials, and others involved in relocation were often concerned about the young single women. At the very beginning of the program in early 1952, three twenty-two-year-olds from Red Lake moved to Chicago. The mother of one, after several months of not hearing from her daughter, wrote to an employee of the BIA office in Chicago. Because she did not know the daughter's new address, the mother asked that her letter to be forwarded and commented on the difficulty she and other parents of young relocatees had in contacting their children. "Our letters keep getting sent back," she wrote. "I thought maybe you'd know where they were at. They haven't written home for a long time. And we would like to locate her. . . . So if it isn't asking too much of you, please forward this letter for me. And if you should see her and those other two girls tell them to write home at least. Their parents are wondering why they never write."[20]

Other observers of reservation life during the 1950s also noted the massive emigration of young people. Opinions about the trend differed, but everyone agreed on its size and scope. One Catholic missionary on the Rosebud Reservation in 1953 commented, "Many of the people have already left the reservation, and the majority of the younger people, graduates from high school and even grade school, continue to leave." Five years later, another missionary, after visiting several reservations across the country, reported, "Adventuresome or restless young people are trying their fortunes elsewhere."[21]

The BIA officials and social workers in Chicago knew that a few well-publicized mishaps involving young Indian women could give the relocation program a permanent black eye. Continually concerned about public relations, the bureau tried to foster an image of relocation that would please the American public and win support for the program. Thus, O. K. Armstrong maintained in a pro-relocation piece in *Reader's Digest* in 1955 that the largest portion of relocatees were between the ages of twenty-eight and thirty-three, married, and had one or two children, although those figures were inaccurate for relocation nationwide and even more so for Chicago.[22] The images of eager Indian families chasing the American dream in Chicago and elsewhere would have pleased non-Indian readers. Those who relocated to Chicago, however, were more likely to be single and younger than Armstrong indicated. He did not mention that groups of eighteen- and nineteen-year-old single Indian women were as prevalent and important in Chicago's developing Indian community as were Indian families.

Although the BIA tried to make the relocation program function in an organized and orderly fashion during the 1950s, some relocatees communicated little with the bureau and came to Chicago on their own. Only after arriving in the city did they contact the BIA about assistance. These "nonscheduled" relocatees made up about one-fifth of the total during the 1950s and received fewer services than scheduled relocatees. That ratio varied greatly at different times, however. In the early years of the program, when Chicago's economy appeared especially robust and bureau officials were struggling to get the program up and running, far more people decided to relocate without BIA scheduling. They would arrange transportation to Chicago and hope to find a job there by themselves. In 1953, 1955, and 1956, about 30 percent of all who relocated to Chicago came without BIA scheduling. During the recession of the late 1950s, however, that number plummeted. By 1958 and 1959 only 3 percent of all relocatees came to Chicago on their own. Evidently, fewer were convinced that the answer to their problems could be found in the city, and almost no one was willing to risk finding out on their own.[23]

Decisions about whether to relocate through formal BIA processes or do so independently also depended upon age, family status, sex, and tribal identity. Because the relocation program was officially designed for those between eighteen and thirty-five, the very young as well as the very old were heavily represented among nonscheduled relocatees. Being single, Chippewa, or female increased the likelihood of a nonscheduled relocation. The combination of two or all of these characteristics increased it more. Forty percent of the single Chippewa women who relocated to Chicago during the 1950s did so without scheduling and thus without full assistance from the BIA (table 10). As late as the mid-1960s, nonscheduled relocatees "include[d] more women and cover[ed] a much wider age span."[24]

*Table 10.* Scheduled and Nonscheduled Participants in Relocation Program to Chicago by Family Status, Tribe, and Sex, 1952–59

|  | Scheduled | Nonscheduled | Totals |
|---|---|---|---|
| Sioux family units | 156 (90%) | 18 (10%) | 174 |
| All family units | 677 (81%) | 154 (19%) | 831 |
| Chippewa family units | 202 (76%) | 64 (24%) | 266 |
| Single Sioux | 158 (76%) | 49 (24%) | 207 |
| Single males | 886 (72%) | 337 (28%) | 1,223 |
| All singles | 1,156 (70%) | 491 (30%) | 1,647 |
| Single females | 270 (64%) | 154 (36%) | 424 |
| Single male Chippewas | 251 (64%) | 139 (36%) | 390 |
| Single Chippewas | 357 (63%) | 211 (37%) | 568 |
| Single female Chippewas | 106 (60%) | 72 (40%) | 178 |

*Source:* Adapted from list of persons provided relocation services to Chicago, box 11, NR, FPROEAR, RG 75, NA-WDC.

Just as Indian urban migrants themselves varied, so did their motivations. For some who were in precarious economic situations, relocation provided a continuation of the seasonal round and was a temporary measure. Others sought to escape the harsh living conditions on their home reservations on a more permanent basis. Many were accustomed to very poor housing; they would paste newspapers onto their cabin walls, for example, to keep out the winter's cold. The housing in Chicago was at least warm and dry. Life in Chicago also offered the possibility of owning a modern automobile. By contrast, on reservations Indian people often relied on Model A Fords and even horse-drawn wagons for basic transportation. Food, too, was sometimes scarce. One observer in 1953 noted that the Rosebud Sioux, who for years had enjoyed communal meals where they ate large amounts of meat, were increasingly reliant on vegetables, including turnips and rutabagas grown in home gardens, for their basic diet.[25]

Residents of many reservations in the Upper Midwest and on the Northern Plains suffered from social as well as economic hardships. Indian communities in Wisconsin and Minnesota were especially isolated, and residents sometimes grew restless. A Chippewa BIA official visiting Minnesota's Red Lake Reservation in 1956 met a young man who observed, "There are only two uses of leisure time young men from Red Lake learn as they grow up—drinking and fighting." From both his experiences growing up and his observation of many reservations in the Upper Midwest, the bureau employee voiced agreement. Elsewhere, some left reservations to free themselves from "the drinking behavior and violence associated with some tribal members."[26]

Some Indian people believed that relocation would improve the lives of their children and gave that as a reason for migration. Among this group were ordinary people like the thirty-six-year-old Chippewa man who relocated to Chicago in 1957 with his family. "I can stand poorness," he said. "I have been poor all my life. It is my children; I want something for them."[27] Others were more forthrightly assimilationist in their thinking and resembled the middle-class leaders of other American ethnic groups. The old ways, they urged, should be abandoned once in new homes.

Ben Reifel was a Rosebud Sioux who went to work for the BIA during the 1930s, served in the military police during World War II, and after the war earned a doctorate from Harvard University. During the 1950s he served as superintendent at both Fort Berthold and Pine Ridge.[28] He championed relocation, although some Indian people resented him because of his education and employment with the bureau. At every opportunity he encouraged others to educate themselves and assimilate. Speaking before a group of Indian political leaders in 1954, Reifel said, "If Indians as groups are to get anywhere they will need to be concerned with the values of the American culture that make for healthy adjustment."[29] Later that same year Reifel suggested to Pine Ridge residents that the process of Indian advancement would be more attainable in cities.

> We Indian people have no time to lose. We must get every school child in a classroom and see that he or she stays in school every day. . . . We must look ahead to better education of our young people. It will not do us any good to keep looking back. We must keep pushing forward. Let's get our kids in school and keep them there. Even if they don't have good clothes, wash up what they have and have them come with what they have. Education is the one way that we can help our children so that they will be better off in the time to come than we are today. It is going to be a hard job because many of the Pine Ridge people are very poor but I know they have what it takes and with God's help I know we are on our way to a great future for ourselves and for America, too.[30]

Political disputes within reservation communities also pushed people into the relocation program. The Indian Reorganization Act of 1934 had established a revolving loan program on participating reservations, but it was insufficiently funded. Moreover, members of tribal councils, who were responsible for distributing tribal loans, often favored relatives, friends, and political supporters. Those who failed to support the tribal politicians failed to receive loans. A Winnebago man remembered the situation on his reservation in Wisconsin: "If you were the chairman or the chairman's uncle or something, all the jobs went to them. Truck driving jobs, all those painting jobs, lawn repair—they went to those guys that were related on the council, and you couldn't say anything." An Apache man had a similar experience with his tribal council: "When I spoke to the tribal council, no one would listen." Some became upset with the Indian Reorganization Act and its legacy, including the favoritism they believed it produced. One man, representing the depth of this distrust, complained that his people were "under Dictatorship" and suffered from treatment at the hands of a "Puppet Council" that spent money "for things that don't help the Indians in any way." Some Indians, then, evidently preferred to attempt a new life in the city rather than endure tribal authorities they considered burdensome.[31]

By the 1950s, some had grown frustrated with the BIA's heavy hand and resentful of its paternalistic attitude. They saw cities as places where they would have more control over their daily lives. Kenneth Philp views this reaction against BIA paternalism as the most important factor in encouraging Indian urban migration. Comparing Indian urbanization to the civil rights movement led by African Americans during the same period, he calls it a "stride toward freedom" and part of Indians' "struggle toward the goal of social equality."[32] Although some Indian migrants fit that model, Philp's explanation too easily conflates the experiences of Native Americans and African Americans and relies on an assimilationist assumption. Reaction against BIA paternalism was only one of many motivations that influenced Indian people.

Some also hoped to escape local white prejudice as well as to enjoy better treatment in Chicago. Native Americans were discriminated against in many areas near reservations. A Sioux man from Minnesota, who believed he had been passed over for jobs, observed, "Metropolitan areas are probably the best bet for an Indian because the next door neighbor probably doesn't care what you are or who you are. And you can have a chance to do what you want to do, work at the job you like to work at." Back home, a Mesquakie who relocated from Iowa to Chicago in 1953 remembered, "The Indians are the last on the job and there is not much chance of advancing to the best of your abilities." From the Southwest came reports that store owners during the 1950s sometimes overcharged Navajos and other Indian people, for example asking 10 cents for a bottle of Coke that cost Anglo customers only 5 cents.[33]

Indians who lived in the South generally encountered the greatest degree of prejudice and discrimination. The white social order considered them "colored" and put them in the same category as African Americans. Lucille Spencer, a Choctaw from Mississippi, moved to Chicago as a girl with her parents. Decades later she remembered going to the local theater in her hometown and watching white people sitting in comfortable seats on the main floor. Her seat was on a wooden bench that blacks and Indians shared in the theater's cramped balcony. Such discrimination influenced her parents' decision to move. Spencer recalled the contrast between North and South when she returned to Mississippi years after the family had moved to Chicago. While visiting in Mississippi, her brother, accustomed to social relations in Chicago, ordered a sandwich at a cafe. Because he was at the window for white customers, however, he was refused service. The incident infuriated him and also left a mark on Spencer, who cannot forget it and the many other humiliations her family suffered in Mississippi. "To this day," she says, "if I have to go into a restaurant, and I see all these whites, I get this funny feeling yet like I'm going to be told to get out."[34]

Some who migrated to urban areas during the 1950s were reacting to family authorities whom they considered unjust or burdensome. Indian migration was often influenced by social and family problems as well as by economic motivation. Single women in particular often moved to cities because of problems with parents, grandparents, or husbands. Urbanization sometimes followed incidents of spousal abuse or stemmed from separation or divorce, which were becoming more common on some reservations by the 1950s. A Catholic missionary at the Rosebud Sioux reservation in 1953, for example, noted that he saw "many broken homes and many neglected children" in the course of his work.[35]

Sharon Skolnick, a Fort Sill Apache from Oklahoma, was among those who came to Chicago because of family difficulties. She and others like her were determined to escape oppressive personal circumstances for a better life in the city. Skolnick, who had experienced the death of a brother from leukemia and her parents' divorce before she was ten, had been placed in the first of what would be several Oklahoma orphanages, where, repeatedly, she and other Indian children were told they "weren't worth a hill of beans." Moreover, local white families would often temporarily adopt the children and use them as servants while receiving financial benefits from the state. Yet Skolnick does not single out the orphanages for blame; they reflected, she believes, Oklahoma society of the era. For her, moving to Chicago was a turning point. As she remembers life in the Oklahoma of her childhood:

> You walk in single file, you do this, you do that, you have your tasks, you're like a little servant. That's how you were brought up in that concept. You had babies, continued to farm, and you grew up. I saw a lot of that after I was adopted in Oklahoma. There were prejudices not only of skin color, but of women trying to get out, to get educated, to get into those jobs that they wanted. . . . If a woman was divorced and she was forty and she decided to go looking for another husband or get a better job, she was thought of as a bad woman. We grew up in a very biblical world there—the Bible belt in Oklahoma—whereas in Chicago, that would be just a normal thing. Back there in that era, a woman . . . was supposed to . . . keep on the farm and die. She could re-marry, but it'd have to be somebody from that area. And again, she steps into a subservient role. And when a woman decided to step out, go to college, get an education, that was a big step. Of course you had to get out of that area because they would condemn you, ridicule you. I grew up with that.[36]

Even when the reservation situation was not so constricting, some Indian people still decided that relationships with family or tribal members were inhibiting and responded by moving. Margaret Curtis, a Sioux, became concerned as she grew up that her grandparents, who were raising her, planned for her to remain permanently with them in South Dakota. As Curtis's interest in the relocation program grew, her grandparents sharply opposed her intention to move. They even attempted to force her to withdraw from high school before she graduated. Yet she persisted and eventually relocated to Chicago. Curtis observes that her grandparents "really didn't like it that I was going away, because I think what they wanted was for me to take care of them for the rest of their lives." In response, she did not return for a visit for ten years after she moved to Chicago. She acknowledges that she might have learned more about her heritage and Indian ways by staying on her reservation but maintains, "I never would have experienced anything else. In a way, I'm happy that I left and made something of myself."[37]

It is clear, then, that a host of factors influenced the Indian people who migrated to Chicago during the 1950s and after. For most, it was not merely a "desperate last resort" but the result of a web of causes.[38] To single out one—even toward the goal of criticizing federal policy—is to simplify a complex process involving thousands of Indian people, all with different hopes for urban life. Some eyewitnesses recognized that many factors lay behind migration. LaVerne Madigan of the Association on American Indian Affairs (AAIA), who traveled the country viewing changes in Indian life during the 1950s, noted that most Indian people had ordinary, day-to-day concerns and were not "humming with discussion of whether Relocation is a brave new way to survive or a way to destroy themselves as Indians" as were many whites on both sides of the issue.[39] Indian people made decisions about migrating in consultation with family and friends, not solely in reaction to federal policy.

---

Relations with fellow tribe members both on the reservation and in various cities were critical in many relocation decisions. Lines of communication were open between reservation and city as people most often moved in groups—sometimes described by historians as "networks" or "chains"—rather than alone. When deciding whether to move, Indian people—like many other migrant groups—considered accounts they had heard about urban life. When deciding where to move, they considered places where they knew they had family or friends.

Stories about Chicago abounded on reservations across the Upper Midwest and Northern Plains. Some emphasized the comparatively wide-open job market and opportunities in Chicago. A Chippewa man who relocated from the Red Lake Reservation at the beginning of the program and enjoyed his job at Republic Steel told friends about it when he returned to his reservation to visit. One observer believed the man was "doing a good job of selling Republic Steel and Chicago to other Indians on the reservation." Other Indian employees at Republic were also "writing back that they like the work and that they fully intend to stay on the job." Some accounts about urban life, however, instilled caution or fear. A Chippewa woman remembers that stories of people who had returned from Chicago often made the city "sound really scary."[40]

Communication also flowed the other way—from reservation to city. While in Chicago, Indians often longed for news from their home reservations. A single woman from Fort Berthold reported that although news had been "rather scarce," she looked forward to opportunities to get together with other Fort Berthold relocatees and "swap news items from home." One way urban Indians kept informed was by subscribing to reservation newsletters, and many in Chicago eagerly awaited every issue, even complaining to the editor when an issue was late in arriving.[41]

Some kept abreast of the relocation program through tribal leadership. A few tribal councils during the 1950s, including the Navajo and San Carlos Apache, expressed great support and communicated positive messages about urban migration to tribal members. Leaders of the two tribes hoped that urbanization would ease overcrowding on their reservations.[42] The council leaders kept in contact with those who had relocated. In 1957 a group of Navajos from the reservation in Arizona visited relocatees in Chicago, St. Louis, and Denver and reported that most were happy and successful. To spur further interest among the Navajos, a local radio station in Arizona broadcast a weekly *Navajo Hour*, which periodically informed reservation Navajos about the relocation program and those who participated in it.[43]

The BIA also discussed many successful relocatees in its more "official" lines of communications to reservation residents. Portions of letters from happy relocatees to relatives were reprinted or summarized to emphasize the quality of housing and the availability of jobs in Chicago. Information about Indian families who had televisions and jobs that provided paid vacations presented an attractive picture of the relocation program to reservation residents.[44]

After making the decision to move, most Indian people chose a city where they already knew people. Often an aunt, brother, cousin, or army buddy played an important role in convincing others to join them in Chicago.[45] Networks of migration developed, with many members of the same family eventually participating. Several Wilkies from North Dakota's Turtle Mountain Reservation, for example, relocated to Chicago during the early 1950s. Three families came in 1952 and 1953, followed by three who came alone the following year. In some cases, single adolescents followed older siblings who were married and had established residence in Chicago. At other times, younger members of a family blazed the trail, only to be followed in later years by older, more cautious relatives. In various ways, family connections played an important role in Indian people's urban migration.[46]

Examples of this trend abounded. In July 1954, for example, a single Mandan woman relocated to Chicago but moved to Milwaukee just a few days later. She wanted above all to be with her aunt in Milwaukee, even though Milwaukee was not an official relocation site and she would receive less BIA assistance there.[47] Family connections also weighed heavily in the Maneys' decision to move from the Winnebago reservation in Nebraska to Chicago in 1937. Rose Maney and her husband followed relatives who had moved there even earlier, found work in a steel mill, and convinced the Maneys that they, too, would be happy in Chicago. The importance of this connection and Rose Maney's long-lasting feeling of obligation is evident in the account of her daughter, Diane, who was born in Chicago and has heard the story of her parents' arrival since childhood. "My mom has said this many, many times: if it wasn't for my dad's sister, they don't know what they would have done. Because she was already here; she knew the city."[48]

----

Initial experiences in Chicago were as varied for Indians as the ways in which they had come to the city and the hopes that motivated them. Many experienced frightening or anxious episodes during their first days of urban life. Susan K. Power, a Sioux who came to Chicago at the age of seventeen to care for an elderly friend of her mother's, recalls being glued to her train seat for the twelve-hour trip, so great was her fear. Once she arrived at Union Station and took a seat in its vast hall, she was intimidated by the size of the crowd. She repeatedly ignored a page of her name on the assumption that there must be several others in the huge crowd who shared her name. After spending an entire day in Union Station's lobby, too frightened to respond to the page meant for her, Power finally bumped into the friend she was to meet and left for her new home.[49]

Some relocatees had difficulties after their initial support networks disintegrated. Josephine Willie, a Choctaw who married in the summer of 1954, discovered three days after her wedding that her new husband had applied for relocation without telling her. Before she knew it, they were on a train bound for Chicago. A few months after the hasty move, her husband got into trouble and lost interest in Chicago just as quickly as he had gained it. Abandoned by her husband, Willie was alone in a city where she had moved not by choice and about which she knew little. It would take several years before she would find stability in Chicago by marrying a non-Indian and starting a new family with him.[50]

Other early experiences were more humorous and years later were remembered with laughter. A Winnebago family, approaching their new Chicago home for the first time, noticed that the roofs of many neighborhood buildings were peaked. Accustomed to the plain and simple structures of their reservation, the family initially believed that Chicago contained more churches than they ever knew existed.[51]

---

Indian people's migration to Chicago, then, was characterized by a great deal of variety. The different urbanization patterns—of Chippewas and Sioux, of men and women, and of single and married people—demonstrate that federal policy was not the only force guiding the urbanization of Indian people. If only a government policy had been necessary for Indian urbanization, one would expect that most who migrated would have had similar experiences. They did not. American Indians took advantage of the relocation program based on their own varied situations and backgrounds. Some migrated to escape authorities they considered burdensome or onerous, whether BIA employees, local whites, tribal leaders, or family members. Others, responding to expectations raised during the war, believed that relocation and urbanization constituted an opportunity for economic improvement. In addition, there were Indian people who incorporated Chicago into a mid-twentieth-century version of seasonal economic activity and hoped to work there only for the harsh winter season. Still others looked to the big city for a brief period of adventure and excitement. Finally, some were drawn by the small Indian community already in Chicago. As they arrived during the 1950s and began to adjust to the city, they faced further challenges—acquiring jobs, finding housing, and building satisfying social and cultural lives in a new urban home.

## Notes

1. Rosebud Agency census, rolls 428–45, M595, Record Group 75, National Archives–Washington, D.C. [hereafter RG 75, NA-WDC]; Rosebud Agency report, Feb. 1958, box 4, Narrative Reports, Field Placement and Relocation Office Employment Assistance Records, Record Group 75, National Archives–Washington, D.C. [hereafter NR, FPROEAR, RG 75, NA-WDC].

2. List of persons provided relocation services to Chicago, box 11, NR, FPROEAR, RG 75, NA-WDC.

3. Blue Clark, "Bury My Heart in Smog," in *The American Indian Experience: A Profile*, ed. Philip Weeks (Arlington Heights: Forum Press, 1988), 283–84; Francis Jennings, *The Founders of America* (New York: Norton, 1993), 400.

4. Cf. Jack D. Forbes, ed., *The Indian in America's Past* (Englewood Cliffs: Prentice-Hall, 1964), 123; Donald L. Fixico, *The Urban Indian Experience in America* (Albuquerque: University of New Mexico Press, 2000), 12–13.

5. Clark, "Bury My Heart in Smog," 282.

6. Kenneth R. Philp, "Stride toward Freedom: The Relocation of Indians to Cities, 1952–1960," *Western Historical Quarterly* 16 (April 1985): 179; BIA press release, 8 July 1954, Robert Rietz Collection, Community Archives, Native American Educational Services College, Chicago [hereafter Rietz Collection, CA, NAES]; "Indians and Industry," *Wall Street Journal*, 28 Dec. 1955, 1.

7. "Minutes of Placement and Relocation Conference," 15–16 Apr. 1953, Rietz Collection, CA, NAES; Brice Lay to Ralph Shane, 18 Mar. 1954, Rietz Collection, CA, NAES.

8. Interview with Phyllis Fastwolf (Sioux-Oneida), Chicago, 8 May 1983, Chicago American Indian Oral History Pilot Project, no. 006, Newberry Library, Chicago and Native American Educational Services College, Chicago [hereafter CAIOHP, NL and NAES]; interview with Margaret Redcloud (Chippewa), Chicago, 12 Feb. 1984, CAIOHP, no. 021, NL and NAES.

9. Nancy O. Lurie, *Wisconsin Indians*, 2d ed (Madison: State Historical Society of Wisconsin, 1980), 8–9.

10. List of reservations with 1950 population estimates, Sol Tax Papers, Community Archives, Native American Educational Services College, Chicago; list of persons provided relocation services to Chicago, box 11, NR, FPROEAR, RG 75, NA-WDC.

11. John Bodnar, *The Transplanted: A History of Immigrants in Urban America* (Bloomington: Indiana University Press, 1985), 56.

12. List of persons provided relocation services to Chicago, box 11, NR, FPROEAR, RG 75, NA-WDC.

13. Ibid.

14. Hasia R. Diner, *Erin's Daughters in America: Irish Immigrant Women in the Nineteenth Century* (Baltimore: Johns Hopkins University Press, 1983).

15. Patty Loew, "The Back of the Homefront: Black and American Indian Women in Wisconsin during World War II," *Wisconsin Magazine of History* 82 (Winter 1998–99): 101; Chicago FRO report, Nov.-Dec. 1951, box 1, Reports on Employment Assistance, Chicago Field Employment Assistance Office, Record Group 75, National Archives–Great Lakes Region, Chicago; "Proposed Plan of Operation, Branch of Relocation, Fiscal Year 1955, Fort Berthold Agency, 2 July 1954," Rietz Collection, CA, NAES.

16. *Fort Berthold Agency News Bulletin*, 25 Aug. 1952, Rietz Collection, CA, NAES.

17. Nellie Baker to Robert Rietz, 10 Dec. 1953, Rietz Collection, CA, NAES.

18. Russell Thornton, "Patterns and Processes of American Indians in Cities and Towns: The National Scene," in *Urban Indians: Proceedings of the Third Annual Conference on Problems and Issues Concerning American Indians Today.* Chicago: The Newberry Library, 1981.

19. List of persons provided relocation services to Chicago, box 11, NR, FPROEAR, RG 75, NA-WDC.

20. Correspondent identified as "52–20" to Mary Nan Gamble, 21 Jan. 1953, case file CH-52–20, Employment Assistance Case Files, 1952–1960, Chicago Field Employment Assistance Office, Record Group 75, National Archives-Great Lakes Region, Chicago [hereafter EACF, CFEAO, RG 75, NA-GLR].

21. Robert M. Demeyer, "The Rosebud Sioux," *Indian Sentinel* (Sept. 1953): 99; J. B. Tennelly, "The Indian Missions, 1958," *Indian Sentinel* (Jan.–Feb. 1958): 5.

22. O. K. Armstrong and Marjorie Armstrong, "The Indians Are Going to Town," *Reader's Digest* 66 (Jan. 1955): 42.

23. List of persons provided relocation services to Chicago, box 11, NR, FPROEAR, RG 75, NA-WDC.

24. Ibid.; "Family Services Report" by Ruth Montague of American Indian Center, Apr. 1964, Welfare Council of Metropolitan Chicago Files, 246–14, Manuscript Collections, Chicago Historical Society.

25. John Kennardh White, "The American Indian in Chicago: The Hidden People," M.A. thesis, University of Chicago, 1970, 13; Demeyer, "The Rosebud Sioux," 100.

26. "Detail of Kent Fitzgerald to Minneapolis," 20 Jan. 1956 to 30 Mar. 1956, box 3, Financial Program, Field Placement and Relocation Office Employment Assistance Records, Record Group 75, National Archives–Washington, D.C. [hereafter FP, FPROEAR, RG 75, NA-WDC]; Anthony M. Garcia, "'Home' Is Not a House: Urban Relocation among American Indians," Ph.D. diss., University of California at Berkeley, 1988, 46–47.

27. Wade B. Arends, Jr., "A Socio-Cultural Study of the Relocated American Indians in Chicago," M.A. thesis, University of Chicago, 1958, 48.

28. *Amerindian* (Nov.–Dec. 1952): 3.

29. Interview with Floyd Taylor (Sioux), 9 Aug. 1968, American Indian Oral History Research Project [hereafter AIOHRP], pt. 1, no. 25, MS 50; Gretchen G. Harvey, "Cherokee and American: Ruth Muskrat Bronson, 1897–1982," Ph.D. diss., Arizona State University, 1996, 195.

30. *The Pine Ridge,* 1 Sept. 1954, Rietz Collection, CA, NAES.

31. Philp, "Stride toward Freedom," 175; interview with Willard LaMere (Winnebago), Chicago, 1 Feb. 1984, CAIOHP, no. 009, NL and NAES; Arends, "A Socio-Cultural Study," 52; *Indian Voices* (Feb. 1964): 8.

32. Philp, "Stride toward Freedom," 190.

33. Interview with Curt Campbell (Sioux), 23 June 1970, AIOHRP, pt. 1, no. 63, MS 504 (first quotation); Arends, "A Socio-Cultural Study," 49–50 (second quotation); "The Changing Fate of the American Indian," *World Today* 13 (Aug. 1957): 351–60 (third quotation).

34. Author interview with Lucille Spencer (Choctaw), Chicago, 22 June 1995.

35. Joan Ablon, "Relocated American Indians in the San Francisco Bay Area: Social Interactions and Indian Identity," *Human Organization* 23 (Winter 1964): 296–304; interview with Cornelia Penn (Sioux), Chicago, 3 Sept. 1983, CAIOHP, no. 017, NL and NAES; Fort Berthold Agency report, Oct. 1952, Rietz Collection, CA, NAES; Francis J. Collins, "Contrasts in Mission Work," *Indian Sentinel* (Oct. 1953): 123.

36. Author interview with Sharon Skolnick (Apache), Chicago, 15 June 1995.

37. Author interview with Margaret Curtis (Sioux), Chicago, 26 Oct. 1993. For more commentary on this interview, see James B. LaGrand, "Whose Voices Count? Oral Sources and Twentieth-Century American Indian History," *American Indian Culture and Research Journal* 21 (Winter 1997): 91–94.

38. Larry W. Burt, "Roots of the Native American Urban Experience: Relocation Policy in the 1950s," *American Indian Quarterly* 10 (Spring 1986): 89.

39. LaVerne Madigan, *The American Indian Relocation Program* (New York: Association on American Indian Affairs, 1956), 10.

40. Emmett Riley to Kurt Dreifuss, 20 Feb. 1952, case file CH-52–5, EACF, CFEAO, RG 75, NA-GLR; interview with Floria Forica (Chippewa), Chicago, 25 Mar. 1983, CAIOHP, no. 004, NL and NAES.

41. Lee Smith to Ben Reifel, 7 Apr. 1953, Rietz Collection, CA, NAES; Bryan Rogers to Robert Rietz, 14 Sept. 1954, Rietz Collection, CA, NAES.

42. *Amerindian* (Sept.–Oct. 1955): 4; Madigan, "The American Indian Relocation Program," 17; Philp, "Stride toward Freedom," 181; Aberdeen Area report, Apr. 1952, box 1, Placement and Statistical Reports, Field Placement and Relocation Office Employment Assistance Records, Record Group 75, National Archives–Washington, D.C.

43. Apr. 1957 reports from Navajo and Crownpoint agencies, box 3, FP, FPROEAR, RG 75, NA-WDC.

44. For examples, see "Chit Chat from the Relocation Office," Turtle Mountain Consolidated Agency, 2 Apr. 1954 and 26 Apr. 1954, Rietz Collection, CA, NAES.

45. Report by Virginia Boardman, 17 Dec. 1959, Church Federation of Greater Chicago Files, 32A-1, Manuscript Collections, Chicago Historical Society; author interview with Lucille Spencer (Choctaw), Chicago, 22 June 1995; author interview with Susan K. Power (Sioux), Chicago, 19 June 1995; interview with Ada Powers (Sioux), Chicago, 19 Apr. 1984, CAIOHP, no. 012, NL and NAES; interview with Rosella Mars (Chippewa), Chicago, 18 Apr. 1984, CAIOHP, no. 013, NL and NAES; interview with Marlene Strouse (Papago), Chicago, 18 July 1983, CAIOHP, no. 011, NL and NAES; George D. Scott, John Kennardh White, and Estelle Fuchs, *Indians and Their Education in Chicago* (Washington, D.C.: Educational Resources Information Center, 1969), 4; White, "The American Indian in Chicago," 2; Clark, "Bury My Lungs in Smog," 159–60.

46. List of persons provided relocation services to Chicago, box 11, NR, FPROEAR, RG 75, NA-WDC.

47. Kurt Dreifuss to Robert Rietz, 14 July 1954, Rietz Collection, CA, NAES; Fort Berthold Reservation census, roll 136, M595, RG 75, NA-WDC; list of persons provided relocation services to Chicago, box 11, NR, FPROEAR, RG 75, NA-WDC.

48. Interview with Rose Maney (Winnebago), Chicago, 2 May 1984, CAIOHP, no. 002, NL and NAES; author interview with Diane Maney (Winnebago), Chicago, 20 June 1995.

49. Author interview with Susan K. Power (Sioux), Chicago, 19 June 1995.

50. Author interview with Josephine Willie and son (Choctaw), Chicago, 14 June 1995.

51. Author interview with Diane Maney (Winnebago), Chicago, 20 June 1995.

# 4   Living and Working in the City

The Chicago of the 1950s that American Indians entered was a city shared by numerous ethnic and racial groups that over many decades had made certain neighborhoods and occupations their own. Near the turn of the twentieth century, for example, Italians dominated Chicago's construction industry from their Near West Side neighborhood. To the south, Irish and Poles lived in Bridgeport, Back of the Yards, Englewood, and other southwest neighborhoods. The Irish were well represented in local politics and on the police force, and a majority of Poles worked in meatpacking plants. Blacks lived in crowded tenements in a rigidly bounded, narrow area that stretched south along State Street. On the North Side, Germans, Swedes, Norwegians, and many other ethnic groups carved out their own residential and economic niches.

This type of segmentation in housing and employment occurred not by accident but as a result of Chicago's developing economy and the efforts of generations of immigrants. During the late nineteenth and early twentieth centuries, immigrants adjusted to Chicago through neighborhoods in which they found jobs, housing, and information about urban life. Fathers acquired jobs for sons alongside them on assembly lines or in various trades. Neighbors from European villages became neighbors in Chicago as older residents found housing for kin. All migrants during the late nineteenth and early twentieth centuries faced the challenge of adjusting to industrial capitalism. It affected not only their jobs but also their homes and families.[1]

By the 1950s, migrant groups had more difficulty trying to cluster in particular occupations or neighborhoods. The very nature of Chicago had begun to change. The central city held preeminent economic and industrial power during the late nineteenth and early twentieth centuries—a symbol of American economic might. In the mid-twentieth century, however, Chicago and other American cities became more and more fragmented as businesses and residents moved to the suburbs. The local economy had come to rely less on heavy industry and more on white-collar, professional, and service jobs. This was the Chicago to which Indian people moved and adjusted during the 1950s. Unlike the city's earlier migrants, they lacked the numbers to control a neighborhood or industry. They faced the challenge of adjusting to a decentralized, dispersed metropolitan region and to an increasingly postindustrial economy.[2]

American Indians who lived and worked in Chicago during the 1950s were blocked from many national economic trends of the time. They only partially benefited from the decade's staggering 37 percent increase in gross national product. Few if any reached the income levels of those employed in booming industries of the 1950s, such as chemicals, plastics, and pharmaceuticals. Likewise, most did not move into homes in the burgeoning suburbs or buy a new Chevrolet every few years, as did some members of earlier migrations.

Yet American Indians were not entirely cut off from all national economic trends. Some participated in the consumer economy of the period in ways that strengthened old identities and values and began to shape new ones. Many experienced the changing nature of Chicago's economy during the 1950s as industrial plants downsized or moved out of the city. In the end, however, the most significant economic change that Indians experienced in Chicago during the 1950s was the most basic—the benefits of urban employment. During the 1950s, the earning power of urban Indians far outdistanced that of their friends and family on reservations. Restricted opportunities for advancement and a lack of prior training put skilled jobs out of reach for all but 5 to 10 percent. A majority, however, was able to find at least unskilled jobs in Chicago, and 30 to 40 percent found semiskilled positions. These jobs brought paychecks—and even benefits—to some. Just over a year after leaving Pine Ridge for Chicago with his young family, for example, Rudy Arcoren was ready to take his first paid vacation. Even the type of employment that he and many other Indians in Chicago took, which lagged behind that of many white Chicagoans, was not available for Indian people on reservations during the 1950s.[3]

The often-repeated claim that American Indians missed out on the prosperity of the 1950s is accurate in one sense but fails to recognize that only urbanization and a closer contact with non-Indians made any comparison possible. Before the 1950s, Indians were even further economically removed from the rest of America, but their reservation existence made their poverty almost invisible. It is ironic that only as Indian people made slow but steady economic progress in Chicago and other urban areas during the 1950s did their deprivation relative to white Americans begin to be noticed.[4]

———

After the difficult adjustments of the first days in the city, an even greater problem became apparent. Many Indians arrived ill-prepared for work in Chicago, and the flexability and resourcefulness that proved useful in finding work near reservations were not as helpful in Chicago. Some had no more than an eighth-grade education and sporadic agricultural work experience. Even those who returned from military service in the 1940s sometimes resorted to short-term jobs with local white farmers at harvest time. Especially if they had reached their forties or fifties, Indian men with minimal education often found nothing better than sporadic work as laborers. Moreover, rural work experiences sometimes contributed to problems in later finding work in Chicago. Some city employers complained that the Indians they hired had physical infirmities and injuries. Years of stoop labor and living in unsanitary work camps left many with injured backs, long-term malnutrition, and other health problems. As a BIA official in South Dakota commented soon after the relocation program began, "Workers from this Area who have performed hard physical labor such as bucking potatoes have been questioned as poor physical risks." In general, Indians and the urban job market were not well matched.[5]

Others who had more education and training sometimes fared better and adjusted more easily to urban life. One-third of both Indian men and women in Chicago in 1959 had graduated from high school; roughly half had attended for a year or two. Chicago Indians were fairly typical of urban Indians nationwide during the late 1950s and ahead of the general reservation population in education. High school graduates were more likely than less-educated Indian people to attain semiskilled jobs in Chicago. A Sioux man who had worked in the boiler room during his years at boarding school, for instance, found work in the boiler departments of both International Harvester and Union Station in Chicago. Some, however, discovered that Indian boarding schools had taught them outdated information that was of little use in competing against a wide cross-section of workers trained in urban schools and workplaces. Especially during the 1940s and 1950s, it was difficult for the remote and understaffed schools in the middle of the Northern Plains or in the North-woods to remain up to date about technology.[6]

Few Indians in Chicago found their jobs to be physically difficult; most had done much harder work in the past. Even when complaints about the relocation program and life in Chicago were frequent, few criticized their jobs or the wages they were paid. Yet the ways in which they were forced to look for jobs did frustrate and alienate many Indians, as did the culture and rhythm of work life. Even those with necessary training were put off by the bureaucratic and competitive nature of urban job hunting. A young Sioux man who had training as a machinist in South Dakota, for instance, responded to a job advertisement in a Chicago newspaper but left when he saw eight other men waiting in line for the job. "What's the use?" he muttered to an onlooker as he left the plant.[7]

Like other Chicagoans before them, Indians were more comfortable acquiring jobs through familiar channels than in relying on impersonal job agencies. Those with minimal knowledge of English especially had reason to rely on family or friends and to bring them along when interviewing or signing papers. A 1956 study of Chippewa and Sioux job-hunting practices in Minnesota showed that fewer than one in twenty-five had ever applied for a job directly in response to an advertisement. The study also claimed that many Chippewas and Sioux had a "strong tendency to undersell themselves" when facing competition, the result of decades of isolation and harsh experiences with non-Indians. The BIA tried to discourage Indians from relying on others to find work and believed that instilling individualism was part of its mandate in conducting the relocation program. One reservation newspaper told those who would soon be moving to cities, "Don't take anyone with you unless you are requested to do so—the employer wants to talk only to you."[8] Such advice, though, would have been daunting and impractical for any newcomer to the city, and few Indians would ever adjust completely to such urban job-hunting practices.

Once on the job, Indians quickly perceived the differences between rural and urban work. Like generations of urban migrants before them, they sometimes adjusted painfully to a world of time clocks and the whistles that divided the working day into different, specified tasks. Little about Chicago work life resembled the seasonal and varying schedule of traditional rural life. The city's noise and congestion made many homesick for prairies or forests, and the demands of urban work, which struck many Indians as unreasonable, resulted in frequent job changes. Few stayed with the same company for long, moving either to another job in Chicago or back to the reservation.[9]

Some mixed old and new cultural patterns while in Chicago. Ann Lim, a Winnebago, deliberately chose seasonal work in order to spend time on the reservation every year. She "couldn't leave Wisconsin during the summer" and found work in a Chicago bakery that regularly laid off workers during those months. Others managed to find jobs in Chicago similar to those they might have had back home. After going through a number of dissatisfying industrial jobs in quick succession, for example, James Quiver from Pine Ridge found work to his liking at a stable on the outskirts of the city. Others worked outside in nurseries or gardens, where at least some sights and smells might evoke pleasant memories of home.[10]

The majority of Indians in Chicago, however, took the types of jobs that other Chicagoans did during the 1950s and worked for more than seven hundred different employers by the middle of the decade. In the unskilled category, they worked as laborers at B&B Enterprises and Paymaster, packed boxes at the Curtiss and Demets candy companies, and washed dishes and cleaned floors at Berghoff's and Stouffer's restaurants. Among the semiskilled, some became factory operatives at Allis-Chalmers, Belmont Radio, Borg-Warner, Caterpillar, Dennison Manufacturing, Elkay Manufacturing, Farmrite Equipment, Hayden Manufacturing, Illinois Tool Works, International Harvester, Stewart-Warner, and Wells Manufacturing. Others clerked and filed and typed at some of Chicago's largest service-sector employers, including Carson Pirie Scott, Montgomery Ward, Sears, and Spiegel. Publisher R. R. Donnelley offered Indians positions binding books and driving trucks. Others became nurses' aides and cooks. A few of the best-trained and most fortunate attained skilled positions. Some became finish laborers and rolling machine operators at U.S. Steel, Inland Steel, and Republic Steel. Other skilled workers were machinists, tool and die makers, welders, draftsmen, and mechanics.

Beginning in August 1956, Indians who lived on reservations across the country could experience Chicago and its labor market through the adult vocational training (AVT) program. Passed by Congress as Public Law 959, the program offered Indians payment for vocational training programs of up to two years if the Indians were between eighteen and thirty-five and lived on restricted or trust reservation lands. In Chicago and the other cities where the BIA had offices, the AVT program soon became more popular than the conventional relocation program. It allowed those interested in building job skills but unsure about settling in a city an opportunity to benefit from modern, urban training temporarily and then take that training back home. By the end of the 1950s, Chicago Indians could choose among forty-two approved vocational courses as part of the AVT program. Some, such as body and fender repair and welding, required as little as four months of training; those who were training to be chefs, accountants, or x-ray technicians needed the maximum two-year period.[11]

Chicago was booming during the 1950s. An average of a hundred new industrial plants a year were put up as soon as the war ended. The city developed a diversified economy and was among the nation's leaders in several categories, including machinery, primary metals, printing and publishing, and meat and confectionery products. Roger Biles, a Chicago historian, has called the 1950s an "era of unparalleled prosperity" for the city, in part because of government money in the way of housing loans, veterans programs, and the G.I. Bill.[12]

Indians, too, enjoyed some economic benefits from working in Chicago and other cities. The median incomes for Indian, black, and white males indicate that the 1950s was a relative boom period for both urban and reservation Indians. Median income for Indian men in cities rose almost twice as quickly as that of those on reservations, 147 percent against 79 percent. No other group experienced a more rapid increase in median income during the 1950s than urban Indian men. That was due in part to their degree of deprivation when they arrived, yet the figures are startling nonetheless. By 1969, urban Indian men boasted a median income just above that of black men after having earned little more than half as much twenty years earlier.[13]

Among cities where Indians lived in large numbers during the 1950s, Chicago was generally above average in the economic benefits achieved by its Native American residents. Only New York, where Mohawk men had worked on skyscrapers and suspension bridges since the 1920s, offered a significantly better economic environment. Chicago's diversified economy, however, gave it some advantages over cities such as Phoenix, Albuquerque, and Minneapolis (tables 11, 12, and 13).

Like many others during the 1950s, Indians in Chicago used some of their earnings to participate in the consumer economy and buy radios, televisions, automobiles, and other items. The availability of both

*Table 11.* Median Income for Males by Race, 1949–69

|      | Urban Indians | Reservation Indians | Blacks | Whites |
|------|---------------|---------------------|--------|--------|
| 1949 | $ 1,198       | $  950              | $ 2,218 | $ 3,780 |
| 1959 | 2,961         | 1,699               | 3,398  | 5,229  |
| 1969 | 4,568         | 2,603               | 4,508  | 7,759  |

*Source:* Adapted from U.S. Bureau of the Census, *Census of Population: 1950; Census of Population: 1960; Census of Population: 1970.*

*Table 12.* Percentage of Indians in Workforce by
City and Sex, 1959

|  | Indian Men | Indian Women |
|---|---|---|
| All Indians | 59 | 25 |
| New York City | 85 | 49 |
| Los Angeles | 78 | 42 |
| San Francisco | 75 | 36 |
| Oklahoma City | 74 | 38 |
| Chicago | 71 | 48 |
| Phoenix | 68 | 28 |
| Tulsa | 66 | 29 |
| Seattle | 65 | 30 |
| Albuquerque | 62 | 42 |
| Minneapolis | 54 | 37 |

Source: Adapted from U.S. Bureau of the Census, *Census of
Population: 1960, Nonwhite Population by Race.*

*Table 13.* Median Income of Indians by City and Sex, 1959

|  | All Indians | Indian Men | Indian Women |
|---|---|---|---|
| All Indians | $1,348 | $1,792 | < $1,000 |
| All urban Indians | 1,950 | 2,759 | 1,227 |
| New York City | 2,902 | 3,660 | 2,069 |
| Chicago | 2,684 | 3,473 | 1,824 |
| Los Angeles | 2,459 | 3,423 | 1,506 |
| San Francisco | 2,292 | 3,349 | 1,223 |
| Tulsa | 2,099 | 2,927 | 1,337 |
| Oklahoma City | 1,836 | 2,658 | 1,435 |
| Minneapolis | 1,743 | 1,978 | 1,335 |
| Albuquerque | 1,698 | 2,392 | 1,335 |
| Seattle | 1,640 | 2,321 | 1,033 |
| Phoenix | 1,245 | 1,845 | < 1,000 |

Source: Adapted from U.S. Bureau of the Census, *Census of Population: 1960,
Nonwhite Population by Race.*

necessities and luxuries was far greater in Chicago than on reservations.
As Chippewa Margaret Redcloud contrasted life in Minnesota and in
Chicago, "We were always scrounging and wearing second-hand clothes
and hand-me-downs. . . . Nowadays, we can go to Sears or anyplace, and
buy what we need." Communication between Chicago and home reservations often carried news about Indians' purchases. The Chippewas at
the Turtle Mountain Reservation in North Dakota, for example, were told
in April 1954 that the Wilkie family, who had moved two years earlier,
"had a television set for entertainment."[14]

Also like other Chicagoans, Indians sometimes over-extended their finances and then fell behind on payments, causing goods they bought on installment to be repossessed. Such incidents concerned the BIA, which in this one area opposed rather than supported Indians' tendency to follow national trends. At a time when millions of Americans were using newly invented credit cards and quickly doubling the nation's total private debt, the BIA urged, "PLEASE don't sign your name agreeing to buy more than your paycheck will pay for, or they will take everything away from you. Talk to the Field Office people about installment buying." Some especially overbearing and paternalistic BIA workers even attempted to dictate what types of food relocatees should buy in Chicago supermarkets. On one occasion, an employee tried to dissuade a Chippewa man from buying a can of fruit cocktail, even after the consumer had placed it in his shopping basket.[15]

Although no exact statistics are available concerning Chicago Indians' purchases of consumer items, numerous references to this subject, together with studies from other cities, suggest the significance of the trend during the 1950s. In Milwaukee, a survey showed that almost all Indians owned a radio, and one-quarter to one-third of all Indian families owned a television set. Likewise, more than half of all Navajos in Albuquerque owned televisions and automobiles in the late 1950s and 1960s. The BIA office in Los Angeles estimated that a majority of Indian families relocated there bought a television soon after arriving.[16]

Some observers believed these trends foreshadowed Indians' rapid assimilation. O. K. Armstrong, for example, who supported relocation, believed that urban Indians' purchase of consumer items signaled a great cultural transformation. Yet he and others exaggerated the extent to which mass consumer culture overwhelmed Indians and stripped them of their identity. They often used the new possibilities to facilitate their urban adjustment and build more satisfying lives. Those who had listened to country and western music on the reservation, for example, searched the dial for Chicago stations that played it. Moreover, they often listened to the radio or watched television together as a group social activity. Indians in Chicago used automobiles not only to drive to workplaces and shopping centers but also to return home to visit families and friends during vacations. For some, the money they earned from urban employment and the ways in which they spent it aided in their adjustment to the city.[17]

Urban life brought a changing job market as well as available consumer goods to Indians. The year 1955 marked an important transformation in this process. Before 1955, blue-collar and industrial workers constituted a majority of the work force; after 1955, white-collar, professional, and service workers gradually did. The Indians in Chicago experienced the trend differently than those in Los Angeles, Denver, and elsewhere. Among cities that had large Indian populations, Chicago led the way during the 1950s in shifting from an strongly industrial to an increasingly service-oriented economy.[18]

The difference between the employment situation for Indians in Chicago and Los Angeles can be seen by comparing a prominent employer of Indians in each city. In Chicago, a few elite Indian workers who had extensive prior training and union membership worked their way into skilled jobs at Inland Steel, Republic Steel, and U.S. Steel. Such employment paid as much as $3.57 an hour, more than the highest wages of Indian men in Los Angeles. Yet as the 1950s wore on, many of these jobs were eliminated through mechanization.

Most who sought work were unable to find jobs that paid wages even approximating those of the steel mills. A wide gap separated elite jobs from those more easily attainable. Many Indians in Chicago during the 1950s were forced to take the types of service jobs offered by Spiegel, a mail order firm that employed hundreds of clerks, packers, billers, and warehouse workers at fairly low wages. Throughout the 1950s, Spiegel wages hovered at about $1 an hour and rose very little over the course of the decade. As soon as the relocation program began, Spiegel began working with the BIA to hire Indians. The firm even sent representatives to reservations in Wisconsin and Minnesota to look for workers and administer the "Wonderlic Mental Alertness Test," which it used to screen applicants. The trips reaped the expected benefits, and several young women in Wisconsin, including the 1952 valedictorian of Flandreau High School, left their reservations to work at Spiegel. Although BIA employees acknowledged that the mail order retailer offered "comparatively low wages," they welcomed the company's participation because Spiegel could put large numbers to work and employed an on-site counselor to help Indian workers adjust to a new workplace and city.[19]

In contrast, Los Angeles offered fewer opportunities than Chicago for Indian people who had minimal skills, although those who were semi-skilled or skilled had greater opportunities. Those with training sometimes thrived in Los Angeles, whereas those without had difficulty finding any job at all. More than other parts of the country, California and the emerging Sunbelt benefited from the general postwar economic boom spurred by defense spending, and North American Aviation offered many Indians in Los Angeles higher wages than those paid by Spiegel. During the late 1950s, defense contracts awarded to North American and other defense plants amounted to 10 percent of the nation's gross national product. In 1953, Indian workers starting at North American Aviation earned a median wage of $1.45 an hour, jumping to $1.60 after just two months. By 1957, the firm employed almost 750 Indians, many of them specially trained for their jobs at the nearby Sherman Institute or the Intermountain Indian School in Utah. A report that year found that North American Aviation was "the first choice of employment among a large percentage of the relocatees."[20]

No employer comparable to North American Aviation existed in Chicago for Indian people. Thus, the earnings of Indian men in Chicago sometimes lagged behind those of their counterparts in Los Angeles. For women, however, Chicago's service economy was often advantageous, and their wages were closer to men's than they were in other cities. Few Indian women in Los Angeles acquired jobs with North American or any other high-paying companies, and their options were often limited in other types of employment as well. Officials at the relocation office in Los Angeles often reported an "over-supply of local women for all job openings," with some working as domestics. Because of Chicago's vast service economy, however, Indian women there had greater access to jobs that required little training.[21]

Indian mothers as well as single women followed a national pattern that saw a fourfold increase in the number of all mothers who took jobs outside their homes during the 1950s. BIA relocation offices offered advice about child care "in case the mother wishes to go to work to augment the family income." Some bureau officials saw even this as part of their mandate to integrate and assimilate their clients. The relocation officer directing Creeks and Seminoles in Oklahoma to Los Angeles, Denver, and Chicago noted that his office encouraged women who had no children or those who had child care to seek full-time employment, "as it is an accelerative step toward the rapid and complete integration of Indian people with the normal life of the nation."[22]

The expectations that urban Indian women faced seemed strange and unjust to recent reservation-dwellers. Even firms interested in hiring Native American women sometimes had strict physical requirements that eliminated individuals considered too short or too heavy. BIA workers on reservations were aware of this and noted appearance and how it might affect a woman's urban job prospects. One wrote approvingly of a Chippewa, nineteen years old and single, from Red Lake in Minnesota: "Reads some, listens to radio, goes to shows and dances. Physically OK. Wears lipstick, clean, well groomed, strong." Another bureau employee instructed that any Indian women who wished to work in a restaurant or in a similar job had to be "neat, well-groomed, and attentive to customers' wishes." They also had to be at least five feet seven inches in height, "as they must be able to reach over the built-in fixtures in back of the counter," and "must be slender." Because of genetics, poor diet, and countless other factors, many Indian women did not meet the general requirements of Chicago's job market during the 1950s.[23]

Others, though, took advantage of the size and flexibility of that market. Charlene Cooper, an Oneida who, with her husband, was among the first to participate in the relocation program to Chicago in 1952, held several jobs over the next fifteen years. She started as a timekeeper at Container Corporation, then took a clerical job at Campbell Soup, and then worked nights at a Christmas card factory. After she separated from her husband, she went to real estate school and then beautician's school at night. Clara Packineau, an Arikara single mother of two, took the opportunity to work nights in Chicago, which she liked "most of all" her new urban experiences. She had a long-term problem, however, in finding child care, especially after her sister left Chicago. Yet despite such problems, life in Chicago presented both women with more job opportunities than they would have found back home in Wisconsin or North Dakota.[24]

As Indian people entered Chicago in increasing numbers during the 1950s, employers such as Spiegel began noticing their presence. Employers sometimes contacted Indians directly but more often spoke with local BIA officials, who toured Chicago workplaces regularly. Many employers reported a wide range of experiences with Indian workers and counted them among their best (as well as worst) workers. Yet even those wary of employing minimally trained Indian workers often became strongly involved in the relocation program.

Some employers hired a few Indians out of a sense of curiosity or romanticism. They were interested in having supposed representatives of the "Wild West" on their shop floors or in their offices. A Sioux man who worked in relocation offices in several different cities noted, "Most of the employers were very nice. They at first were interested only in [that] you were really an Indian, [that] you were from a reservation. They wanted to visit with you. You went there with the idea: 'Will you hire a few Indians if we get them out here?' And their attitude was: 'Could you get me a beaded tie or ash tray?' And I did this; I used to order ash trays from Pipestone. I'd give them one, and they'd hire four or five."[25]

The majority of Chicago employers who participated in the relocation program, however, did so because low-wage clerical and industrial workers were in demand during the early 1950s. After talking with the BIA's Kurt Dreifuss, director of the Chicago office, about the relocation program and the available work force it provided, Burt Muldoon, personnel director of the electrical equipment manufacturer Stewart-Warner, sent an appreciative letter to Commissioner of Indian Affairs Dillon Myer in December 1952. "After one has tried every trick in the bag to entice qualified applicants into our Employment Department," he wrote, "it is indeed gratifying, and I might add a bit surprising, to answer the phone and have someone ask you if you can use a good, clean, intelligent young man who is looking for work." Harry Scheidt from Wells Manufacturing likewise appreciated the BIA office's assistance, especially its streamlining of the hiring process through assuming some tasks usually left to personnel departments. He said that he hired Indians sent by the Chicago relocation office "because we know they aren't recommended unless they have been carefully screened." A third factory representative, explaining his interest in the relocation program, spoke for many when in 1955 he said that he looked on Indians "as a great untapped source of workers in a tight labor market."[26]

Occasionally, Indians' willingness to take low-wage jobs combined with their unfamiliarity with urban labor relations to make them especially attractive to employers. In December 1955 the *Wall Street Journal* announced in a front-page story, "Factories reach for reservation red men to ease labor pinch." With some amusement, the newspaper reported on two Indian factory workers in Los Angeles who were somewhat confused about the strike at their plant. One followed his co-workers to the picket line and marched behind them during the day but in the evening reported for his swing-shift job. A second also crossed the picket line and began operating several idle machines near his post to make up for the loss of production caused by absent workers. Observing this "one-man assembly line," his delighted supervisor stated, "He'd never said 'boo' to anyone, and it's the first time we had any idea he could run any machines but his own."[27]

In implementing the relocation program in Chicago, Kurt Dreifuss worked closely with local business leaders. He quickly organized the Citizens' Advisory Board to give leading civic figures greater authority and responsibility in administering the program. Dreifuss placed personnel directors from several large Chicago firms on the board's "subcommittee on employment." These business leaders acted as loyal allies and mimicked the rhetoric emanating from the Chicago and Washington BIA offices about integration and urban employment for Indian people. As Muldoon, a member of the board, said in 1952, "I think it is high time we gave Indians a better break and started giving them jobs the same as other people."[28]

Sitting on the subcommittee on employment also helped personnel directors funnel Indian employees into low-wage job slots. Spiegel, whose personnel director G. S. Sargent sat on the board, and the Curtiss Candy Company both viewed the relocation program as a godsend. The two companies employed many Indians to answer telephones and pack boxes—often for less than $1 an hour. The firms represented on the board attempted to maintain good relations with Chicago's Indian community. For one Christmas party attended by a group of Indian people, for example, Curtiss Candy donated 144 candy bars and Spiegel provided eighty more pounds of candy. Sporadic donations, however, would not make up for the persistently low wages paid to Indian workers throughout the 1950s.[29]

Although most Indians depended on the BIA office in Chicago to find them initial jobs, over time many looked for work independently. Word spread quickly about how much various employers or industries paid. Indians in Chicago talked about their wages and noted when someone else earned more for similar work, sometimes making frequent job changes. One Winnebago woman who worked in the office of a gasket factory wandered upstairs during a break and discovered that a sandwich company had moved in. The company needed workers and asked if she was interested in working evenings on a part-time basis. She agreed because "you could make some good money by doing this, and they paid you by the sandwich." Eventually, she quit her job at the gasket factory and went to work full time making sandwiches.[30]

BIA employees at the Chicago relocation office hoped that the jobs they found for clients—often at completely non-Indian workplaces—would help them adjust to the city. Yet Indian-led job-hunting expeditions and workplaces where several Indians worked were usually more successful in this process. Although Indians in Chicago never dominated any industry or workplace, as did other ethnic groups, they found solace in having at least a few other Indian people nearby. One such place was R. R. Donnelley, which employed more than ten Indians in 1957. Union Station, where most had first stepped foot in Chicago, also hired a number of Indians to sort mail and do maintenance work throughout the 1950s. People from different tribal backgrounds sometimes met at on the job and helped each other adjust to their new lives. Marlene Strouse, a Papago, met her future husband when her father introduced her to the young Pima who worked with him at Union Station.[31]

Indians took many different paths to adjusting to Chicago's employment environment, not all of them necessarily profitable. Poorly paying day-labor jobs, for which workers were hired for only one day at a time and paid at the end of that day, introduced many to the urban work world. Indeed, some Indians followed this pattern for years. Although in time the BIA would officially oppose day-labor jobs for Indians, it initially perceived them as necessary. In 1953 Kurt Dreifuss placed fifteen unscheduled relocatees—all young, single men—in casual day-labor jobs. Some were with Readymen, Inc., which would place hundreds more Indian laborers from its office at One North LaSalle and become the preeminent day-labor agency in Chicago over the course of the 1950s.[32]

For some, the day-labor experience was a destructive one. In exchange for finding jobs for workers, Readymen and other daily-pay offices took as much as 20 percent of workers' already slim paychecks. Day-labor sometimes perpetuated a cycle of desperation, leading a later BIA employee to condemn the offices as "slave labor markets." More important, daily-pay work was tied to drinking problems and alcoholism for many Indian people (as well as non-Indians). A drinking problem would often prevent acquisition of a better-paying job but could be fed by the small amount of money a daily-pay job brought in. Moreover, most daily-pay workers did not have bank accounts and often cashed their checks in local taverns and transient hotels where their daily-pay employers had made arrangements. Their marginal financial status resembled that of earlier mine or factory workers who were paid in scrip. Edward E. Goodvoice, a Sioux from the Rosebud Reservation, worked daily-pay jobs and suffered from alcoholism for more than ten years in Chicago. Even after leaving Chicago to serve in the elite 101st Airborne Division he returned to his old habits after coming back to Chicago. Now a successfully recovering alcoholic and well-respected substance abuse counselor, Goodvoice still has some ill-will toward the BIA and Readymen. "Some of us who were prone to drink too much would just sit there and drink up the eight-hour check. It wasn't a good idea," he recalls.[33]

For others, though, daily-pay labor was a satisfying way to combine old and new cultural patterns. It provided a gradual means toward adjustment without the shock and anxiety of working at conventional, full-time, industrial or office jobs. Some exchanged financial benefits for freedom, which was used to socialize within the city or back home on the reservation. The "traditional" as well as those who were more "acculturated" were represented in semiskilled employment positions in Chicago, but daily-pay work was primarily the domain of traditional people who lived in extended families. Some in that category took on full-time employment after awhile, but daily pay became a way of life for most. Similar to their ancestors, they lived lives of constant mobility.[34]

As more Indians began working daily-pay jobs for Readymen, the firm developed a reputation for employing Indians. Ada Powers, a Sioux, observed that it was the place to be "with the Indians," and that fact enabled them to "follow the Indian life." Some left regular jobs to join the group of Indians that worked out of Readymen; others found they belonged there after going through a number of dissatisfying jobs. Either way, daily-pay employment was one of the many ways in which some Indians began to adjust to Chicago during the 1950s.[35]

In housing as in employment, Indians often had difficulty adjusting to Chicago during the 1950s. They faced not only neighborhoods and blocks segmented by race and ethnic group but also the fact that limited construction during the 1930s and early 1940s had created a very short supply of housing after World War II that by late 1945 was further taxed by returning veterans. About one-fifth of all families were forced to double up in the first few years after the war. Two hundred fifty families in Chicago temporarily moved into the streetcars the city had converted into homes.[36]

As it worked to find housing in this tight market, the BIA's Chicago relocation office also heeded its mission to assimilate and integrate Indians into the city. During the early years of the relocation program, Kurt Dreifuss deliberately tried to spread Indian people throughout the city—to speed their assimilation, he claimed. His office, he noted, "found it desirable to find apartments which are scattered about the entire city rather than having individuals and families clustered in a few congested buildings." This approach would "facilitate a more normal and happy integration of persons into the life of the community." To further his goals, he also used neighborhood councils and other civic and religious organizations to help Indians "take root in their local communities."[37]

Some observers in Chicago noticed this housing policy pursued by the BIA. A member of the clergy who worked with Indians in Chicago noted in 1956 that there was "no large concentration of Indian population in any given spot in the city," with exceptions of a few areas in which "several families are to be found in a given block or two." Relocatees themselves observed Dreifuss's strategy and were often upset about it. As Phyllis Fastwolf, a Sioux, observed, "They placed us so that we never lived together. . . . They put us on the south side, others on the north side. That was their policy—to scatter us out over the city."[38]

Initially, the Chicago relocation office placed many relocatees in hotels and rooming houses near its location in the Loop. Some stayed there on a temporary basis and others more permanently. The BIA office often used the Isham Memorial YMCA at 1508 North Larabee Street on the Near North Side. There relocatees found beds as well as recreational facilities for a few weeks while they adjusted to the city. Soon, a small group of Indians—acquiring housing both through the BIA and on its own—began to converge around 1500 Larabee, a few blocks east of the cluster of industrial plants that hugged the Chicago River. Another group on the Near North Side emerged on North Clark Steet between Chicago and Grand avenues. Much of the housing here—especially that used for temporary purposes—was poor, and it quickly soured some relocatees on urban life. The BIA worked at upgrading its sources of temporary housing but achieved only limited success. After a visit to the Dorset Hotel where some Indians were staying in the late 1950s, an employee acknowledged with some embarrassment, "Our skirts are not neat and clean on temporary housing."[39]

To the west of the Loop lay the famous skid row on Madison Street, where Indians and others could rent three-by-seven-foot cubicles for as little as 75 cents a night. Some in this area also slept under bridges or in railroad yards. Although life here was hard and dangerous, one resident described it as no worse than reservation life, mentioning the availability of hot and cold running water and public bath houses on skid row. Further west, some Indians lived in the West Town neighborhood and near Garfield Park. Most were long-time Chicago residents who had arrived before the relocation program began. They enjoyed better housing than those along Madison Street, and some had achieved middle-class status.[40]

In addition to their many other disadvantages, the neighborhoods near downtown offered very little housing for big families. The hotels and YMCAs of the Near North Side could be sufficient for young, single people but not for large groups. Although the average family participating in the relocation program during the 1950s had only four members, many were larger. One in five of all families (one in four of all Sioux families) that relocated to Chicago had six or more members, and some had as many as ten. To acquire housing for them, the Chicago relocation office turned to the South Side during the 1950s and built on the small community that already existed there. Some Indians had moved to Kenwood and Hyde Park near the University of Chicago's campus during the war. During the 1950s, those neighborhoods were in transition as large numbers of blacks moved in. The BIA took advantage of the anxiety that transition created—and the low rents the anxiety produced.[41]

Even those who found spacious apartments at reasonable rents on the South Side, however, sometimes encountered problems. Some Indians, accustomed to interacting primarily with other tribe members and a few whites on home reservations, feared living close to large numbers of African Americans. In Hyde Park, several families were the only non-black tenants in their buildings. Some feared venturing out their apartments and spent most of the time inside.[42]

A second and related problem with Indians taking up residence on the South Side was the advent of urban renewal. As blacks and other poor migrants flocked to Chicago during the 1950s and 1960s and whites increasingly moved to outlying suburbs, Mayor Richard J. Daley and other local officials grew worried about the city's weakening economy. They responded with proposals designed to rid the city of slums, build new and highly concentrated housing, and raise the tax base. During the late 1950s and early 1960s, Chicago was second only to New York in the amount of money received for urban renewal projects—almost $52 million by 1962. Among them were the Robert Taylor Homes, twenty-eight identical, sixteen-story buildings that stretched for two miles along State Street, from Fortieth to Fifty-fourth streets. In part because of the location of such projects, almost all public housing tenants in Chicago by the end of the 1950s were black. The urban renewal projects the city undertook in Hyde Park during the 1950s also displaced some of the American Indians who lived there.[43]

Those displaced from the South Side—and many other Indians, as well—moved to the North Side during the mid- and late 1950s. The Uptown and Lakeview neighborhoods in particular become home for hundreds. As early as the late 1940s and at the beginning of the relocation program in 1952, small pockets of Indians lived in Uptown around the intersections of Lawrence and Kenmore avenues and Wilson and Clarendon avenues just to the west of Lake Shore Drive. As the 1950s progressed, even more Indian people made the North Side their home.[44]

Uptown had become part of Chicago in 1889 and had grown quickly during the early twentieth century, with Swedes, Germans, and others moving there. By the 1920s developers began to tear down single-family homes and build high-rise apartments and apartment hotels. This occurred especially in the southeastern section east of Broadway, where after 1930 new residential construction almost came to a halt and the division of existing buildings into ever-smaller apartments continued. The neighborhood became a port of entry for poor migrants, a transient district where people of many ethnic groups came and went frequently. World War II saw even more single-family homes converted to rooming houses. The typical structures in Uptown during the early twentieth century— three-story buildings containing six apartments of six or eight rooms—

were usually converted to twenty or more two-room kitchenette apartments during the 1940s and 1950s.[45]

As a result of these conversions, Uptown had become the second most densely populated neighborhood in Chicago by 1950. Two-thirds of its apartment buildings had ten or more units. Such crowding was not as common in the other areas where Indians lived. Only half of Lakeview's structures and one-tenth of West Town's, for example, had ten or more units in 1950. Moreover, those neighborhoods—and Chicago at large— also had far more modest-sized apartment buildings of two, three, or four units (table 14). The Uptown neighborhood and the city of Chicago as a whole continued in their opposite trajectories through 1960. By then, Uptown had even higher-density housing and Chicago more single-family units than a decade earlier.[46]

Many large apartment buildings in Uptown and elsewhere in Chicago had five or six stories, and Indians were often unhappy and fearful about living so high. A Sioux woman, for example, who had moved from the Cheyenne River Reservation in South Dakota into a small, third-floor apartment that had no screens feared that her children would fall through its windows. Others felt trapped and disconnected from the world. Before city officials began to publicly acknowledge the problems of large, multistory housing units in the 1960s, the Indians who lived in them understood intuitively that being separated from nature sapped the human spirit.[47]

Beyond being forced to live in intimidating high-rise buildings, many Indians in Uptown lived in apartments judged to be "sub-standard" or "dilapidated" by city housing officials. Although Uptown as a whole had roughly the same proportion of sub-standard dwelling units as did Chicago at large, its southeastern section had far more housing in poor condition than did areas in the northern part of the neighborhood. Most In-

*Table 14.* Types of Dwelling Structures in Uptown, Lakeview, West Town, and Chicago, 1950

|            | Uptown | Lakeview | West Town | Chicago |
|------------|--------|----------|-----------|---------|
| 1 unit     | 5.1%   | 4.8%     | 6.0%      | 17.9%   |
| 2 units    | 6.9    | 14.6     | 20.7      | 21.8    |
| 3–4 units  | 9.8    | 19.3     | 34.0      | 19.3    |
| 5–9 units  | 12.3   | 13.4     | 30.4      | 14.6    |
| 10+ units  | 65.9   | 47.9     | 8.9       | 26.4    |
|            | 100.0  | 100.0    | 100.0     | 100.0   |

*Source:* Adapted from Philip M. Hauser and Evelyn M. Kitagawa, eds., *Local Community Fact Book for Chicago, 1950.*

dians in Uptown lived in an area of roughly fifty blocks, between Lawrence Avenue to the north, Montrose Avenue to the south, Clarendon Avenue to the east, and Clark Street to the west, an area city surveyors labeled as census tracts twenty-two, twenty-three, and twenty-four. Here, problems with plumbing, heating, insects, and general deterioration were far more common than in the rest of Uptown or Chicago at large. Moreover, buildings in these tracts were even more divided than those elsewhere in Uptown. Dwelling units between Racine Avenue and Sheridan Road in tract twenty-three contained an average of 1.4 rooms in 1960, which meant that few if any three-room apartments existed in the sixteen-block area. Almost all had either one or two rooms (tables 15 and 16).[48]

In some ways, it is surprising that so many Indian people congregated in Uptown during the 1950s, but even that housing, with all its problems, was often superior to that available to Indians elsewhere. At the same time Indians in Chicago were moving into cramped Uptown kitchenette apartments, for example, a group of Chippewas who worked on Minnesota's iron range was living in tents. In other cities, too, housing conditions were as bad as or worse than in Chicago. In Los Angeles, many

*Table 15.* Selected Characteristics of Dwelling Units in Chicago and Uptown, 195

| | Substandard | 1.51+ Persons per Room | Median Rent | Median Famil Income |
|---|---|---|---|---|
| Chicago | 19.6% | 6.4% | $44 | $3,956 |
| Uptown | 23.1 | 10.5 | 55 | 4,258 |
| Uptown census tract no. 22 | 37.0 | 13.0 | 53 | 3,683 |
| Uptown census tract no. 23 | 70.0 | 18.0 | 43 | 3,245 |
| Uptown census tract no. 24 | 44.0 | 18.0 | 54 | 3,868 |
| Uptown census tract no. 27 | 40.0 | 20.0 | 53 | 3,460 |

*Source:* Adapted from Philip M. Hauser and Evelyn M. Kitagawa, eds., *Local Community Fact Boo for Chicago, 1950.*

*Table 16:* Selected Characteristics of Dwelling Units in Chicago and Uptown, 196

| | Substandard | 1+ Persons per Room | Median Rent | Median Fami Income |
|---|---|---|---|---|
| Chicago | 14.0% | 11.7% | $88 | $6,738 |
| Uptown | 20.5 | 9.1 | 91 | 6,780 |
| Uptown census tract no. 22 | 28.3 | 15.4 | 81 | 5,891 |
| Uptown census tract no. 23 | 60.5 | 19.5 | 64 | 4,648 |
| Uptown census tract no. 24 | 28.9 | 14.1 | 83 | 5,444 |
| Uptown census tract no. 27 | 44.3 | 13.4 | 72 | 5,158 |

*Source:* Adapted from Evelyn M. Kitagawa and Karl E. Taeuber, eds., *Local Community Fact Boo Chicago Metropolitan Area, 1960.*

families lived in trailer courts described as dangerous and "unsuitable for children," and low-rent housing for larger families was even more scarce than in Chicago. Indians in St. Louis, Oakland, and Dallas lived in large housing projects that were crowded and sometimes dangerous.[49]

Moreover, within Chicago, Indians had limited options in finding housing. Either because of excessive rents or ethnic or racial composition, many neighborhoods were closed to them. Throughout the 1950s, rents for Uptown apartments rose more slowly than for apartments in other parts of Chicago. In the city as a whole, median income and median rent doubled during the 1950s. In the parts of Uptown where Indians most often lived, both figures only rose by an average of 50 percent (tables 15 and 16).

Indians approached housing in Chicago from a different perspective than did other urban-dwellers, which helps explain their settlement in Uptown during the 1950s. Because they moved frequently, they often were uninterested in spacious housing and made do with cramped quarters in Uptown and other parts of the North Side. They believed that being with friends and family was more important and made sacrifices to achieve that goal. Groups often moved together within the city, intent on remaining together even in the face of various challenges. Marlene Strouse remembers that a friend of her father's led them in moves around the city— "Wherever he moved, we moved with him."[50]

By the end of the 1950s, Uptown was becoming the primary area where Indians clustered. Various family members acquired apartments on the same floor, in the same building, or within the same block. Sometimes many members of a widely extended family—including grandparents, cousins, uncles, and aunts—lived close by one another. Single young people also frequently moved in together after they had been in the city for a while. A small, two-room apartment that had six, seven, or eight tenants was not unusual. Close quarters could lead to drinking and fights, but this approach to urban living allowed young people to save on rent and also provided social comforts. After a day filled with frustrating, frightening, or alienating experiences, newly urbanized Indians were reassured to know that there were others who understood their problems.[51]

By the end of the 1950s, Uptown had become an Indian neighborhood of sorts. It stood somewhere between the BIA's early vision of a completely even geographical distribution of Indian people across all parts of the city and the classic neighborhoods formed by ethnic and racial groups of the nineteenth and early twentieth centuries. Indians were not as geographically concentrated in Chicago as they were in cities such as Minneapolis or in smaller towns near reservations. They continued to live on the South and West sides as well as in parts of the North Side, including Lakeview and Lincoln Park. Moreover, many other groups—including people from Appalachia, Puerto Rico, and Asia—shared Uptown with them and made them a numerical minority there.[52]

Despite these limitations, Uptown began to take on special status as a place to be with other Indians. Although some have viewed the concentration of Indians there as a sign of poor adjustment, it rather should be seen as fostering adjustment, somewhat as late-nineteenth and early-twentieth-century neighborhoods did among Europeans. Although their numbers remained relatively small compared with those of other ethnic and racial groups, Chicago Indians who lived in Uptown were more likely to interact with Native people from different parts of the country and different tribal backgrounds than were those who lived elsewhere in Chicago. It was a first, realistic step in urban adjustment, more so than being dropped in a sea of non-Indians elsewhere.[53]

Although scholars have made negative complaints about "Indian ghettos" in places like Chicago, it seems that most Indian people wanted to live among each other in what could be described as Indian neighborhoods or ghettos.[54] A report from 1957 acknowledged that observers repeatedly heard Indians complain about being "lonesome because city Relocation Offices will not permit them to live in Indian neighborhoods." Their problem, then, was not consolidation itself but the specific characteristics of the housing they had to accept in developing Indian areas. Urban renewal, the lack of new construction in parts of the North Side, and the ongoing process of dividing buildings into ever-smaller units worked against Indians who tried to find housing in Chicago. Yet they persisted in order to be with each other and enjoy the types of social benefits that Ada Powers recognized when she came to Uptown in the 1950s. Powers recalled that initially she "never really got acquainted with the Indians. There were Indians on the south side. I met a few, and then we heard there were Indians on Clark Street. So we went down there and we met some. They were strangers to us. But we got acquainted with them and made friends. And then we decided to move on the north side because that's where the Indians were gathering."[55]

Whether they lived in Uptown, the West Side, or South Side, Indians in Chicago encountered a far wider range of people than in reservation communities. A new pattern of race relations emerged. As Indians observed whites and blacks, they not only came to conclusions about those people but also began to rethink their own place in the city and in American society as a whole.

Indians did not generally complain much about discrimination or prejudice in Chicago. Relations with non-Indians in the city were less stressful than in rural Wisconsin or South Dakota. The BIA was greatly pleased by this and crowed about it frequently. When bureau employee Peter Walz stated in 1953 that "there is no discrimination against American Indians in Chicago," he may have been exaggerating somewhat, but Indians in Chicago and other large cities voiced few complaints about racial bias during the 1950s.[56]

Indians took different approaches to interaction with non-Indians. Many successfully avoided extensive contact with them—at least outside work—and largely associated with other Indian people. Others had grown accustomed to people from different backgrounds as a result of work experiences or military service before coming to Chicago. A Sioux who fought in the Korean War before coming to Chicago in 1957 stated that he had "not run into any kind of problems with race—just the usual things." Still others, such as Diane Maney, a Winnebago, genuinely enjoyed the experience of meeting a wide variety of people in Chicago's neighborhoods. "When we lived on the Near North Side," she recalled, "it was the League of Nations. All my girlfriends were from different ethnic groups—Greek, Japanese, Spanish, Puerto Rican, Polish. My sister had a real good Polish girlfriend. She started talking Polish and she could even dance. So I mean it was like a League of Nations. And when we moved west of there, it was mostly Italians. So I learned how to do a lot of good Italian cooking. I had a lot of Italian girlfriends and boyfriends."[57]

Although Indians generally got along satisfactorily with whites, relations varied. Middle-class whites often were interested in the Native American migrants in their midst. If Indians could look past the patronizing attitude that sometimes came with these relationships, interactions were usually cordial. As a Winnebago woman said of meeting whites, "Everybody treated me good when they saw me. It seemed like they were more interested in me because I was an Indian."[58] Within Uptown, however, Indians interacted mostly with poor whites from Kentucky and Tennessee. The two groups of migrants—American Indian and Appalachian—shared some of the same problems. They both had trouble finding acceptable housing and jobs that did not require extensive training and skills and difficulty avoiding trouble when getting together to drink. Tensions, however, were frequent, and violence occasionally broke out. One man claimed, "Every time you see an Indian and a hillbilly, you can expect a fight."[59]

Chicago Indians had some tensions with the large numbers of Appalachian migrants they lived near, but another group loomed even larger in their consciousness despite infrequent interaction. Uptown, Lakeview, and West Town had strikingly few black residents—fewer than 1 percent of the total population. From 1945 to 1965, Chicago's black population increased 65 percent, yet most areas in which Indians lived were almost untouched by that massive migration stream.[60] The already minuscule black population of Uptown and Lakeview actually diminished during the 1950s, and most Indians who had lived on the South Side moved north by the end of the decade. In Chicago and other cities, Indians were often adverse to living near blacks, sometimes claiming that their children would be picked on and beaten. An Apache man who lived with many blacks in a public housing unit on the South Side claimed they were "always looking for a fight."[61]

The BIA's Chicago relocation office recognized Indians' opposition to living in mixed and black neighborhoods and tried to accommodate it when possible. Integration of Indians and blacks was not as great a priority for the bureau as integration of Indians and whites. A Choctaw man, for example, complained about being housed in a black area. In reaction, a relocation office employee quickly and forcefully defended herself and her office, writing that the man's family had initially been placed in a "building occupied by one other Indian and white workers . . . in a section that is completely non-Negro." She maintained that the family must have moved to a black neighborhood on its own to save money. "At no time," she stated emphatically, "has an Indian worker and his family been placed in an area of the city that is predominantly Negro, Latin, or Oriental. . . . Every attempt has been made to house people to their own satisfaction."[62]

Even if the Indians did not see an increase in the number of blacks in their neighborhoods during the 1950s and the bureau stopped placing them in black neighborhoods, Indians remained concerned. They recognized that much of Chicago and the nation was talking about issues of race relations and worried about how the public perceived them in the racial hierarchy of mid-twentieth-century America. Richard LaRoche, a former tribal chair at South Dakota's Lower Brule Sioux reservation, never participated in relocation or moved to a city like Chicago, yet he heard what some of his tribe discovered there. Speaking of urban Indian migrants, he said, "They got over there just the same time [as] the white man and the colored man was having the troubles. And they was right in the center and they didn't know which way to turn."[63]

Many dark-skinned Indians in Chicago feared being confused for African Americans and were quick to correct those who misidentified them. One observer reported that it was such a "traumatic occurrence" for Indian children to be asked by teachers if they were black that they often refused to go back to school. The identities of children of black and Indian parents were sometimes challenged. After her husband left her, Josephine Willie, a Choctaw from Mississippi, married a black man and started a family with him. Later, as the couple's grandchildren were growing up in Chicago, she told a grandson, "You're Indian because I'm Indian. Don't ever be ashamed of that." Yet other Indians told him that he was black, not Indian. In other cities as well, Indians took pride in having more status than blacks in the eyes of white society. A Pueblo woman who lived near Richmond, California, during the 1950s noted that when she visited the downtown commercial district in the evening, "the Blacks would be gone after a certain time from restaurants, but we [could stay and] had credit and everything."[64]

Some Indians feared that whites might come to view them as just another of the city's minority groups and, moreover, that they might conflate the concerns, demands, and rights of Indians and blacks. The idea of integration—which by the late 1950s had become tainted and compromised in the minds of many Indian people because of how termination-minded federal officials had used it—was reconsidered and even dismissed by more people as a result of race relations in the city. Benjamin Bearskin was quick to refute assumed similarities between Indians and blacks, claiming that the Indian "still retains his own culture" but that the "Negro's culture . . . is obtained from the white man." Bearskin even dismissed the civil rights demonstrations of the late 1950s and early 1960s and their focus on integration. The Indian, Bearskin claimed, "possesses values that the white man never dreamed of, which are much more important to him." Others also came to oppose relocation, which seemed to further the process of clustering Indians and blacks together. At a national meeting of Indians in 1952, a Chippewa man claimed that through relocation the BIA was "treating Indians like Negroes and herding them into Negro communities." The enthusiastic reception his statement received demonstrated that many were anxious about their position in American society, yet another product of Indian urbanization during the latter half of the twentieth century.[65]

---

Important as it was, adjustment in the areas of employment and housing was not of ultimate significance to most Indians in Chicago. The process also included forming organizations, participating in community life, and following family and religious practices. Yet employment and housing were not unimportant issues either. To pretend otherwise both portrays Indians as somehow above human needs and desires and misses the connections between work, neighborhood, and community life.[66] In many cases, having a job or an apartment contributed to social and cultural adjustment. Experiences related to finding employment and housing were also important in how Indians intersected with such major patterns of American life in the mid-twentieth century as affluence and consumerism, the rise of a service economy and the post-industrial city form, urban renewal, and changing race relations. Despite the importance of this process and the successes experienced, though, adjusting to Chicago through employment and housing was challenging for most Indian people, and unsuccessful and demoralizing for some, because of the cultural perspectives they brought to such matters and the way cities like Chicago were changing at mid-century.

## Notes

1. John Bodnar, *The Transplanted: A History of Immigrants in Urban America* (Bloomington: Indiana University Press, 1985).

2. Jon C. Teaford, *The Twentieth-Century American City*, 2d ed. (Baltimore: Johns Hopkins University Press, 1993); Raymond A. Mohl, "Shifting Patterns of American Urban Policy since 1900," in *Urban Policy in Twentieth-Century America*, ed. Arnold R. Hirsch and Raymond A. Mohl (New Brunswick: Rutgers University Press, 1993), 1–45; Kenneth R. Philp, "Stride toward Freedom: The Relocation of Indians to Cities, 1952–1960," *Western Historical Quarterly* 16 (April 1985): 185.

3. Elaine M. Neils, *Reservation to City: Indian Migration and Federal Relocation*, University of Chicago Department of Geography Research Paper no. 131 (Chicago, 1971), 93, 181; John Kennardh White, *Patterns in American Indian Employment: A Study of the Work Habits of American Indians in Chicago, Illinois* (Chicago: St. Augustine's Center for American Indians, 1971), 9; John Kennardh White, "The American Indian in Chicago: The Hidden People," M.A. thesis, University of Chicago, 1970, 22–41; "A Little Newspaper about Indians," June 1953, Robert Rietz Collection, Community Archives, Native American Education Services College, Chicago [hereafter Rietz Collection, CA, NAES]; Warren Spaulding to Selene Gifford, 13 Oct. 1950, box 1, Placement and Statistical Reports, Field Placement and Relocation Office Employment Assistance Records, Record Group 75, National Archives, Washington, D.C. [hereafter PSR, FPROEAR, RG 75, NA-WDC].

4. For studies that emphasize Indians' continued poverty after migrating to cities, see Blue Clark, "Bury My Heart in Smog," in *The American Indian Experience: A Profile*, ed. Philip Weeks (Arlington Heights: Forum Press, 1988), 286; Grace Mary Gouveia, "'Uncle Sam's Priceless Daughters': American Indian Women during the Depression, World War II, and Post-War Era," Ph.D. diss., Purdue University, 1994, 172; Tom Holm, *Strong Hearts, Wounded Souls: The Native American Veterans of the Vietnam War* (Austin: Uni-

versity of Texas Press, 1996), 112; Ann Metcalf, "Navajo Women in the City: Lessons from a Quarter Century of Relocation," *American Indian Quarterly* 6 (Spring–Summer 1982): 71–89; Margaret Connell Szasz, *Education and the American Indian: The Road to Self-Determination* (Albuquerque: University of New Mexico Press, 1974), 137–38; John R. Wunder, *"Retained by the People": A History of American Indians and the Bill of Rights* (New York: Oxford University Press, 1994), 105–7; and David W. Yaseen, "Settlement Patterns of Relocated American Indians," M.A. thesis, University of Chicago, 1962.

5. Aberdeen Area report, Feb. 1954, box 3, Narrative Reports, Field Placement and Relocation Office Employment Assistance Records, Record Group 75, National Archives–Washington, D.C. [hereafter NR, FPROEAR, RG 75, NA-WDC]; Paula Verdet, "Summary of Research on Indians in St. Louis and Chicago" (1961), 11 pp. unpublished ms., box 16, American Indian Chicago Conference Records, National Anthropological Archives, Smithsonian Institution, Washington, D.C. [hereafter AICC Records, NAA, SI].

6. U.S. Bureau of the Census, *Census of Population: 1960, Nonwhite Population by Race* (Washington, D.C.: Government Printing Office, 1960); interview with Phyllis Fastwolf (Sioux-Oneida), Chicago, 8 May 1983, Chicago American Indian Oral History Pilot Project, no. 006, Newberry Library, Chicago, and Native American Educational Services College, Chicago [hereafter CAIOHP, NL and NAES]; Robert S. Weppner, "Urban Economic Opportunities: The Example of Denver," in *The American Indian in Urban Society*, ed. Jack O. Waddell and O. Michael Watson (Boston: Little, Brown, 1971), 245–73.

7. LaVerne Madigan, *The American Indian Relocation Program* (New York: Association of American Indian Affairs, 1956), 8–9; "How Newcomer Navajo Finds Life in Chicago," *Chicago News*, 10 Aug. 1959, Clip File: "Ethnic Groups-Chicago-Indians," American," Harold Washington Public Library, Chicago [hereafter CF, HWPL].

8. "Detail of Kent Fitzgerald to Minneapolis," 20 Jan. 1956 to 30 Mar. 1956, box 3, Financial Program, Field Placement and Relocation Office Employment Assistance Records, Record Group 75, National Archives–Washington, D.C. [hereafter FP, FPROEAR, RG 75, NA-WDC]; E. M. McCauley to Dillon Myer, 20 Oct. 1950, box 1, PSR, FPROEAR, RG 75, NA-WDC; *Fort Berthold Agency News Bulletin*, 2 June 1951, Rietz Collection, CA, NAES.

9. Herbert G. Gutman, *Work, Culture, and Society in Industrializing America: Essays in American Working-Class and Social History* (New York: Knopf, 1976); House Subcommittee on Indian Affairs, "Indian Relocation and Industrial Development Programs," 85th Cong., 2d sess., 1957, 14; William H. Kelly, "The Economic Basis of Indian Life," *Annals of the American Academy of Political and Social Sciences* 311 (May 1957): 75.

10. Interview with Ann Lim (Winnebago), Chicago, 7 Feb. 1984, CAIOHP, no. 019, NL and NAES; Chicago FRO report, July 1955, box 2, Reports on Employment Assistance, Chicago Field Employment Assistance Office, Record Group 75, National Archives-Great Lakes Region, Chicago [hereafter REA, CFEAO, RG 75, NA-GLR].

11. Minneapolis Area report, July 1958, box 13, NR, FPROEAR, RG 75, NA-WDC; Chicago FRO report, 1961, folder 22, box 14, Stanley D. Lyman Papers, Marriott Library, University of Utah, Salt Lake City [hereafter Lyman Papers, ML, UU]; Larry Burt, *Tribalism in Crisis: Federal Indian Policy, 1953–1961* (Albuquerque: University of New Mexico Press, 1982), 74–75; Donald L. Fixico, *The Urban Indian Experience in America* (Albuquerque: University of New Mexico Press, 2000), 16–18.

12. *A Survey of the Resources of the Chicago Industrial Area* (Chicago: Chicago Association of Commerce and Industry, 1950), n.p.; Roger Biles, *Richard J. Daley: Politics, Race, and the Governing of Chicago* (DeKalb: Northern Illinois University Press, 1995), 4.

13. Alan L. Sorkin, "The Economic and Social Status of the American Indian, 1940–1970," *Journal of Negro Education* 45 (Fall 1976): 433–47. See also Terrel Rhodes, "The Urban American Indian," in *A Cultural Geography of North American Indians,* ed. Thomas E. Ross and Tyrel G. Moore (Boulder: Westview Press, 1987), 259–74.

14. Interview with Margaret Redcloud (Chippewa), Chicago, 12 Feb. 1984, CAIOHP, no. 021, NL and NAES; "Chit Chat from the Relocation Office," Turtle Mountain Consolidated Agency, 2 Apr. 1954, Rietz Collection, CA, NAES.

15. Case file CH-52–37, Employment Assistance Case Files, 1952–1960, Chicago Field Employment Assistance Office, Record Group 75, National Archives–Great Lakes Region, Chicago [hereafter EACF, CFEAO, RG 75, NA-GLR] (quotation); minutes of Joint Committee on Indian Work, 21 Mar. 1960, Church Federation of Greater Chicago Files, 28–5, Manuscript Collections, Chicago Historical Society [hereafter CFGC Files, MC, CHS]; Brice Lay to Aberdeen Area superintendents, 12 Oct. 1956, box 4, NR, FPROEAR, RG 75, NA-WDC; Wade B. Arends, Jr., "A Socio-Cultural Study of the Relocated American Indians in Chicago," M.A. thesis, University of Chicago, 1958, 44.

16. Robert E. Ritzenthaler and Mary Sellers, "Indians in an Urban Situation," *Wisconsin Anthropologist* 36 (Dec. 1955): 159; William H. Hodge, *The Albuquerque Navajos,* Anthropological Papers of the University of Arizona, no. 11 (Tucson: University of Arizona Press, 1969); "Indians and Industry," *Wall Street Journal,* 28 Dec. 1955, 1.

17. O. K. Armstrong and Marjorie Armstrong, "The Indians Are Going to Town," *Reader's Digest* 66 (Jan. 1955): 42; Peter Z. Snyder, "The Social Environment of the Urban Indian," in *The American Indian in Urban Society,* ed. Jack O. Waddell and O. Michael Watson (Boston: Little, Brown, 1971), 222–27; Anadarko Area report, May 1953, box 2, NR, FPROEAR, RG 75, NA-WDC; "A Little Newspaper About Indians," May 1953, Rietz Collection, CA, NAES. On the limited power and influence of mass culture among various urban dwellers, see also Joseph H. Stauss and Bruce A. Chadwick, "Urban Indian Adjustment," *American Indian Culture and Research Journal* 3 (Spring 1979): 23–38; and Lizabeth Cohen, "The Class Experience of Mass Consumption," in *The Power of Culture: Critical Essays in Amer-*

*ican History,* ed. Richard W. Fox and Jackson Lears (Chicago: University of Chicago Press, 1993), 135–60.

18. Raymond A. Mohl, "Shifting Patterns of American Urban Policy since 1900," in *Urban Policy in Twentieth-Century America,* ed. Arnold R. Hirsch and Raymond A. Mohl (New Brunswick: Rutgers University Press, 1993), 13.

19. Madigan, *The American Indian Relocation Program,* 6, 13; Minneapolis Area reports, June and Aug. 1952, box 2, NR, FPROEAR, RG 75, NA-WDC; Consolidated Chippewa Agency reports, Aug. and Sept. 1952, box 2, NR, FPROEAR, RG 75, NA-WDC.

20. Harold Mann to Dillon Myer, 1 Apr. 1952, box 1, FP, FPROEAR, RG 75, NA-WDC; Los Angeles FRO report, July 1952, box 1, NR, FPROEAR, RG 75, NA-WDC; "Indian Relocation and Industrial Development Programs," 85th Cong., 2d sess., 1957, 6; Philp, "Stride toward Freedom," 184; Alida Bowler, "A Brief Study of Relocation Activities and Results in California," 1 Apr. 1952 through 31 Mar. 1953, Rietz Collection, CA, NAES.

21. U.S. Bureau of the Census, *Census of Population: 1960, Nonwhite Population by Race;* Chicago FRO reports, Jan. 1953–Nov. 1957, boxes 1–3, REA, CFEAO, RG 75, NA-GLR; Alida Bowler to Kurt Dreifuss, 5 Sept. 1952, box 1, NR, FPROEAR, RG 75, NA-WDC.

22. "Indian Relocation and Industrial Development Programs," 85th Cong., 2d sess., 1957, 5; Anadarko Area report, Sept. 1952, box 2, NR, FPROEAR, RG 75, NA-WDC.

23. Case file CH-52–27, EACF, CFEAO, RG 75, NA-GLR; Los Angeles FRO report, Feb. 1952, box 1, NR, FPROEAR, RG 75, NA-WDC.

24. "Indians vs. the City," *Chicago Magazine* (Apr. 1970), CF, HWPL; Packineau to Rietz, 6 Aug. 1953, Rietz Collection, CA, NAES; Report by Rietz, 1 Sept. 1953, Rietz Collection, CA, NAES.

25. Interview with Gordon Jones (Sioux), 2 June 1971, American Indian Oral History Research Project [hereafter AIOHRP], pt. 1, no. 34, MS 684.

26. Burt Muldoon to Dillon Myer, 29 Dec. 1952, box 1, REA, CFEAO, RG 75, NA-GLR (first quotation); "Indian Relocation and Industrial Development Programs," 85th Cong., 2d sess., 1957, 15 (second quotation); "Indians and Industry," *Wall Street Journal,* 28 Dec. 1955, 1 (third quotation).

27. "Indians and Industry."

28. "Summary of Area Directors' Conference," 12–16 May 1952, Rietz Collection, CA, NAES.

29. Chicago FRO reports, July and Oct. 1952, box 1, NR, FPROEAR, RG 75, NA-WDC.

30. "Agenda: Placement and Relocation Field Meeting, Bismarck, North Dakota," 24–26 June 1953, Rietz Collection, CA, NAES; author interview with Diane Maney (Winnebago), Chicago, 20 June 1995.

31. "Indian Relocation and Industrial Development Programs," 85th Cong., 2d sess., 1957, 16; interview with Marlene Strouse (Papago), Chicago, 18 July 1983, CAIOHP, no. 011, NL and NAES.

32. Charles Miller to John Cooper, 16 Mar. 1953, box 1, FP, FPROEAR, RG

75, NA-WDC; Chicago FRO report, Feb. 1953, box 1, REA, CFEAO, RG 75, NA-GLR.

33. George D. Scott, John Kennardh White, and Estelle Fuchs, *Indians and Their Education in Chicago* (Washington, D.C.: Educational Resources Information Center, 1969), 8; Stanley Lyman to files, 7 Jan. 1960, folder 20, box 14, Lyman Papers, ML, UU; Virgil J. Vogel, "Chicago's Native Americans: Cheechakos, Old-Timers and Others in the City of the Wild Garlic," in *Indians of the Chicago Area*, ed. Terry Straus (Chicago: NAES College, 1990), 183–87; author interview with Edward E. Goodvoice (Sioux), Chicago, 14 June 1995.

34. White, "The American Indian in Chicago," 15, 33, 43; John W. Olson, "Epilogue: The Urban Indian as Viewed by an Indian Caseworker," in *The American Indian in Urban Society*, ed. Jack O. Waddell and O. Michael Watson (Boston: Little, Brown, 1971), 402–3.

35. Interview with Ada Powers (Sioux), Chicago, 19 Apr. 1984, CAIOHP, no. 012, NL and NAES; interview with Floria Forica (Chippewa), Chicago, 25 Mar. 1983, CAIOHP, no. 004, NL and NAES; interview with Cornelia Penn (Sioux), Chicago, 3 Sept. 1983, CAIOHP, no. 017, NL and NAES; Edward E. Goodvoice, "Relocation: Indian Life on Skid Row," in *Native Chicago*, ed. Terry Straus and Grant P. Arndt (Chicago: Native Chicago, 1998), 131.

36. Karl B. Lohmann, *Cities and Towns of Illinois: A Handbook of Community Facts* (Urbana: University of Illinois Press, 1951), 37–38; William L. O'Neill, *American High: The Years of Confidence, 1945–1960* (New York: Free Press, 1986), 12.

37. Chicago FRO reports, Feb. 1952 and Jan. 1953, box 1, REA, CFEAO, RG 75, NA-GLR.

38. Report by Rev. E. Russell Carter, 23 May 1956, CFGC Files, 28–4, MC, CHS; interview with Phyllis Fastwolf (Sioux-Oneida), Chicago, 8 May 1983, CAIOHP, no. 006, NL and NAES.

39. "The Chicago Story," 9 Apr. 1962, folder 23, box 14, Lyman Papers, ML, UU; Stanley Lyman to files, 20 Nov. 1959, folder 20, box 14, Lyman Papers, ML, UU (quotation); "Transition Hard for Indians Here," *Chicago Sun-Times*, 20 May 1957, CF, HWPL; Arends, "A Socio-Cultural Study," 8–9, 79. See also Felix M. Padilla, *Puerto Rican Chicago* (Notre Dame: University of Notre Dame Press, 1987), 84.

40. Arends, "A Socio-Cultural Study," 103–6; author interview with Edward E. Goodvoice (Sioux), Chicago, 14 June 1995; author interview with Lucille Spencer (Choctaw), Chicago, 22 June 1995; minutes of the Joint Indian Committee, 15 July 1957, CFGC Files, 28–4, MC, CHS.

41. Chicago FRO reports, Apr. 1955 and Apr.–May 1957, boxes 2 and 3, REA, CFEAO, RG 75, NA-GLR; list of persons provided relocation services to Chicago, box 11, NR, FPROEAR, RG 75, NA-WDC; interview with Ada Powers (Sioux), Chicago, 19 Apr. 1984, CAIOHP, no. 012, NL and NAES; "Transition Hard for Indians Here"; Madigan, *The American Indian Relocation Program*, 12; Neils, *Reservation to City*, 60; Janusz Mucha, "From Prairie to the City: Transformation of Chicago's American Indian Community," *Urban*

*Anthropology* 12 (Fall 1983): 348; Arnold R. Hirsch, *Making the Second Ghetto: Race and Housing in Chicago, 1940–1960* (New York: Cambridge University Press, 1983).

42. Arends, "A Socio-Cultural Study," 56–58.

43. Jon C. Teaford, *The Rough Road to Renaissance: Urban Revitalization in America, 1940–1985* (Baltimore: Johns Hopkins University Press, 1990); Teaford, *The Twentieth-Century American City*, 118–24; Biles, *Richard J. Daley*, 11–13, 50–52, 74–78, 87, 96; Hirsch, *Making the Second Ghetto;* Lohmann, *Cities and Towns of Illinois*, 38–39; Devereux Bowly, Jr., *The Poorhouse: Subsidized Housing in Chicago, 1895–1976* (Carbondale: Southern Illinois University Press, 1978), 112–24; Arends, "A Socio-Cultural Study," 79–80. See also Padilla, *Puerto Rican Chicago*, 78–98.

44. "Transition Hard for Indians Here"; Neils, *Reservation to City*, 60; Mucha, "From Prairie to the City," 348.

45. Dominic A. Pacyga and Ellen Skerrett, *Chicago, City of Neighborhoods: Histories and Tours* (Chicago: Loyola University Press, 1986), 109–12; David K. Fremon, *Chicago Politics: Ward by Ward* (Bloomington: Indiana University Press, 1988), 303–9; Philip M. Hauser and Evelyn M. Kitagawa, eds., *Local Community Fact Book for Chicago, 1950* (Chicago: Chicago Community Inventory, University of Chicago, 1953), 18; White, "The American Indian in Chicago," 5–6.

46. Biles, *Richard J. Daley*, 7; Hauser and Kitagawa, eds., *Local Community Fact Book for Chicago, 1950*; Evelyn M. Kitagawa and Karl E. Taeuber, eds., *Local Community Fact Book: Chicago Metropolitan Area, 1960* (Chicago: Chicago Community Inventory, University of Chicago, 1963).

47. Madigan, *The American Indian Relocation Program*, 12; Gouveia, "Uncle Sam's Priceless Daughters," 172–73.

48. Kitagawa and Taeuber, eds., *Local Community Fact Book: Chicago Metropolitan Area, 1960.*

49. Consolidated Chippewa Agency report, June 1952, box 2, NR, FPROEAR, RG 75, NA-WDC; Los Angeles FRO Bulletin, 10 Mar. 1953, Rietz Collection, CA, NAES; Alida Bowler, "A Brief Study of Relocation Activities and Results in California," 1 Apr. 1952 through 31 Mar. 1953, Rietz Collection, CA, NAES; Anadarko Area report, Oct. 1952, box 2, NR, FPROEAR, RG 75, NA-WDC; Madigan, *The American Indian Relocation Program*, 12; Verdet, "Summary of Research on Indians in St. Louis and Chicago" (1961), box 16, AICC Records, NAA, SI; Ablon, "Relocated American Indians in the San Francisco Bay Area," 296–304; "National Council of Indian Opportunity Dallas–Fort Worth Public Forum on the Condition of Urban Indians," 13–14 Feb. 1969, box 88, Record Group 220: Records of the National Council on Indian Opportunity, National Archives II [hereafter RG 220, NA II].

50. Interview with Marlene Strouse (Papago), Chicago, 18 July 1983, CAIOHP, no. 011, NL and NAES.

51. Scott, White, and Fuchs, *Indians and Their Education in Chicago*, 31–32; undated report, CFGC Files, 32A-1, MC, CHS.

52. Merwyn S. Garbarino, "Indians in Chicago," in *Urban Indians: Proceed-*

*ings of the Third Annual Conference of Problems and Issues Concerning American Indians Today* (Chicago: Newberry Library, 1981), 57–58.

53. Tony Lazewski takes the position that living in Uptown tended to diminish Indians' adjustment to Chicago. See Tony Lazewski, "American Indian Migrant Spatial Behavior as an Indicator of Adjustment in Chicago," in *Geographical Perspectives on Native Americans: Topics and Resources,* ed. Jerry N. McDonald and Tony Lazewski (Washington, D.C.: Association of American Geographers, 1976), 105–19; Tony Lazewski, "American Indian Migration to and within Chicago, Illinois," Ph.D. diss., University of Illinois, Urbana-Champaign, 1976, 142.

54. Donald L. Fixico, *Termination and Relocation: Federal Indian Policy, 1945–1960* (Albuquerque: University of New Mexico Pres, 1986), 155; Fixico, *The Urban Indian Experience in America,* 24; Larry W. Burt, "Roots of the Native American Urban Experience: Relocation Policy in the 1950s," *American Indian Quarterly* 10 (Spring 1986): 89–90; James J. Rawls, *Chief Red Fox Is Dead: A History of Native Americans since 1945* (Fort Worth: Harcourt Brace, 1996), 50.

55. Madigan, *The American Indian Relocation Program,* 8–9; interview with Ada Powers (Sioux), Chicago, 19 Apr. 1984, CAIOHP, no. 012, NL and NAES.

56. "Agenda: Placement and Relocation Field Meeting, Bismarck, North Dakota, June 24, 25, and 26, 1953," Rietz Collection, CA, NAES (quotation). On the relative lack of discrimination against Indians in large urban centers, see Verdet, "Summary of Research on Indians in St. Louis and Chicago" (1961), box 16, AICC Records, NAA, SI; Merwyn S. Garbarino, "Life in the City," in *The American Indian and Urban Society,* ed. Jack O. Waddell and Michael Watson (Boston: Little, Brown, 1971), 182–83; Janusz Mucha, "American Indian Success in the Urban Setting," *Urban Anthropology* 13 (Winter 1984): 338; Ritzenthaler and Sellers, "Indians in an Urban Situation," 157–58; Mary Patrick, "Indian Urbanization in Dallas: A Second Trail of Tears?" *Oral History Review* (1973): 57; James Goodner, *Indian Americans in Dallas: Migrations, Missions and Style of Adaptation* (Minneapolis: University of Minnesota, Training Center for Community Programs, 1969). Some scholars have disagreed and emphasized frequency of discrimination against Indians in cities. See Patricia K. Ourada, "Indians in the Work Force," *Journal of the West* 25 (Apr. 1986): 53; and Burt, "Roots of the Native American Urban Experience," 91.

57. Author interview with Edward E. Goodvoice (Sioux), Chicago, 14 June 1995; author interview with Diane Maney (Winnebago), Chicago, 20 June 1995.

58. Interview with Rose Maney (Winnebago), Chicago, 2 May 1984, CAIOHP, no. 002, NL and NAES.

59. Hal Bruno, "Chicago's Hillbilly Ghetto," *The Reporter,* 4 June 1964, 28–31; Todd Gitlin and Nanci Hollander, *Uptown: Poor Whites in Chicago* (New York: Harper and Row, 1970); Garbarino, "Life in the City," 175.

60. Hauser and Kitagawa, eds., *Local Community Fact Book for Chicago,*

*1950*; Kitagawa and Taeuber, eds., *Local Community Fact Book: Chicago Metropolitan Area, 1960*; Teaford, *The Twentieth-Century American City,* 115; Hirsch, *Making the Second Ghetto*; Nicholas Lemann, *The Promised Land: The Great Black Migration and How It Changed America* (New York: Knopf, 1991).

61. Patrick, "Indian Urbanization in Dallas," 59; Arends, "A Socio-Cultural Study," 53.

62. Madigan, *The American Indian Relocation Program,* 8–9; Mary Nan Gamble to Robert Cullum, 21 Aug. 1952, case file CH-52–55, EACF, CFEAO, RG 75, NA-GLR.

63. Interview with Richard LaRoche (Sioux), 25 Aug. 1971, AIOHRP, pt. 1., no. 41, MS 784.

64. "Survey of vocational and on-the-job training," 7 Aug. 1951, box 5, NR, FPROEAR, RG 75, NA-WDC; Madigan, *The American Indian Relocation Program,* 12; Scott, White, and Fuchs, *Indians and Their Education in Chicago,* 52; author interview with Josephine Willie and son (Choctaw), Chicago, 14 June 1995; Kurt Peters, "Santa Fe Indian Camp, House 21, Richmond, California: Persistence of Identity among Laguna Pueblo Railroad Laborers, 1945–1982," *American Indian Culture and Research Journal* 19 (Summer 1995): 51.

65. Interview with Benjamin Bearskin in Studs Terkel, *Division Street America* (New York: Pantheon Books, 1967), 109; Chicago FRO report, Nov. 1952, box 1, REA, CFEAO, RG 75, NA-GLR.

66. Looking at a period earlier in the twentieth century, Brian C. Hosmer similarly argues for the necessity of carefully examining Indians' responses—both successful and unsuccessful—to capitalism and the American economic system in *American Indians in the Marketplace: Persistence and Innovation among the Menominees and Metlakatlans, 1870–1920* (Lawrence: University Press of Kansas, 1999).

# 5   Surviving the City

Beyond employment and housing, Indians' adjustment to Chicago in the 1950s and early 1960s involved matters great and small. Patterns of cultural, religious, social, and economic behavior were all affected by urbanization, as were day-to-day expectations. As Indians spent more time in Chicago, some even discovered that they became accustomed to the sounds of the city. Benjamin Bearskin found that when he returned to Nebraska to visit, he would "wake up in the middle of the night, feeling that there was something drastically wrong." Then he would realize the problem: "It was too quiet—that's what was wrong. There's no fire engines or police sirens passing by, no street noises."[1]

Adjustment also varied by degree. Some Indians were only minimally affected by urban life and tried whenever possible to live exactly as they had before. They usually chose not to pursue conventional full-time employment or participation in mainstream organizations, and they frequently traveled back and forth between Chicago and their reservation. Others swung radically in the other direction, leaving everything on their journey from reservation to city. Isaac Stands, a Sioux who had spent much of his life off the reservation, clearly preferred Chicago to Pine Ridge, saying that he was "fairly secure" financially and could "look forward to advances and raises." In Chicago, "What a man earns he can keep for himself and family. I can even plan on having a savings account like other people, which is something impossible to most reservation Indians. That really means opportunity to get ahead the same as Whites." Another Indian man reflected on his life—all of it spent in Chicago—and said, "I think it is something you can choose, whether to be an Indian or not ... if you have grown up in the city. It's probably not the same thing if you are reservation-bred because there would be stronger ties to Indian identity, whatever that is. But anyhow, in my case, you can say that I am just a Chicagoan." These people represented the exceptions and not the rule, however. Most Indians in Chicago carefully balanced valued old ways with attractive new ones.[2]

Although scholars have examined Indians' experiences adjusting to cities, they have disagreed about how the experiences compared with those of other ethnic groups. Some have emphasized Indians' dislike of competition and confrontation, arguing that their experience was uniquely difficult.[3] These accounts, though, often misunderstand the experiences of European immigrants, who also frequently struggled with reconciling mutualistic and collectivist cultural patterns with urban life.[4] Other accounts have emphasized the similarities between American Indian adjustment patterns to cities and those of other groups.[5] They point to the common practices of forming ethnic neighborhoods and migrating back and forth between city and homeland. In looking at Indians' adjustment to Chicago during the 1950s and early 1960s in comparative context, both unique and familiar patterns emerge.

---

During the 1950s, people associated with the relocation program and American Indian urbanization argued frequently about the "return rate," the percentage of relocatees who soon abandoned city life and returned to the reservation. Both the BIA and its opponents fervently believed that arriving at an accurate figure and publicizing it would vindicate their position on relocation and bring about their side's success. At times, the BIA boldly claimed that only one-quarter of all those participating in the relocation program later returned home. The bureau's fiercest critics sometimes reversed that figure, claiming that three-quarters of all relocatees returned and only one-quarter remained in the city. Later observers and scholars, also caught up in this numbers game, have suggested a range of return rates that in part reflect their opinions of the program.[6]

Best estimates show that approximately 35 to 45 percent of relocatees to Chicago during the 1950s soon returned home to the reservation. Yet that figure does not deserve the importance and symbolic weight sometimes given to it. First, American Indians' practice of return migration was not unique; return migration has been common among many migrant groups in the United States. In the nineteenth century, for example, most Italians migrated to America with the intent of making enough money to return home for a fresh start. American Indians' return migration, then, should come as little surprise if migration is examined in comparative context.[7] Second, focusing on only the numbers can deflect attention from important issues tied to return migration, including the reasons for it and the ways in which it influenced Indian communities both in Chicago and on reservations across the Upper Midwest and Northern Plains. Continuing attention to return rates among American Indian urban migrants places the focus on government policy and its success or failure. A social history perspective on Indian urbanization shifts the focus to the experiences of Indians who stayed in Chicago and other cities.

Many American Indian people who lived in Chicago from a few months to a few years never thought of the city as their true home. Social, psychological, and spiritual ties to the reservation remained vital and strong. Nagging, long-term feelings of tension were often replaced by a welcome sense of peace when Indian people returned to their reservations. Most who decided to leave Chicago, then, did so because of homesickness and loneliness. Single people tended to succumb slightly more often than families, yet no group was untouched. For some, experiences in Chicago were marked by a total absence of adjustment or increased comfort. Marlene Strouse's Papago family stayed for four years, a period almost exclusively marked by fear and anxiety. She recalls, "My mother I don't think really liked Chicago that well. She was unhappy, she lost a lot of weight, and she wouldn't leave the apartment." Others came to tolerate city life more successfully, yet preferred many aspects of reservation life. As a Winnebago woman explained, "I like the laid back activities that they have. Everything is not so: 'Hurry up! Do it tomorrow!'" And a Sioux man watching tribespeople return to his Crow Creek Reservation heard them talk about how "it isn't quite as nice out in the city as it is at home."[8]

Feelings of homesickness welled up even more than usual during holidays and on other special occasions. On days of religious, tribal, or familial importance, few wanted to be in Chicago among millions of people who did not understand—and perhaps did not care to understand—their culture and traditions. In some years the "Fourth of July exodus" of Chicago Indians to their home reservations took place as early as late June. During the Christmas season, too, many returned home to spend time with family and friends. Some went back to Chicago after their visit, but others could not bear to leave the reservation again. More personal events, such as births and deaths, also resulted in returns. Most Indians thought that the beginning and end of life could not be marked appropriately in a foreign land of noise and skyscrapers.[9]

Numerous people returned home because they had drinking problems—and resulting legal problems. Although some Indians used alcohol, and the taverns that served an Indian clientele, to try to adjust to Chicago, drinking more often had destructive effects. Those accustomed to drinking publicly on reservations often got into trouble with police when they did that in Chicago. When asked why Indians left the city, Edward E. Goodvoice, a Sioux, replied unhesitatingly, "Because of drinking—number one problem." Sometimes, entire families would leave because of a member's drinking problem. At other times, families would divide. After a few months in Chicago, a Mandan woman whose husband had used his weekly paycheck on liquor and spent time in jail for public drunkenness decided to leave him and return to the Fort Berthold Reservation in North Dakota with her children. In another case, a Choctaw man who had a drinking problem returned home but his wife stayed.[10]

Other types of family strain also caused people to leave Chicago for home. Many parents complained and worried about the difficulty of raising children in Chicago. Adult sons who had benefited from training programs sometimes earned more than their unskilled fathers, which limited parental authority. Some discovered that other children, too, were difficult to raise and discipline in the city. At home, uncles, grandparents, and other community members helped parents with upbringing. No one could become invisible or escape attention on a small reservation. In Chicago, children were often out of sight and subject to new and—to parents—frightening influences. The Amarok family returned to Alaska after a year in Chicago following a series of events that included a teenaged son being sent to an institution for juvenile delinquents and a teenaged daughter being offered beer by her employer. Exhausted after a taxing year in the city, the father stated, "Mostly, I want to go home because I want to keep the family together."[11]

The economic problems that plagued American Indians in Chicago during the 1950s also helped convince some to leave the city. Those without a high school diploma, especially those who had dropped out of school much earlier, had difficulty finding and keeping work. Although Chicago was booming in the early 1950s, a recession hit the city and the rest of the nation near the end of the decade and put Indian residents at further disadvantage. Fewer decided to come to Chicago, and more left for reservations from late 1957 through the end of the decade. Many Indian people followed news of the recession. Creeks in Oklahoma read local newspapers, and Chippewas in North Dakota listened to radio broadcasts to learn of rising unemployment and the bread lines forming in some cities. Indians who returned home during this period often complained about the effects of the recession. One bureau employee referred to such information as "adverse free publicity." Some Indian leaders grew angry when the relocation program charged ahead in difficult economic times. At the 1958 annual meeting of the American Association of Indian Affairs, the tribal chair from Fort Berthold asserted that Commissioner Glenn L. Emmons was "completely oblivious to the business recession."[12]

For some, the economic downturn combined with their anger at the BIA convinced them to return to the reservation. From their preliminary educational sessions on the reservation and interactions with employees of the Chicago relocation office, Indian people realized that the bureau was intent on relocation being a permanent arrangement. They also knew that an effective way of opposing the BIA if they felt aggrieved, ignored, or misled was to oppose the logic of the policy and return home. Indians and bureau employees often sparred over the amount of assistance that would be given. One frustrated BIA official in 1958 complained that relocatees "expect[ed] to be met with a band and everything brought to them on a silver platter." Indians saw things differently. Their experiences in cities rarely resembled the images of urban life they had seen or the accounts they had heard before leaving their reservations. A Pawnee relocatee angrily criticized the relocation policy for failing to live up to its billing. "I told the lady [a bureau employee], 'Well, we didn't have much where we came from, but we had better than this and we were supposed to come out here to improve ourselves!'"[13]

Some returned home not because they had failed in Chicago but because they had acquired skills in the adult vocational training program or elsewhere that would be useful on the reservation. Rural areas often had greater need for auto mechanics and beauticians than Chicago during the 1950s. Others continued to move back and forth between Chicago and their home reservation periodically, staying home when work could be found there and coming to Chicago when economic conditions required. Chippewas from Turtle Mountain especially incorporated Chicago into their seasonal round. One observer, watching a group of young and single Chippewa men return home from the city, noted that they "felt too strongly the pull of an established seasonal employment pattern" in coming back to the ore boats and the work they had "been doing for years."[14]

Still others returned home only to find that their urban experiences had influenced them more than they realized and seemed more attractive in hindsight. Ernie Peters, a Sioux, went to Los Angeles on relocation in 1957 from his home reservation in Minnesota but returned home after two years. "I couldn't take it," he explained. When he arrived, however, he saw rural Minnesota with new eyes. Now even more dissatisfied with life there, he returned to Los Angeles—this time to stay. "It was worse back there [Minnesota], after living here [Los Angeles], so I came back again," he concluded. Although bureau officials often maintained that people like Ernie Peters, and all the others who did not immediately set down roots and permanently stay in cities where they relocated, had failed, that was not true from the Indians' perspectives.[15]

In general, Indians remained very mobile during the 1950s. One survey found that rather than being "isolated and geographically fixed on reservations, in rural non-reservation areas, or in inner-city Indian ghettos," Native Americans born between 1944 and 1952 were "exceptionally mobile" as children. Nearly one-fourth of them moved frequently between urban areas and reservations. The pattern is evident among many relocatees to Chicago who had numerous stays there or in other cities. A Choctaw man, for example, who had spent his life doing miscellaneous work in the woods, moved his family to Chicago in 1953; quickly returned to Oklahoma; soon moved again to New Mexico, where he found work at a sawmill; and finally went to Dallas, where he found a better-paying job. The practice of moving from Chicago to another city or town was even more common among single people. One-sixth of those who relocated to Chicago between 1952 and mid-1954 later moved to another urban center, compared with one-tenth of those who came in families.[16]

Indian mobility in the 1950s reshaped both urban and reservation communities to some extent. In Chicago, Native residents set about building lives and identities. But with anywhere from 35 to 45 percent of those who came to Chicago soon returning home, the city's Indian community was fragile and fragmented in the 1950s. Return migration and a longing for home even among those who stayed minimized commitment to social and political developments in Chicago. Despite return migration, reservation Indian communities were affected by urbanization as well. Over time, the demographic structure of some changed, and they became the homes of primarily the very old and very young. Some tribal elders, worried that the leaders of the future were leaving, tried to stem the tide of urban migration, but they were usually unsuccessful.[17]

Those who left often received less than encouraging send-offs. Reservation residents often thought those leaving were foolish dreamers, materialists, or even traitors to the tribe. A tribal chair at Lower Brule bade farewell to Sioux migrants with some condescension. Their motives, he suggested, were frivolous and their return imminent. They would realize the error of their ways. Recalling the incident years later, he said, "I told the boys as they was leaving, 'Go on, go on and have fun. Then come home. We'll stay here and try to make something.' We stayed and kept the home fires burning."[18]

Those who did stay in their new urban homes during the 1950s often found that relationships grew strained between Indians in cities and those on reservations. Each group worried that the other was enjoying the lion's share of BIA money and programs. Some in Chicago who returned home for visits found their tribespeople now were guarded and distant around them, jealous of their financial gain or suspicious they had abandoned their Indian ways. On some reservations, those who returned from the city had trouble finding jobs. Disputes arose over the status of Indian children born in cities, and reservation groups often argued that they should be ineligible for some of the tribe's financial benefits.[19]

Likewise, urban Indians sometimes worried that their tribespeople back on the reservation were enjoying luxuries while they scrimped and saved to get by. Lee Smith and his family, who relocated from Fort Berthold to Los Angeles, had run up debt as a result of several family illnesses. After hearing rumors from home, his wife responded to the reservation superintendent: "I've heard that persons who have stayed on the reservation and are as able to meet bills as we are have had medical bills paid—in fact—have gotten the most expensive glasses because the government was paying for them. When I heard this I felt that even though we are no longer on the reservation my husband is still an enrolled member and should receive as much help as these people have."[20]

Although some of the suspicions that city and reservation Indians held toward each other proved unfounded, they reveal a important trend. By the end of the 1950s, urban Indians had developed the beginnings of a separate identity. The people increasingly known as "urban Indians"— both among themselves and by reservation residents—were becoming a distinct group that had its own experiences, struggles, and hopes. Even when the relocation program failed in the eyes of BIA officials and a relocated family returned to its home reservation, the broader social transformation of urbanization—even temporary urbanization—continued to reshape American Indian life.

Although some Indians found even the neighborhoods of Uptown or Lakeview unsatisfactory and alienating compared with their home communities on reservations, a smaller number followed a markedly different adjustment pattern and settled in places even more devoid of other Indians. They found homes and jobs in Chicago's suburban ring. Among the suburbs inhabited by Indians beginning in the 1950s were Joliet, Waukegan, and Elgin, all roughly an hour's drive from downtown Chicago. These "suburban Indians" often did not present much of a distinct Indian identity in public; many blended into suburban civic life quite thoroughly. Feeling few tugs from their older way of life, they followed an adjustment strategy opposite to those relocatees who eventually returned to the reservation.

The BIA partly contributed to Indian suburbanization when it opened relocation offices in Joliet and Waukegan, Illinois, and began to support relocation to both places in 1954. It was a response to the geographical patterns of postwar America and to specific requests made by Indian people familiar with the BIA's relocation program. Throughout the postwar period, U.S. suburbs grew in population, political strength, and economic power. During the 1950s, the population of Chicago slightly decreased, whereas many of its suburbs grew at rates ranging from 10 to 40 percent. Between the end of the war and 1954, the number of manufacturing plants in suburban Chicago doubled.[21]

Indian families had their own personal reasons for preferring suburban life. Large families in particular often requested relocation to Joliet or Waukegan rather than to Chicago because of the difficulty of finding housing in Uptown and other city neighborhoods where many apartment buildings had been carved into small kitchenettes. In 1960, when 63 percent of Waukegan residents and 68 percent of Joliet residents lived in one-unit or single-family structures, only 24 percent of Chicago residents, and 4 percent in the Uptown neighborhood, shared that same experience. Ernest Parisien, a Turtle Mountain Chippewa, wrote home to praise the space and freedom his family had found in Waukegan. "Our children have a nice big yard to play in," he reported. "There's an automatic washing machine in the basement for our use. It's just like back home. There are big trees in the yard." Although the trees and bushes of the suburbs perhaps reminded some of home and helped them adjust, others continued to be overwhelmed by the number of suburbs that ringed the central city. The BIA office in Chicago tried to acclimate relocatees and described suburbs in terms Indian people could understand. Those from the wide-open spaces of South Dakota were informed that Chicago's suburbs were like "Sioux Falls, Aberdeen, Huron, Pierre, Redfield, Kadoka, Yankton, Murdo, Rapid City, and Mitchell all in one place."[22] Even in the relatively uncrowded suburbs of Chicago, Indian people were struck by the differences between their old surroundings and the new ones.

————————

The Indian people who stayed in Chicago rather than move to the suburbs or return home after a short time faced challenges beyond acquiring a job or finding housing. These things were certainly necessary, but by themselves they did not necessarily make Indian people feel at ease in the city. Material well-being alone seldom brought a satisfactory adjustment to urban life. Many Native Americans needed opportunities to express their Indian identity socially and culturally, and various Indian organizations established in Chicago throughout the 1950s provided those opportunities for some. The largest and most significant was the American Indian Center.

The center emerged from a variety of sources. The BIA, through the Chicago relocation office, was involved from the beginning and hoped the center would further its assimilationist goals for Indian people. Various religious and philanthropic organizations also participated. The Church Federation of Greater Chicago and the Welfare Council of Metropolitan Chicago were usually less determined than the bureau that Indians become completely like Chicago's white citizens. Yet they, too, pursued an agenda that focused on the importance of contributing to a pluralist Chicago. Over time, however, the center truly came to belong to Indian people, and it served their needs for contact and solidarity with other Indians of various tribes, for social and cultural activities, for developing leaders, and for a forum in which to discuss and often oppose BIA policy. The center was often used in ways the BIA and various civic organizations had not foreseen or intended.

The earliest beginnings of the American Indian Center came when the Citizens' Advisory Board's subcommittee on leisure-time activities first met in 1952 with Kurt Dreifuss, director of Chicago's relocation office, and found that most Indians did not participate in the city's recreational or entertainment activities, either because of a lack of interest or money. That concerned the committee and the BIA, which hoped to develop a "sense of belonging" among Chicago Indians, particularly the many young and single ones. The group set about organizing a social organization for Indians, the American Indian Club. Backed by the BIA's Chicago relocation office, the club soon had branches on the north, side, and west sides of town. It held meetings in Uptown's Chase Park Field House and the South Side's Ogden Park Field House.

The American Indian Club soon outgrew those cramped meeting places. Dreifuss and the Citizens' Advisory Board then planned for a more permanent American Indian Center that would allow the club's activities to take place more frequently and reach more people. The Citizens' Committee for an "All-Tribes American Indian Center" was established. It held its first meeting in July 1953, with representatives from the Indian Council Fire, American Indian Club, First Daughters of America, the Chicago BIA office Citizens' Advisory Board, and other groups. John Willard, executive director of the American Friends Service Committee's Chicago office, was named chair of the committee, and Toni Omen, a

Sioux woman, became secretary. The center began fundraising and soon had almost $9,000, enough to rent space in the Loop. The Friends Committee acted as financial steward of the center until it incorporated in 1955 as a nonprofit organization and had the legal ability to accept money.

The All-Tribes American Indian Center (as it was first called) opened in September 1953, the first urban Indian center of its kind. It occupied two floors of an office building at the corner of LaSalle and Kinzie streets, a block north of the Chicago River. Thomas Segundo, a Papago law student at the University of Chicago, was the center's first executive director, and John Willard moved from the Citizens' Committee to serve as the first president of the board of directors. Joining him on the board were Segundo, Babe Begay (Navajo), Eli Powless (Oneida), Felix Chico (Papago), Daniel Gloyne (Cherokee), Hiawatha Hood (Yavapai), Mrs. Elmer Luckow (a non-Indian), and Ernest Naquayouma (Hopi). The board and representatives of various other civic organizations drafted a constitution that illustrated the center's somewhat ambiguous mandate to showcase Native American cultures and help Indian people integrate into mainstream American society. The constitution's preamble read:

> We, the American Indians of Chicago, in co-operation with our non-Indian friends, do hereby affiliate ourselves and our common interests, in a civic and cultural organization to be known as the All-Tribes American Indian Center of Chicago, to promote fellowship among the Indian people of all tribes living in metropolitan Chicago, and to create bonds of understanding and fellowship between Indians and non-Indians in this city; to stimulate the natural integration of American Indians into the community life of Metropolitan Chicago; to foster the economic and educational advancement of Indian People; to encourage membership in artistic and avocational pursuits; and to preserve and foster arts and crafts and Indian cultural values.[23]

Soon, Indians living in different parts of Chicago and from various tribal backgrounds were assembling at 411 North LaSalle for powwows, club meetings, athletic contests, and other games, dinners, and social events. The center's opening in September 1953 excited Indian people in Chicago and elsewhere. That month, the reservation newsletter at Fort Berthold in North Dakota announced: "Perhaps never before in the history of America have so many American Indians from all parts of the country, from many different tribes, often with different cultural and language backgrounds, come to live together in one place as has happened this past year and a half in Chicago."[24]

The mix of tribes at the center was indeed impressive. Nowhere was that more evident than at powwows. The center began holding a large annual powwow in 1954 and smaller ones throughout the year. Even those knowledgable about their own tribe's history and culture were often humbled upon encountering the dozens of tribes represented at the powwows. That was the experience of Samson Keahna, a Mesquakie who came to Chicago from Iowa as a young boy with his family and was immediately impressed with the center.

> One of my first vivid experiences was being taken down to the Indian Center. . . . The program director at that time asked my brother and me if we still had our regalia, and we said, "Yes." They said, "We're having a powwow. You should bring it down." I remember the shocking part of it: when the powwow began, we had come down to the dance arena, and lo and behold, the song that was being sung, I didn't know it. I did not know it. And I'm going around the drum trying to pick it up. Being ten years old, I had learned all my tribal songs before I came here—songs that we needed to know back there.[25]

In Chicago, Keahna and others learned the songs and dances of other tribes. As the number of Indians in Chicago and the tribes they represented increased during the 1950s, more cultural traditions were added. The center's 1958 powwow, for example, had Yakima, Hopi, Pueblo, Winnebago, Omaha, Sioux, Mesquakie, and Kiowa dances as well as the Friendship Dance, Kids' Dance, Round Dance, and War Dance, which did not originate from any one tribe. Other artistic expressions also fostered knowledge of various tribal traditions. Artists from different tribes sold their wares to both Indian and non-Indian customers. One Sioux woman who later became an artist got her start in this way. Every year she would save for months before the annual Indian Center powwow in order to buy jewelry from the vendors there.

Powwows sponsored by the center combined traditional and modern elements in ways that aided Indians' adjustment to life in Chicago. The costumes, music, and food all testified to Chicago Indians' practices of borrowing from urban life while carving out distinct niches for their own purposes. For example, a Miss Indian Chicago was crowned for the first time at the American Indian Club powwow in 1952, and the center continued that annual practice, beginning at its first powwow in 1954. Soon, Miss Indian Chicago would also be known as the American Indian Center Princess. Yet this innovation was not an imitation of beauty pageants of the time. Community members emphasized that Miss Indian Chicago was chosen because of her ability to be a spokesperson for the community and a role model of Indian culture and values. In 1958 the young woman crowned Miss Indian Chicago received a scholarship to the Patricia Stevens Finishing School in Chicago in addition to enjoying the honor of representing the city's Indian community in the Miss American Indian contest in Wyoming along with dozens of other Indian women. Those named Miss Indian Chicago during the 1950s and 1960s frequently traveled throughout Indian Country to promote Chicago's Indian community.[26]

In addition to powwows, those who joined the center enjoyed other activities as well. By 1954 the center had produced six groups: a baseball team ("the Braves"), a teenaged girls' club, a photography club, a dancing class, an arts and crafts club, and a group that met Friday evenings to view and discuss educational films. Two very popular basketball teams, a canoe club, a Boy Scout troop, an Alcoholics Anonymous chapter, and other groups soon followed. In addition to helping Indians meet each other within Chicago, these activities also brought them into contact with Native Americans who lived elsewhere. The canoe club in particular traveled widely. It paddled in all five Great Lakes with Indians from nearby reservations and also participated in a race around Manhattan Island. Moreover, the center enabled members to meet Indians who lived in other cities. The dance group, for example, helped inaugurate an Indian center in Detroit by participating in the organization's first powwow. Baseball and basketball teams from the center often challenged their counterparts in Milwaukee, and the games were closely watched by each team's fans. Some of these athletic contests were all-day affairs, with ceremonials between the girls' and boys' games and a powwow in the evening to honor the winning teams.[27]

These activities helped Indians adjust to life in Chicago as Indians and not as people who had abandoned their culture and history in their move to the city. Samson Keahna discovered that after his initial reluctance to join his family in Chicago. Before the move, his cousins on the reservation often teased him, claiming that he would lose a part of himself in the city. "You're going to lose your ways," they would say. "You won't speak your language anymore, you're going to become a white man." Yet after attending his first powwow at the center and becoming involved in community life through it, Keahna realized that his cousins were wrong. He continued to value his tribal traditions and learned of others, remaining involved in Chicago's Indian community for decades thereafter.[28]

Either serving on the board of directors or working in some other capacity, many Indian people developed valuable leadership skills at the center. Indeed, the experiences of urban Indians who came together from many different tribal backgrounds resembled those of students at Indian boarding schools. In both contexts, people met challenges and obstacles by uniting and sharpening their political skills. When asked about the beginnings of the Chicago American Indian Center, Daniel W. Battise spoke of the similarities to his experiences at Chilocco Indian School in Oklahoma, where Indian people from various tribal backgrounds congregated. "The early days of the Center were just like when I went to school in Chilocco; had some good leaders there," he reminisced. "When we first started the Indian Center here, we had some good leaders."[29]

Indian leaders on the center's board of directors discussed many issues, among them the BIA policies of termination and relocation. Increased criticism of the bureau resulted in a growing rift between the center and the BIA's Chicago relocation office. In April 1954 Segundo resigned as executive director of the center because of his studies at law school. He was replaced by Theodore White, of Sioux and Oneida lineage and from Green Bay, Wisconsin. White had attended the University of Wisconsin and served four years in the U.S. Air Force. He came to the directorship from the staff of United Charities of Chicago and had also done casework for the Chicago Welfare Department and the Veterans Administration. Yet some viewed him with suspicion because of his cordial relationship with the BIA's Kurt Dreifuss. Dorothy VandeMark, who had written an influential attack on the BIA's practice of termination and who continued to take pride in hectoring the bureau throughout the 1950s, became a board member in 1955. She quickly came to distrust the new executive director, calling him "a white man's Indian used by Kurt Dreifuss."[30]

The lengthy, sometimes all-night, board meetings became increasingly occupied with the center's relationship with the bureau. Some board members complained about the BIA's implementation of the relocation program and its willingness to send people unprepared for urban life in Chicago. Over time, the debate about relocation became polarized. Dreifuss believed that VandeMark and others critical of the BIA were trying to make the center "a forum for airing their hostility." He responded by rallying his own troops in the propaganda war—the upper-middle-class white friends and associates he had met during years of civic work in Chicago. Dreifuss placed them on various boards and committees working on Indian issues, but he quickly grew frustrated when they were outnumbered and neutralized by bureau opponents. By 1957 he was worried that his foes were winning and that the relocation program was falling into disrepute. At one point he wrote that his allies were "unfortunately busy in their own professions and businesses, which leaves control with a few militant individuals from whom the relocation program has nothing to gain."[31]

Earlier, in July 1955, Theodore White had resigned after months of disagreements with the board of directors over the direction of the center. In November the board named Allen Seltzer, a non-Indian, and Hollis Chough, a Pima, as co-directors. Soon, the BIA's Chicago relocation office stopped sharing the names and addresses of newcomers with the center. In an increasingly tense climate, Chough resigned after only five months, and Willard resigned as chair of the board in mid-1956. As problems between the center's staff and board members increased, Seltzer, too, resigned in 1957, and Segundo again became director. Soon thereafter and in the midst of a chaotic period, the center received a three-year, $45,000 grant from the Emil Schwarzhaupt Foundation. The funds were to be used broadly to "promote civic competence of American Indians," specifically for staff development. But that did not solve the problems between staff and board members, and in September 1958 all of the center's staff members, including Segundo, resigned. The board named anthropologist Robert Rietz as the new executive director.[32]

Intent on weakening the center, the Chicago relocation office helped establish a new organization through the Mayor's Committee for Newcomers. Dreifuss relied on his allies to staff the new Kenmore Uptown Center, which opened at 4228 North Kenmore Avenue in November 1956 and took a decidedly more assimilationist approach than the American Indian Center on LaSalle. Dreifuss gave the new organization lists of relocatees and $50 for every Indian family that joined. The Kenmore Uptown Center paid little attention to Native arts and culture and instead taught classes on modern home economics and child rearing. Those attending the two centers soon became just as divided as the organizations' leaders. Although few in number, the participants at the Kenmore Uptown Center who were more interested in pursuing a middle-class lifestyle looked down at those affiliated with the American Indian Center downtown. They, in turn, laughed at the Kenmore Uptown Center's snobbery. At its first meeting, a representative from the gas company taught Indian women how to cook broccoli on a gas stove. After that, members of the American Indian Center derisively referred to the Kenmore Uptown Center as "the broccoli club." Rivalry between the two organizations almost escalated into violence when both sides vied to be featured in a May 1957 broadcast of the NBC television show *Wide, Wide World*. Shortly thereafter, the Kenmore Uptown Center closed its doors due to lack of interest and funds, although civic and church groups hoped to "preserve the values of the Kenmore Uptown Center" on the North Side by continuing to emphasize assimilation.[33]

Other Indian organizations also operated in Chicago during the 1950s. The Indian Council Fire continued to appeal to a handful of assimilated Indians and non-Indian civic leaders. Soon after the center was established, the Indian Council Fire cut back on its social service activity and focused on its annual Indian Achievement Award. Some Indians also joined Albert Cobe's organizations. Cobe, a Chippewa from Lac du Flambeau, arrived in Chicago in 1930 and soon started a basketball team that included Indians and members of many other ethnic groups. In 1951 he founded the Indian Service League, which had its beginnings in a group of nearly thirty Indians who met in YMCAs to play basketball, pool, or swim. By 1953 the group had two hundred members. Cobe was often distant toward the center, which once described him as a "one-man show" unwilling to cooperate with any other Indian organization in Chicago. Cobe later helped organize the Off-the-Streets-Club and then The Longhouse. The groups Cobe associated with all shared a generally assimilationist outlook, a fierce opposition toward the BIA and its policies, and a firm belief in Indian uplift. In this, Cobe resembled Carlos Montezuma, the Indian leader who had lived in Chicago a half-century earlier.[34]

In 1961 a second major center for American Indians emerged in Uptown, increasingly the area of Indian settlement in Chicago. St. Augustine's Center for American Indians at 4718 North Sheridan Road was fostered by Fr. Peter John Powell, a parish priest at St. Timothy's Episcopal Church on the West Side. Interested in Native American history and culture from an early age, when Powell was a young priest he began work among the small number of Indian people coming into Chicago. In 1954 he established a Native American assistance center in the parish hall and financed it with speaking engagements and mailed appeals. He also began publishing *The Cross and the Calumet,* a newsletter that conveyed news concerning Indian people, both in Chicago and on reservations nationwide. The project exemplified Powell's interest in the parallels between Native religions and Christianity; a cross and a calumet were shown intertwined on the cover of each issue. In the late 1950s, Powell sat on the Church Federation of Greater Chicago's Joint Indian Committee, where he and others attempted to improve the BIA's relocation program. Along with Dorothy VandeMark and Thomas Segundo, Powell developed a reputation for being a critic of the bureau. On one of many occasions when the impetuous Kurt Dreifuss attempted to quiet his critics, he called Powell a "well-known opponent of the program."[35]

In 1961 Powell also founded the Committee on American Indian Work of the Diocese of Chicago, which provided counseling, food, clothing, and short-term loans to Indians in need. Just a year later, convinced the committee was still not doing enough, Powell received permission from Chicago church officials to found the St. Augustine's Center for American Indians. Powell's work expanded in scope there, and he built a chapel for Indian worshippers. He continued to emphasize the parallels between Native religions and Christianity and commissioned Cheyenne artist Richard West to craft a crucifix, to be placed above the chapel altar, that depicted Christ as a Cheyenne. Although open to Indian people of all tribes as well as to local non-Indians in need, St. Augustine's appealed to those who had already encountered Episcopal missionaries and churches. In particular, Chippewas from Wisconsin frequented St. Augustine's for aid, fellowship, and spiritual guidance.[36]

Two years after St. Augustine's opened, the American Indian Center relocated to the neighborhood where most of its members lived. In 1963 it moved to 738 North Sheridan Road, and four years later it took over the Ravenswood Masonic Temple at 1630 West Wilson Avenue. Once in Uptown, the center became a more important community institution and gathering place. Summer camps, various classes, and tutoring services were set up, and some couples married at the center. In 1964 the center also initiated an annual buffalo dinner as a fund-raiser. At the inaugural event, more than one hundred people paid $50 a plate and gathered at the Palmer House Hotel. Several prominent Chicagoans were in attendance, including Gen. Robert E. Wood, the president of Sears and Roebuck and former chair of the America First Committee. After a meal of buffalo steak, a mixed group of Indians and non-Indians listened to a talk by Commissioner of Indian Affairs Philleo Nash. The 1964 dinner and those held in the following years raised much-needed funds for the center.[37]

By the mid-1960s, much of this money went to social services at the center. Initially, many Indians considered St. Augustine's as the place to receive aid, whereas the center was the place to socialize. Yet the center moved increasingly toward social welfare activities. Some Chicago Indians became uncomfortable with that trend and hesitated to frequent the center because of its new emphasis. That limited the center's ability to reach out to all Indians in Chicago and meet its original pan-tribal mandate. As one woman stated, "Lots of Indian people I know don't go to the Center. One reason I think is that they associate it with welfare, and people don't want other people to think they are on welfare. I know that there are lots of things going on at the Center besides welfare work, but

I hear people with good jobs say that they wouldn't go to the Center because they don't need any services."[38]

The center was also becoming more involved in tribal affairs by the mid-1960s. Lines of communication developed between it and reservations in the Upper Midwest and on the Northern Plains and West Coast. A group of Sioux leaders interested in coordinating the political action of separate Sioux communities in South Dakota, for example, visited the center and spoke with Thomas Segundo about how his tribe, the Papagos, was undertaking a similar project. Meanwhile, reservation communities developed and strengthened their methods of communicating with the center. In 1957 a board member announced that "the ties between our Center and the reservations are so close that the people at Fort Hall know the rages of the Center within hours."[39]

The center helped Indians learn about each another in a variety of ways. The connections they formed in Chicago were unique and differed considerably from those of reservation communities, where the vast majority of people were from the same tribal background. Informal newsletters published by the center facilitated these contacts. Many had loose publishing schedules and went through a series of name changes over a short span of time—from *American Indian Center News* to *Indian News* to *Tom Tom Echoes* to *Teepee Topics* to *The Warrior.*[40] Despite the publications' casual nature, however, many people relied on them for news and information. They contained sections describing the upcoming schedule of events at the center and featured a section of classified advertisements. Purses, necklaces, earrings, pins, moccasins, belts, powwow regalia, and other Native American arts and crafts items were all bought and sold in the pages of the newsletters. In addition, the advertisements had an educational function. Even those who did not buy or sell items through the classifieds learned of other tribes and cultural traditions by looking through them. Whatever the form of exchange they led to, the advertisements helped Indians in Chicago learn more about members of other tribes, stimulated interests in other tribal cultures, and strengthened the growing pan-Indian movement.[41]

Sporting events also played an important role in Chicago Indian community. Teams from the center, St. Augustine's, and other organizations frequently played counterparts from Milwaukee, Minneapolis–St. Paul, and reservation communities in Wisconsin, Minnesota, and North and South Dakota. In February 1965 the Warriors from the center won the thirty-third Midwest All-Indian Basketball Tournament, besting a team from Neopit, Wisconsin, in the final game. Art Elton, a Sioux from South

Dakota and member of the center's team, won the Jim Thorpe Memorial Trophy, which was given to the tournament's most valuable player.
Elton and his teammates, who came from many tribes—Sioux, Chippewa,
Crow, Blackfoot, and Navajo—took great pride in their victory and in
representing Chicago's Native American community and the American
Indian Center. In years to come the center would sponsor additional basketball teams for men and women. The frequent success of those teams
would earn the center great fame among Indians in Chicago and in urban and reservation communities across the United States.[42]

Many Indian people joined or associated with organizations that
helped them adjust to the city and begin to think about their places
there. A poem by Patricia Miller, a young Chippewa, in honor of the
center illustrates that:

> To be an Indian is really the most
> I know sometimes I seem to boast,
> But it's only because I'm so proud.
> My people are great, our Tom-Tom's loud.
> No one could be more United States
> Our home to all has open gates.
> You'll find it at 411 North LaSalle
> We welcome you, the great and small.
> See our ceremonies and study our race—
> Watch us work or play, whatever the case!
> To you, who, so long ago, invaded our land—
> Again we offer a most welcome hand.
> Savage we aren't and no scalps we'll take—
> But lots of friends we hope to make.[43]

Patricia Miller's poem illustrates well the mindset of many Indians
in Chicago during this time, combining adjustment to American society
with cultural continuity and pride. This sentiment comes closer to describing Indian people in Chicago during the 1950s than does the center's
constitution, which speaks primarily of integration. Miller's poem, too,
suggests that Indians were interested in interacting with non-Indians and
claims they were more American than any other group. Yet it also ex-
presses racial pride apart from the dominant BIA and mainstream philosophy of integration. Both integration and separatism are on display here,
a microcosm of many Indians' relationship with mainstream American
society in Chicago. The American Indian Center and other Indian organizations in Chicago allowed these complex sentiments to be voiced and
in many cases cultivated.

Although they came from a wide variety of religious backgrounds, Indians often managed to find a religious home in Chicago. Religion, like other experiences, helped them adjust to the city, but it seldom fostered a common Indian identity or pan-Indianism. Most Indians in Chicago remained wary of those who professed different faiths or belief systems.

Most reservations from which Indians in Chicago had come had long histories of Christian missionary activity. Some wished to continue along the Christian path they had begun on the reservation, whereas others saw urban migration as a way to escape from missionary-imposed control. Among the latter group was a Native Presbyterian minister who, after relocating, stopped attending church. Working closely with churches and church workers in the relocation program, the BIA urged relocating Indians to fill out a form before they left their reservations and list their religious preferences. The names and addresses of those who indicated they were Catholic were sent to the cardinal's office in Chicago. The forms of those who said they were Baptist, Methodist, Presbyterian, or from any other mainline denomination were sent to the Church Federation of Greater Chicago, a Protestant ecumenical organization.[44]

Some Indian people accepted assistance from the Church Federation of Greater Chicago and even became actively involved with the organization. One Eskimo man looking for a new church home to replace his Southern Baptist church in Anchorage, for example, contacted the Church Federation after arriving in Chicago. The organization pointed him to the Lake Shore Baptist Church on Clark Street. After helping a Creek woman meet other Baptist women, the Church Federation was delighted when she said, "I really feel at home in my new church. They come and pick me up for Sunday School and church every Sunday morning, [and] take me to ladies' aid during the week. They make me feel at home." Although the number of Baptists among Chicago's Indians was relatively small, the American Baptist Association still placed a "Christian Friendliness Worker" in the city, as it did in other urban Indian centers, to find Christian homes for interested Indians and provide more general types of aid.[45]

Many American Indians in Chicago, however, frustrated the Church Federation in their responses to the group. Some had no interest in its Protestant Christian religion. Others were put off by its single-minded emphasis on integration. The liberal clergy active in civic affairs with the Church Federation often viewed Indians as pieces to be added to their city's cherished ethnic and racial jigsaw puzzle. Although going to great pains to express their opposition to racism, members of the Church Federation and other philanthropic groups had a clear agenda: Native Americans were to contribute to the city's pluralistic community. Many Indian people rejected that role, however, and remained uninterested in the Church Federation's pluralist and integrationist program. In time, the Indians' tepid response caused the Church Federation to retreat from its insistence on integrated and inter-racial congregations that included Indian people. By the mid-1960s the group reluctantly acknowledged that it "might have to organize Indian congregations."[46]

Indians' location within Chicago also limited the success of the Church Federation. Well connected in the city's downtown and affluent suburbs, the group had little clout in Uptown and Lakeview, where Methodist, Presbyterian, and other mainline churches were often outnumbered by small storefront Baptist, Pentecostal, or independent churches that were more popular among active Indian Christians. At a 1961 meeting, one minister expressed continued support for "strengthening churches in ports of entry" such as Uptown but cautioned colleagues against excessive optimism. "Most churches in these areas are sectarian, nonrelated churches," he explained, "and we have no influence with them." Into the mid-1960s, one of the most popular churches among active Indian Christians was the theologically conservative American Indian Bible Church on Clark Street, which had no connection to the Church Federation. It served as one of the most important institutions and means of adjustment in the lives of its members.[47]

Catholic Indians, or at least those with some Catholic experience or training in their upbringing, outnumbered Protestant Indians of whatever denomination or organizational affiliation in Chicago. For decades, priests working throughout the Upper Midwest and Northern Plains had established mission stations on the Chippewa and Sioux reservations from which many migrants would come. In this regard, Chicago was different from western cities such as Denver and Los Angeles, where Protestants, particularly Baptists, dominated Indian communities. Some Indians in Chicago with Catholic backgrounds (as many as half the population according to one estimate) became involved with their local Catholic church. One man, a Turtle Mountain Chippewa, when writing home made note of the convenient three-block walk to church in listing the attractive features of his new Chicago apartment.[48]

Yet the great majority of Indians in Chicago who had Catholic backgrounds were only "nominal Catholics" according to Chicago archdiocese reports. Church officials bemoaned the small number who attended mass, even in the two parishes within the heavily Indian southeastern section of Uptown, St. Mary of the Lake at 4200 North Sheridan Road and St. Thomas of Canterbury at 4827 North Kenmore Avenue. For a time, the archdiocese considered starting a Catholic Indian center in Chicago, but the plan never came to fruition, in part because of lack of interest and involvement among Indians themselves. Because of its limited influence in the lives of most, Catholicism played only a minor role in Indians' adjustment to Chicago.[49]

In addition to Protestants and Catholics, Chicago's Indian community contained many who followed traditional religious ways. Many Winnebagos, for example, followed the Medicine Lodge. By the mid-1960s, the Native American Church also had a presence in Chicago. Begun in the early twentieth century in the Southwest, the church mixed Christianity and aspects of traditional Native religions into a new, syncretic structure. Perhaps its most significant aspect was the use of peyote as a sacrament.[50]

The exposure to new religions in Chicago had important effects on Indian people. Some were swayed by competing faiths, whereas others embraced previous religious beliefs more firmly. The experiences of Diane Maney, a Winnebago, mirrored this enlarged perspective. As a youngster, she developed interest in the various religions represented in Chicago. After feeling "left out" when Catholic friends from school went to catechism, she started attending instructional meetings with them and frequently interrupted lessons with questions about Catholic doctrine. With unflagging interest, she also visited Baptist, Pentecostal, and other denominations in Chicago. She depicts this as part of her urban education and recalls asking questions and paying attention wherever she went: "Why they did this and why they did that—some places you couldn't cut your hair, you couldn't wear makeup, you couldn't do this or that." Interest and involvement in non-Indian affairs did not usually result in complete assimilation and loss of Indian cultural patterns, however. After describing her many experiences while studying religions in Chicago, Maney reports that none permanently won her over. She continued to follow the traditional religious ways of her parents and grandparents. After describing her many adventures with Catholic and Protestant friends, she says, "When you come right down to it, I'm still going to Medicine."[51]

The groups of Indian people in Chicago who followed Protestantism, Catholicism, or traditional religious ways persisted through the mid-1960s and in general remained divided. The religions often aided in adjustment to the city, but sometimes tensions between people of varying religious beliefs caused strife and conflict. The BIA's Chicago relocation office and other groups that crossed swords from time to time with the American Indian Center often charged that its leadership and programs were hostile to Christianity. After being replaced as the director of the center in 1959, Thomas Segundo joined with a group of Indian Baptists who attempted to gain control of the center. When that failed, he began working with the Church Federation to renovate Woodlawn Baptist Church and prepare it for Indian programs meant to compete with those of the center.[52]

By the mid-1960s, the center appeared to be increasingly used by traditionalists and those for whom religion was relatively unimportant. An informal study conducted at the center on Chicago Indians' church activity revealed that only four of thirty people surveyed attended church (two Catholics and two Baptists). The majority consisted primarily of Chippewas and Menominees who had exposure to Catholic missionaries on their reservations but did not attend church in Chicago.[53]

An uneasy relationship developed between some Christian Indians and the center. They made use of it for certain social events but often avoided dances and powwows and shunned meetings of religious groups other than their own. Josephine Willie, who grew up in a Christian family on the Choctaw reservation in Mississippi, soon learned that other Indians in Chicago came from different backgrounds and had "a religion of their own." She left when Native American Church groups conducted peyote ceremonies at the center.[54]

To some extent, the religious factionalism prevalent in some reservation communities in the early twentieth century was carried to Chicago. Religion seldom brought together all or even most of the Indians in the city. Their religious adjustment usually occurred on one of three tracks: Indian Protestantism, Indian Catholicism, and Indian traditionalism.

Just as there was no single pattern of religious observance, so, too, among Indians in mid-twentieth-century Chicago there was no single pattern of family life, no single way of adjusting the family to urban life. Some clung to traditional extended family patterns and relied on kin relations that affected the planning of everything from potluck meals to bowling teams. Others began to gravitate toward nuclear family patterns and companionate marriages. As Indian women in Chicago learned more about the marriage arrangements of their non-Indian friends and co-workers, they tended to favor the nuclear family more than their husbands did. Among the Navajo and some other tribes, furthermore, women were often much better educated than men and sometimes found more employment opportunities. The new demands on the marriage relationship and women's growing power sometimes produced marital tension. A 1968 study found that one-quarter of Indian spouses in Chicago were separated or divorced and that separations (not divorces) were even more frequent among poorer families. Those statistics reflected a national trend, for in other urban relocation centers as well anywhere from one-fifth to one-half of Indian marriages ended in separation or divorce.[55]

As they attempted to adjust or just survive in Chicago, Indian parents remained concerned about their children. Most were relatively pleased with the education the children received, particularly compared to reservation schools. Similarly, Indian children and youths were even more pleased with Chicago's schools, including Senn and Lakeview high schools on the North Side. Some parents, though, believed that contact with white and black youths made their children more brash and outspoken, patterns of behavior they opposed as "non-Indian." Other children seemed to rediscover their heritage, exceeded their parents in their interest in Indian ways, and readily questioned parents about traditional languages and cultural patterns. As Margaret Redcloud, a Chippewa, said of her youngest daughter, she "really wants to know everything about the Indian ways and she'll sit for hours with me when I talk about our lives."[56]

Although adjustment by Chicago Indians in both pan-Indian and other directions proceeded apace during the early 1960s, some residents became ambivalent about the forms it took. Differences between old-timers and newcomers mirrored similar conflicts among other ethnic groups that had migrated to U.S. cities. Some long-standing residents resented the increase in federal financial support for relocatees who came after the 1950s. Marlene Strouse, who relocated to Chicago from Arizona in 1952, questioned BIA payments for clothing, tools, and other items furnished to later relocatees. "That wasn't so when we first came up," she observed.[57]

Others looked beyond individual gains or losses and focused on how newcomers seemed to change the city's Indian community. Indian identity was altered by Native Americans' urban experiences, and Indians in Chicago shared in those changes. Yet some members of the Chicago community remained ambivalent about the adjustments they saw other Indian people undertaking. On the one hand, these changes often resulted in economic advancement; on the other hand, they sometimes appeared to alter what it meant to be an Indian in significant and seemingly dangerous ways.

Susan K. Power, a Sioux who came to Chicago during the 1940s, was one of the earliest residents to worry about how Indians could remain "traditional" and "real Indians" in the city amid the habits and values of later generations of urban migrants. Although she highly valued education, she had a dismissive attitude toward what she called "city smarts" or "Chicago smarts," which she characterized as being able to take advantage of welfare and becoming involved in community affairs solely for financial gain. Although she had lived in Chicago for years, the experience had not detrimentally affected her. Power thought that others, though, had allowed urban life to foster selfishness and opportunism. She contrasted her generation's devotion to the work ethic and self-help strategies with that of later arrivals, whom she depicted as less committed to hard work and sacrifice. She was implicitly uncertain about the ability of tribal people to adjust to Chicago's environment.

Power compares the closeness of the early Indian community in Chicago and its devoted, self-sacrificial nature with the more individualistic late-comers, whom she believes have negatively influenced not only the Indian community in Chicago but also those on reservations. "We all knew each other," she says, "and we did what everybody's talking about—grassroots—we pulled ourselves up." Responding to frequent discussions among Indian people—young and old—about how to remain traditional in changing circumstances, Power invokes the name of Vine Deloria, Sr., an Episcopal minister and Sioux leader whom many of his generation revered. Deloria made regular visits from South Dakota to Chicago while the Indian community there was still young and relatively small. Power refers to those visits in discussing traditionalism:

> This is being a traditional—you looked up your people, not just necessarily your people, but other Indians. You checked up on them, in other words, and those people were honored when you came to their place. Nowadays, even on the reservation, you go home and you say, "I'm looking for so-and-so." And they say, "I don't know her." You go to seven different places and . . . they don't even know each other. In the city here, Old Vine [Deloria, Sr.] would come and check on us. He knew every Sioux that was here. Maybe he was here just for a short time, but he'd find them.

Increasingly, though, Power believes that Indians have lost that vision and commitment and been lured by negative urban influences ranging from television to junk food. When she was a child on the Standing Rock Reservation, the distribution of "commodities" or basic foodstuffs was an important ritual tied to tribal and kinship obligations. Now, she asks, "How many of them sit and cook the commodities? You see the kids walking down the streets of Chicago, eating fries and chips and pop." In this and other ways, Power worries, some urban Indians have not retained their traditional ways and have lost what was most valuable.[58]

---

Despite concerns about the losses suffered by Indian people in the city and Indians' frequent movements in and out of Chicago, many survived and even thrived there. Social centers, religion, family, and community all contributed to this process. A dual identity, one between city and reservation, developed in urban centers such as Chicago. Some observers, such as government officials interested in Indians' complete assimilation, failed to see the transformation. Yet examination of the early years of Chicago's American Indian Center in particular reveals this new identity. Indians faced a new environment in Chicago. They had to come to terms with a dizzying array of tribal backgrounds, the city's variety of racial groups, and outsiders who had their own plans for how Indian people should live. Through it all, urban Indians developed an identity that would reshape even broader notions of Indian identity.

## Notes

1. Interview with Benjamin Bearskin in Studs Terkel, *Division Street America* (New York: Pantheon Books, 1967), 109.

2. Pine Ridge Agency Placement Record, 25 May 1953, Robert Rietz Collection, Community Archives, Native American Education Services College, Chicago [hereafter Rietz Collection, CA, NAES] (quotations); Merwyn S. Garbarino, "Life in the City: Chicago," in *The American Indian in Urban Society,* ed. Jack O. Waddell and Michael Watson (Boston: Little, Brown, 1971), 173–74.

3. Joan Ablon, "American Indian Relocation: Problems of Dependency and Management in the City," *Phylon* 26 (Winter 1965): 362–71; Joan Ablon, "Cultural Conflict in Urban Indians," *Mental Hygiene* 55 (Apr. 1971): 199–205; Joan Ablon, "Relocated American Indians in the San Francisco Bay Area: Social Interactions and Indian Identity," *Human Organization* 23 (Winter 1964): 26–304; Blue Clark, "Bury My Heart in Smog," in *The American Indian Experience: A Profile,* ed. Philip Weeks (Arlington Heights: Forum Press, 1988), 278–91; Donald L. Fixico, *Termination and Relocation: Federal Indian Policy, 1945–1960* (Albuquerque: University of New Mexico Press, 1986), 191; Anthony M. Garcia, "'Home' Is Not a House: Urban Relocation among American Indians," Ph.D. diss., University of California at Berkeley, 1988, 2–32; Madelon Golden and Lucia Carter, "New Deal for America's Indians," *Coronet* 38 (Oct. 1953): 74–80; Janusz Mucha, "American Indian Success in the Urban Setting," *Urban Anthropology* 13 (Winter 1984): 329–54; Patricia K. Ourada, "Indians in the Work Force," *Journal of the West* 25 (Apr. 1986): 52–58; Virgil J. Vogel, "Chicago's Native Americans: Cheechakos, Old-Timers and Others in the City of the Wild Garlic," *City: A Journal of the City Colleges of Chicago* (Winter 1986): 183–87.

4. John Bodnar, *The Transplanted: A History of Immigrants in Urban America* (Bloomington: Indiana University Press, 1985).

5. Merwyn S. Garbarino, "Indians in Chicago," in *Urban Indians: Proceedings of the Third Annual Conference on Problems and Issues Concerning*

American Indians Today (Chicago: Newberry Library, 1981), 54–77; Roger L. Nichols, "Something Old, Something New: Indians since World War II," in *The American Indian Experience: A Profile*, ed. Philip Weeks (Arlington Heights: Forum Press, 1988), 292–312; Rosalyn R. LaPier and David R. M. Beck, "Linking the Past and the Present," in *Indians of the Chicago Area*, ed. Terry Straus (Chicago: NAES College, 1990), 191.

6. Cheyenne River Agency report, Aug. 1957, box 4, Narrative Reports, Field Placement and Relocation Office Employment Assistance Records, Record Group 75, National Archives–Washington, D.C. [hereafter NR, FPROEAR, RG 75, NA-WDC]; LaVerne Madigan, *The American Indian Relocation Program* (New York: Association on American Indian Affairs, 1956), 6; Wade B. Arends, Jr., "A Socio-Cultural Study of the Relocated American Indians in Chicago," M.A. thesis, University of Chicago, 1958, 27; O. K. Armstrong and Marjorie Armstrong, "The Indians Are Going to Town," *Reader's Digest* 66 (Jan. 1955): 43; John A. Price, "The Migration and Adaptation of American Indians to Los Angeles," *Human Organization* 27 (Summer 1968): 168–75; Kenneth R. Philp, "Stride toward Freedom: The Relocation of Indians to Cities, 1952–1960," *Western Historical Quarterly* 16 (Apr. 1985): 175–90; Clark, "Bury My Heart in Smog," 287; Ablon, "Relocated American Indians in the San Francisco Bay Area," 296–304.

7. On return migration among European immigrants, see Mark Wyman, *Round-Trip to America: The Immigrants Return to Europe, 1880–1930* (Ithaca: Cornell University Press, 1993); and Bodnar, *The Transplanted*, 53. In discussing this phenomenon in comparative context, Richard White and Francis Jennings recognize its prevalence among both European immigrants and Indian urban migrants, while Nancy Lurie and Russell Thornton somewhat exaggerate the differences between these two groups' return migration patterns. See White, *"It's Your Misfortune and None of My Own": A History of the American West* (Norman: University of Oklahoma Press, 1991), 448–49; Jennings, *The Founders of America* (New York: Norton, 1993), 401; Nancy O. Lurie, *Wisconsin Indians*, 2d ed. (Madison: State Historical Society of Wisconsin, 1980), 8; and Russell Thornton, "Patterns and Processes of American Indians in Cities and Towns: The National Scene," in *Urban Indians: Proceedings of the Third Annual Conference on Problems and Issues Concerning American Indians Today* (Chicago: Newberry Library, 1981), 29.

8. "Summary of Relocations with Financial Assistance, f.y. 1952–1953," box 2, NR, FPROEAR, RG 75, NA-WDC; interview with Marlene Strouse (Papago), Chicago, 18 July 1983, Chicago American Indian Oral History Pilot Project, no. 011, Newberry Library, Chicago, and Native American Educational Services College, Chicago [hereafter CAIOHP, NL and NAES] (first quotation); author interview with Diane Maney (Winnebago), Chicago, 20 June 1995 (second quotation); interview with William Isburg (Sioux), 26 July 1968, American Indian Oral History Research Project [hereafter AIOHRP], pt. 1, no. 22, MS 54 (third quotation). See also Mary Patrick, "Indian Urbanization in Dallas: A Second Trail of Tears?" *Oral History Review* (1973): 55; Peter Iverson, *When Indians Became Cowboys: Native Peoples and Cattle Ranching in the Amer-*

156     *Indian Metropolis*

*ican West* (Norman: University of Oklahoma Press, 1994), 205–7; Arends, "A Socio-Cultural Study," 64–65; William H. Hodge, "Navajo Urban Migration: An Analysis from the Perspective of the Family," in *The American Indian in Urban Society*, ed. Jack O. Waddell and O. Michael Watson (Boston: Little, Brown, 1971), 350–51; Garcia, "'Home' Is Not a House."

9. Chicago FRO report, June 1952, box 1, Anadarko Area report, Dec. 1952, box 2, and Pierre Agency report, Dec. 1956, box 4, all NR, FPROEAR, RG 75, NA-WDC; interview with Rose Maney (Winnebago), Chicago, 2 May 1984, CAIOHP, no. 002, NL and NAES.

10. Author interview with Edward E. Goodvoice (Sioux), Chicago, 14 June 1995; Mary Nan Gamble to Robert Rietz, 14 Apr. 1953, and Robert Rietz to Kurt Dreifuss, 2 June 1953, both Rietz Collection, CA, NAES; author interview with Josephine Willie and son (Choctaw), Chicago, 14 June 1995. See also Garbarino, "Life in the City: Chicago," 186.

11. Chicago FRO report, Apr. 1952, box 1, NR, FPROEAR, RG 75, NA-WDC; "Family Life of Indians Suffers Here," *Chicago Daily News*, 25 Jan. 1963, Clip File: "Ethnic Groups-Chicago-Indians, American," Harold Washington Public Library, Chicago [hereafter CF, HWPL] (quotation). On relationships between Indian parents and children in the city, see also author interview with Ronald Bowan, Sr. (Menominee), Chicago, 15 June 1995; Ablon, "American Indian Relocation," 365.

12. James O. Palmer, "A Geographical Investigation of the Effects of the Bureau of Indian Affairs' Employment Assistance Program upon the Relocation of Oklahoma Indians, 1967–1971," Ph.D. diss., University of Oklahoma, 1975, 94–105; minutes of the Joint Indian Committee, 7 Oct. 1958, Church Federation of Greater Chicago [hereafter CFGC] Files, 28–5, Manuscript Collections, Chicago Historical Society [hereafter MC, CHS]; Muskogee Area report, F.Y. 1959, box 13, NR, FPROEAR, RG 75, NA-WDC; Turtle Mountain Consolidated Agency report, Feb. 1958, Turtle Mountain Consolidated Agency report, Jan. 1958, and Aberdeen Area report, Apr. 1958, all box 4, NR, FPROEAR, RG 75, NA-WDC; *Indian Affairs* (May 1958): 7 (quotation). See also Garbarino, "Life in the City: Chicago," 178; Philp, "Stride toward Freedom," 185; and Larry W. Burt, "Roots of the Native American Urban Experience: Relocation Policy in the 1950s," *American Indian Quarterly* 10 (Spring 1986): 94.

13. Menominee Agency report, June 1958, box 13, NR, FPROEAR, RG 75, NA-WDC (first quotation); second quotation from interview with Lois Knifechief, Pawnee, 26 Oct. 1970, Doris Duke Oral History Center interview no. 984, Special Collections, Marriott Library, University of Utah, Salt Lake City, cited in Clark, "Bury My Lungs in Smog," 160.

14. Minneapolis Area report, Mar. 1952, box 2, NR, FPROEAR, RG 75, NA-WDC; Elaine M. Neils, *Reservation to City: Indian Migration and Federal Relocation* (Chicago: University of Chicago Department of Geography Research Paper no. 131, 1971), 91 (quotation); Patrick, "Indian Urbanization in Dallas," 56; Kathryn L. MacKay, "Warrior into Welder: A History of Federal Employment Programs for American Indians, 1878–

1972," Ph.D. diss., University of Utah, 1987, 212; James O. Palmer, "A Geographical Investigation of the Effects of the Bureau of Indian Affairs' Employment Assistance Program upon the Relocation of Oklahoma Indians, 1967–1971," Ph.D. diss., University of Oklahoma, 1975, 24.

15. NCIO, *Public Forum before the Committee on Urban Indians in Los Angeles, California* (Washington, D.C., 1968), 97.

16. Tom Holm, *Strong Hearts, Wounded Souls: The Native American Veterans of the Vietnam War* (Austin: University of Texas Press, 1996), 110; Muskogee Area report, Oct. 1953, box 3, NR, FPROEAR, RG 75, NA-WDC; Chicago FRO report, June 1954, box 2, Reports on Employment Assistance, Chicago Field Employment Assistance Office, Record Group 75, National Archives–Great Lakes Region, Chicago [hereafter REA, CFEAO, RG 75, NA-GLR].

17. "Indian Relocation and Industrial Development Programs," 85th Cong., 2d sess., 1957, 20.

18. Interview with Richard LaRoche (Sioux), 25 Aug. 1971, AIOHRP, pt. 1, no. 41, MS 784.

19. Interview with Amy Lester Skenandore (Stockbridge), Chicago, n.d., CAIOHP, no. 003, NL and NAES; interview with Willard LaMere (Winnebago), Chicago, 1 Feb. 1984, CAIOHP, no. 009, NL and NAES; interview with Josephine Spotted Hawk (Sioux), 1 Sept. 1971, AIOHRP, pt 1. no. 43, MS 787.

20. Mrs. Lee Smith to Robert Rietz, 17 July 1953, Rietz Collection, CA, NAES.

21. Jon C. Teaford, *The Twentieth-Century American City*, 2d ed. (Baltimore: Johns Hopkins University Press, 1993), 107–9; *A Social Geography of Metropolitan Chicago* (Chicago: Northeastern Illinois Metropolitan Planning Commission, 1960), n.p.

22. Evelyn M. Kitagawa, Donald J. Bogue, and Karl E. Taeuber, eds., *Local Community Fact Book: Chicago Metropolitan Area, 1960* (Chicago: Chicago Community Inventory, University of Chicago, 1963), 3, 5, 234; Ernest Parisien to Turtle Mountain Consolidated Agency, 4 Feb. 1957, box 5, NR, FPROEAR, RG 75, NA-WDC; "Chicago—A City of Many Communities," 1961, folder 22, box 14, Stanley D. Lyman Papers, Mariott Library, University of Utah, Salt Lake City [hereafter Lyman Papers, ML, UU].

23. Chicago FRO report, Sept. 1952, box 1, REA, CFEAO, RG 75, NA-GLR; "History of the American Indian Center," undated unpublished ms., American Indian Center, no. 0400, sec. 1, Urban Records Collection, Community Archives, Native American Educational Services College [hereafter URC, CA, NAES]; "Constitution of the All-Tribes American Indian Center," Welfare Council of Metropolitan Chicago [herafter WCMC] Files, 246–13, Manuscript Collections, Chicago Historical Society [hereafter MC, CHS]. Other accounts on the beginnings of the American Indian Center include Grant Arndt, "'Contrary to Our Way of Thinking': The Struggle for an American Indian Center in Chicago, 1946–1953," *American Indian Culture and Research Journal* 22, no. 4 (1998): 117–34; Merwyn S. Garbarino, "The Chicago American Indian Center: Two Decades," in *American Indian Urbanization*, ed. Jack O. Wad-

dell and O. Michael Watson (West Lafayette: Institute for the Study of Social Change, 1973), 77–79; and Janusz Mucha, "From Prairie to the City: Transformation of Chicago's American Indian Community," *Urban Anthropology* 12 (Fall 1983): 349–50.

24. *Fort Berthold Agency News Bulletin*, 21 Sept. 1953, Rietz Collection, CA, NAES.

25. Author interview with Samson Keahna (Mesquakie), Chicago, 27 Oct. 1993. For more commentary on this interview, see James B. LaGrand, "Whose Voices Count? Oral Sources and Twentieth-Century American Indian History," *American Indian Culture and Research Journal* 21 (Winter 1997): 94–97.

26. Debra Valentino, "The History of the American Indian Center Princess," in *Native Chicago*, ed. Terry Straus and Grant P. Arndt (Chicago: Native Chicago, 1998), 148–54; Program for Fifth Annual AIC Spring Bazaar, 3 and 4 May 1958, American Indian Center, no. 0400, sec. 11–D-2, URC, CA, NAES; author interview with Candace Ryan (Sioux), Chicago, 13 June 1995.

27. "Purpose and Activities," June 1954, American Indian Center, no. 0400, sec. 3, URC, CA, NAES; "Chicago Indians Have Active Canoe Club," *Amerindian* (Mar.–Apr. 1968): 6; interview with Joe White (Winnebago), Chicago, n.d., CAIOHP, no. 022, NL and NAES; Edmund Jefferson Danziger, *Survival and Regeneration: Detroit's American Indian Community* (Detroit: Wayne State University Press, 1991), 60; *Tom Tom Echoes*, 26 Aug. 1954, Rietz Collection, CA, NAES; *Teepee Topics* (Nov. 1956) no. 5925, URC, CA, NAES.

28. Author interview with Samson Keahna (Mesquakie), Chicago, 27 Oct. 1993.

29. K. Tsianina Lomawaima, *They Called It Prairie Light: The Story of Chilocco Indian School* (Lincoln: University of Nebraska Press, 1994); Lurie, *Wisconsin Indians*, 50–51; author interview with Daniel W. Battise (Alabama-Coushatta), Chicago, 15 June 1995.

30. Dorothy VandeMark to John Collier, 18 Dec. 1955, reel 42, Collier Papers, Archives and Manuscripts Division, Sterling Memorial Library, Yale University, New Haven, Conn.

31. Chicago FRO reports, Feb. 1955 and Mar. 1957 (quotations), boxes 2 and 3, REA, CFEAO, RG 75, NA-GLR.

32. "History of the American Indian Center," undated, unpublished ms., American Indian Center, no. 0400, sec. 1, URC, CA, NAES; Garbarino, "The Chicago American Indian Center," 77–79; Mucha, "From Prairie to the City," 349–50. The 1957 Schwarzhaupt grant to the center was later increased to $67,500 and extended through 1961, one of eight grants totaling $350,700 given from 1954 through 1961 "to promote civic competence of American Indians." On the Schwarzhaupt Foundation, see Carl Tjerandsen, *Education for Citizenship: A Foundation's Experience* (Santa Cruz: Emil Schwarzhaupt Foundation, 1980), esp. 23–75, 687–88.

33. Dorothy VandeMark to John Collier, 22 Feb. 1957 and 20 May 1957, reel 58, Collier Papers, Archives and Manuscripts Division, Sterling Memorial Library, Yale University, New Haven, Conn.; Minutes of the Joint Indian Committee on Indian Work, 15 July 1957, CFGC, 28–4, CHS.

34. Revised Indian Council Fire bylaws, 1 May 1955, box 1, ICF, SC, NL; "Albert Cobe: 'I Must Step Up,'" *Chicago Tribune*, 20 May 1971, CF, HWPL; Elaine Switzer to Bernie Shiffman, 10 Jan. 1958, WCMC Files, 246-13, MC, CHS.

35. Chicago FRO report, Oct. 1956, box 3, REA, CFEAO, RG 75, NA-GLR (quotation); Peter Powell to Philleo Nash, 6 Sept. 1962, folder 24, box 14, Lyman Papers, ML, UU.

36. Peter Powell and Mrs. Harold Fey to Members of Joint Indian Committee, 27 Feb. 1958, CFGC, 28-5, MC, CHS; "Chicago's Indian Priest," *Newsweek*, 23 Jan. 1967, 91; Mucha, "From Prairie to the City," 363-65; Neils, *Reservation to City*, 66-67.

37. *Indian Voices* (June 1964): 6.

38. Garbarino, "Life in the City: Chicago," 197; see also Garcia, "'Home' Is Not a House," 24-25.

39. Dorothy VandeMark to John Collier, 9 Apr. 1956 and 20 May 1957 (quotation), reels 42 and 58, Collier Papers, Archives and Manuscripts Division, Sterling Memorial Library, Yale University, New Haven, Conn.

40. The most complete collection of these newsletters is in the Urban Records Collection of NAES College's Community Archives. It has partial runs of *American Indian Center News* (no. 5100), *Indian News* (no. 5375), *Teepee Topics* (no. 5925), and *The Warrior* (no. 5965). A few issues of *Tom Tom Echoes* are in the Robert Rietz Collection, also in NAES College's Community Archives.

41. Chicago was not the only place during this time where arts and crafts played an important role among American Indians. Peter Iverson discusses their role among the Navajos and other tribes in the Southwest in "Building toward Self-Determination: Plains and Southwestern Indians in the 1940s and 1950s," *Western Historical Quarterly* 16 (Apr. 1985): 171.

42. *Amerindian* (Mar.–Apr. 1965): 5; Goodner, *Indian Americans in Dallas*.

43. *Tom Tom Echoes*, 16 July 1954, Rietz Collection, CA, NAES.

44. Paula Verdet, "Summary of Research on Indians in St. Louis and Chicago" (1961), 11 pp. unpublished ms., box 16, American Indian Chicago Conference Records, National Anthropological Archives, Smithsonian Institution, Washington, D.C.; Arends, "A Socio-Cultural Study," 82.

45. Report by Virginia Boardman, 13 Dec. 1959, CFGC Files, 32A-1, MC, CHS; "Summary Report on Student Visitation among American Indians," Apr. 1960, CFGC Files, 32A-1, MC, CHS (quotation); Anadarko Area report, Sept. 1952, box 2, NR, FPROEAR, RG 75, NA-WDC.

46. Minutes of the Joint Committee on Indian Work, 8 June 1961 and 26 June 1962, CFGC Files, 28-5, MC, CHS.

47. Minutes of Newcomer Commission, 27 Nov. 1961, CFGC Files, 28-1, MC, CHS; Minutes of Chicago Indian Ministry Committee, 31 Aug. 1965, CFGC Files, 29-4, MC, CHS.

48. "Proposal for Community Action Program among Chicago's American Indians," n.d., CFGC Files, 35-2, MC, CHS; "Indian's Life in 'Promised Land'

Here," *Chicago Daily News*, 24 Jan. 1963, CF, HWPL; "Chit Chat from the Relocation Office," Turtle Mountain Consolidated Agency, 2 Apr. 1954, Rietz Collection, CA, NAES.

49. "Proposal for Community Action Program among Chicago's American Indians," n.d., CFGC Files, 35–2, MC, CHS; "The Indian: His Politics, Religion," *Uptown News*, 13 Dec. 1972, CF, HWPL.

50. Robert E. Bieder, *Native American Communities in Wisconsin, 1600–1960: A Study of Tradition and Change* (Madison: University of Wisconsin Press, 1995), 170–72.

51. Author interview with Diane Maney (Winnebago), Chicago, 20 June 1995.

52. Dorothy VandeMark to John Collier, 20 May 1957 and 12 Mar. 1959, reel 58, Collier Papers, Archives and Manuscripts Division, Sterling Memorial Library, Yale University, New Haven, Conn.; Marion Obenhaus to CFGC board, 18 Jan. 1960, CFGC Files, 28–5, MC, CHS.

53. Working Paper by Dorothy W. Davids, "The Ministry of the Churches to Off-Reservation Indians," n.d. (1967?), CFGC Files, 34–9, MC, CHS.

54. Author interview with Josephine Willie and son (Choctaw), Chicago, 14 June 1995; George D. Scott, John Kennardh White, and Estelle Fuchs, *Indians and Their Education in Chicago* (Washington, D.C.: Educational Resources Information Center, 1969), 25. On the religious environment among Indians in Los Angeles, see Joan Weibel-Orlando, *Indian Country, L.A.: Maintaining Ethnic Community in Complex Society* (Urbana: University of Illinois Press, 1991).

55. Scott, White, and Fuchs, *Indians and Their Education in Chicago*, 26–33; Garbarino, "Life in the City: Chicago," 187; Arends, "A Socio-Cultural Study," 70–71; Joyce Griffen, "Life Is Harder Here: The Case of the Urban Navajo Woman," *American Indian Quarterly* 6 (Spring–Summer 1982): 90–104.

56. Leonard Rascher, "Urban Indian Attitudes toward Education," Ph.D. diss., Northwestern University, 1977; Scott, White, and Fuchs, *Indians and Their Education in Chicago*, 44; Garbarino, "Life in the City: Chicago," 184; John Kennardh White, "The American Indian in Chicago: The Hidden People," M.A. thesis, University of Chicago, 1970, 9–10; interview with Margaret Redcloud (Chippewa), Chicago, 12 Feb. 1984, CAIOHP, no. 021, NL and NAES.

57. Interview with Marlene Strouse (Papago), Chicago, 18 July 1983, CAIOHP, no. 011, NL and NAES.

58. Author interview with Susan K. Power (Sioux), Chicago, 19 June 1995.

# 6 A New Type of Indian

By the end of the 1950s, some Indian people had achieved a measure of success in adjusting to Chicago through jobs, homes and neighborhoods, and involvement in various organizations and community life. They attempted to build on this foundation in the early 1960s. During this time, Chicago's Indian community continued to develop while the connections between Indians' experiences in the city and their ethnic identity further solidified. Noting these trends as well as the general stability of the period, one scholar has called the early 1960s the community's "golden age" following an earlier era when Indian people struggled to find their way in Chicago.[1]

It would be inaccurate, however, to see complete unity in Chicago's Indian community during this time despite progress on many fronts. Although various organizations helped foster a common identity within the community, none proved to be a perfect catalyst; unity and division occurred simultaneously. The urban environment, which increasing numbers of Indian people experienced during this time, contributed to these trends. In addition, the particular nature of Chicago's Indian population—shaped by its early migration patterns—helped determine the type of community that developed there. Tribal affiliation often influenced the route that people took toward urban adjustment. Although Chicago's Indian community shared some characteristics with contemporary urban Indian communities in Los Angeles and Denver, it also differed from them in significant ways.[2]

By the mid-1960s a new type of Indian had emerged in cities such as Chicago, one increasingly connected to members of other tribes living in the city. Sometimes called "pan-tribal" or "pan-Indian" or "ethnic," this identity began to partially replace traditional, strictly tribal, identities. Both day-to-day community activities and a prominent national conference held in Chicago in 1961 contributed to the transformation.

The older, more traditional notions of identity that many urban Indians absorbed while growing up in reservation communities preceded the new identity, however. Elements of identity often changed during Indians' migration from reservation to city, among them ideas concerning race, assimilation, and individualism. In contrast with urban life, which in many ways highlighted race and racial identity, on reservations the notion of race was not salient. Identity instead revolved around membership in a particular family or band. The social, cultural, and economic pressures of assimilation that were evident in the city were less apparent on most reservations. To be sure, government officials and missionaries tried to push Indian people toward assimilation, but the stakes were smaller, and assimilation—at least total assimilation—remained an unattractive prospect for most. Even in the city, many shared that perspective, although it seemed as if assimilation might bring greater material benefits individually and communally. Indians could conceivably connect it to a comfortable apartment, a white-collar office job, or a high-quality education for their children. In reservation communities, assimilation often could not offer even those modest material benefits. Individualism, which some believed to be more necessary in cities, was seen as socially destructive on reservations, and traditional communities often discouraged it by means of complex social ceremonies and mores. In general, the older, traditional Indian identity that urban migrants carried with them was formed in isolation and had no need to respond to outside groups and influences. The experience of the new types of Indians in Chicago and other cities would be quite different.

———————

The developing pan-Indianism or pan-tribalism among American Indians in Chicago was influenced by both old and new experiences. In some ways it resembled the ethnic identity that other immigrants have created in American cities, described by one group of scholars as "continuously being reinvented in response to changing realities both within the group and the host society." To paraphrase a historian of Chicano urban experiences, ethnicity was not "a fixed set of customs" brought to Chicago from reservation communities but rather "a collective identity that emerged from daily experience" there. Pan-Indianism, as it developed in Chicago and elsewhere, drew on both reservation and urban experiences.[3]

Just as New York, San Francisco, and other cities made "Italian Americans" out of Sicilians, and Los Angeles created a unique Mexican American identity for Mexican migrants, Chicago helped create "Indians" with some variety of pan-Indian identity out of Chippewas, Sioux, Winnebagos, and members of other tribes. By the late 1950s a student doing fieldwork in Chicago noted, "The Indians are beginning to develop a new identity. Rather than exclusive tribal identity the Indians are beginning to identify themselves as 'Indians' rather than 'Apaches' or 'Navahos.'" Another observer commented, "An 'urban' Hopi may be able to associate more readily with an 'urban' Sioux than with a 'tribal' person of his own tribal background." Indians interviewed during this time discussed their changing sense of identity and championed strategies by which "Indians of all tribes should work more closely together."[4]

In later years, observers also noted the trend in other cities and described it in different ways. Various anthropologists, sociologists, geographers, historians, and Indian political leaders indicated that "a neo-Indian social identity," "a new ethnic group," or "a new urban tribe" had emerged. Others described it as "supratribal reorganization" or "supratribal amalgamation." Its practical, everyday result was that American Indians in Chicago began to take more interest in "Indian ways" as a result of proximity to one another. They were drawn to, and grew attached to, the city's Indian community for various reasons.[5] Some, like Floria Forica, a Chippewa, did so out of necessity, having been cut off from their reservations. Others were drawn to Chicago and truly began to consider it home. Phyllis Fastwolf, from both Sioux and Oneida backgrounds, described the city's Indian community as "a great big family" where "we all came together and we all needed each other." Likewise, Ada Powers admitted that she never seriously considered returning to her Santee Sioux reservation in Nebraska "because even though I'm here, I'm with the Indians. . . . Every day I'm with the Indians. So, I'm not missing out on anything." And when asked about her birthplace on the Rosebud reservation and whether she planned to return some day, Cornelia Penn replied, "To tell the truth, no. . . . I've been gone so long. I left in 1941 when my father died. Now my mother is gone, too. My aunts and, of course, some sisters [are there], and my only brother is living there. Still, I don't know. I guess I've been gone too long. It just doesn't seem like home anymore."[6]

Many other Indians in Chicago during the early 1960s also assumed an identity apart from the mainstream of Chicago through their association with the city's Uptown neighborhood, its various Indian centers, and its other informal Indian organizations. This Indian identity conflated the traditions, histories, and cultural ways of various tribes. An observer in the late 1960s who spent time in Chicago's Indian community observed that every person with whom he talked was quick to differentiate "Indian" and "non-Indian" behavior. "There are constant references," he wrote, "to some particular action being an 'Indian thing to do.' There are Indian values and white values, Indian ways of acting and white ways of acting."[7]

The definitions of "Indian" behavior and pan-tribal culture were part of a national pattern, and other urban communities also shared many of these values. Moreover, the growing pan-Indian identity influenced how Indians in Chicago related to those who lived on reservations. As Benjamin Bearskin and his wife reared their children, they fostered pan-tribalism, whether deliberately or not, by frequently visiting not only their home, Winnebago, reservation but also the reservations of various other tribes. "Four of our children were born here in this city," he said, "and yet, I think, they're oriented as American Indians. I make it a point to take them on my vacation trips in the summer, always to a different reservation to get acquainted with the people of the tribe. We take photographs, we record the songs that are sung, we participate in dancing and compete for prizes."[8]

Proximity to other Indians and Indian events made a vibrant Indian self-identity more possible in Uptown than elsewhere in Chicago and fostered the growth of pan-Indianism. After leaving the area for a short time, Edward E. Goodvoice commented, "I finally started living in Uptown again where I had originally lived prior to joining the army, and I began to become more involved with Native American social activities."[9]

The demographics of Chicago's Indian community also contributed to its pan-Indian characteristics. By the early 1960s, some who had come to Chicago in the 1950s as adolescents were ready for marriage. Even those inclined to marry a member of their tribe or band often were unable to do so in Chicago. Inter-tribal marriages became the norm, and many married non-Indians. Apartment buildings that housed several Indian families often fostered tribally mixed couples because the young people would become acquainted after commuting together to schools, jobs, and stores. Lucille Spencer, a Choctaw, met her Navajo husband in this way, and many other intertribal marriages also resulted from similar contacts.[10]

Although anti-Indian prejudice in cities near large reservation communities—including Minneapolis, Denver, and Phoenix—contributed to pan-Indianism in those communities, such discrimination played a less-important role in Chicago.[11] Yet members of the Chicago community were aware of the prejudice in other regions of the country, and their reaction to such hatred strengthened their Indian identity. Moreover, some engaged in activist protests in neighboring states. After leaving Mississippi for Chicago, Spencer believed she was also leaving rampant prejudice and discrimination. Yet when her teenaged children began traveling with groups of friends to Wisconsin, she realized she had been wrong. Indians in Wisconsin who attempted to exercise their treaty-guaranteed fishing rights often faced angry groups of whites and responded by holding "fish-ins" that followed the model of the first one conducted in Washington state in 1964. Fish-ins produced camaraderie among those who participated and also fueled pan-Indian feelings. Spencer explains, "My daughter usually goes to Wisconsin with her boyfriend and her friends, rafting and camping and fishing. And it never dawned on me until I learned that there is a lot of prejudice over there, too. One time, my son experienced it because he was there as a supporter for the fishermen. And he was sick because he never thought people could talk like that. They were talking bad at the Indians. So they're aware that there are some prejudices, too, over here."[12]

The epitome of pan-Indianism in Chicago, as elsewhere, was—and still is—the powwow. Powwows much like the one described at the beginning of this book were held frequently during the early 1960s and continue to be held. At powwows, the beat of the drum drives away frustrations and fears and strengthens a sense of Indian identity. When asked why he attended powwows, Menominee Ronald Bowan, Sr., responded quickly, "Number one—I go to hear the drum; it revitalizes me." As Gloria Young, an anthropologist, puts the importance of powwows, "To dance Indian dances is to 'be Indian.'" Powwows enable Indians to live the communal, kin-dependent type of life that many desire but which seems more difficult in the city. Robert Thomas explained that he readily participated in powwows while he lived in Chicago because they allowed his family to do something together. "In these times," he wrote in 1965, "going to Powwows is about the only thing my whole family and myself can do together. . . . Powwows are one of the few genuine family and community affairs that's still going strong." Powwows also convince urban Indians that theirs is a vibrant, legitimate community that does not need to depend upon reservation communities. An Arapaho man explained, "I used to have to wait 'til my vacation to get my fill of powwows. I would go back to Oklahoma and just go from one to another 'til it was time to come back. Now the powwows around here have built up to where I don't have to miss them anymore. There's one some place just about every week now."[13]

At powwows and on other occasions, Indians in Chicago emphasized learning from other tribes. Part of the pan-Indian experience was to become educated in the ways of other tribes. As Diane Maney, a Winnebago, describes it, "When you do something as a Winnebago, when you're doing something on the res, people know why you're doing it. They don't ask questions or anything; they know what's going on. Whereas being here in the city with all different tribal groups, they do things differently. So in order to understand, you more or less have to step back and watch and learn from other tribes. But I like it because you're learning something new every day; you're learning from a different tribe."[14]

Urban pan-Indian communities fostered self-assertion and pride among Indian people. The opportunities to establish and operate various organizations, to acquire jobs in the city, and to educate non-Indians about aspects of Indian culture encouraged Indians to publicize their successes and the virtues of their history and culture. During the Kennedy administration, the American Indian Center became involved in the National Service Corps project but was displeased with the focus of press coverage on the organization. One board member wrote to Washington, D.C., to complain that American Indians had been "lumped together with juvenile delinquency, refugee status, and other undesirable things which are to be eliminated." He attempted to correct this perspective, because Indians "do not look forward to being done away with as a problem, nor do they feel that Indian identity is anything but a very real asset of which they can continue to be proud."[15]

Although a pan-Indian spirit grew among Native Americans in Chicago during the early 1960s, its intensity varied by tribe. Pan-Indianism, despite its vitality as a social force, was often fragile and could coexist with tribal or other identities that individuals still held. Urban Indians were often bicultural—they possessed multiple identities that could be more, or less, pan-Indian in orientation.[16]

Pan-Indianism's characteristics differed from city to city, depending in part on its tribal composition. In many western cities, Indian communities were pan-Plains in cultural form. Sioux, Kiowas, or Comanches formed the nucleus of pan-Indian organizations and greatly influenced powwows and other cultural events. Members of these Plains tribes correspondingly benefited more from urban activities because their cultural patterns dominated them. A Sioux man and leader of Tulsa's Indian community observed that powwows "erase alienation, especially for members of the Plains tribes." In this, he demonstrated both the extent of pan-Indianism among urban Indians as well as its limits, depending on tribe, region, or culture group. Of the Plains tribes, only the Sioux had a large population in Chicago, and they were outnumbered by the Chippewas and other tribes from the Upper Midwest.[17]

Yet few of the many Chippewas in Chicago were inclined to pour all their energies into pan-Indian activities and enterprises. Close to their reservations in Wisconsin, the Chippewas in Chicago more than other tribes tended to retain ties with home reservations and often did not fully commit to their new home. During the late 1960s, observers noted that some Chippewas and others "whose residence in the city is of a more transitory nature are still emotionally tied to their home communities." By contrast, the Chippewas in San Francisco appear to have been much more involved in pan-Indian activities.[18]

In Chicago, the Navajos, although far from home, initially were particularly reluctant to become fully involved in pan-Indian activities. In western cities such as Denver, Albuquerque, and Los Angeles, they were accustomed to dominating the urban Indian scene and not sharing the stage with other tribes. The immense size of the Navajo tribe relative to others also mitigated against ceding much tribal identity. The Navajos often became more self-assured and adjusted in Chicago over a period of time, but they continued to think primarily in tribal terms. While other groups developed pride in being an Indian, the Navajos often completely retained their traditional categories and ways of thinking. One described how he had adjusted to life in Chicago yet clung to his tribal identity: "I learned a lot of things here in Chicago. I learned how to speak. I learned how to walk on the sidewalk. I told myself, 'You're a Navajo. Hold your head up.'" While walking the streets of Chicago, his point of reference remained two thousand miles away on the Navajo reservation.[19]

Their dominant tribal identity often made Chicago's Navajos reluctant to involve themselves actively in the Indian Center. In 1964 the center reported many contacts with Indians from the Upper Midwest and Northern Plains but not as many with Indians from the Southwest. "Although the Bureau of Indian Affairs reportedly brings a large number of members of Southwest tribes to Chicago," the report read, "these people have not come in significant numbers for services—nor for other Center activities." When Navajos did become involved in the center, rifts quickly developed. Their persistent tribal identity, according to one member of the center's board, resulted in some general animosity and two long-lasting feuds: "Navajo versus everybody else—and vice versa" and "the Southwest Indian tribes versus the Sioux groups." Despite their tribal pride, Navajos never became the political influence within Chicago and its Indian Center that they did in San Francisco and other western cities.[20]

In contrast to the Chippewas and the Navajo, the relatively few Winnebagos in Chicago, who came from Nebraska and Wisconsin, enjoyed influence beyond their numbers. From 1959 through 1965 the center's board of directors was chaired by either Chippewas or Winnebagos. Winnebagos were also the first tribe to form a separate tribal club at the center in 1962. Furthermore, they were renowned dancers who influenced urban cultural activities. Even some Sioux children learned to dance from Winnebagos, so great was their reputation. Although Chicago powwows and other activities were characterized by pan-Plains culture, the Winnebagos' presence created a hybrid cultural situation that was distinct from that of cities in either the Plains states or the Far West. Chicago's geography and early migration patterns greatly influenced the shape of the city's Indian community and the extent and limits of its pan-Indianism.[21]

---

This urban pan-Indianism was evident in June 1961, when Chicago hosted one of the most important Indian meetings of the twentieth century. More than 450 American Indian delegates from seventy tribes across the United States converged for the American Indian Chicago Conference (AICC). One hundred or more of the Indians who lived in Chicago also participated in the conference, both officially and unofficially.[22] Events that led to the AICC and the conference itself reveal much about the shape of pan-Indianism during the 1960s within Chicago's Indian community and among Indians nationwide.

In the early 1960s, many Indian people on reservations were fearful of the federal government's attempts to terminate more tribes from federal status. They were also frustrated at the continuing control that the BIA exercised over their reservations and lives. Urban Indians shared those fears and also had concerns of their own. They faulted the relocation program for trying to move too many people too quickly to cities that could not always provide satisfactory housing and employment for them. Anger continued over the bureau's rumored quotas for relocation. With the change in presidential administrations in 1961, some considered it an opportune time to make a statement to the nation.

Sol Tax, a professor of anthropology at the University of Chicago, shared many Indians' concerns about termination and the shortcomings of the relocation program. Tax was also dissatisfied with trends in his professional discipline that were leading colleagues to think of themselves as aloof and removed from their subjects. He believed that too many scientific-minded anthropologists were undertaking projects that failed to contribute to the communities being studied and sometimes even offended or harmed them. In response, Tax developed a model of anthropological work that he called "action anthropology." Anthropologists would consult with the people they were studying, both before starting a project and as it progressed. Moreover, they would only undertake work that the people they studied deemed helpful. "Community research is justifiable," Tax maintained, "only to the degree that the results are imminently useful to the community and easily outweigh the disturbance to it." Tax and his students—including Nancy Lurie, Joan Ablon, and many others—used the techniques of action anthropology in numerous projects, including one with the Fox Indians of Iowa.[23]

It was not long before Tax's concerns about Indian policy became part of action anthropology. By 1960 he had decided to use the concepts of action anthropology to organize a national conference for the political, economic, and social improvement of Indian people. Ultimately, he hoped that conference participants would write and ratify a document that would define Indian policy in the Kennedy administration. Tax soon acquired the assistance of Robert Rietz, Albert Wahrhaftig, Joan Ablon, and Nancy Lurie. Lurie, who served as assistant coordinator, shared her mentor's interest in action anthropology and later explained, "There is the need for fundamental faith coupled with much patience that the people involved are better able to solve their own problems, given the opportunity, than anyone else." Tax's and Lurie's shared belief led American Indian people from across the country to participate in planning the meeting and also contribute to the drafts of the document that would emerge from it.[24]

Tax then set about building support for the project. He immediately contacted his friend Carl Tjerandsen at the Emil Schwarzhaupt Foundation, which had helped fund both the Chicago American Indian Center project in the late 1950s and Tax's own Fox Indian project. In November 1960 Tjerandsen offered Tax $10,000 for the new project, later to be increased to $14,800. The Wenner-Gren Foundation and the University of Chicago also donated money for the conference.[25]

Among American Indian political leaders as well, Tax built support for his developing project. In November 1960 at the annual meeting of the National Congress of American Indians (NCAI) he discussed the conference with friends Helen Peterson and D'Arcy McNickle, who enthusiastically endorsed the idea. Although the National Congress did not officially sponsor the project for fear that Indian people who thought the

NCAI too conservative and closely tied to the bureau would be offended, Tax asked Peterson, McNickle, and other NCAI leaders to help "write the first draft of policy statement to send out," the genesis of what after several months and a series of revisions would become the conference statement.[26]

In order to publicize the meeting and Indian people's demands, Tax began contacting media outlets, including *Life* magazine and the NBC television network. At NBC, he talked with Chet Hagen about the conference and "pressed for a regular network half-hour to develop." In late 1960 Tax also initiated plans to develop a document from the conference that would formally be presented to President John F. Kennedy. In addition, he tried to convince Kennedy to attend the conference in person. He was encouraged when Helen Peterson told him that she had "turned on" writer Alvin Josephy of *American Heritage* magazine to the conference and asked him to use his contacts at the White House to arrange for an invitation after the conference.[27]

Tax next set about securing a location for the conference. Although Milwaukee was briefly considered, Tax's position and Chicago's many railroad and airline connections made it the choice. Knowing the Chicago Police Department's reputation for renegade behavior, Tax talked with representatives of Mayor Richard J. Daley's office to ensure that the conference would not have any "police troubles." He then negotiated with University of Chicago officials to hold the conference on campus, a location that had the advantage of being independent from the government. Tax knew that if Indian people began to suspect, even incorrectly, that the federal government and BIA were involved in the conference it would fail. He finally determined a convenient time for the event: Tuesday, June 13, through Tuesday, June 20, 1961. That week fell between the University of Chicago's spring and summer terms and would ensure the availability of dormitory space and meeting rooms. With the site selected, in February 1961 Tax invited a group of Chicago Indians to meet with him at his home, including Benjamin Bearskin, Frank Fastwolf, Tom Greenwood, Robinson Johnson, Willard LaMere, and Melvin Walker. Dorothy Holstein and Thomas Segundo were also invited but were unable to attend.[28]

As Tax worked to fulfill his vision of action anthropology for the conference, several committees formed to work toward the creation of a document to ratify at the meeting. Both general and regional committees formed and submitted proposals. The process revealed a tension between those supporting a strong nationalist, supra-tribal, pan-Indian approach and those opposing it. The tension would linger throughout the conference and play an important role in late-twentieth-century Indian life, both in Chicago and across the United States.

Regional meetings held in the spring of 1961 in various cities across the country revealed widespread excitement about the upcoming conference and its potential to help American Indian people. Shuttling between her home in Ann Arbor, Michigan, and Chicago, Nancy Lurie sifted through mountains of preliminary drafts that slowly helped shape the statement to be ratified. What impressed her was the "growing recognition, with each successive version of the charter, of the rights of all Indians: reservation, non-reservation, non-federally recognized, relocated, and terminated Indians."[29]

Indians in Chicago and other cities were excited about the upcoming conference and the ways in which it appeared to be fostering pan-Indianism and general Indian unity. They were involved in the planning of the AICC, both as hosts and members of the "Lakes region," which also encompassed Wisconsin and Michigan. Eight other regions also sent delegations from across the United States, and Melvin Walker at the center headed a committee to handle housing arrangements. The group canvassed all the Indians they could find in Chicago and asked them for help. Benjamin Bearskin, the Winnebago chair of the center's board of directors, was the regional organizer of the Lakes region.

Indians in Chicago particularly called for improvements in the implementation of the relocation program, including better screening, more financial assistance, better services available to those who relocated on their own, and greater economic opportunities on reservations so relocation did not become a necessity. In addition, the Chicago American Indian Center's statement to the AICC echoed the conference theme of Indian self-determination and participation. Urban Indian centers, a group of Indians who lived in Chicago wrote, "can function best if their operation is the responsibility of the Indian people themselves. It would be a great error to see these centers as places where things are done to Indians and for Indians 'for their own good' as so much of our past Indian Affairs policy has been carried out." As in Chicago, the relocation program was on the minds of urban Indians everywhere. One Oglala Sioux man who taught engineering in Kansas City urged that the program be improved quickly because relocatees were "becoming a 'black mark' on the whole of American Indianism in public viewpoint."[30]

The regional meetings that took place in other cities with significant Native populations echoed the Chicago community's insistence upon self-determination and racial unity. Those attending a regional meeting in Portland, for example, urged, "Remember the adage: one arrow is easily broken, but a handful cannot be broken." They also hoped that the AICC would bring Indian people publicity and be "another step forward in our effort to become able to step in our rightful place among world people." Education was high on the list for many urban Indians; those in Los Angeles called it "our most urgent need."[31]

As plans for the AICC progressed, developing tensions threatened to stifle any expression of pan-Indian sentiment. Many Native people remained concerned about the conference's position toward the BIA. Although most Indians agreed that the bureau needed to be reformed and deserved criticism for its paternalism and lack of responsiveness to Indians, some worried about offending the BIA and tried to dampen opposition to it. One person who attended the February 1961 Advisory Committee meeting warned that "the group might alienate the Indian Bureau and that before incorporating anything in the Charter they should consult with the Bureau and Secretary of Interior." This proved to be a minority position, however. The group voted down his proposal because they viewed it as too acquiescent toward the BIA.[32]

Far greater, however, were the tensions over representation. Months before the conference, many groups of urban Indians and non-federally recognized Indians were already anticipating the meeting and having the opportunity to express their opinions and vote on issues of interest. Many tribes living on reservations and recognized by the federal government, however, worried about these groups having too much influence. They knew that their interests often differed from those of urban or federally unrecognized communities and feared being outvoted at the AICC. A month and a half before the conference, the planning committee, after "extensive discussion," determined that tribal delegations from federally recognized tribes would have 60 percent of the voting power "in the event that matters requiring a vote should occur at the June conference"; non-federally recognized tribes or bands and organized urban groups would have the remaining 40 percent. Committee records indicate that opposition to equal representation for all groups of Indians at the AICC "stemmed from fear of reservation groups that urban, relocated groups from reservations could dictate reservation policy."[33]

Other divisions between urban and reservation Indians also emerged from the suggestion sheets that Tax distributed widely before the AICC in order to get feedback. Marvin Pine, president of the White Buffalo Council of American Indians in Denver, wrote that he thought the AICC should take up the "problems faced by Indians who leave reservation for better economic development in making a new and successful life." Robert Burnette, chair of the Rosebud Sioux, gave Tax the opposite advice. He returned not just the single suggestion sheet but the entire mailing, and his comments, scrawled in the margins, constituted a ongoing dialogue with Tax and his project. Near a section of the report that addressed how all Indians would have opportunity to express their views, Burnette wrote in large letters, "We are oppressed in this because most of those people present will be city Indians and will clash with the official voice of the tribes."[34]

The AICC began, hopes high among its participants, on Tuesday, June 13, 1961. The afternoon sun beat down on the University of Chicago's Stagg Field as Benjamin Bearskin opened the conference with a solemn calumet ceremony of welcome; he then offered prayers and passed the peace pipe to Tax and the other organizers of the event. Delegates already in Chicago then participated in the first of many powwows that would be held during the week, which was followed by a formal dinner. The hundreds of chickens Nancy Lurie had stored in refrigerators across campus because of the unexpected early summer heat were retrieved and barbecued. The American Indian Chicago Conference, and American Indian Week in Chicago as proclaimed by Mayor Daley, had begun.[35]

That night, delegates heard Edward P. Dozier, a Santa Clara Pueblo and professor of anthropology at the University of Arizona, deliver the keynote address. Dozier was one of several prominent young Indian leaders during the 1960s. The first words he spoke likely cheered those in the audience from cities and non-recognized tribes but worried many from reservation communities. Dozier's speech also signaled urban Indians' important role at the AICC and within twentieth-century American Indian society in general. He opened with the following words: "This is an historic and memorable occasion. We have here a gathering of Indians from many tribes and from vast areas of the American continent to discuss problems that affect us all. This is not simply a gathering of reservation Indians, but also of Indians now living in off-reservation locations as well as of Indians who have lived for many years without federal recognition."

Dozier pointed out that the AICC had been organized in part so these groups of often-neglected Indians might be heard. "Government responsibility for Indians," he stated, "does not apply solely to reservation Indians." Dozier and the speakers who would follow him during the week ahead put conference objectives not in the context of charity but rather of justice from the federal government. Addressing American Indians and the media covering the conference, Dozier noted that Indians did not want a "free ride" but rather "ask[ed] only for the aid to enable us to build and revitalize our communities and enrich our ways of life for a better America."

Finally, Dozier called for the United States to honor its tradition of pluralism with respect to American Indians. In the cold war context of the early 1960s, African Americans were urging the United States to protect freedom at home while attempting to defend it abroad. Many American Indians, such as Dozier, also drew on cold war themes and concerns, yet they often pursued goals different from those of African Americans. Although blacks protested to achieve legal and social integration—to be served at lunch counters and seated on busses the same as other American citizens—Dozier argued against federal Indian policy focused solely on assimilation or integration. "It is the inherent right for Americans to be different," he maintained. "Our free nation can no more insist that Jews stop being Jews and that Catholics give up their religion than it can insist that Indians stop being Indians."[36]

After Dozier's keynote address, some AICC delegates retired to their dormitory quarters for the night. Others, energized by the speech and excited at being in the midst of a large group of American Indian people, attended late-night powwows and more informal social gatherings. Sioux and Crow delegates especially took the nightly powwows at the AICC very seriously. These tribes had been rivals for more than a century, and in Chicago the rivalry took the form of trying to outdo one another in drumming, singing, and dancing. The more ardent powwow participants stayed late into the night and got no more than a few hours' sleep before committee meetings began at 9 A.M. Groups of Indians from the Chicago area who had continued with their daily employment and not registered for the AICC often visited the Hyde Park campus at night in order to participate in the powwows. Other AICC delegates took a more casual approach to socializing as they drank coffee together and talked about the challenges Indian people who lived in different parts of the country faced. As Lurie noted, "Many Indians met members of tribes they had not even heard of before, and names and addresses were exchanged between these newfound friends." At AICC powwows as at other conference events, pan-Indianism mixed with the continued boundaries that existed among the various groups of Indian people.[37]

The trend continued in the daily committee meetings held on June 14, 15, and 16. Here, AICC delegates wrote, revised, and debated about what would become the conference's official highlight, the "Declaration of Indian Purpose." During the three days of meetings, disagreements reemerged that had been expressed in the months before the AICC. Reservation Indians recognized by the federal government, those groups not recognized, and Indians in urban areas all had moments when they sus-pected each other's motives. The last two groups in particular resented the reservations' 60 percent voting bloc, which guaranteed its victory in any official balloting.

Yet despite these differences, many observers were struck by the un-precedented level of unity at the AICC. Shirley Witt, a Mohawk and an experienced political activist, remembered that "at the outset [of the con-ference], each tribe was prepared to do battle for its own personal aims; by meeting's end, virtually all were working as Indians first and tribal mem-bers second." Likewise, one of Tax's assistants at the conference, Joan Ablon, saw American Indians at the AICC drawn together by common challenges and the kinship ties between city and reservation. As a result of Indians looking out for the welfare of relatives in other situations, she observed, "Reservation people, rural and urban dwellers alike, were able to see the whole range of problems of their Indian brothers, and it appeared that each Indian voted in the interests of all Indians." One female delegate from a reservation admitted, "When I came here, I thought only of my people and our problems, and now I think of all the Indian people and all their problems."[38]

On Saturday, June 17, AICC delegates enjoyed some time away from University of Chicago lecture halls. Some chose to tour an exhibit set up by the Indian Arts and Crafts Board from Washington, D.C. Many Native American artists at the time were concerned about counterfeit, non-Indian-made items undercutting the integrity of Indian art, and the exhibit helped boost pride in their artistic heritage. Among its other attractions, the Arts and Crafts Board's showcase contained a "true-false exhibit" that prom-ised to demonstrate the "superiority of genuine Indian artistry and crafts-manship over inferior imitations and importations." Delegates could also browse through commercial booths that exposed them to American Indi-an culture in every part of the country. Everything from food items to Bi-bles translated into Native American languages were offered for sale. An-other group of delegates spent Saturday afternoon watching the Chicago White Sox play at nearby Comiskey Field. As a result of Tax's prior nego-tiations, AICC delegates were admitted free of charge by showing their registration badges. Some also accepted the ball club's offer to "come with your costumes to demonstrate an Indian Dance out on the ball field a few minutes before game time."[39]

After a variety of religious services and a mass powwow on Sunday, AICC delegates voted on the Declaration of Indian Purpose on Monday, June 19. The declaration began with the "American Indian Pledge," a response to the patriotism Indian people had expressed during World War

II and to the climate in which the AICC took place—just two months after the failed Bay of Pigs invasion. The delegates reminded all Americans of their loyalty to the U.S. government:

> We are steadfast, as all other true Americans, in our absolute faith in the wisdom and justice of our American system of Government. We join with all other loyal citizens of our beloved country in offering our lives, our property, and our sacred honor in the defense of this country and of its institutions. We denounce in emphatic terms the efforts of the promoters of any alien form of government to plant upon our shores or within any of our institutions the dubious ideology or way of life which inflicts slavery, trial and punishment without the sanction of a jury, denies free speech, abhors free choice of religious worship, or through force and fear threatens the peace and safety of mankind. At this critical hour of human history the American Indians arise as one in pledging to the President of the United States and to our fellow citizens our fervent assurance that upon these principles we and our children shall forever stand.

The declaration then asked that steps be taken to ensure that "the Indian people will grow and develop as members of a free society." These included reform of the relocation program and improvements in Indian education, health, and housing. At the most basic and general level, though, the declaration demanded Indians' right to be Indians. "We, the Indian people," it declared, "must be governed by principles in a democratic manner with a right to choose our way of life." That demand emerged from and contributed to the increasingly pan-Indian spirit of the mid-twentieth century. After spending a week talking and dancing together, the AICC delegates steadfastly reaffirmed the right and responsibility to preserve their "precious heritage" against the threat of "being absorbed by the American society."[40]

The delegates approved the declaration on Monday, June 19, and the next day the conference officially closed. Acting for all the AICC delegates, Chicago resident Nathan Bird, a Winnebago, presented Sol Tax with an enormous peace pipe he had carved to resemble the one that had adorned the AICC's publications. Lurie called it one of many "spontaneous expressions of pleasure at the progress of the Conference."[41]

The AICC had one remaining task—to officially present President Kennedy with the Declaration of Indian Purpose. Despite Tax's best efforts, Kennedy did not attend the conference—due to other commitments, he asserted. As the months passed after the AICC, Tax continued to work with Kennedy's representatives, Secretary of the Interior Stewart Udall and Commissioner of Indian Affairs Philleo Nash, to arrange a formal ceremony in Washington. When the initial effort to hold the ceremony immediately after the conference failed, Tax made plans to meet with Kennedy in June of 1962 to mark the one-year anniversary of the AICC. When that date also was canceled, Tax became frustrated and wrote his friend Sen. Paul Douglas, "Many are waiting for the White House invitation. The Indians have long since chosen their representatives. When I spoke to Philleo Nash the last time, he said that the administration is aware of the importance of this commitment, and would arrange the presentation soon. Months pass. Please do not think that this is forgotten; and it could be politically damaging for Udall and Kennedy to show so obviously that they do not keep simple promises." Finally, on August 15, 1962, thirty-five delegates from the AICC—including Robert Burnette and three Winnebagos from Utica, Illinois—came to the White House to present Kennedy with the Declaration of Indian Purpose. In officially receiving the document, the president emphasized "how interested all of us are in the conference which was held in Chicago."[42]

---

Throughout the 1960s the pan-Indian movement that owed so much to urban Indian communities such as Chicago's continued its powerful position among Native Americans. Yet despite its prominence, the movement was also fragile and fractured in some ways, both within Chicago and nationwide.

Anonymous questionnaires returned by delegates to the AICC revealed that tension, as people described hope as well as concern about pan-Indianism. Urban Indians who had attended the conference generally were more committed to pan-Indianism than were delegates from reservation communities. As a result, they were more excited about the event. When asked why he had attended the AICC, one relocatee replied, "In the hopes that the Indians would all agree as a race rather than tribes. Also that this conference would be 100 percent the voice of the Indian." Another relocatee wrote in large, bold letters, "Because I am an Indian." Some urban Indians had other tribespeople's interests at heart but also believed that their situations were different and might require different strategies. Among them was a forthright individual who stated he had come "in the interest of *all* Indian problems, but mainly urban Indians."[43]

The questionnaires completed by tribal delegates and others from federally recognized tribes revealed much more suspicion of urban and non-recognized Indians. One delegate who had not approved of the tone of the conference from the moment the keynote address began wrote, "So far all the meetings I have attended have been about relocatee, self-relocatee, and non-reservation Indians. I have not heard a thing about *Reser-*

*vation Indians.*" Three other tribal delegates indicated that they, too, worried that other groups of Indians whose identity they did not fully support might deprive them of rights and benefits. When asked why they had attended the conference, one said, "[To] defend the rights of my tribe." Another wrote, "For the welfare of my people on our reservation." A third responded, "Hope in some way serving my people." That attitude would become more popular within the National Congress of American Indians during the 1960s as new leaders came to view the established organization as representing a reservation constituency.[44]

Yet even some reservation residents acknowledged the importance of the pan-Indian spirit and agreed with the urban resident who said he had attended the AICC simply because he was an Indian. One such delegate referred to "his people" as "the American Indians." Another wrote, "I think it the opportune time, the 'Indians' in unity, *to act and determine policy concerning them.*" A third stressed the common situation facing all Indians and said he came "to learn about other tribes and learn their problems compared to ours and to see if we can solve our problems together." Finally, one delegate who epitomized the hopes of pan-Indianism stated that he had come to the conference "in hopes that a common bond other than our Indian blood can be a bond of perpetual peace, harmony and unity of purpose."[45]

The attempt at American Indian unity by members of various tribes—however precarious—would remain one of the legacies of the Chicago American Indian Conference and Chicago's American Indian community during the middle of the twentieth century. It would also have momentous effects in years to come.

## Notes

1. Janusz Mucha, "From Prairie to the City: Transformation of Chicago's American Indian Community," *Urban Anthropology* 12 (Fall 1983): 353.

2. Joan Dorothy Laxson, "Aspects of Acculturation among American Indians: Emphasis on Contemporary Pan-Indianism," Ph.D. diss., University of California, Berkeley, 1972, 149; Alfonso Ortiz, "Summary of Conference," in *Urban Indians: Proceedings of the Third Annual Conference on Problems and Issues Concerning American Indians Today* (Chicago: Newberry Library, 1981), 183.

3. Kathleen Neils Conzen et al., "The Invention of Ethnicity: A Perspective from the U.S.A.," *Journal of American Ethnic History* 12 (Fall 1992): 4–5 (first quotation); George J. Sánchez, *Becoming Mexican American: Ethnicity, Culture, and Identity in Chicano Los Angeles, 1900–1945* (New York: Oxford University Press, 1993), 11–12 (second quotation). See also

Russell A. Kazal, "Revisiting Assimilation: The Rise, Fall, and Reappraisal of a Concept in American Ethnic History," *American Historical Review* 100 (Apr. 1995): 437–71; and Joane Nagel, "Constructing Ethnicity: Creating and Recreating Ethnic Identity and Culture," *Social Problems* 41 (Feb. 1994): 152–76.

4. Wade B. Arends, Jr., "A Socio-Cultural Study of the Relocated American Indians in Chicago," M.A. thesis, University of Chicago, 1958, 49–50 (first and third quotations); "Research Design, Ministry to American Indians in Chicago," n.d., Church Federation of Greater Chicago [hereafter CFGC] Files, 29–4, Manuscript Collection, Chicago Historical Society [hereafter MC, CHS] (second quotation).

5. Joan Ablon, "Relocated American Indians in the San Francisco Bay Area: Social Interactions and Indian Identity," *Human Organization* 23 (Winter 1964): 296–304 (first quotation); Robert K. Thomas, "Pan-Indianism," in *The American Indian Today*, ed. Stuart Levine and Nancy O. Lurie (Deland: Everett, 1968), 77 (second quotation); Elaine M. Neils, *Reservation to City: Indian Migration and Federal Relocation* (Chicago: University of Chicago Department of Geography Research Paper no. 131, 1971), 128 (third quotation); Joane Nagel and C. Matthew Snipp, "Ethnic Reorganization: American Indian Social, Economic, Political, and Cultural Strategies For Survival," *Ethnic and Racial Studies* 16 (Apr. 1993): 212 (fourth and fifth quotations); Tom Holm, *Strong Hearts, Wounded Souls: The Native American Veterans of the Vietnam War* (Austin: University of Texas Press, 1996), 109.

See also Howard M. Bahr, "An End to Invisibility," in *Native Americans Today: Sociological Perspectives*, ed. Howard M. Bahr, Bruce A. Chadwick, and Robert C. Day (New York: Harper and Row, 1972), 409–10; James Hirabayashi, William Willard, and Luis Kemnitzer, "Pan-Indianism in the Urban Setting," in *The Anthropology of Urban Environments: Monograph Series No. 11*, ed. Thomas Weaver and Douglas White (Washington, D.C.: Society for Applied Anthropology, 1972), 77; Laxson, "Aspects of Acculturation among American Indians, 166; Shirley Hill Witt, "Nationalistic Trends among American Indians," in *The American Indian Today*, ed. Stuart Levine and Nancy O. Lurie (Deland: Everett, 1968), 53–75; Margaret Sanford, "Pan-Indianism, Acculturation, and the American Ideal," *Plains Anthropologist* 16 (Aug. 1971): 222–27; Stephen E. Cornell, *The Return of the Native: American Indian Political Resurgence* (New York: Oxford University Press, 1988); Joane Nagel, *American Indian Ethnic Renewal: Red Power and the Resurgence of Identity and Culture* (New York: Oxford University Press, 1996); and Roger W. Lotchin, "The Impending Western Urban Past: An Essay on the Twentieth-Century West," in *Researching Western History: Topics in the Twentieth Century*, ed. Gerald D. Nash and Richard W. Etulain (Albuquerque: University of New Mexico Press, 1997), 62.

Some scholars—such as anthropologist William K. Powers in *War Dance: Plains Indian Musical Performance* (Tucson: University of Arizona Press, 1990)—have disputed the concept of pan-Indianism or pan-tribalism. Powers, though, does so by reacting against a definition of pan-Indianism that sees it obliterating all tribal distinctives. Few who have written about pan-Indianism would share Powers's definition and have acknowledged the coexistence of continuing tribalism with important changes across tribal lines.

6. Interviews with Floria Forica (Chippewa), Chicago, 25 Mar. 1983, Phyllis Fastwolf (Sioux-Oneida), Chicago, 8 May 1983, Ada Powers (Sioux), Chicago, 19 Apr. 1984, and Cornelia Penn (Sioux), Chicago, 3 Sept. 1983, Chicago American Indian Oral History Pilot Project, nos. 004, 006, 012, and 017, Newberry Library, Chicago, and Native American Educational Services College, Chicago.

7. John Kennardh White, "The American Indian in Chicago: The Hidden People," M.A. thesis, University of Chicago, 1970, 9.

8. Interview with Benjamin Bearskin, in Studs Terkel, *Division Street America* (New York: Pantheon Books, 1967), 105.

9. Author interview with Edward E. Goodvoice (Sioux), Chicago, 14 June 1995.

10. Author interview with Lucille Spencer (Choctaw), Chicago, 22 June 1995. See also "A Little Newspaper about Indians," Jan. 1954 and Mar. 1954, Robert Rietz Collection, Community Archives, Native American Education Services College, Chicago [hereafter CA, NAES].

11. Peter Iverson, "Building toward Self-Determination: Plains and Southwestern Indians in the 1940s and 1950s," *Western Historical Quarterly* 16 (Apr. 1985): 169.

12. Author interview with Lucille Spencer (Choctaw), Chicago, 22 June 1995. On the fish-ins, see Nancy O. Lurie, *Wisconsin Indians*, 2d ed. (Madison: State Historical Society of Wisconsin, 1980), 59–60.

13. Author interview with Ronald Bowan, Sr. (Menominee), Chicago, 15 June 1995; Gloria A. Young, "Powwow Power: Perspectives on Historic and Contemporary Intertribalism," Ph.D. diss., Indiana University, 1981, 331; *Indian Voices* (July 1965): 1; James Hirabayashi, William Willard, and Luis Kemnitzer, "Pan-Indianism in the Urban Setting," in *The Anthropology of Urban Environments: Monograph Series No. 11*, ed. Thomas Weaver and Douglas White (Washington, D.C.: Society for Applied Anthropology, 1972), 82.

14. Author interview with Diane Maney (Winnebago), Chicago, 20 June 1995.

15. Nathan Bird to National Service Corps, 18 Dec. 1962, American Indian Center, no. 0400, sec. 13, Urban Records Collection, Community Archives, Native American Educational Services College, Chicago [hereafter URC, CA, NAES].

16. Paula Verdet, "Summary of Research on Indians in St. Louis and Chicago" (1961), 11 pp. unpublished ms., box 16, American Indian Chicago Conference Records, National Anthropological Archives, Smithsonian Institution, Washington, D.C. [hereafter AICC Records, NAA, SI]; Young, "Powwow Power," 77; Ann Metcalf, "Navajo Women in the City: Lessons from a Quarter Century of Relocation," *American Indian Quarterly* 6 (Spring–Summer 1982): 71–89. See also Melissa L. Meyer, "'We Can Not Get a Living as We Used To': Dispossession and the White Earth Anishinaabeg, 1889–1920," *American Historical Review* 96 (Apr. 1991): 368–94.

17. Hirabayashi, Willard, and Kemnitzer, "Pan-Indianism in the Urban Setting," 84; Young, "Powwow Power," 378–79, 390.

18. George D. Scott, John Kennardh White, and Estelle Fuchs, *Indians and Their Education in Chicago* (Washington, D.C.: Educational Resources Information Center, 1969), 25; Hirabayashi, Willard, and Kemnitzer, "Pan-Indianism in the Urban Setting," 84.

19. Donald L. Fixico, *The Urban Indian Experience in America* (Albuquerque: University of New Mexico Press, 2000), 54; "Indian's Life in 'Promised Land' Here," *Chicago Daily News*, 24 Jan. 1963, Clip File: "Ethnic Groups–Chicago-Indians, American," Harold Washington Public Library, Chicago.

20. "Family Services Semi-Annual Report, Jan.–June 1964," American Indian Center, no. 0400, sec. 3, URC, CA, NAES (first quotation); Dorothy VandeMark to John Collier, 21 Dec. 1959, reel 58, Collier Papers, Archives and Manuscripts Division, Sterling Memorial Library, Yale University, New Haven, Conn. (second quotation); Anthony M. Garcia, "'Home' Is Not a House: Urban Relocation among American Indians," Ph.D. diss., University of California at Berkeley, 1988, 62–63.

21. Program Report, Mar. 1966, AIC, no. 0400, sec. 3, URC, CA, NAES; Mucha, "From Prairie to the City," 360; author interview with Susan K. Power (Sioux), Chicago, 19 June 1995.

22. Author interview with Nancy O. Lurie, Milwaukee, 21 June 1995.

23. First presented as an address at the University of Michigan on 20 Mar. 1958, Sol Tax's paper, "Action Anthropology," was printed in the Mar.–Sept. 1959 issue of *Journal of Social Research* (Bihar, Ranchi, India) and reprinted in *Current Anthropology* 16 (Dec. 1975): 514–17 (quotation). On the influence of Tax and action anthropology, see Leonard D. Borman, "Action Anthropology and the Self-Help Mutual-Aid Movement," in *Currents in Anthropology: Essays in Honor of Sol Tax*, ed. Robert Hinshaw (New York: Mouton Publishers, 1979), 487–511.

24. Nancy O. Lurie, "The Voice of the American Indian: Report on the American Indian Chicago Conference," *Current Anthropology* 2 (Dec. 1961): 481; Sol Tax diary entry, 14 Nov. 1960, box 1, AICC Records, NAA, SI.

25. Sol Tax diary entry, 14 Nov. 1960, box 1, AICC Records, NAA, SI; Carl Tjerandsen, *Education for Citizenship: A Foundation's Experience* (Santa Cruz: Emil Schwarzhaupt Foundation, 1980), 687–88.

26. Sol Tax diary entry, 15 Nov. 1960, box 1, AICC Records, NAA, SI; Thomas W. Cowger, *The National Congress of American Indians: The Founding Years* (Lincoln: University of Nebraska Press, 1999), 133–40.

27. Sol Tax diary entries, 22 Nov. and 20 Dec. 1960, box 1, AICC Records, NAA, SI.

28. Lurie, "The Voice of the American Indian," 482; author interview with Nancy O. Lurie, Milwaukee, 21 June 1995.

29. Lurie, "The Voice of the American Indian," 483.

30. Sol Tax to Margaret Perry, 11 Apr. 1961, box 1, AICC Records, NAA, SI; "Chicago Meeting, February 1961," box 1, AICC Records, NAA, SI; "American Indian Center Statement to the AICC," 23 May 1961, folder 1, box 50,

Stanley D. Lyman Papers, Mariott Library, University of Utah, Salt Lake City [hereafter Lyman Papers, ML, UU] (first quotation); AICC suggestion sheet by S. William Salway, Jr., box 2, AICC Records, NAA, SI (second quotation).

31. "AICC Progress Report No. 4," 26 Apr. 1961, box 1, AICC Records, NAA, SI; "AICC Progress Report No. 5," 26 May 1961, box 1, AICC Records, NAA, SI; "AICC Progress Report No. 6," 7 June 1961, box 1, AICC Records, NAA, SI.

32. "Notes on AICC Meeting of Indian Advisory Committee, Chicago," 10–14 Feb. 1961, Sol Tax Papers, Community Archives, Native American Education Services College, Chicago [hereafter Tax Papers, CA, NAES].

33. "AICC Committee Meeting—Drafting, Steering, Regional Organizers," 26–30 Apr. 1961, box 1, AICC Records, NAA, SI (quotations); Laurence M. Hauptman and Jack Campisi, "The Voice of Eastern Indians: The American Indian Chicago Conference of 1961 and the Movement for Federal Recognition," *Proceedings of the American Philosophical Society* 132 (Dec. 1988): 316–29.

34. AICC suggestion sheets by Marvin Pine and Robert Burnette, box 2, AICC Records, NAA, SI.

35. Lurie, "The Voice of the American Indian," 490; author interview with Nancy O. Lurie, Milwaukee, 21 June 1995; proclamation by Mayor Richard J. Daley, 22 May 1961, box 6, AICC Records, NAA, SI.

36. AICC Keynote Address, folder 1, box 50, Lyman Papers, ML, UU.

37. Author interview with Nancy O. Lurie, Milwaukee, 21 June 1995; Lurie, "The Voice of the American Indian," 498. On powwows, see also Mark Mattern, "The Powwow as a Public Arena for Negotiating Unity and Diversity in American Indian Life," *American Indian Culture and Research Journal* 20 (Fall 1996): 183–201.

38. Shirley Hill Witt, "Nationalistic Trends among American Indians," in *The American Indian Today*, ed. Stuart Levine and Nancy O. Lurie (Deland: Everett, 1968), 65; Joan Ablon, "The American Indian Chicago Conference," *Journal of American Indian Education* 1 (Jan. 1962): 22.

39. "Final Report of the Coordinator," 26 May 1961, Tax Papers, CA, NAES.

40. "Declaration of Indian Purpose," AICC, no. 3150, URC, CA, NAES.

41. Lurie, "The Voice of the American Indian," 498; author interview with Nancy O. Lurie, Milwaukee, 21 June 1995.

42. Sol Tax to Sen. Paul Douglas, 16 Mar. 1962, box 6, AICC Records, NAA, SI; "Delegates to the White House," box 6, AICC Records, NAA, SI; *Indian Voices* (Dec. 1962): 1.

43. AICC questionnaires no. 169 and unnumbered, box 4, AICC Records, NAA, SI.

44. AICC questionnaires nos. 176, 188, 191, and 195, box 4, AICC Records, NAA, SI; Cowger, *The National Congress of American Indians*, 142–43.

45. AICC questionnaires nos. 181, 196, 211, and 215, box 4, AICC Records, NAA, SI.

# 7  New Indians in a New America

After the delegates at the 1961 American Indian Chicago Conference returned to their homes on reservations or in urban communities, after makeshift powwow venues set up in the University of Chicago fieldhouse were dismantled, and after hardworking organizers finally succeeded in officially presenting President John F. Kennedy with the Declaration of Purpose, few concrete reminders of the conference remained. There was, however, a new publication, *Indian Voices*, that emerged from the meeting in Chicago. First published in April 1963, it was a "newsletter for all the opinions and voices of all American Indians" said its editor Robert K. Thomas, a Cherokee. Although fairly unimpressive at first glance and with a relatively small subscription base and irregular publication schedule, it contributed to an important and enduring trend. The monthly publication frequently revealed the emerging Indian identity that had led to the AICC and was strengthened by it. In October 1963 Thomas reported that "he had been asked by many of our readers to print some of the famous speeches by Indian chiefs." Happy to oblige and meet readers' needs for a shared public memory and cultural affirmation, he began by printing a speech given in 1906 by the Creek leader Crazy Snake. Thomas, an intellectual and academic who also acknowledged appreciation for the simple pleasures of powwows and conversations with friends over coffee, resisted giving a textual or historical analysis of the speech. Instead, he commented, "I guess there isn't any more to say after such a touching portrayal of Indian wisdom except to feel proud!"[1]

Pride seemed to run deep among Indians during the 1960s and 1970s. New Indians emerged, not only from the AICC but also from experiences that made them think of themselves and their identities in new and different ways. Although the experiences cut across generational and geographical lines they especially occurred among young people and among Indians in cities. Resistance to complete assimilation and an identity marked out against the nation and mainstream America, trends rooted in urban Indian communities since the 1950s, continued in the 1960s and continued to rely on pan-tribal patterns.

Strikingly, Indians in urban communities and elsewhere by the late 1960s were part of a new social environment and were not alone in their thinking about group identity. Others, particularly African Americans, were also reacting against assimilation and allegiances directed primarily toward the nation. African Americans, Mexican Americans, and various European ethnic groups moved, in the words of historians David R. Colburn and George E. Pozzetta, "beyond issues of individual rights and equality" and in the process began to challenge the basis of the American political system, which was rooted in individual rights and equal opportunity.[2] Indians, although not as numerous and visible as other racial and ethnic groups and thus less noticed by American historians, led the way in this influential inward turn toward what would be called "identity politics" by drawing on pan-tribal patterns already in place. In so doing they became harbingers of a new America as they worked to make a better life for their people.

---

Young Indian people served notice that their voices would be heard even during the waning days of the Chicago conference in 1961. A number of college-educated Indians, including Clyde Warrior (Ponca), Melvin Thom (Paiute), Herbert Blatchford (Navajo), and Shirley Hill Witt (Mohawk), had been asked by members of the National Congress of American Indians (NCAI) to work as pages at the event. They watched the deliberations, carried messages from subcommittee to subcommittee, and in the end were unimpressed. They believed the conference would have almost no effect on their lives and communities. The young Indians viewed NCAI members as too cautious and satisfied with the status quo, both because of their ages and because of their many connections to the Bureau of Indian Affairs (BIA). Thom labeled the NCAI members at the conference as "Uncle Tomahawks," a name that would endure long after the conference ended. Thom described these establishment figures as "fumbling around, passing resolutions, and putting headdresses on people" but in the end as being unwilling to take what he considered a "strong stand" for their people.[3]

A division was becoming evident. All sides involved—old and young, establishment and outsider—agreed that Indians must represent themselves, and all spoke the language of "Indian self-determination," talk that had been popular in much of Indian Country for many years. What divided the parties was the question of which Indians in particular would represent their people.

Impromptu meetings in hallways and dormitories at the University of Chicago built on earlier activity by Indian students in the Southwest and soon helped produce a new Indian organization. In August 1961, just weeks after the AICC ended, a number of young Indian people dissatisfied with existing leadership and polices met in Gallup, New Mexico, where they established the National Indian Youth Council (NIYC). The group, initially led by Melvin Thom, would chart a more aggressive course of action in Indian politics. Members focused from the beginning on self-determination and Indian sovereignty. They sought a world in which Indians would make choices for themselves. They also advocated direct action, believing that in doing so they were returning to "the traditional way that Indians got things done." "It was," they said, "time to raise some hell," but "it had to be done in the Indian way."[4]

As he led the group in its early years Thom continued to promote a common Indian identity. He challenged the notion of a homogeneous national American identity, claiming that Indians "were the only people that the American melting pot cannot melt." Attempts to assimilate Indians in the past, he argued, had met with disaster. Only hunger, alienation, and loss had resulted from the "civilization" programs brought to Indians in the nineteenth century. Throughout the 1960s the NIYC looked for opportunities to publicize its stance on Indian identity and politics, such as at a U.S. Army ceremony in 1965 to present medals to the few men still living who had fought in the Indian wars of the late nineteenth century. Thom argued that, at the very least, Indian warriors should also receive medals in honor of their attempts to protect their homeland.[5]

Other activist groups of young people who had split with their elders and established organizations also emerged during the 1960s. In 1966 young blacks in the civil rights movement were chanting "black power!" to express dissatisfaction with the approach taken by the National Association for the Advancement of Colored People (NAACP) and black church leaders such as Martin Luther King, Jr. Focused on the goals of integration and political equality, the leaders, most of them middle-aged, pursued a strategy of nonviolent resistance in order to reveal the injustices of Jim Crow and bring about its demise. The Student Non-Violent Coordinating Committee (SNCC), including its early leader Stokely Carmichael, balked at that approach in the mid-1960s and broke away from the political coalition forged decades earlier with liberals and the Democratic Party. Carmichael eventually concluded that nonviolent resistance did not work in a society too callused to be moved by even the most blatant cases of racial injustice. In his essay "What We Want" (1966) Carmichael argued that blacks who followed in the footsteps of Gandhi and King "demonstrated from a position of weakness." By the end of the 1960s, part of the black power movement would become even more focused on violence as both real threat and political theater. "Take up the gun" became a slogan intended to frighten white America while informing the integrationist, nonviolent wing of the movement that its day had passed. Carmichael also opposed the goal of integration because he said it implied the need for assistance from whites and thus indicated weakness on the part of blacks. In the end, he concluded, "Integration is a subterfuge for the maintenance of white supremacy."[6]

Black power, as practiced by Carmichael and others, combined self-love and an embrace of black culture with a sharp oppositional stance against whites and white power structures. In that way it was both positively and negatively defined. In explaining what he and other like-minded black activists wanted, Carmichael wrote that they "don't want to 'get whitey'; they just want to get him off their backs." He, "a person oppressed because of my blackness," had common cause with other blacks for that reason. Although he held out the possibility for some cooperation with whites, the initial step was to work with blacks and only then perhaps to address themselves to "friends from the oppressing group." Furthermore, Carmichael and the nationalist figures who followed him expanded their list of potential allies, adding all nonwhite people in the United States and worldwide. They, too, Carmichael suggested, suffered a similar "colonizing treatment" by the United States, which he described as "an octopus of exploitation" whose tentacles stretched near and far. The "colored masses," whatever their particular background and identity, he maintained, were in the same powerless relationship against the "powerful few" and should unite when appropriate.

Among the "colored masses" of whom Carmichael spoke were American Indians, and among the prominent young American Indian leaders coming of age during the 1960s was Clyde Warrior. Born into a traditionalist Ponca family in 1939, Warrior pursued what was both a family and tribal tradition by becoming an accomplished fancy-dancer at powwows near his Oklahoma home and across the nation. Warrior had developed an award-winning technique but was remarkably modest and never boasted. Rather, he eagerly and respectfully approached members of different tribes, always asking about other traditions. He never missed an opportunity to immerse himself in tribal and pan-tribal culture. Paul Chatt Smith and Robert Allen Warrior describe him, even as a young man, as an "always-growing walking library of intertribal songs and stories."[7] Although he never lived in urban Indian communities where pan-Indianism had deep roots, Clyde Warrior was an important contributor to this movement culturally as he followed the powwow circuit. Also deeply committed to Indian politics, Warrior assumed the presidency of the NIYC at the age of twenty-eight. In February 1967 he testified before a presidential commission, testimony that within a few weeks would be printed in *Indian Voices* and then in many other publications and collections. The title would come from a climactic line in the testimony: "We Are Not Free."

In some ways, Clyde Warrior's testimony sounded like an Indian variation of Stokely Carmichael's essay, published just a few months before. Warrior, too, expressed frustration with white "friends" who spoke the "not-so-subtle racist vocabulary of the modern middle class." He suggested that he had often experienced paternalistic demonstrations of sympathy and offers to help "deprived" Indians.[8] Also like Carmichael, Warrior criticized assumptions of assimilation, especially those that advocated the complete disappearance of diverse groups into American society.

Yet the differences between Carmichael's and Warrior's landmark statements were as striking as their parallels, and they illustrate the particular nature of Indian nationalism and how it had been shaped by a developing pan-Indian identity. Warrior notably said little about white injustice or oppression. His version of identity politics and Indian activism appeared not to rely on an outside foe for inertia. It was more deeply rooted in his people and their traditions—both tribal and pan-tribal. Clyde Warrior's political activism in a sense sprang more from his love of fancy dancing and powwows than from his opposition to white America. It was a natural, inherent part of who he was.

Perhaps the most striking characteristic of "We Are Not Free," given at a time when countless political activists and organizations were running off position papers and manifestos, was the way in which it avoided the prideful and shrill tone of so many other contemporary statements. Warrior was under no illusion that he stood alone, surrounded by unenlightened masses who needed to get out of the way so a newer, more progressive chapter in Indian history could unfold. Rather, he effectively located his vision within a larger and longer story that crossed generations. Speaking before both Indians and non-Indians, his first words were:

"Most members of the National Indian Youth Council can remember when we were children and spent many hours at the feet of our grandfathers listening to stories of the time when the Indians were a great people, when we were free, when we were rich, when we lived the good life."

At a time when many Americans were focused on the nation's prosperity and how it might be extended to even more people, Warrior notably spoke not of economics but of family. He implicitly dismissed the material improvement that was reaching even some Indian people and instead drew a connection for Indians in the audience between the good life and following the ways of their grandfathers. He then looked forward to the generation of Indian children who were growing up and even to those not yet born. Raising new generations of Indians, he argued, was among the most important work that his people faced. He warned, however, that challenges faced them in this work. As in the late nineteenth century when boarding schools attempted to remove every last vestige of tribal identity and culture from Indian children, so, too, in the late twentieth century some wanted to raise Indian children and shape their cultural values in place of Indian parents. Educators and politicians, Warrior stated, believed that Indians were "not capable of handling our own affairs and even raising our own children." Schools, he said, were teaching Indian children that they were not worthy, attacking their identity and their culture.

Even before his testimony, Warrior worked toward building Indian unity around ideas of self-determination, nationalism, and Indian pride. For years he had longed for a world in which Indians indeed would be free. By 1964 he and other members of the NIYC had been hearing for some time about the challenges posed to tribes in the Pacific Northwest that tried to exercise their treaty rights to fish in the places and manner of their ancestors. Non-Indian fishermen sabotaged Indian fishing nets and harassed and even beat Indian fishermen while conservation officers and local officials looked the other way. The incidents seemed to provide an opportunity to defend unique Indian treaty rights as well as demonstrate Indian pride and unity. In March 1964 several Indians from many different tribal backgrounds arrived in Washington state to exercise fishing rights in the first of many protest demonstrations that the media dubbed "fish-ins."[9]

Warrior's beliefs and his role in positioning NIYC during the fish-ins and after shed light on the nature of Indian activism in the 1960s and 1970s. Increasingly, that activism appeared to be not a dramatic break with the past but rooted in old values and traditions. Young Indians opposed assimilation in large part because of a conscious and strengthened identity often rooted in pan-tribalism. Increased pride in Indian identity, which NIYC and Clyde Warrior did so much to bolster, would continue to spread. By the early 1970s even one-time opponents of NIYC, such as the leaders of NCAI, had begun focusing intently on Indian pride. Leon Cook (Chippewa), president of the National Congress in 1971, spoke that year of government-sponsored assimilation policies as attempts to force Indians into the "polluted mainstream of American life."[10] Although comments similar to Cook's are often used rightly to demonstrate that assimilation was not held in high regard in some Indian circles during the 1970s, that observation can also be extended back to Clyde Warrior and like-minded young people in the early 1960s, who in turn recognized and cherished their ties with generations past and drew on them in crafting political stances.

Despite the growing strength of a pan-Indian identity in the 1960s, relatively few in America as a whole noted this development. Given the Indians' small numbers and the prominence of blacks, that is no surprise. Despite the emergence and growth of Indian-style identity politics, Native people realized that the sit-ins of the civil rights movement rather than the fish-ins of the NIYC grabbed most of the headlines in the United States during the 1960s. Indeed, some Indians saw the civil rights movement, the ideas driving it, and the legislation it produced as more than competition for public attention. What was at stake was the very model America would use in majority-minority relations.

The NCAI in particular reacted nervously as the Civil Rights Act of 1964 made its way through the legislative process. This measure, giving every individual American, regardless of race, equal access to buses, restaurants, hotels, and all public spaces, did not produce much enthusiasm among Indians. Integration and individual rights had never resonated with them as they did with blacks and others. Indeed, some, like John Cummings of the Crow tribe, were concerned that the act might threaten tribal autonomy and the tribes' right of self-government. A year after the legislation passed, the leadership of NCAI announced that "the great issue for Indians was not individual rights as such but the continuation of tribe and the preservation of the people." As the group's leaders sensed civil rights drowning out their own unique perspective on political and legal issues, they warned darkly, "Unless Indians make their position crystal clear and LEAD the thinking of this country, they will undoubtedly be swept away in the ongoing movement."[11]

Even the Indian Civil Rights Act of 1968, which enjoyed Indian support because of its effort to weaken states' jurisdiction that began in 1953 with the advent of termination, drew criticism for giving individuals the power to challenge tribal authority.[12] The values of individual freedom and equality under the law, so much the focus of the rest of America in the 1960s, had a potential to dismantle political and social bonds—and even an entire way of life for many Indians.

Many Indians in the 1960s decided that blacks' goals were completely different from their own.[13] A member of NCAI characterized blacks as "pleading for equality" while arguing that Indians should continue to fight for their "superior rights as guaranteed . . . by treaties and agreements." In 1964, when much of the nation was changing its view on civil rights and the government's responsibilities toward blacks, Melvin Thom went so far as to state that Indians' specific rights, which emerged from their government-to-government relationship with Washington, D.C., were "more sacred than civil rights." As an urban Indian resident contrasted blacks' and Indians' relations with whites, Indians "always had the reverse problems from the Negroes: too much government attention instead of too little." Black politics and Indian politics clearly were moving in different directions in the 1960s.[14]

Some Indians who resisted the civil rights movement and its tactics presented Indians as the model minority group—calm, stable, and law-abiding. One Indian man who lived in Los Angeles in the late 1960s contrasted blacks with Indians, whom, he said, were too "proud" to "tear up schools and universities" and instead used diplomacy "given to us by our heritage." W. W. Keeler, chief of the Cherokee Nation and vice president of Phillips Petroleum in Oklahoma, told NCAI members in 1966 in the same manner that Indians should not imitate blacks, especially civil rights demonstrators, whom he characterized as trying to influence Indians "from the outside to preach hate."[15]

Most NCAI members, many of them middle-aged, seemed to agree with Keeler and in general lacked enthusiasm for the civil rights movement and for the political developments led by young blacks during the 1960s. Yet even many young Indian people who were attracted to some aspects of the civil rights movement remained cautious in their allegiance to it because of their traditions, cultures, and outlooks. NIYC was the sort of young, activist Indian group that Stokely Carmichael likely had in mind when he wrote of a coming alliance among the "colored masses." Indeed, the relationship between NIYC and NCAI was sometimes compared to that between SNCC and the NAACP, in part because young Indians and blacks both increasingly rejected their elders' advice and found direct action appealing. Yet even though members of NIYC disagreed with their NCAI counterparts on many issues, they often reacted to race relations in the same manner. Young Indians, too, resisted wholeheartedly following the dominant model of social and racial reform of the mid-1960s that focused on integration and equal rights under the law. At a 1964 meeting, NIYC members did vote to support the Civil Rights Act of 1964, in part because they believed that Indians, as a "small minority group," suffered "the same injustices as other minorities." Yet they also emphasized that the "Indian cause is something different" and that much of their energy would be directed toward gaining public support "to let Indians exist as a people."[16] Members of the NIYC and many other Indians would not willingly allow their cause or their evolving identity to be lumped in with that of black Americans or any other minority group.

Beyond publicizing their causes on the national stage, Indians during the 1960s also demonstrated changing and strengthening notions of identity in their increased efforts to influence their children's lives against outside challenges. Even those unfamiliar with Clyde Warrior's 1967 address were aware of the importance of building bonds across generations and the profound connection between their children's upbringing and the future of their people. That recognition was evident at a July 1968 press conference when five Sioux mothers from the Fort Totten Reservation in North Dakota, supported by officials from the Association on American Indian Affairs (AAIA), charged the child welfare system in North Dakota with misconduct. All five women reported having children unjustly taken from them and placed in non-Indian foster homes. One illustrated her understanding of the issue and its importance in maintaining Indian identity when she stated, "They want to make white people out of the Indians. They're starting with the kids because they couldn't do it to us." The executive director of the AAIA spoke following the women's testimony and maintained that one-quarter of all Sioux children born at Fort Totten were eventually taken to adoptive homes, foster homes, or other non-Indian institutions.[17]

The challenge to Indian families also spread beyond reservations. Another Sioux, Clem Janis, who had moved from the reservation to Los Angeles, charged that in the city, too, local government and social service structures treated Indian families unjustly. Janis reported instances of Indians applying for welfare and being pressured to give up their children. He had helped set up a foundation in Los Angeles that temporarily assisted these parents while they went through hard times, but he still worried about a "racket" that tried to separate children from their families. In San Francisco, another Indian man described the adoption of children out of Indian families and Indian tribes as a process of emasculation. In part because of pressure exercised by Indian parents and families, the AAIA called for federal agencies to investigate child welfare and adoption procedures and also called for more use of Indian foster homes. The process culminated in the Indian Child Welfare Act of 1978, which gave Indian parents the right to withdraw consent to adoption at any time and formally promised to "promote the stability of Indian tribes and families."[18]

Changes in the nation's social and cultural climate by the late 1960s meant that many Indians felt compelled to defend their identity from not only old foes but also new ones. Much had changed since relocation began to swell urban Indian populations. During the early 1950s, government officials encouraged American Indians to become like white Americans through termination and relocation programs. By the late 1960s, however, some white Americans were newly interested in Native American history and culture, giving rise to "Indian chic." There was a new, although no more realistic, concept of the "noble savage" during the 1960s. Some, such as Robert F. Kennedy, were attracted to Indians because they seemed to represent the underdog and the romantic outsider. While on a speaking tour in Oklahoma in 1967 Kennedy stated that he wished he had been born an Indian. He was greeted with overwhelming applause by a primarily white audience.[19]

Young people in the antiwar movement and the counterculture of the late 1960s and early 1970s also gravitated to the image of "the Indian." Some white student protestors considered Indians as they did southern blacks or Vietnamese peasants—symbols of U.S. government oppression—and believed they had solidarity with them. Indians were one of the groups through whom young people tried to live vicariously. An even more demeaning role came by way of the counterculture, which saw Native people as unacknowledged trailblazers for the drug culture. Trying to appropriate something Indian, for example, members of a commune in New Mexico would yell a supposed war cry after smoking a joint. Still others compared hallucinogens and narcotics to "the herbs and cactus and mushroom of the American Indians." Both the LSD that white hippies used to achieve mind-altering experiences and the peyote that members of the Native American Church employed in religious ceremonies, commune members believed, made it "possible to live in peace."[20]

Indians during this time were well aware of attempts by liberals, hippies, and others to appropriate their culture, and they responded to that trend. The experiences of Candace Ryan, a young mixed-blood Sioux who lived in Chicago, illustrate how Indians responded to the era's identity politics. The daughter of a Santee Sioux mother and white father, Ryan was a happy, well-adjusted student at a Chicago public high school during the late 1960s. When another Sioux girl transferred into the school

from South Dakota, she immediately suspected the light-skinned Ryan—
who frequently wore turquoise jewelry—of being among the increasing
numbers of "Indian wannabees" she had encountered since moving to
Chicago. During classes the newcomer would frequently shoot dirty looks
at Ryan, assuming that she was trying to appropriate another people's
culture. Only when the newcomer was informed of Ryan's Indian heritage, and thus her legitimate reason for wearing Indian-style jewelry, was
the matter resolved. After the misperception had been corrected, Ryan
recalls, "She was nice and cordial to me. It made all the difference in the
world."[21] This Sioux girl recently arrived at an urban high school, long-
time Chicagoan Candace Ryan, and many others played a part in an important process for Indians during the 1960s and early 1970s—further
development of a changing Indian identity and its defense against new
challenges.

The political changes of the 1960s also influenced ideas about Indian
identity and contributed to the growth of one type of pan-Indianism.
Among the most significant political change was the Johnson administration's approach to poverty. Sharing widespread confidence that the
power of the nation and the national government could meet any challenge, Lyndon Johnson in January 1964 called for an "unconditional war
on poverty," with "total victory" as the objective. Toward that end, within
a few months he had pushed through the Economic Opportunity Act. The
War on Poverty, fought through the newly formed Office of Equal Opportunity (OEO), attempted to bring new opportunity to the nation's poor and
allow them to reach the limits of their capacities with the help of government programs. Between 1965 and 1970 the OEO received almost $10
billion from the federal government to defeat poverty. To some extent
Johnson was borrowing from his hero Franklin Roosevelt as well as from
earlier liberals, but over time the program took on a structure unlike previous antipoverty programs. Rather than being centrally organized by
officials in Washington, D.C., War on Poverty programs, especially the
influential community action programs (CAPs), would be organized and
run at the local, grass-roots level. "Maximum feasible participation" in
which the poor would plan and operate programs for themselves would
be the mantra of community action.[22]
    Although the problem of urban poverty among blacks was foremost
in the minds of Johnson administration officials, Indians, too, became
involved in the War on Poverty. As the Economic Opportunity Act made
its way through the legislative process, a group that included roughly four

hundred Indians traveled to Washington in May 1964 to participate in a four-day American Indian Capital Conference on Poverty and request that Indians be included in OEO programs being developed.[23] Sen. Hubert H. Humphrey (D-Minn.), who only months later would be steering the Civil Rights Act of 1964 through the Senate and then accepting the Democratic Party nomination to run with Johnson in the 1964 presidential election, gave the keynote speech at the conference and supported the Indians' request. Furthermore, he incorporated Indians and Indian policy into a broad range of ventures to be undertaken by the nation at home and abroad. "Failure in coping with Indian problems," Humphrey announced, "mitigates against our success in any part of the world."[24] Humphrey and those attending the conference were successful, and Indians soon were included in the War on Poverty.

Although not immediately apparent, the principle of maximum feasible participation that guided the CAPs would become an ally for many Indians in the ongoing struggle toward self-determination. With the passage of the Equal Opportunity Act, several government agencies created separate sections, "Indian Desks," which had responsibilities specifically toward Indians. In the process, policies affecting Indians were discussed and pursued, bypassing the BIA, which was accustomed to controlling interagency programs. The OEO, the Department of Labor (DOL), the Department of Housing and Urban Development (HUD), and the Department of Health, Education, and Welfare (HEW) would all take part in this experiment in more specifically tailoring policy for Indian people.[25]

By 1965 CAPs had been funded in more than thirty reservation communities. The largest tribe, the Navajo, not surprisingly received the largest OEO grant; $920,000 was to be used to establish preschool classes, a job training center, and recreation programs. The grant also allowed for a feasibility study to establish a community college on the reservation, and three years later Navajo Community College was founded. In addition, the OEO in 1965 awarded the White Earth Chippewa Reservation $176,000, the Leech Lake Chippewa Reservation $157,000, and the Turtle Mountain, Pine Ridge, Nez Perce, Nett Lake, and Mille Lacs reservations each between $75,000 and $100,000. To provide technical assistance in implementing and operating the CAPs, the OEO also awarded grants in 1965 to three universities near large reservations: Arizona State University, the University of Utah, and the University of South Dakota. Three more universities in Indian Country were later added.[26] By 1968 total funding for the OEO had dropped, but funding for Indian projects had increased. In that year, sixty-three CAPs served 129 reservations across the country, and just over $22 million in OEO money was sent to reservations. Almost half went to the Navajo reservation, with both Pine Ridge and Rosebud receiving almost $1 million each.[27] War on Poverty programs, in addition to addressing economic and educational problems in Indian communities, also provided valuable training and experience for many Indians. In the late 1960s, anthropologist Alfonso Ortiz (San Juan Pueblo) has reported, many Navajos returned home from Los Angeles and San Francisco because they had opportunities to use skills developed in the city to administer CAPs on the reservation. New and newly expanded programs addressing areas such as mental health and alcoholism also provided opportunities for Indians to gain expertise and help their people. Women in particular were able to set up and run community programs. Fourteen were on the fifteen-person staff that established a Head Start program at a Phoenix church, for example.[28]

The bulk of the OEO money earmarked for Indian communities went to reservations, especially early in the War on Poverty. The Office of Housing and Urban Development, despite its name, built housing projects on the Rosebud Sioux, Pine Ridge Sioux, White Mountain Apache, and Blackfeet reservations, miles from urban areas. Model Cities, another War on Poverty program, also provided money to rural reservation communities.[29]

As time went on, however, more OEO money was sent to urban Indian communities, even as the OEO as a whole enjoyed less political support in Washington circles and was eventually shut down in 1974. In 1968, $300,000 was sent to the Intertribal Council in Los Angeles, and in 1970 the Model Urban Indian Center Project was established, jointly funded by the OEO and the Departments of Health Education and Welfare, Labor, and Housing and Urban Development. In attempting to alleviate poverty and social problems through a "network of vigorous Indian centers through which Indians can improve service delivery and develop their self-help potential," the project remained true to the original idea of community action.[30]

The Model Urban Indian Center Project selected Los Angeles, Minneapolis, Fairbanks, and Gallup to house the first four Indian centers it funded. They received a total of $730,000 to develop programs in employment, youth counseling, housing, recreation, and economic development. Additional centers were later added in Omaha, Denver, Phoenix, and Lincoln. Even those projects, however, did not convince all urban Indians that the OEO was giving them fair and equitable treatment. There were many calls in the late 1960s and early 1970s for more OEO money, programs, and technical assistance for urban Indians. An administrator at the Los Angeles Indian Center during a 1968 forum compared the situation of urban Indians to the more favorably treated reservation Indians, saying, "We need the same type of technical assistance and training that the Indian Desk of OEO provides."[31]

As the War on Poverty continued, more disputes arose about how OEO money should be spent. Early on, officials seemed to believe that putting power and money in the hands of "the poor" would solve most problems, but in time they experienced difficulty in deciding exactly who would represent the poor. The question could and did produce a great deal of contention and conflict.[32] Because of such debates, the War on Poverty contributed further to the development of a pan-tribal identity for urban Indians. Many began to think of themselves as being set against other racial groups in cities as well as the Indians who lived on reservations. Both groups had become potential competitors for government money. Urban Indians, who saw many of the concrete manifestations of the War on Poverty close at hand in the wide range of social programs starting up in their cities, believed that other urban groups, especially blacks, received a disproportionate share of federal money. That helped produce greater identification with other Indians and strengthened Indian identity over and against blacks and other minority groups. As an Indian man in Los Angeles complained at a forum in 1968, "The black and the brown voices of California are much louder, much more militant and they get a much greater share of the dollar." Likewise, Charles Deegan from Minneapolis in 1969 called poverty programs "a farce as far as the Indians are concerned" because they were "mostly black-controlled and black-oriented." And Ernie Stevens from Los Angeles in 1969 expressed his view on race relations and the prospect of alliances among minority groups: "You know, it's a sad thing. It's bad enough when you are getting it from white people, but when the Mexicans and Blacks crunch you, that's too much. And they can have their damned coalitions, as far as I'm concerned."[33]

Among Indians themselves, the flow of money from the OEO led to new arguments. On reservations that petitioned successfully for OEO money, tribal councils began to lose some of their autonomy. More and more they became administrators of federal programs, even to the point of creating special stationary for tribal CAPs. The War on Poverty caused social and political restructuring among Indians. Old organizations, including religious ones, gave way to secularized bureaucracies. At Rosebud, the Rosebud Christian Social Action Group was replaced by the OEO-created and funded Rosebud Economic Opportunity Commission. Tribes became more dependent on the federal government as they were further incorporated into the national and mainstream social welfare system. Furthermore, some on reservations that received OEO money believed it, and the power that accompanied it, was not shared fairly. Rifts and cliques emerged on several reservations during the 1960s. A member of the Committee on Poverty won the chairmanship of the Rosebud Sioux in 1967, for example, but his defeated opponent afterward charged that Sioux OEO workers had played an inappropriate role in the campaign and rigged it for their candidate.[34]

The War on Poverty further divided urban and reservation Indians, increasing mutual suspicion between the two groups. Some residing on reservations grew accustomed to OEO funds, and when they perceived them decreasing they feared that more federal funds were being directed to urban residents. That increased the resentment of reservation Indians for urban Indians. In his presidential address at the 1966 NCAI meeting, Wendell Chino, an Apache, bemoaned the fact that rural America—which he equated with Indian Country—was "rapidly becoming a forgotten country."[35] In fact, urban Indians received relatively little War on Poverty money during the late 1960s, although reservation-dwellers perceived them to be diverting funds that could go to them or, more generally, as representing cities that were doing so.

Periodic disputes between urban and reservation Indians extended beyond how War on Poverty money should be dispersed. The BIA continued to be a focus of attention and debate for Indian people as it responded to an increasingly diverse Native population by the 1960s. All Indians had mixed feelings about the bureau—frustration at its paternalism and the control it exercised but also a measure of reassurance that it was the only agency that at least occasionally looked out for the particular interests of Indians. Urban Indians' opinions about the BIA soon changed, shaped specifically by urban life. Their reactions would drive much of the activism and militancy that ended the 1960s and began the 1970s.

Since the early 1950s, many urban Indians had resented what they saw as the BIA's negligence and inflexibility. As the prime example of this, they pointed to the relocation program. Indians in the 1960s continued to complain that bureau employees failed to provide complete information about urban life, did not work hard enough to find satisfactory jobs and housing, and stuck too close to the letter of the law when relocatees asked for more financial aid or other types of help. Further frustration occurred when non-Indians frequently told them to go to the BIA for help, not knowing the history of relocation and that the bureau intended the program to end federal responsibilities for urbanized Indians.

Urban Indians also recognized and sometimes tried to change the BIA's overwhelming reservation orientation. From its inception, the bureau had organized itself around the reservation system, and that remained unchanged even when almost half of all Indian people no longer lived on reservations. When official relocation began in 1952, the BIA hoped that responsibility for urbanized Indians would disappear. In many cases, tribal governments supported that notion as they worried about competition from urban Indians for federal dollars. Because of continuing Indian urbanization, though, questions surfaced periodically during the 1960s and 1970s about the proper place of the BIA. Urban and reservation Indians responded to such questions very differently, further demonstrating the developing distinct identity of urban Indians. When there was talk in early 1970 about the possibility of transferring the BIA to the Department of Health Education and Welfare from the Department of the Interior, NCAI leader Bruce Wilkie expressed strong opposition, in part because of the connection between Indian reservations and the conservation of natural resources. "The functional set-up and purposes of HEW are unsuited to the management of Indian reservations," he argued. Wilkie seemed to recognize that such a change might serve urban Indians better but would likely put those on reservations at a disadvantage.[36]

Such complaints helped produce a new agency whose goal it was to better coordinate federal programs for Indians. On March 6, 1968, President Johnson addressed Congress on the subject of American Indians. He wished to end "the old debate about 'termination' of Indian programs" and promised to stress self-determination. He soon followed by creating the National Council on Indian Opportunity (NCIO). Because the NCIO was chaired by Vice President Humphrey (and, following him, Vice Presidents Spiro Agnew and Gerald Ford), it gave Indians direct access to the executive branch. Humphrey believed that many greatly valued this change and recalled that those with whom he worked on the council viewed it as "a real communication vehicle." The council began with seven government representatives (the vice president and the secretaries of agriculture, commerce, HUD, interior, labor, and the OEO) and six Indian representatives. Later during the Nixon administration, the number of Indian representatives expanded to eight. Much like the CAPs granted to Indian communities, the NCIO held out the promise of effecting change while minimizing or entirely bypassing the BIA. The NCIO would provide opportunities for self-determination on the part of both urban and reservation Indians and set higher standards in that regard for the future, especially by 1970 when President Richard Nixon was promising Indians greater control over federal programs and money.[37]

Initially, the NCIO addressed six areas of concern to Indian people: jobs and unemployment, local schools and hospitals near reservations, industrial development on reservations, Indian involvement in program planning, housing, and the problems of urban Indians. The last area was the responsibility of NCIO member LaDonna Harris, a Comanche, administrator with various War on Poverty programs, and wife of Sen. Fred R. Harris (D-Okla.). To learn about urban Indians and the problems they faced, the NCIO's Committee on Urban Indians chaired by Harris scheduled public forums in late 1968 and early 1969 in five cities that had a significant Indian population: Los Angeles, Dallas, Minneapolis, San Francisco, and Phoenix. The forums in part allowed urban Indians publicly to express complaints about the BIA and further strengthened the voice of urban Indians. Virginia Edwards spoke for many in Dallas and in urban Indian communities across the nation when she said, "I would like to thank you for letting an Indian have his say-so for once."[38]

The Committee on Urban Indians gave Indians in Los Angeles their first opportunity to comment and voice concerns on December 16 and 17, 1968. Los Angeles, which along with Chicago had received some of the first participants in the relocation program in 1952, had a widely dispersed Indian community. One witness at the public forum told the committee that Indians in the area were scattered over three counties: Los Angeles, Orange, and San Bernardino. The region had three Indian centers in 1968, but all were fairly small. Like other cities, Los Angeles's Indian population was from a variety of tribal backgrounds, although the Five Southern Tribes and tribes from the Southwest were strongly represented. A survey taken in 1966 found the Los Angeles region's Indian population to be 14 percent Navajo, 12 percent Sioux, 6 percent Cherokee, and 6 percent Creek. Pueblos, Choctaws, Seminoles, Cheyennes, Chippewas, Apaches, and Kiowas each numbered between 3 and 5 percent of the total. Although the community was diverse tribally and in other ways as well, it tended to be moderate to conservative in political matters. Militants never composed a significant portion of Los Angles's Indian community.[39]

One group that contributed to this orientation was the Urban Indian Development Association (UIDA), described by Director A. David Lester as an "association of Indian businessmen whose goal is the development of a viable Indian business community." The agency tried to help Indians through financial counseling, offering small loans, and management training. The UIDA enjoyed the support of the NCIO and the executive branch during the Nixon administration as its leaders cultivated a friendly relationship with Spiro Agnew, sharing his distaste for radical groups. The UIDA, they assured the vice president, agreed that "violent demonstrations, accusations, and bitterness are poor substitutes for self-help, professionalism, and meaningful dialog."[40]

Half a continent away, the urban Indian community in Cleveland was developing in a different direction than Los Angeles's. Cleveland's Indian population was quite small (only 391 in 1960, according to the census) and compact, a result of the BIA's decision to house most relocatees on the city's near-east side in a predominantly black neighborhood. Cleveland also had no formal Indian center until 1969, when Russell Means (Sioux) and Sarge Old Horn (Crow) together started one. Beginning in April 1969 and for the first four and a half years of its existence, the Cleveland American Indian Center was located in the basement of St. John's Episcopal Church, known locally for involvement in liberal politics and social reform. Soon, the OEO funded a grant for $18,000, allowing for a full-time director. Means left another OEO job elsewhere in Cleveland and became the first to lead the center, drawing a salary of $10,000 paid by the grant. During its first years, the center in Cleveland established cultural programs, employment programs, a burial program, a medical clinic, and programs that helped people apply for welfare. Means cut his sideburns, grew out his shoulder-length hair, exchanged his hipster clothes for a fringed leather jacket and became an identifiably militant Indian. In the process, he influenced the Cleveland American Indian Center and part of its community to adopt a radical orientation. [41]

Despite these differences in the makeup of Los Angeles's and Cleveland's Indian communities, they were strikingly similar in important ways. Parents in both cities revealed a sense of Indian pride and grew frustrated at the way their children's education in urban public schools undermined it. This was communicated at many of the NCIO's urban forums, including one in Los Angeles where a witness complained that "the majority of the textbooks contain almost nothing about the character of Indian culture prior to the coming of the white man" and that "some of the materials used in schools do much damage to the Indian child's sense of identity and personal worth." In Cleveland, too, the Indian Center recognized a need for cultural education programs to counteract what it considered the inaccurate and damaging information taught in schools. Another group, the American Indian Policy Review Commission, also conducted hearings in several cities during this time and found much discontent toward schools. Many teachers were characterized as "insensitive, poorly informed about Indian heritage and culture, and . . . basically incompetent to provide such services." In part because of such complaints, the federal government established the National Indian Education Advisory Committee in 1967, and Indian teachers started the National Indian Education Association in 1969. [42]

Indian communities in Los Angeles, Cleveland, and many other cities also often were alike in their frustration with the BIA, and they shared a demand for self-determination. The NCIO hearings heartened many who attended them, in part because witnesses saw the new agency as having the potential to play a very different role than the BIA. Suanne Wright called for the NCIO to help work toward the nationalism she and others were building in Los Angeles. She also explained what she meant by that term: "When we talk about restoring Indian culture, Indian dances, this is nationalism. This means self-determination of a people." The UIDA in Los Angeles focused on the implications of promised self-determination for the delivery of social services to urban Indians. After the NCIO hearings again seemed to promise greater Indian control, the UIDA proposed to contract with the BIA to more effectively manage relocation services in Los Angeles and find housing and jobs for relocatees. The UIDA was concerned, though, that the local BIA office and its director D. L. Maloney were trying to torpedo the deal for fear of losing power and money. In Cleveland, where Russell Means cut a very different figure than the Indian businessmen leading the UIDA in Los Angeles, self-determination also took root. Although Means's goals differed from those of the UIDA, he, too, demanded that Indians help Indians and that the BIA be phased out. "We wanted the BIA to leave town" he explained later. "We were providing almost all the services that it was supposed to be doing, and many that it never did."[43]

---

By the 1960s, then, Indians in general and urban Indians in particular had developed and defended a particularly Indian form of identity politics, strengthening Indian pride and demands for self-determination and further developing pan-Indian identity through cultural developments and struggles in the political sphere. In the late 1960s and early 1970s these elements contributed to the emergence of well-publicized incidents of Indian activism. At first glance, episodes such as the occupation of Alcatraz Island in 1969, the establishment of the American Indian Movement (AIM) in 1968, the occupation of the BIA headquarters in Washington, D.C., in 1972, and the occupation of Wounded Knee, South Dakota, in 1973 seem to fit comfortably in any list of examples of "1960s radicalism" that appears in general surveys and documentaries on the period. Considered more carefully, however, each incident reveals roots in the experiences of Indian people during the 1950s and early 1960s. The type of cultural activism that Clyde Warrior and many others fostered had led the way to political activism.

Furthermore, urbanization lay behind much Indian activism and militancy, both where it might be expected (in San Francisco and Minneapolis) and where it might not (at Wounded Knee). Urban life was a necessary condition for much Indian activism of the 1960s and early 1970s. Many of the causes that drove it—from the policies of BIA officials in urban relocation offices, to the actions of city police officers, to conditions in city housing projects, to the education offered in city schools—sprang from an urban environment. The way in which activist Indians conducted protests often relied on tactics that Indian people in the past had either not used at all or had not been able to use effectively because of their distance from mainstream centers of power and communication. After watching civil rights and antiwar protests either firsthand or through the media, though, some Indians learned how they might attract attention to their causes and bring about change. The use of the media, interest group lobbying, and "grievance politics"—what might be called "urban tactics"—was important in Indian activism.[44]

San Francisco, site of one of the most important Indian protests of the late 1960s, was home to a group of somewhere between ten and fifteen thousand Indians at the beginning of the decade, some of whom had come on relocation and some who had come on their own. Among the tribes represented in the largest numbers were the Navajos, Sioux, and Chippewas. Unlike the Chippewas in Chicago, most of whom came from reservations in Wisconsin and Minnesota, in San Francisco most Chippewas were from North Dakota's Turtle Mountain Reservation.

The city also saw the type of pan-Indianism, with some limits and constraints, that was developing in Chicago and other cities. Joan Ablon, an anthropologist who did participant-observation research among Bay Area Indians in 1961 and 1962, has noted that several organizations and institutions brought many Indians together.[45] Among them were the Intertribal Friendship House in Oakland, the San Francisco American Indian Center, the Four Winds Club in Oakland, the Oakland American Indian Baptist Church, the San Jose Dance Club, and the American Indian Council of the Bay Area. Church groups, apartment buildings, workplaces, and bars also connected Indian people.

Despite the evident possibilities for Indian socializing in San Francisco, Ablon has estimated that only about one-sixth of adult Indians participated in organizational activities, and she describes the Indian community as "tenuous." The Navajos, as in Chicago, generally kept to themselves and limited their pan-Indian activity. Chippewas from Turtle Mountain also spent most of their socializing time together as a group at baseball games, New Year's Eve parties, and other events. Many Turtle Mountain Chippewa in San Francisco were of French Canadian descent, which in-

fluenced their leisure and recreational choices. They seemed more interested in continuing traditional French Canadian family visiting rituals
than learning new Sioux or Winnebago dances at powwows.

Even with different tribal and cultural factors limiting unity, Indians in the San Francisco Bay area shared many trends taking root across
the country in other Indian communities. In her interactions with Indians during the early 1960s, Ablon repeatedly witnessed great frustration
with the BIA, the way in which it advertised and operated the relocation
program, and its sharp differentiation between Indians in cities and those
on reservations. She also identified a strong sense of identity that might
be described as pan-tribalism (although Ablon does not use that term).
Several parents emphasized to her that their children had been "raised
as Indians." Although that meant different things to different parents, it
suggested pride in a pan-Indian identity. Ablon also pointed out for non-
Indian readers that Indian pride could sometimes operate in surprising
ways. For those expecting radical caricatures, she noted meeting with
many who combined a "fierce pride in Indian identity" with the ability
"to form close personal ties with individual white friends."

By the late 1960s Indian opposition to the BIA had deepened, as had
Indians' pride in their identity. At the April 1969 NCIO public forum in
San Francisco, several witnesses criticized the BIA. One described the
bureau as a "colonial institution controlled by the white establishment"
and said that "people in the BIA don't see themselves as advocates for
Indians. They're bureaucrats who know what's best for Indians." National political leaders and Indians themselves had raised the bar for self-
determination and made BIA paternalism all the more unbearable. Some
were also frustrated with the BIA's lack of power, because the War on
Poverty had shown them federal agencies with far more clout. One witness captured both sentiments. The acronym *BIA*, he said, stood for the
"Bureau of Indian Annihilation" as well as the "Bureau of Inefficient Administration."[46]

In San Francisco as elsewhere, schools were one of the battlegrounds
that either strengthened or weakened Indian pride. Parents of youngsters
and college-age students alike desired educations for their children that
used Indian history and culture and that served the particular needs of
Indians. At the NCIO public forum, one parent stated that Indian children needed "to be taught that it's cool to be Indian," and another touted the recently formed California Indian Education Association, which
was an all-Indian, privately funded organization that had emerged out of
dissatisfaction with public schools. In higher education, schools such as
San Francisco State University were establishing Native American Stud-

ies programs. As a student in the program defended it before the NCIO, "We don't want to be whitewashed, to become . . . puppets and utter the words of somebody else."[47]

First briefly in 1964 and then for a longer period from 1969 through 1971, Alcatraz Island would be a symbol of self-determination and Indian pride for Native Americans in the San Francisco Bay area. On March 8, 1964, just a few months after the prison closed, a small group of Sioux, including Allen Cottier and Walter Means, landed on Alcatraz Island and staked their claim to the land, claiming that the Fort Laramie Treaty of 1868 gave them right to the now-surplus federal land. In addition to seizing hold of Sioux history to make their claim, they also drew upon the history of California tribes and illustrated the effects of pan-tribalism in their offer to the federal government. The group said they would buy the land for the "going federal set price for California lands claimed by the Indians back in the gold rush days, 47 cents an acre." The protestors left the same day and never had their day in court to argue their legal right to the land, yet they recognized that their action would attract attention that other Indians might capitalize upon in the future. The Sioux were already influenced by their urban experiences and recognized the power of the press. Russell Means, twenty-six when his father went ashore at Alcatraz in 1964, remembered that after returning to the mainland his father and the others went directly to the San Francisco American Indian Center "to wait for early editions of the next day's papers."[48]

By 1969 San Francisco's Indian population was growing, often by attracting young people like Richard Oakes, a Mohawk. He had spent much of his young life traveling in the Northeast, but in the late 1960s he went west and enrolled in the Native American Studies program at San Francisco State University. At the same time that Oakes and other Indian college students were being inspired by their classes, they also learned more about San Francisco's population and were impressed by Indians' poverty relative to other groups. When the San Francisco Indian Center burned in October 1969, frustrated Indians believed they had nowhere to gather. The idea of re-occupying Alcatraz—which had increasingly been the focus of conversations in classrooms and at bars and Indian Center meetings—was beginning to take shape. Oakes and many others began to link the island that loomed in the San Francisco Bay with the ideal of self-determination, but the goal, as before, was interpreted in different ways. During the summer of 1969, both Oakes and Adam Nordwall, a Chippewa businessman in San Francisco, worked separately on establishing an Indian center on Alcatraz Island. The men viewed each other with the suspicion that had marked many relationships be-

tween youths and establishment Indian groups. Nordwall saw Oakes as
an irresponsible young radical, and Oakes viewed Nordwall as too conservative and connected to the city's business class to be able to bring
about real change. But during a social occasion Oakes heard Nordwall
discussing his plans to move on Alcatraz, and he agreed to join in.[49]

A small group landed at Alcatraz on November 9, 1969, and were
quickly removed by federal marshals, but on November 20, seventy-eight
Indians landed again. This time they stayed for the long term. As the
number of reporters covering the Alcatraz story swelled, the occupiers
cleverly reversed some of the island's signs with terminology that had
shaped Indian life. A sign that once warned visitors "you are on federal
land" now read "you are on Indian land." Satirizing the rhetoric of Indian reformers and officials, the group pledged to protect and help whites
on Alcatraz by establishing a "Bureau of Caucasian Affairs" and by changing their culture. The group promised, "We will offer them [whites] our
religion, our education, our life-ways, in order to help them achieve our
level of civilization and thus raise them and all their white brothers up
from their savage and unhappy state." The occupiers hoped to pursue
Indian self-determination further through educational, spiritual, and
ecological centers they proposed establishing on the island.[50]

A powerful pan-Indian spirit hung over Alcatraz during the early days
and weeks of the occupation. The group that had begun calling itself Indians of All Tribes soon issued a statement: "We want all Indian people
to join with us. . . . We are issuing this call in an attempt to unify all our
Indian Brothers behind a common cause. . . . We realize . . . that we are
not getting anywhere fast by working alone as individual tribes. If we can
gather together as brothers and come to a common agreement, we feel
that we can be much more effective, doing things for ourselves, instead
of having someone else doing it, telling us what is good for us."[51]

This unity was particularly apparent on Thanksgiving Day 1969,
when the Indians of All Tribes held an open house for visitors from the
Bay Area and all over the country. Some of the fervor began to wane in
time as students wished to return to school, tensions and violence increased on the island, and the media started paying less attention to the
occupying group. Finally, on June 11, 1971, federal marshals forced the
last fifteen Indians off Alcatraz. Still, the earlier powerful and inspiring
cries of "We hold this rock!" would not be forgotten.

One place they were heard was Minneapolis. Like Chicago, Minneapolis had attracted many Chippewas and Sioux, particularly Chippewas
from the White Earth Reservation, during the early and mid-twentieth
century. Most settled in South Minneapolis and established various po-

litical and social organizations. Some were tribally oriented, and some, such as the Ojibway-Dakota Research Society established in 1944, were pan-tribal in nature. Beginning during the war years and continuing throughout the 1950s, Indians in Minneapolis felt the effects of a housing supply that failed to keep up with demand. By the late 1960s Minneapolis's Indian population had reached approximately ten thousand, a larger group than lived on any Indian reservation in the state.[52]

Over the years Indians felt crowded in their South Minneapolis neighborhood centered along East Franklin Avenue, and they developed the type of Indian identity politics shared with others elsewhere. As community members watched city police hang around Indian bars, waiting to arrest Indian drunks, many became frustrated and angry. They believed that Indians were the objects of police mistreatment and furthermore that Indian self-determination was being compromised. On August 23, 1968, they responded by forming the "Indian patrol." On that night and on many nights following, the patrollers (which included Indians as well as non-Indians) walked up and down East Franklin Avenue, monitoring police activity and helping Indians. When they saw individuals who were recognizably drunk, they tried to get them a ride home in a cab or in a patrol member's car. The patrol operated periodically and had varying numbers of participants over the next two years, depending on weather, community interest, and other factors. What energized the group and got it out on the streets in force were incidents where, they believed, the police had overstepped their bounds and infringed on Indians' right to govern and regulate their own community. After the police responded to a call about a fight between two Indian boys at a Minneapolis powwow, for example, patrol activity increased markedly. The Indian patrol intended to show that the city's Indians could look after and help their own.[53]

A new organization soon grew out of the Indian patrol. From a meeting in the summer of 1968 attended by about 250 Minneapolis Indians who belonged to different organizations came the American Indian Movement (AIM). Led in its early days by Chippewas Dennis Banks, Clyde Bellecourt, and George Mitchell, AIM from the beginning focused on specifically urban concerns. It continued to publicize police harassment against Indians. It criticized poor public housing and pressured the city to improve it. And it tried to foster Indian pride in an increasingly public, aggressive fashion. As AIM grew in popularity, particularly among Indian youths, late-model cars cruising South Minneapolis began to display bumper stickers that boasted "Custer Had It Coming," "Better Red Than Dead," and "Kemo Sabe Means Honky." An unofficial AIM uniform developed that centered around long hair and a jean jacket. Clothing and appearance in general soon became a way to establish personal and political identity for young Indians in Minneapolis and in cities such as Cleveland and Milwaukee as the organization spread nationwide. Russell Means, who would help lead AIM into the early 1970s, was initially attracted to the group because of Banks's and Bellecourt's aura of Indian identity and pride, as symbolized by their aggressiveness with white authorities and their long hair and Indian clothing.

AIM especially focused on schools as it attempted to strengthen Indian pride. When the NCIO came to Minneapolis in 1969 and conducted a public forum there for a government report, Clyde Bellecourt accused local schools of teaching the Indian child "to know himself as a savage" and blamed them for Indian dropouts. AIM attracted attention and emboldened local Indians by protesting against demeaning treatment in public schools. In November 1969, for example, when Bellecourt heard that a local school was rehearsing a play about the first Thanksgiving and that the Indian characters had been given lines that amounted to no more than grunts, AIM protested and the play was cancelled. AIM established the Heart of the Earth Survival School in Minneapolis in 1971, and in 1972 it founded the Little Red School House Survival School in St. Paul so Indian children might have an alternative to local public schools. The Indian-run schools were viewed proudly by like-minded Indians in urban communities across the nation. The facilities hosted many groups of visitors interested in what was happening in Minneapolis and curious about introducing similar schools elsewhere.[54]

AIM also demonstrated Indian power during this time by protesting injustices against Indians nationwide. One of the most infamous involved the killing of Raymond Yellow Thunder in February 1972 in Gordon, Nebraska, near the Pine Ridge Reservation. Gordon was notorious among the Sioux at Pine Ridge because previous attacks on Indians there had gone largely unnoticed by local authorities. Most Sioux who visited Gordon tried to keep their heads down and escape notice. The murder of Raymond Yellow Thunder produced a powerful response, however, sparked by AIM. After being informed of his death and his humiliating final hours during which he was forced to dance for his white tormentors, hundreds of AIM members descended on Gordon, where they joined hundreds of emboldened Pine Ridge residents. The unprecedented scene sent a wave of panic through the town as white merchants closed down their stores and most residents remained huddled in their homes while Indians marched in the streets demanding justice. The protest produced federal intervention, and eventually five local men were charged with manslaughter and false imprisonment. A new day for Indians in rural Nebraska and elsewhere seemed to be dawning, in part due to AIM's show of power.[55]

Some AIM protests were more symbolic in nature and directed not at a specific contemporary injustice but at the prevailing patterns of Indian-white relations. AIM was behind short-term protests at national icons such as Ellis Island, Plymouth Rock, and Mount Rushmore during the early 1970s that garnered ever-increasing media attention. Cleveland's AIM chapter, housed in the city's Indian Center run by Russell Means, saw an opportunity for such protest in the summer of 1971. As part of the 175th anniversary pageant celebrating the founding of the city by Moses Cleaveland in 1796, city officials planned a reenactment of Cleaveland's original trip down the Cuyahoga River and his landing on the river's east shore. As the date of the pageant approached, Means and other Indian Center members expressed indignation at being left out and were asked if they would participate as the Indians who had greeted Cleaveland. They consented but departed from the script on the day of the reenactment. Some produced protest signs claiming that the land on which the city was built belonged to Indians, and others kept the man impersonating Cleaveland from landing and delivering his lines. The pageant finally continued when the event's organizer promised that three AIM members could be the first to speak. Afterward, Means was pleased to learn that the protest had been covered by CBS News and the *Wall Street Journal* as well as by local media.[56]

In dealing with churches, AIM applied the lessons it had learned in public relations and interest group politics. Both at the local level in Cleveland and at the national level, liberal Protestant church groups were becoming increasingly interested in social and political issues and were intent on demonstrating allegiance with groups that had been mistreated. As a result, some became benefactors of AIM and other new Indian organizations. Means accompanied Banks and Bellecourt to the annual National Council of Churches meeting in Detroit in 1970. During a general meeting, Bellecourt seized the floor and demanded that all donations for Indian organizations be controlled by Indian-run boards and organizations, cutting out denominational mission boards. Staying on the offensive in the same way that had originally inspired Means, Bellecourt went on to charge the audience with hypocrisy and, because of their role in the loss of Indian lands in generations past, with violating the commandment against stealing. Despite his accusations, the National Council of Churches paid all its critics' expenses during the conference, including shoes and a new suit for Means and rooms at Detroit's exclusive Ponchartrain Hotel for Means, Banks, and Bellecourt. The group even picked up the room-service charges associated with an impromptu party given by the three AIM leaders. In years to come AIM would make frequent demands of Protestant denominations and para-church organizations, often with great success. AIM members became fixtures on the religious boards that controlled charitable donations for Indians. Means would remark on churches' liberalness with money in the early 1970s. They acted, he said, "like the Christians they claimed to be."[57]

By the early 1970s, then, AIM had become successful at exposing injustices in Minneapolis and elsewhere through new tactics and building Indian pride in general. When it began to appear that AIM might eclipse NCAI in importance and clout, the more venerable and reservation-based Indian organization responded defensively. It increasingly viewed AIM and urban Indians as one and the same and believed that both were trying to take money that would otherwise be available to the older group. Although that was an exaggeration, many young people in particular saw urban Indian identity as being bound up in AIM. That was the experience of Russell Means, who was transformed by his first meeting with Banks and Bellecourt. He concluded that AIM represented the best interests of Indians, and therefore, when he took a job with AIM, he decided that he was working "full-time on behalf of the Indian community." Membership in AIM was "a way to be a *real* Indian."[58]

There were costs as well as benefits in the way urban Indian identity was bound up with AIM and AIM-style activism. AIM sometimes followed the example set by some in the black power movement and cashed in on white guilt through "grievance politics." Black power leader H. Rap Brown argued during the late 1960s that stealing or looting white-owned property was acceptable because whites had stolen it from oppressed people. "I figured it belonged to me anyway," he explained. Likewise, Russell Means describes AIM members occasionally stealing clothes, food, and money from white storekeepers, a practice he calls "AIM shopping." Describing it later, he wrote, "We did that with clear consciences: we were repossessing, in another form, that which had been taken from us."[59]

As AIM became emboldened by political victories it also occasionally practiced a theatrical or symbolic type of violence. One such example punctuated a national conference on urban Indians sponsored by the NCIO in December 1970 as a follow-up to the public forums it had held in urban Indian centers. It was attended by 150 urban Indian delegates, among them several AIM members. Held on the grounds of the plush Airlie House in Warrenton, Virginia, the meeting got off to a rocky start. On its first night, about a dozen of the more militant Indian delegates got into an argument with a group of white businessmen staying at the facility and then set up a drum, antagonizing other white guests, before raiding the Airlie House kitchen for food and alcohol. The next night, real trouble developed as the small group of Indians, most of them drunk, took over the entire center. They vandalized much of the Airlie House's grounds, removing or destroying every one of twenty-five large U.S. flags. They also briefly took three members of Airlie House staff as hostages. The NCIO, as sponsor of the meeting, eventually paid $30,000 to Airlie House for the damages sustained, and the Indian delegates and the government publicly downplayed the vandalism and violence. Dennis Banks even praised the Airlie House conference as a "very successful meeting and a real beginning of a dialogue between the Federal Government and the urban Indian people."[60]

As AIM grew more powerful it began to imply that it was the true—perhaps the only true—representative of Indian people. That led to attempted takeovers of groups that got in its way. Dismissing groups that opposed or competed with AIM for money and media attention as "window dressing," "sell-outs," and "apples" (red on the outside but white on the inside), AIM leaders often tried either to remove or hijack them. In the process, AIM violated its claim that it only acted when called upon by the people. As a result of AIM's strong-arm tactics, its reputation began to change among some Indians. Mark Monroe, a Sioux community leader in Alliance, Nebraska, was initially enthusiastic after hearing about AIM's reputation for bringing Indians together to lobby more effectively. He became disenchanted, however, after AIM members came to Alliance to take over the American Indian Council he had established and made successful. When Monroe resisted, a group of AIM members first tried to alienate the group from its supporters on the city council and then physically attacked Monroe and shot up his house to intimidate him and his family.[61]

AIM sometimes exhibited smug confidence in its presumed preeminence as Indian representative and in the illegitimacy of any person or organization that differed from the group in any way. An example of this occurred at a meeting attended by both AIM members and the revered Pueblo anthropologist and spokesperson Alfonso Ortiz. During Ortiz's speech, AIM members paid little attention, in part because Ortiz failed a "test" that had become critical to some in AIM. In wearing a three-piece suit, he did not look Indian. The body language of AIM members who sat through Ortiz's speech communicated that they thought his words and the man himself were irrelevant. After the speech, AIM members took control of the meeting and redirected it toward their style of Indian politics. At the end of Ortiz's speech, Means remembered, AIM members "started to beat a drum and sing a traditional melody." If AIM at its best gave Indian children hope for the future and a passionate interest in their history and culture, this was AIM at its worst. It did not matter to AIM leaders that Ortiz knew more about Indian culture and traditions than anyone else in the room. Totally convinced that they were the *"real* Indians," AIM members felt that they had nothing to learn from Ortiz.[62]

In the early 1970s, AIM leaders and other young urban activists increasingly were making connections and finding common cause with traditionalists on reservations. Both groups—young and old—took issue with the existing leadership that enjoyed power on many reservations due to BIA connections and willingness to work within the system. Both groups, furthermore, shared an increasingly passionate anger at the BIA and resented its actions in cities and on reservations. Each group had something the other desired. The elders and traditionalists seemed to hold the key to unlocking what it meant to be an Indian, and AIM members in the early 1970s eagerly desired their guidance for the Sun Dance and other rituals. AIM members, for their part, had something elders and traditionalists desired—an ability honed in their urban environment to organize and carry out protest movements that could catch the nation's eye.

In 1972 AIM leaders met with Sioux spiritual leaders at the Rosebud Reservation to discuss the next move for the new and tentative alliance. Former Rosebud chair Robert Burnette proposed a large march from all parts of the country, converging on Washington, to be called the "Trail of Broken Treaties." As AIM leaders took more control in organizing the "trail," however, they increased the demands that the group would make of the government, including repeal of the 1871 ban on future treaties, a sizable increase in the Indian land base, and cancellation of most leases held by non-Indians. All were issues that dated back to the nineteenth century, and government officials considered them closed.

After arriving in Washington on November 1, 1972, the march participants stayed in a cramped and unsanitary church basement due to a lack of advance planning. Only as an afterthought did the group the next day decide to seize the BIA building, which it renamed the "Native American Embassy," signifying the group's demand for Indian sovereignty. The group, frustrated by constant trips back and forth across Washington trying to find lodging and by zealous federal guards who tried to push them outside the building, became violent. They blocked all doors to the building and occupied it for six days, and during that time offices were vandalized and files seized. Although some Indians saw the occupation as an impressive show of power that forced the nation to notice Indians, many decried the violence, particularly the loss of important documents on Indian history and government policy. In the end, the occupiers agreed to leave, and the OEO gave the group $66,650 to help Indians return home.[63] Another dramatic example of the developing alliance between young urban militants and traditional elders and chiefs occurred a few months later and proved the most effective use of the media to date by Indians. On the Pine Ridge Sioux reservation in South Dakota, both AIM members and traditionalists had become sworn enemies of tribal chair Dick Wilson and formed the Oglala Sioux Civil Rights Organization as a means of opposing him. After Wilson and his supporters harassed AIM members at Pine Ridge and the BIA police arrested Russell Means, the new alliance took action. On February 28, 1973, Dennis Banks and Russell Means took control of the trading post in the small village of Wounded Knee, which they called the Independent Oglala Nation, arguing that it was a sovereign nation operating under the Fort Laramie Treaty of 1868. Armed federal marshals soon arrived to seal off the town. The occupiers, many of them veterans who drew on experiences gained during the Vietnam War, held off the marshals and the FBI for weeks, demanding that the Senate Foreign Relations Committee review all Indian treaties the federal government had broken and then that the Independent Oglala Nation be admitted into the United Nations. None of these demands were met, however, and when the last occupier finally left in May 1973 the government firmly refused to revisit treaty-making.[64]

---

Whether feelings of pride caused Indians to join new organizations, take children into their homes, resist demeaning symbols, participate in direct-action protests, or become involved in a range of other less-visible activities, this development of the 1960s and early 1970s was frequently rooted in urbanization and its by-products. The slowly developing pantribalism that had been germinating in urban Indian communities like Chicago's for years now led to increased activism and militancy. In the process it reshaped Indian society as a whole and influenced the ways in which many Native people thought of their relationship to other groups of Americans and to the nation itself.

## Notes

1. *Indian Voices* (Apr. 1963): 1, and (Oct. 1963): 1.
2. David R. Colburn and George E. Pozzetta, "Race, Ethnicity, and the Evolution of Political Legitimacy," in *The Sixties: From Memory to History*,

ed. David Farber (Chapel Hill: University of North Carolina Press, 1994), 121. David Steigerwald, too, has noted the significance of Indians' ethnic identity within the context of the ethnic nationalism of the late 1960s. See Steigerwald, *The Sixties and the End of Modern America* (New York: St. Martin's Press, 1995), 229–31.

3. Stan Steiner, *The New Indians* (New York: Harper and Row, 1968), 36.

4. Steiner, *The New Indians*, 40.

5. "Indian Leadership Accent on Youth Program," 11–13 June 1964, Ritzenthaler Field Notes, box 1, folder 23, Milwaukee Public Museum [hereafter MPM]; *Amerindian* (July–Aug. 1965): 3.

6. Stokely Carmichael, "What We Want," *New York Review of Books*, 22 Sept. 1966, 5–7. Subsequent quotations are also from this essay. The view of the black power movement expressed here is informed by David Burner, *Making Peace with the Sixties* (Princeton: Princeton University Press, 1996), 49–83.

7. Those interested in twentieth-century American Indian history are indebted to Paul Chatt Smith and Robert Allen Warrior for bringing Clyde Warrior's story to light and demonstrating his important role within the broader Indian activist movement. See *Like a Hurricane: The Indian Movement from Alcatraz to Wounded Knee* (New York: Free Press, 1996), 36–59, quotations on 70. See also Robert Allen Warrior, "Clyde Warrior," in *Encyclopedia of North American Indians*, ed. Frederick E. Hoxie (Boston: Houghton Mifflin, 1996), 665–66.

8. Clyde Warrior, "We Are Not Free," in *Red Power: The American Indians' Fight for Freedom*, ed. Alvin M. Josephy, Jr. (New York: McGraw-Hill, 1971), 71–77, quotations on 73; subsequent quotations are also from this essay.

9. James S. Olson and Raymond Wilson, *Native Americans in the Twentieth Century* (Urbana: University of Illinois Press, 1984), 160; Smith and Warrior, *Like a Hurricane*, 42–44; Peter Iverson, *"We Are Still Here": American Indians in the Twentieth Century* (Arlington Heights: Harlan Davidson, 1998), 146–48.

10. Roger L. Nichols, "Something Old, Something New: Indians since World War II," in *The American Indian Experience: A Profile*, ed. Philip Weeks (Arlington Heights: Forum Press, 1988), 304–5.

11. *Indian Voices* (Feb. 1964): 5; *NCAI Sentinel* (Fall 1965): n.p.; *NCAI Sentinel* (Winter 1965): 10.

12. Francis Paul Prucha, *The Great Father: The United States Government and the American Indians* (Lincoln: University of Nebraska Press, 1984), 1106–10; James J. Rawls, *Chief Red Fox Is Dead: A History of Native Americans since 1945* (Fort Worth: Harcourt Brace College Publishers, 1996), 60–63; George Pierre Castile, *To Show Heart: Native American Self-Determination and Federal Indian Policy, 1960–1975* (Tucson: University of Arizona Press, 1998), 65–66.

13. Among those who have made this observation are Nancy O. Lurie, "An American Indian Renascence?" in *The American Indian Today*, ed. Stuart

Levine and Nancy O. Lurie (Deland: Everett, 1968), 191; Vine Deloria, Jr., "Identity and Culture," *Daedalus* 110 (Spring 1982): 18–19; Richard White, *"It's Your Misfortune and None of My Own": A New History of the American West* (Norman: University of Oklahoma Press, 1991), 582.

14. Rawls, *Chief Red Fox Is Dead*, 118 (first quotation); "Indian Leadership Accent on Youth Program," 11–13 June 1964, Ritzenthaler Field Notes, box 1, folder 23, MPM (second quotation); "Indians vs. the City," *Chicago Magazine* (Apr. 1970) (third quotation).

15. National Council on Indian Opportunity, *Public Forum before the Committee on Urban Indians in Los Angeles* (Washington, D.C., 1968), 261; *Amerindian* (Jan.–Feb. 1966): 3.

16. *Indian Voices* (Apr. 1964): 10.

17. "AAIA and Devils Lake Sioux Protest Child Welfare Abuses," *Indian Affairs* (June–Aug. 1968): 1–2; *Rosebud Sioux Herald*, 12 Aug. 1968, 1.

18. National Council on Indian Opportunity, *Public Forum before the Committee on Urban Indians in Los Angeles*, 268; "NCIO San Francisco Public Forum on the Condition of Urban Indians," 11–12 Apr. 1969, box 89, Record Group 220: Records of the National Council on Indian Opportunity, National Archives II [hereafter RG 220, NA II]; Iverson, *"We Are Still Here,"* 171; Rawls, *Chief Red Fox Is Dead*, 72–73.

19. Arthur M. Schlesinger, Jr., *Robert Kennedy and His Times* (Boston: Houghton Mifflin, 1978), 793.

20. Philip J. Deloria, *Playing Indian: Making American Identities from the Boston Tea Party to the New Age* (New Haven: Yale University Press, 1998), 154–62, quotations on 160–61.

21. Author interview with Candace Ryan (Sioux), Chicago, 13 June 1995.

22. James T. Patterson, *Grand Expectations: The United States, 1945–1974* (New York: Oxford University Press, 1996), 530–42; Steigerwald, *The Sixties and the End of Modern America*, 200–209; Nicholas Lemann, *The Promised Land: The Great Black Migration and How It Changed America* (New York: Knopf, 1991), 111–221.

23. *The Warrior* (June 1964): 2; Prucha, *The Great Father*, 1093; Castile, *To Show Heart*, 23–42; Alvin M. Josephy, Jr., *Now That the Buffalo's Gone: A Study of Today's American Indians* (New York: Knopf, 1982), 224–26; Daniel M. Cobb, "Philosophy of an Indian War: Indian Community Action in the Johnson Administration's War on Poverty, 1964–1968," *American Indian Culture and Research Journal* 22, no. 2 (1998): 71–102.

24. "Capitol Conference on Indian Poverty Sets Forth Needs and Aims," *Amerindian* (May–June 1964): 1.

25. Castile, *To Show Heart*, 23–42; Josephy, *Now That the Buffalo's Gone*, 224–26; Cobb, "Philosophy of an Indian War," 71–102.

26. "The War on Poverty Continues," *NCAI Sentinel* (Summer 1965): 3; "$920,000 Granted for Anti-Poverty Program," *Indian Voices* (Apr. 1965): 7; "Indians Participate in All AO Act Programs," *Amerindian* (Sept.–Oct. 1965): 4; Cobb, "Philosophy of an Indian War," 85.

27. W. Dale Mason, "The Carl Albert Collection: Resources Relating to

Indian Policy, 1963–68," *Chronicles of Oklahoma* 71 (Winter 1993): 423; OEO budget for F.Y. 1968, box 66, RG 220, NA II.

28. Alfonso Ortiz, "Summary of Conference," in *Urban Indians: Proceedings of the Third Annual Conference on Problems and Issues Concerning American Indians Today*, 178; Mark Monroe, *An Indian in White America* (Philadelphia: Temple University Press, 1994), 145–89; Päivi Hoikkala, "Feminists or Reformers? American Indian Women and Community in Phoenix, 1965–1980," in *American Indians and the Urban Experience*, ed. Susan Lobo and Kurt Peters (Lanham: Rowman and Littlefield, 2000), 163–85.

29. Rawls, *Chief Red Fox Is Dead*, 58.

30. National Council on Indian Identity, *Public Forum before the Committee on Urban Indians in Los Angeles*, 168; "Proposal for Model Urban Indian Center Project, n.d. (1970?), box 88, RG 220, NA II.

31. "Strengthening Neighborhood Center Services for Urban Indians," 8 Sept. 1970, box 89, RG 220, NA II; "Summary of the Model Urban Indian Center Project," 21 Apr. 1971, box 88, RG 220, NA II; "Agenda: Ad Hoc Interagency Task Force on Off Reservation Indians," 22 May 1973, box 17, RG 220, NA II; National Council on Indian Identity, *Public Forum before the Committee on Urban Indians in Los Angeles*, 153.

32. Steigerwald, *The Sixties and the End of Modern America*, 205.

33. "NCIO Los Angeles Public Forum on the Condition of Urban Indians," 16–17 Dec. 1968, box 89, RG 220, NA II; National Council on Indian Opportunity, *Public Forum before the Committee on Urban Indians in Minneapolis* (Washington, D.C., 1969), 90; Report from 1969 American Indians–United Conference, Church Federation of Greater Chicago Files, 34–2, Manuscript Collection, Chicago Historical Society.

34. Folder: "Community Action Programs," box 21, RG 220, NA II; *Rosebud Sioux Herald*, 1 Aug. 1966, 1, and 20 Nov. 1967, 1.

35. *NCAI Sentinel* (Fall 1966): 11.

36. Bruce Wilkie to Richard Nixon, 9 Jan. 1970, box 25, RG 220, NA II.

37. "Council—Executive Order 11399—3/6/68," box 24, RG 220, NA II; Hubert Humphrey to Gerald Ford, 8 Apr. 1974, box 24, RG 220, NA II; Prucha, *The Great Father*, 1098–99, 1111–13; Castile, *To Show Heart*, 68–69, 86–98.

38. "Press Conference of Federal and Indian Members," 16 July 1968, box 24, RG 220, NA II; National Council on Indian Opportunity, *Public Forum before the Committee on Urban Indians in Dallas* (Washington, D.C., 1969), 45.

39. National Council on Indian Opportunity, *Public Forum before the Committee on Urban Indians in Los Angeles*, 143; John A. Price, "The Migration and Adaptation of American Indians to Los Angeles," *Human Organization* 27 (Summer 1968): 168–75; Joan Weibel-Orlando, *Indian Country, L.A.: Maintaining Ethnic Community in Complex Society* (Urbana: University of Illinois Press, 1991), 103.

40. Memo by David Lester, n.d., box 87, RG 220, NA II; Eugene Stewart to Spiro Agnew, 20 Mar. 1970, box 87, RG 220, NA II.

41. Russell Means and Marvin J. Wolf, *Where White Men Fear to Tread: The Autobiography of Russell Means* (New York: St. Martin's Press, 1995), 145–

57; Lynn R. Metzger, "Cleveland American Indian Center: Urban Survival and Adaptation," Ph.D. diss., Case Western Reserve University, 1989, 118–22; Philip Weeks and Lynn R. Metzger, "American Indians," in *The Encyclopedia of Cleveland History,* ed. David D. Van Tassel and John J. Grabowski (Bloomington: Indiana University Press, 1996), 29–30.

42. "NCIO Los Angeles Public Forum on the Condition of Urban Indians," 16–17 Dec. 1968, box 89, RG 220, NA II; American Indian Policy Review Commission, *Report on Urban and Rural Non-Reservation Indians: Final Report to the American Indian Policy Review Commission* (Washington, D.C.: U.S. Government Printing Office, 1976), 65; Prucha, *The Great Father,* 1101–2.

43. National Council on Indian Opportunity, *Public Forum before the Committee on Urban Indians in Los Angeles,* 207; "UIDA Proposal for a Relocation Assistance Program," 12 June 1970, box 87, RG 220, NA II; David Lester to Louis Bruce, 22 June 1970, box 87, RG 220, NA II; Means and Wolf, *Where White Men Fear to Tread,* 158.

44. Among studies that have effectively illustrated the pan-Indian and urban background to Indian activism are Olson and Wilson's *Native Americans in the Twentieth Century* and Smith and Warrior's *Like a Hurricane.*

45. Joan Ablon, "Relocated American Indians in the San Francisco Bay Area: Social Interactions and Indian Identity," *Human Organization* 23 (Winter 1964): 296–304. Subsequent quotations are from this essay.

46. "NCIO San Francisco Public Forum on the Condition of Urban Indians," 11–12 Apr. 1969, box 89, RG 220, NA II.

47. The struggle for self-determination is the focus of Troy R. Johnson's *The Occupation of Alcatraz Island: Indian Self-Determination and the Rise of Indian Activism* (Urbana: University of Illinois Press, 1996).

48. "Sioux Indians Claim Alcatraz," *Indian Voices* (Apr. 1964): 4; Johnson, *The Occupation of Alcatraz Island,* 16–25; Means and Wolf, *Where White Men Fear to Tread,* 106.

49. Johnson, *The Occupation of Alcatraz Island,* 49–75; Smith and Warrior, *Like a Hurricane,* 12–13.

50. Johnson, *The Occupation of Alcatraz Island,* 53–55.

51. Indians of All Tribes, "We Must Hold on to the Old Ways," in *Red Power: The American Indians' Fight for Freedom,* ed. Alvin M. Josephy, Jr. (New York: McGraw-Hill, 1971), 187–89.

52. Nancy Shoemaker, "Urban Indians and Ethnic Choices: American Indian Organizations in Minneapolis, 1920–1950," *Western Historical Quarterly* 19 (Nov. 1988): 431–47; Olson and Wilson, *Native Americans in the Twentieth Century,* 167.

53. Fay G. Cohen, "The Indian Patrol in Minneapolis: Social Control and Social Change in an Urban Context," *Law and Society Review* 7 (Summer 1973): 779–86.

54. National Council on Indian Opportunity, *Public Forum before the Committee on Urban Indians in Minneapolis,* 172; Smith and Warrior, *Like a Hurricane,* 127–37; Metzger, "Cleveland American Indian Center," 194–95;

Donald L. Fixico, *The Urban Indian Experience in America* (Albuquerque: University of New Mexico Press, 2000), 148–49.

55. Smith and Warrior, *Like a Hurricane*, 112–17.

56. Means and Wolf, *Where White Men Fear to Tread*, 192–93; Metzger, "Cleveland American Indian Center," 130.

57. Means and Wolf, *Where White Men Fear to Tread*, 149–55; Henry Endress to Robert Robertson, 29 June 1973, box 19, RG 220, NA II.

58. Means and Wolf, *Where White Men Fear to Tread*, 153.

59. Burner, *Making Peace with the Sixties*, 62–63; Means and Wolf, *Where White Men Fear to Tread*, 225.

60. List of delegates, box 1, RG 220, NA II; NCIO press release, 17 Dec. 1970, box 1, RG 220, NA II; Robert Robertson to Charles Wilson, 19 Nov. 1971, box 1, RG 220, NA II; Smith and Warrior, *Like a Hurricane*, 102–5.

61. National Council on Indian Opportunity, *Public Forum before the Committee on Urban Indians in Minneapolis*, 12; Means and Wolf, *Where White Men Fear to Tread*, 164, 175; Monroe, *An Indian in White America*, 202–8.

62. Means and Wolf, *Where White Men Fear to Tread*, 173.

63. Smith and Warrior, *Like a Hurricane*, 149–68.

64. Ibid., 194–268; Stanley David Lyman et al., *Wounded Knee 1973: A Personal Account* (Lincoln: University of Nebraska Press, 1991), xxxi–xxxii.

# 8  Activists and Institutions

The late 1960s and early 1970s brought challenges to the social patterns established earlier by Indians who lived in Chicago. In a changed environment they again had to address the question of how to be an Indian in the city. The changing nature of the era's political protests and the media attention they attracted seemed to value not merely individual action and commitment but even a theatrical type of self-expression. Would that tactic make American society more aware of Indians' needs, or would it inevitably lead to the abandonment of the most central elements of Indian identity? These and other questions faced Indians in Chicago as the process of reconciling urban life with Indian identity continued.

Indian activism in Chicago, as in San Francisco and Minneapolis, responded to the urban context—including housing, schools, and political officials—and used urban tactics. Yet this activism by no means characterized Chicago's Indian community as a whole. As elsewhere, splits and angry confrontations often developed over political strategy and relationships with other groups. Furthermore, some of the momentum the Indian community in Chicago had recently gained was lost as institutions turned upon each other. Old ones were challenged, and new groups emerged.

Yet in some ways there is less here than meets the eye. Much of the rhetoric produced during what some have called the "Indian wars" of the late 1960s and early 1970s dealt with "angry young radicals" on the one hand and "middle class sell-outs" on the other. It was overwrought and failed to acknowledge a common emphasis on self-determination, Indian pride, and identity politics. Many Indians in Chicago affiliated with a range of different organizations that shared these attributes, but varying understandings and practices of identity politics led to factionalism and division. In the end, the development of Indian pride and a demand for self-determination—which had preceded its most visible manifestations during the late 1960s—would survive a time of trouble and continue to distinguish Chicago's Indian community.

In many ways, social and cultural events held at the American Indian Center throughout the 1960s continued to be important symbols of the Chicago Indian community. The center still demonstrated the ways in which Indian people negotiated life in urban America through a combination of mainstream influences and tribal ones. Powwows continued to be highly anticipated events. The center's powwows on the second Saturday of every month drew anywhere from three to five hundred people by the late 1960s; for many, the annual fall powwow was the high point of the year. A participant at the twelfth annual American Indian Center powwow in the fall of 1965 noted that "to be able to have a powwow like this in a large city like Chicago is a part of being Indian in an urban center. This, along with many other things, are we able to perpetuate and maintain, keeping alive those things of our Indian heritage anywhere we go." Indian people from as far away as Cleveland who were "hungry to meet other Indian people" came to Chicago for these fall powwows.[1]

Although powwows and other events continued to foster pan-tribalism, the American Indian Center also developed several tribal clubs, indicating that some Indians were unwilling to meld their tribal identity completely into a pan-tribal model. The Winnebago Club was the first to emerge in 1962, followed by the Sioux/Lakota Club, the Six Nations Club, the Council of the Three Fires (a social group for Menominees, Pottawatomis, and Chippewas), and clubs formed by Southwestern tribes and the Oneidas. Frank Fastwolf, who helped establish the Sioux/Lakota Club in 1965, said he and other Sioux wished to "express our own type of singing, dancing, and our own types of meals" and hand down the "fine heritage" of the Sioux to their children. The new organization attempted to combine both tribal and pan-tribal activities. The group, which enjoyed some popularity during the 1960s, appealed most to suburban tribal members who lived in Barrington and Waukegan, Illinois. Sioux who lived in Chicago were able to frequent the center to participate in its pan-tribal activities and draw from a new urban, pan-tribal identity.[2]

Sports continued to be popular at the center into the late 1960s, and new teams joined the well-established basketball teams that had achieved almost legendary status. A local Golden Gloves champion offered his services and trained young Indian men to box. The Canoe Club picked up in popularity after a period of inactivity, paddling year-round in Chicago and throughout the Midwest. In January 1967 forty club members filled three war canoes and paddled the fifteen miles from Skokie to the Michigan Avenue Bridge in the Loop. Although the weather was subfreezing and some had to chop their way through the ice with their paddles, the group's persistence was rewarded by greetings from center members awaiting them at the bridge. The center also started a bowling league in the early 1960s that included the Frybreads, the Buckskins, and the Crazy Horses among its teams.[3]

The powwows, clubs, and teams, and especially the extensive social service work done at the center, all cost money, which always seemed in short supply, even after a $45,000 grant from the Emil Schwarzhaupt Foundation put the center back on its feet during a difficult time in the late 1950s. By the mid-1960s the center was also hurt by the competitive job market for social service workers during the War on Poverty. Between 1964 and 1967 two program directors and one caseworker left the center to direct community action programs elsewhere, adding to the already frequent turnover of staff. By 1967 the center's annual budget had grown to $96,000. Almost half came from the Metropolitan Crusade of Charity, a local civic organization with which the center had worked hard to build trust and good relations. The rest of the budget came from private donations. Among the center's prominent patrons were Robert E. Wood of Sears Roebuck, W. Clement Stone of the Combined Insurance Company of America, and the Fourth Presbyterian Church of Chicago. An unexpected bequest allowed the purchase of a building for its permanent home. Verna Ewen of Evanston, who had developed a deep friendship with her Indian housekeeper, left money in her will for that purpose, and in November 1967 the center moved into the former Ravenswood Masonic Temple, an imposing five-story building at 1630 West Wilson Avenue in the middle of Uptown. Because the center initially needed only the first two floors, the top three were leased out for Masonic lodge meetings. On the first floor, the center made use of two large meeting rooms (one holding four hundred people and the other two hundred), a full kitchen, a casework office, several small group-work offices, and a lounge. On the second floor was a five-hundred-person auditorium with a stage, a balcony that sat 150, and other small rooms for meetings, offices, and storage.[4]

St. Augustine's, which had started in 1954 as an Indian assistance center and was located in the parish hall of Fr. Peter Powell's West Side Episcopal church, also expanded its work into the late 1960s and early 1970s. It continued to emphasize social services somewhat more than the American Indian Center, which traditionally focused more on social and cultural activities. In 1965 alone, caseworkers from St. Augustine's interviewed more than five thousand Indians and provided emergency cash assistance to more than two thousand to help pay bills or get through various financial emergencies. Later, St. Augustine's added an alcohol treatment program and a child welfare program to its extensive social services offerings. The center also fostered Indian leadership. In 1971 St. Augustine's came under Indian leadership when Matthew Pilcher, a Winnebago, assumed the director's position. He was followed shortly thereafter by Amy Skenandore, a Stockbridge Indian.[5]

Besides offering a variety of services and social and cultural events, both centers allowed Indians in Chicago to continue to define their identities and gave them forums for demanding self-determination. Some of this activity revolved around Indian children and young people. Recognizing that they would be the future leaders of the community, the two centers developed programs designed to help them meet the challenges they faced as Indians and as Chicagoans. The center began holding "back-to-school parties" to encourage Indian schoolchildren who sometimes faced frustrations in dealing with non-Indian teachers and students. Some at the center became involved in an emerging national movement that focused on placing Indian foster children and adoptees in Indian homes, among them Nathan and Sandy Bird (Winnebago), who took a thirteen-year-old Chippewa boy into their home.[6]

The center made efforts to incorporate young people into the life of the institution during the late 1960s, in part through the work of program director Tony Machukay (Apache). He initiated youth group meetings "aimed towards stimulating participation and involvement of other Indian youths" who seemed detached from the center and the broader Indian community. Throughout his tenure, Machukay emphasized the importance of self-determination, arguing that the Indian "should be allowed to run his own affairs." Machukay helped organize meetings that brought together young Indian people, some of whom were politically transformed by the experiences. One young man who attended a "being Indian in an urban situation" meeting at the center in the summer of 1969 developed new awareness. "For years and years," he reflected, "white Americans and some negroes have told us about American Indians, where to live, what to eat, how to educate our children, and just about everything, come to think of it." The meeting had caused him to reflect more on the injustice of that situation and on the importance of Indian self-determination.[7]

Many young people at the center in the late 1960s were influenced by the Indian pride movement. The pages of *The Warrior* in 1968 and 1969 contained increasing references to Indian identity. In September 1968 a report on a summer camp staffed by young adults at the center explained that in addition to the importance of education and hard work, campers had been taught the necessity of "knowing their Indian heritage and being proud of it." The report concluded that "all of us from the Center who were there at the camp know that we ran a camp that was really different from the usual white-man's camp." In the April 1969 issue of *The Warrior*, a young poet began a poem by describing how the sun, mountains, trees, animals, and birds were looking at him and asking, "Who are you?" In the final line the author concluded, "I am an Indian." Francesca Veltri, a youth group worker at the center, also provided a column on the particular importance of Indian pride for young women. "I suppose that most our girls have heard or read 'Black is Beautiful.' Well, have you ever stopped to think that 'Red is Beautiful?' The negroes have awakened to the fact that they too are beautiful people meaning being themselves and bringing out their natural beauty and not trying to be somebody they are not. Going back years ago, most Indian girls had long hair. Each tribe had their own hairstyle. The natural way is the healthier and most attractive way. Be what you are—Indian."[8]

In addition to Tony Machukay, the Rev. Richard Lupke also worked in the late 1960s to allow young Indian voices to be heard at the center and in other forums. Lupke, who had been engaged in church work on the Lac du Flambeau Reservation in Wisconsin, came to Chicago in 1965 to direct the Church Federation's Chicago Indian Ministry committee. He brought with him a strong commitment to community organization and even criticized some community action programs for being insufficiently responsive to the grass-roots community. Lupke's primary goal for the Chicago Indian Ministry committee was to have Indians "create a structure for themselves that will utilize the tested concepts of community organization." His desire for community feedback led him to invite many people, including young people, to meetings so other committee members could hear their opinions. Some meetings apparently included a great deal of input from the young Indians. The harried secretary who took the minutes for a March 1969 meeting wrote: "Many questions asked; much discussion. Objection to use of the word 'help' or any suggestion of continued paternalism. Indian youth spoke freely."[9]

Lupke also worked with participants in the BIA's adult vocational training program. Because bureau guidelines restricted the program to people between the ages of eighteen and thirty-five, most with whom Lupke worked were fairly young. Vocational students became the first of several groups to make a public issue of the poor housing in Uptown. The issue would shortly become publicly well-known and increasingly contentious as housing demands were taken up by more militant and activist groups. Yet the housing issue had its start in a group that was fairly moderate and mainstream. Vocational students began modestly by focussing on housing costs. In 1968 they received a stipend of $36 a week from the bureau to cover their living costs, although the YMCA in which the BIA placed almost all of them had been increasing its rates, so that rooms there cost between $14 and $17 a week. Many students, including Karen Crowshoe, a young Sioux who led the student group, complained that this left very little for food, books, and other items. She and other vocational students asked the BIA to increase the weekly stipend to $49, which they considered a more realistic figure. Within a few months the bureau increased the stipend to $42 a week.[10]

Energized by their success, in June 1968 some of the vocational students formed the Young Tribal Organization (YTO), again with the help of Lupke and the Chicago Indian Ministry committee, and turned their attention from lowering housing costs to constructing new housing in Uptown. YTO members began meeting with non-Indian residents of Uptown, who had also expressed concern about the lack of affordable housing in their neighborhood. The new coalition contacted an architect, and together they developed a plan for a hundred-unit building that they tentatively referred to as "The Village." This time, however, there was no prompt and successful conclusion, because the BIA did not support the proposal from the Young Tribal Organization. The problem of insufficient housing in Uptown remained.[11]

---

Ever since the first relocatees had begun arriving in Chicago in the 1950s a new sense of Indian identity and self-awareness had been developing. So much of life before urbanization had been tied up with reservations and villages. What now was to be the identity for urban Indians? Could the city be home for those who kept their Indian identity, or were they to become displaced persons? These questions became more impor-

tant nationally as more Indians began to live in cities than on reservations. In Chicago during the late 1960s urban Indian leaders responded
by forming a national organization, American Indians–United, for the
purpose of representing all urban Indians and urban Indian centers.[12]

The group emerged out of conversations over many years between
urban Indian leaders and officials of the National Congress of American
Indians (NCAI). Throughout the 1960s urban Indians accused the NCAI
of ignoring them. At the American Indian Chicago Conference in 1961
some of the divisions between urban and reservation Indians had been
evident, and as the government started spending more money on antipoverty programs in the mid-1960s the rifts increased. The NCAI responded to charges from those claiming to be disenfranchised and engaged in
a debate over the role of urban Indians within the organization, including the possibility of giving them equal representation. At a December
1967 meeting in Omaha the group's leaders rejected that idea, however,
and decided that the NCAI could be most effective by continuing to rely
on reservation-based leadership and focusing on reservation-based programs. At the same time, the NCAI started conversations about the possibility of a new group that would serve as its urban counterpart. This
approach had some apparent advantages. Such a group could efficiently
go its own way on specifically urban issues and would leave reservation
issues in the hands of the NCAI; the two groups would come together to
work in unity on issues pertinent to all Indians.[13]

From the perspective of those who would affiliate with American
Indians–United, the most significant part of this plan was the freedom it
offered Indians in cities to tackle problems they saw as distinctly urban.
Jess Sixkiller, a Cherokee and the first Indian detective hired by the Chicago Police Department, became American Indians–United's initial director. At an annual convention he addressed urban Indian identity and
in the process argued for the necessity of the new organization. "In the
urban areas of the country today," he noted, "we're faced more and more
with a different kind of crisis than our reservation brothers."[14]

The new organization began with a meeting of what was called the
National Urban Indian Consultation in January 1968 at Seattle's Indian
Center. Seventy-nine Indians and nineteen non-Indians came together for
an opening-night salmon dinner and then a discussion of future political
involvement by urban Indians. Of the Indians, half were from Washington and California. Four came from Chicago: Benjamin Bearskin and Edith
Johns from the center, Karen Crowshoe from the YTO, and Jess Sixkiller. At the meeting's end, Sixkiller was elected chair of the twelve-person
committee that next met in May at the Cook Christian Training School

in Tempe, Arizona. There the committee renamed the new urban organization American Indians–United and elected Sixkiller as director after he said he would be willing to take a year's leave from his job. After a long discussion, the committee decided that urban Indian centers would serve as the means of representation in the new organization. Those in the Central and Pacific time zones would each have three members on American Indians–United's board of directors, those in the eastern and mountain time zones would each have two, and those in the Alaska time zone would have one member on the board.[15]

During its short lifetime American Indians–United focused on what it saw as the special needs of urban Indians and the need for unity among all Indians who lived in cities. The first item on the list of goals adopted at the Tempe meeting was "articulate the need for jobs, job training, vocational counseling, housing, education opportunities, and related services for the off-reservation Indians." Some members expressed frustration about their inability to get extensive OEO funding during the War on Poverty. In order to voice these issues and the other needs of urban Indians, members realized they needed unity. Even when American Indians–United was in decline, Sixkiller said, "We try to bridge those ill feelings among the tribes and I believe the urban Indian, thrown together with Indians from other tribes, is forming a new culture, borrowing from the best that exists in the tribes now."[16]

Like so many other Indian organizations and movements at the time, American Indians–United emphasized self-determination and identity politics. Its goals were to inform government officials of the needs of Indians and support the kinds of "programs they, *as Indians,* want and need." As a confederation of urban Indian centers, the group was particularly mindful of the need for Indians to control these important institutions, and it gave those with majority-Indian boards of directors more voting power than centers where most board members were non-Indians. Sixkiller's grand hopes for the future of American Indians–United included establishing a national Indian bank and writing Indian history textbooks. Like many others, he was dissatisfied with the textbooks of the time, which, he said, "take away an Indian child's past and make him feel he's not an Indian." In other ways as well, American Indians–United said it would encourage identity politics and Indian pride by supporting "proposed improvements in Indian education that will strengthen, *not weaken,* Indian personality and cultural identification."[17]

After returning to Chicago from the Tempe meeting in May 1968, Sixkiller and George Effman, a Klamath Assemblies of God pastor who served as American Indians–United's assistant director, moved into an office offered by the American Indian Center in its new building at 1630 West Wilson Avenue. Board members at the center were enthusiastic at first about a new urban Indian organization that had so much potential being housed in their building. After settling in, Sixkiller and Effman were further encouraged when the Ford Foundation in 1969 awarded American Indians–United a grant for $88,500 to develop a program for urban Indian centers. The new program began with an effort to develop and strengthen Tucson's Indian center.[18]

As American Indians–United's annual convention approached in October 1969, though, the organization was faltering, still undecided about a comprehensive strategy. It was also under attack from other Indian organizations. Some members believed that American Indians–United had not used its Ford Foundation grant effectively, and there also seemed to be some resentment from similar and competing organizations about a newcomer receiving such a large grant. As delegates arrived in San Francisco to meet at that city's Indian center, the organization was far from unified. Sixkiller was on the defensive for much of the three days of the convention as AIM leaders Dennis Banks, Clyde Bellecourt, and Russell Means criticized his leadership. Banks warned that unless the new group made drastic changes it would sink into irrelevance and become another "do-nothing organization" like the NCAI. He also criticized the organization's bookkeeping and budgeting, claiming that much of the Ford Foundation's grant had gone to administrative costs. At one meeting Banks charged, "You have less than $40,000 left to be administered to Indian programs throughout the United States. And when you divide that up by 750,000 Indians you are ending up with less than 15 cents per Indian. This is what the Ford Foundation is doing for 15 cents an Indian: they are controlling a national organization." Toward the end of the convention, Banks and other AIM leaders tried to declare the meeting illegal. They were, they said, responding to the board's "dictatorial" behavior and poor bookkeeping. Others, however, saw the pioneering urban Indian group trying to co-opt or eliminate a new organization with which it might have to compete for money and allegiance. When Banks's constitutional maneuver failed, AIM cut ties with American Indians–United.[19]

After the feud with AIM, any institutional strength that American Indians–United had was further sapped by its increasingly tense relationship with Chicago's American Indian Center and its board of directors. Gene Begay, a board member at the center, also criticized Sixkiller at the San Francisco convention. Sixkiller did not, Begay claimed, communicate enough with urban Indians, not even those at the center. The board of directors appeared to be upset that the new organization, housed under its own roof and recently flush with money, was reluctant to take its advice and view it as a mentor. After the meeting in San Francisco, another center board member claimed numerous improprieties on the part of American Indians–United, ranging from a "lack of responsiveness" to his suggestions to accusations of sloppy bookkeeping. He concluded that "Mr. Jess Sixkiller does not have the support of most of the Indians living in the Chicago metropolitan area." By a year later American Indians–United had disbanded.[20]

---

Other Indian organizations and institutions in Chicago also fell on hard times during the early 1970s. As Indians in Chicago continued to be influenced by national events and trends as well as by issues rooted in their own homes and neighborhoods, it became clear that there would be no unified idea of the urban Indian identity. Forms of it diverged more and more, and, finally, the already fractured Indian community could no longer hold together in any meaningful way. By 1971 the American Indian Center had broken into factions, a situation that would persist for the rest of the decade.

It was becoming increasingly difficult to keep all different interests under one roof. Debates took place in 1969 in the pages of the center's newsletter about how Indians should pursue individual objectives and how they should relate to other protest movements. Most of the space was taken by writers suspicious of political changes among young Indians and the increasing influence of white and black youths. The other side is largely silent in these pages, an imbalance that illustrates which groups tended to feel at home at the center and which had come to believe that the institution no longer represented them. One unsigned editorial noted the stark contrast between those in American society "burning down buildings, rioting, fighting, and killing other human beings" and Indians "maintaining harmony and understanding and peace." It implied that Indians' separation from more militant and violent movements was natural and appropriate.[21] Another editorial addressed those who labeled Indians at the center, and others who held similar views, as "establishment Indians":

> It may be that the creators of the "Establishment Indian" mean to place in that category those Indians who coincide with what the white establishment signifies: a new car, a home in suburbia, an 8 to 5 job, bowling leagues, etc. It would be well to consider that this type of Indian, even if he fits the "Establishment" category, has overcome great psychological and perhaps racial barriers to achieve that status. And it doesn't mean

that he has rejected his Indian values to do so. It may be that the creators of the "Establishment" category mean to say: "those who do not believe as I do what an Indian should be."[22]

These calls for Indians to protect themselves from outside militant influences and embrace establishment figures did not convince everyone, however. In December 1969 a group of young people established the Native American Committee (NAC), claiming that the center no longer represented all Indians in Chicago, particularly those who were poor and young. Founders included Steve Fastwolf, Mike Chosa, Bill Whitehead, Helen Whitehead, Dennis Harper, Judith Harper, and Norma Stealer. While NAC gave young people an organization of their own, it likely also prevented AIM from taking root in Chicago at the time, because the Native American Committee served a function similar to AIM's in Minneapolis, Cleveland, and Milwaukee. Many of NAC's founders were particularly interested in Indian education and served on the education committee at the center. They helped bring an outpost of Senn High School to the center so Indian children could take basic courses in mathematics, science, and English and later learn about Indian history and Indian dancing. Even after NAC had established itself following vigorous debate with leaders at the center, it continued to run some programs there.[23]

NAC developed its own patrons, mostly from groups different than those that helped the center. It ignored the established local civic leaders allied with the center and found individuals and organizations looking to support some part of the activism of the late 1960s. Early on, NAC received support from students at nearby Northeastern Illinois University; some founders even received college credit for starting NAC and planning its programs.[24] Richard Lupke also assisted NAC from the time it was formed by finding office space, paying for three members to travel to Alcatraz, and helping members find positions on the Lutheran church's Board of American Missions. Lupke got in trouble with his supervisors at the Church Federation after they discovered that NAC members used his office telephone to make lengthy long-distance calls. As Lupke increasingly appeared to give more support to NAC and other radical groups than to their mainstream competitors, he came under increasing scrutiny and eventually was fired by the Church Federation.[25]

What most distinguished the Native American Committee from its counterparts at the center was its willingness, and in some cases eagerness, to participate in direct-action protests, a practice fostered in part by the fact that some members had taken college classes on protest movements. NAC members staged several direct action–style confrontations at Northwestern University, the Model Cities Program office, and, most dramatically, at the local BIA office. On December 26, 1969, a group occupied the bureau office in support of the Alcatraz occupiers. Then, on March 23, 1970, twenty-three members again staged a sit-in, this time in support of Indians protesting the BIA's lack of response to their needs after "dumping" them in Denver. The NAC protestors demanded more influence in bureau decisions affecting Indians. Steve Fastwolf went further, saying the local BIA office should be "all-Indian." All twenty-three protestors were arrested for criminal trespass but were later acquitted.[26]

The Native American Committee again saw opportunity for a dramatic and media-friendly direct-action protest when it learned that the National Conference of Social Welfare was planning to hold its annual convention in June at the Conrad Hilton Hotel in Chicago. For some young activist Indians, this organization represented the frustrating and paternalistic welfare system, and when they learned that the BIA would also participate to report on its work among Indians, it seemed like the perfect protest opportunity. Fastwolf called AIM leaders in Milwaukee and Cleveland, and they agreed to participate, as would the Turtle Mountain chapter of the National Welfare Rights Organization.

At the Hilton, the coalition of activist groups began by challenging the BIA convention exhibit, which boasted of the bureau's good work on reservations. Protestors replaced photographs in the BIA exhibit with their own, which they claimed were more realistic, and marked up the bureau's pamphlets "to correct the lies." Then, during a large plenary session, they coordinated efforts to interrupt the convention. Russell Means seized the podium while four others took control of floor microphones. Having gained a captive audience, Means then spoke for all four groups and demanded $250,000 from the National Conference of Social Welfare to start programs for Indians in Chicago, Milwaukee, and Cleveland and at Turtle Mountain. The audience of social workers compliantly voted on the demand and approved it by a vote of 399 to 93, although the vote was not binding. Later, NAC members brought in cardboard boxes filled with old clothes, used pantyhose, and mismatched tennis shoes and dumped the boxes in front of the audience—an act that they said symbolized their contempt for a paternalistic welfare system.[27]

Protests like the episode in the hotel ballroom and the reactions of militant young Indians would be repeated many times in Chicago and elsewhere during the early 1970s. Yet the situation was fraught with a frustrating contradiction. On the one hand, the young people believed that white organizations, and perhaps whites in general, owed Indians special attention and resources. On the other hand, they became frustrated and angry when such exchanges or discussions of exchanges were quickly overlaid with paternalism. The apparent contradiction proved difficult to solve.

Native American Committee protests in 1969 and 1970 at the Chicago BIA office and the National Conference of Social Welfare revealed the differences between the new organization and the American Indian Center. But the center, although perhaps weaker, still held a prominent position throughout this time. That would change in May 1971 with the death of long-time executive director Robert Rietz and with the turmoil that would plague the center during the period that followed. Rietz had devoted much of his life to the center and regularly put in extraordinarily long days, but when he died at the age of fifty-seven it became obvious that he had not groomed a successor. Indeed, he had not been very successful at developing Indian leadership in general.

Suddenly, all the center's problems came to the forefront. Some of the most prominent families there had been carrying on rivalries and feuds, in some cases for many years. Moreover, the center's financial situation continued to be precarious. Donations came in irregularly, and the organization's bookkeeping had always been haphazard, in part because money was lacking to hire a professional bookkeeper. Finally, within the center there festered a personal rift that pitted the majority of the board against the staff.[28]

Faith Smith, a young Chippewa who had assisted Rietz, was named acting executive director after his death. In the months that followed, the board, led by their chair Marvin Tahmahkera, turned against Smith. On August 20, 1971 the board voted seven to six to fire her for insubordination and questionable bookkeeping and banking practices. She had, they said, failed to comply with a board resolution to close a bank account and refused to turn over the center's books to the treasurer who sat on the board. A few days later Smith's outraged supporters, who viewed Tahmahkera as high-handed and authoritarian, called a meeting of center members. They voted to reinstate Smith and replace the seven members of the board who voted against her. The existing board and its allies at the center declared the supporters' meeting illegal, and the issue was argued for months, eventually ending in the courts.[29]

The center remained profoundly divided for much of the 1970s. Some thought tribal differences were the most powerful and harmful during this time. Recalling her experiences with the center, Phyllis Fastwolf, a Sioux-Oneida, compared the early, happy times with the period in the 1970s, when she remembered "all this tribal fighting." Another Sioux woman also viewed the troubles as revolving around tribal rivalries. The Win-nebagos, she maintained, were the "dominant people at the American Indian Center" for a long time.[30]

Religious differences also contributed to factionalism. The Begay brothers, Gene and Duane (Navajo-Chippewa), took on prominent roles at the center in the late 1960s and early 1970s, a fact that produced var-ied reactions. Gene, who worked as an architect and served as an elder in a local Presbyterian church, was a frequent board member and sat on the Chicago Indian Ministry committee. Duane left his job as an engi-neer in 1972 to become the full-time pastor of the American Indian Church, which met at the center, and over time earned a degree from Moody Bible Institute. Other leaders of the American Indian church were also active at the center. Roger Harper, a Chippewa, for example, was a church deacon as well as a board member. Some at the center believed the Begays and the rest of the group they called "the church people" held too much power. Center funds, they said, were "all in the hands of the Moody deacons," despite denials from Duane Begay and Moody officials of any ties between Moody and the center. Critics also charged that all center activities not endorsed by the American Indian church were be-ing dropped.[31]

Meanwhile, financial problems persisted. By early 1973 the situation was so severe that it appeared the center might have to close. Some do-nors who had helped it for many years had become nervous at the con-stant turmoil there and cut back their funding. Neither staff members nor creditors had been paid in months. One attempt to stave off bank-ruptcy was an eighteen-mile "walk of survival" in the spring of 1973. Although the center's financial difficulties occupied the time and ener-gies of many leaders in the Indian community, they still managed to re-spond to and speak on social and political movements of the time. The center, although weakened, continued in this way to fulfill a role it had played from its beginning. In the early 1970s, center leaders often respond-ed to Indian activism nationally. As many watched the tense stand-off at Wounded Knee, one member was quick to emphasize that the center's walk "wasn't a protest" and that some of the center's financial problems were caused by whites' distaste for the radicalism led by the Wounded Knee occupiers and other Indians.[32]

While the feuding between NAC and the center continued and the factionalism within the center showed no signs of ending, a new organi-zation came forward, hoping to serve as a broker between radicals and conservatives and unify Indians in Chicago. In 1970 Al Cobe, who had started a number of small organizations since arriving in Chicago as a young man in 1930, and Gene Bearbow began a group they called Indians for Indians. Cobe believed that those who were unskilled and poor were suffering while organizational leaders sniped at each other. He promoted the development of programs that would have Indians train other Indians in job skills. Indians for Indians was successful in winning some grants in the early 1970s. One for $56,300 in 1972 permitted employment of thirty Indians and was funded by the Department of Labor, the Office of Equal Opportunity, and the Presbyterian church. A 1974 grant for $348,000 from the Department of Labor allowed the group to train clients for the building trades. Yet other than win grants, Indians for Indians had a minimal presence in the community's everyday social and cultural life and was unable to bring together the opposing factions represented in the center and NAC.[33]

The two organizations carried on their war of words throughout the early 1970s, even trying to outdraw each other at powwows.[34] At the heart of the matter was a debate about identity and who was the "true Indian." This was a debate that could only have taken place within an urban Indian community. As in the 1950s and 1960s, the city continued to play a key role in shaping Indian identity throughout the 1970s. A challenging and foreign environment, the prospect of being misidentified by others, new economic and political obstacles, and the sheer diversity and heterogeneity of the population made presentation of an Indian identity an issue of utmost importance in the city. Urbanization and urban Indian communities such as Chicago's had contributed enormously to developments in Indian identity, especially the growth of pan-tribalism. That development, in turn, led to a greater sense of pride and power among Indians. In the early 1970s, though, the same processes turned on urban Indian communities and challenged their solidarity.

Unforeseen results of the developing urban Indian identity were threatening to tear apart Chicago's Indian community. On the one side, some at the center argued that the idea of "Indian power," as usually understood, was un-Indian and appropriated from non-Indian society. After various militant slogans were spray-painted on the walls of the center, presumably by Indian youths, a member used the center's newsletter to decry the "vandalism" and instruct young Indians that "those of you who profess to advocate 'Indian Power' are only borrowing these words from the non-Indian." Those affiliated with NAC, however, believed they represented the Indian community and filled their speeches and writings with references to the "community" and the "grass-roots" while suggesting that the center's programs were directed "from the outside" and thus not products of true self-determination and not truly Indian. Some, like Norma Stealer, a Winnebago-Sioux who was a mental-health worker with NAC, believed that the professional and middle-class status of a few at the center in itself discredited their Indian identity. She boldly challenged the Indian identity of hundreds, asserting, "As a rule, Indians are poor people; they have no money and no power." Others believed the center to be compromised because of weakness and a lack of independence because of its work with Chicago civic organizations. As one observer favoring NAC described the relationship between it and the center, "On the one side, there are those who choose to accept what the white world offers and, on the other, there are those who are committed to the maintenance and growth of the Indian community." Forgotten now by many was the center's long history of not accepting what white BIA officials and others offered. Overlooked as well was the evidence that more than one group or ideology was at work for the growth of the Indian community. Yet in the Indian community of Chicago during the early 1970s factions had become polarized. [35]

Through the mid-1970s NAC developed more programs out of its office at 1362 West Wilson Avenue, a few blocks from the center. Its newsletter, *Redletter*, focused on education, and through the publication NAC hoped to build Indian identity and Indian pride. Helen Whitehead, a Winnebago-Chippewa, said of NAC, "Our main thrust is to start at the time they're very young and to build a positive self-image." For some, education extended through adulthood as they earned their G.E.D. through NAC's Adult Learning Center. NAC also continued to enjoy success in winning grants while the center struggled to keep its doors open. In 1976 NAC received a $294,000 grant from the Department of Health Education and Welfare to improve Indian education, and the next year a $42,000 Comprehensive Employment Training Act grant to expand programs for elderly Indians. [36]

The split between the center and NAC was not the only one within Chicago's Indian community. NAC itself faced challenges, beginning in the early summer of 1970 in the wake of a housing protest. On May 5, 1970, Carol Warrington, a thirty-five-year-old Menominee who was separated from her husband and raising six children on her own, was evicted from her apartment for failure to pay rent. Warrington said that conditions in her building on North Seminary Avenue in the Lakeview area near Wrigley Field were very poor and that withholding rent was the only way to pressure the landlord into improving conditions. NAC members came to Warrington's aid by helping her get back clothing and household items that had been removed from the apartment. Then they borrowed the center's large ceremonial teepee used for powwows and set it up in an empty lot across the street from Warrington's building, in view of Wrigley Field. In a show of solidarity, a number of other Indians who had learned of Warrington's situation and were sympathetic with her struggle to find housing pitched smaller tents around the large teepee. Between thirty and sixty gathered, some staying only a few hours but others settling in. Two days after the tent village was set up, Steve Fastwolf led most NAC members in pulling out of the protest, believing they had made their point and NAC's efforts could be better used elsewhere. Others who decided to stay called themselves the Chicago Indian Village (CIV). Thus another faction was born, and a fateful division among Chicago's Indian community first surfaced.[37]

Among those who split with NAC and stayed with CIV was Mike Chosa, a thirty-three-year-old Chippewa who would become the new group's leading spokesperson and strategist. Born on Wisconsin's Lac du Flambeau Reservation in 1936, Chosa lived briefly in Chicago as a young man before he served in the army and then traveled west in 1964. There he worked at various jobs and sometimes supported himself as a pool hustler. Chosa became interested in labor organizing and spent some of his time in California working in lemon groves and organizing the mostly Hispanic labor force there. He orchestrated a plan by which workers took advantage of a key element of production that they controlled—ladders. To protest low wages and poor working conditions, Chosa had the workers climb into lemon trees and pull their ladders up behind them. They then refused to work until their employers agreed to their terms. Returning to Chicago in 1969, Chosa joined NAC and continued to pursue his interests in community organization and activism, also becoming a student at Saul Alinsky's Industrial Areas Foundation. In May 1970, huddled with Warrington and her supporters in a vacant lot on the city's north side, he found a cause that would occupy him for much of the next two years.[38]

In its first weeks, CIV focused on protesting the poor housing conditions of many Indians in Chicago. Speaking for "the American Indians of Chicago," CIV issued a manifesto declaring "war on the slum conditions in and near the Uptown area" and demanding that local politicians force landlords to repair properties within sixty days of receiving notice. If slumlords failed to comply, the city should fine them and, if necessary, seize their property. When members were arrested for disorderly conduct a month after the protest began because they were beating their drum loudly and late at night, Chosa had another opportunity to publicize his group's demands. "We will stay on this land," he pledged, "until the city does something about our housing problems." A week later more CIV members were arrested after nearby residents again complained about noise. This time Chosa alleged that police had overreacted and beaten a young Indian boy they believed to have thrown rocks at them. Meanwhile, residents continued to complain that CIV members were breaking local ordinances by burning huge bonfires day and night and tossing beer cans on their lawns. Throughout the early period CIV attempted to expand its tent village. Two months after the protest began, members moved onto a privately owned parking lot used by Cubs fans and adjacent to the vacant lot they had been occupying. The lot's owner, who had originally allowed CIV to camp on part of his property, became frustrated with their litter and constant attempts to expand. Chosa, however, claimed that the action was justified and alluded to the Alcatraz occupiers and other Indian activists. The parking lot owner, he claimed, had "broken a treaty" with CIV.[39]

By responding to conditions in Uptown and other neighborhoods where Indians lived in Chicago, CIV members had identified a serious problem. Poverty seemed to have a firm grip on the neighborhood. The Model Cities Program, which had started in Uptown in 1967 with such high hopes, had only hurt the poor there further. With the federal government providing aid, Uptown residents who suddenly could afford to leave often did, leaving the poorest of the poor behind. Communities like Uptown had suffered from overcrowding after World War II, but by the 1970s population there was actually declining. There were 13 percent fewer residents in Uptown at the end of the decade than at its beginning.[40]

The easing of population pressure did not help Uptown, however. Many larger apartments had been subdivided into kitchenettes and could not easily be restored. Marilou Hedlund, alderwoman for Chicago's Forty-eighth Ward, which included Uptown, acknowledged in 1972 that the neighborhood had a "desperate need for family-sized units." Moreover, as Uptown's declining population became more uniformly poor there was little incentive to build up the neighborhood's economic or housing base. Many buildings started to deteriorate. In just a ten-block stretch of North Kenmore Avenue, one of Uptown's major thoroughfares, seven large apartment buildings were condemned and scheduled for demolition, including one a few doors down from the building that had housed the short-lived Kenmore Uptown Indian Center in the 1950s. Indians and others in Uptown were also hurt by changes in the economy as the city lost a third of its manufacturing jobs between 1967 and 1977.[41]

Despite the aggressive stance CIV took toward some of the problems Chicago's Indians faced, many in the community disapproved of the group's approach and style. In June 1970 two members from St. Augustine's, women who had been active for years in trying to meet the social and spiritual needs of Chicago Indians, presented a petition against CIV to the press. They maintained that the new radical organization presented a "distorted picture of Indian life and Indian needs in Chicago." The more than 270 signers also stated that, contrary to what CIV said, many had managed to find "good jobs, decent homes, and lives of dignity and decency." Some petitioners also expressed concern about reports of drunkenness and drug use at CIV.[42]

Chosa's Chicago Indian Village further polarized Chicago's Indians. The camp and its environment embarrassed some, whereas others were indignant that any Indian person would feel ashamed about a fellow Native participating in the protest. In this environment, Chosa and other CIV members decided to meet with members of the center. From the beginning of the meeting, each side employed terminology that indicated the width of the divide between CIV and the center. Chosa, who had sometimes referred to the center as the "American Apple Center," characterized the meeting as being between "street Indians" and "educated Indians," the latter label used disparagingly. Marvin Tahmahkera of the center's board of directors, in turn, angered some CIV residents when he characterized himself and others opposed to the protest as "working Indians" who should have more time to present their position. Tahmahkera and some other board members were especially opposed to CIV's continued use of the center's teepee as their camp symbol and asked that it be returned. Chosa responded with annoyance and treated the center's leaders as he had previous opponents among landlords and politicians. The teepee would be returned, Chosa told Tahmahkera, only after CIV's demands for better living conditions had been met.[43]

Disagreements among those in the center's auditorium on a June 1970 evening corresponded to Chicago Indians' differing reactions to Indian activism and militancy during the 1960s and 1970s. One thirty-six-year-old man acknowledged that Indians could try to improve their conditions in various ways, but he himself would be embarrassed to join a march. If he felt strongly enough about an issue he "would find some quieter way of getting [his] ideas across." Some were particularly disappointed that Indians had resorted to violence or threatened it. Edward E. Goodvoice, a Sioux who had served in the 101st Airborne Division during World War II, recalled following the Alcatraz story in the media and hearing "these supposedly well-educated Indians talking about getting guns and shooting up the place. . . . For me that was an empty statement—getting the guns." The older generation, especially those who fought in World War II, often had reservations. Daniel W. Battise, also a veteran, no doubt expressed the views of many others when asked about Alcatraz and AIM and Wounded Knee. He paused for a long time, and when he responded it was in a way that implicitly and humbly suggested that no one group had a monopoly on Indian power and Indian pride. "I'm an older person," he observed calmly, "and I fought the war, and I fought to protect the people. The war is dead; we did it; nothing can run over us. We got power already; we can stop anything. Maybe they were just trying to make their voice known. I believe in a different way myself."[44]

Others, however, welcomed the new Indian activism and militancy and identified it as essential to their Indian identity. Such was the experience of Phyllis Fastwolf, who in 1971, at the high point of the activism, turned fifty and decided that "this was the time for me to blossom." With most of her children grown and out of the house, she felt free to involve herself in Indian protest movements. Traveling throughout the country, she went to Alcatraz and to Wounded Knee and testified on behalf of Dennis Banks and Russell Means. She also emphasized that the primary motivation for her new life was that it "gave my boys a strong feeling of what an Indian is all about."[45]

After the June 1970 meeting at the center, Chosa and roughly thirty other CIV members continued to camp out near Wrigley Field, making their case to anyone—Indian or non-Indian, curious bystander or reporter—that the city and the city's landlords had treated Indians unjustly. Meanwhile, city officials tried to resolve the issue or at least make it go away. In July, Mayor Richard J. Daley appointed Deton Brooks to take care of the CIV problem. Daley had already named Brooks to administer and control community action programs in Chicago, and the mayor knew Brooks shared his appreciation for centralized municipal government and distrust for those who tried to work outside the system. By the time Brooks met with Chosa, the Indian leader had increased his demands. The discussion between the two grew testy. No longer interested in simply ameliorating the behavior of unscrupulous landlords, Chosa now demanded an entire housing complex for Indians so they could stay together. "You are trying to disperse us so that we will not have strength," Chosa told Brooks, "and we are not going to let you do it." When Brooks was noncommittal about a separate urban progress center for Indians, Chosa accused him of saying that Indians were incapable of running their own affairs. "Please don't put words in my mouth!" Brooks shot back. "Please don't put Saul Alinsky words in my mouth!"[46]

Brooks was well aware of the work of Saul Alinsky and his influence on community organizers such as Chosa. Alinsky had built a reputation of being an effective, grass-roots community organizer and activist and proved to be Mayor Daley's nemesis. Alinsky's usual pattern was to look for grievances that could unite an entire neighborhood in protest and then use them to pressure centers of power, including businesses, property owners, and politicians. By this time it had become apparent that Chosa—both because of his training with Alinsky and for personal reasons—was not eager for the dispute to end, or at least for it not to end with limited results. He saw some advantages to prolonging the protest. Among other things it would allow him to continue to make his case for the media, something at which he was growing increasingly adept. When Brooks said that he had a list of available housing in Uptown for all the residents of CIV, Chosa rejected the offer, saying he did not believe such a list existed. He continued to press for a separate Indian housing complex in Uptown. Five families from CIV accepted the city's offer of housing, but the others and Chosa refused. The dispute would continue. Later, an official from the city met with Carol Warrington and asked for information to fill out the necessary forms to obtain housing for her and her family. Warrington laughed and said, "You know you're not going to get me anything" before turning away. She and others had grown increasingly certain that the white establishment would not help them and that further radical action would be necessary.[47]

In early 1971 Chosa began to take more direct action to irritate and undermine the center. CIV targeted a pair of benefactors who had been generous to the American Indian Center and the Indian community in general. In January CIV residents gathered at the headquarters of the Combined Insurance Company of America, owned by W. Clement Stone, a longtime friend and benefactor of the Chicago Indian community. CIV demonstrators marched around the building, and when Stone himself came out Chosa greeted him with an ultimatum. Claiming that the land where the building stood "was originally ours," Chosa said CIV would be willing to give Stone a ninety-nine-year lease in exchange for $50,000 to aid CIV. Stone said he would like to be of help but would not be threatened. Indeed, he later guaranteed a $7,500 loan for a landscaping firm started by CIV.[48]

A few weeks later, after CIV's "first annual convention" in March 1971, members started planning a sit-in at the Fourth Presbyterian Church. Because he had received a stipend of $450 a month from the National Presbyterian church while a student at Saul Alinsky's foundation, Chosa was familiar with the Presbyterian leadership in Chicago. After church officials discovered thirty Indians from both CIV and Indians for Indians occupying the church basement and chanting slogans, the Indian leaders issued their demands. They said they wanted a long-term mortgage loan to finance a housing development for Indians, money for an Indian school, changes in the Chicago Indian Ministry committee, and $2,500 in emergency funds to house destitute families in CIV. While one of the ministers negotiated with CIV members, Chosa found the church telephone and used it to summon the news media to the sit-in. Even after CIV members were given $2,500 and had left the church Chosa continued to reap theatrical benefit from the event. He later told church officials, whom he had accused of misusing money raised for Indian missions, "We thought very seriously of going down to the police station and swearing out a warrant for you people for misappropriation of funds."[49]

In just under a year CIV's rhetoric and demands had sharply escalated from talking about taking the property of slumlords to threatening to take the property of long-time benefactors of Chicago Indians. Chosa was surely aware of the much larger demands that black activist James Forman had made at New York's Riverside Church two years earlier. In what he called the "Black Manifesto," Forman had demanded that white Christian churches pay $500 million in reparations to establish a black land bank, book publisher, television network, university, think tank, and labor fund.[50]

The negotiations with Clement Stone and with the Presbyterians illustrated the conflict CIV never managed to escape. The group needed funding and appeared sincerely interested in economic self-determination, as evidenced by the two small, Indian-controlled businesses it started. CIV members became frustrated, though, in early 1971 about the attitude of whites who were willing to help Indians. In one sense Chosa represented the most dramatic and dynamic form of Indian pride as he boldly entered into debates with political officials, journalists, and others. Clearly, most members of CIV viewed him in this way. Yet to those at the center and to those caught between the two dueling factions of Chicago Indians, Chosa's version of Indian pride seemed strained and frayed due its ties to white organizations and the need to go to them, no matter how boldly, for aid.

Soon after the sit-in at Fourth Presbyterian Church in March 1971, CIV again refused relocation assistance from the city, claiming that officials offered only run-down housing in dangerous neighborhoods. They then occupied an abandoned three-story building at 1142 West Ainslie Street that had recently gone into receivership. While in that building, CIV members endured periodic power outages, police raids, and other challenges. By June, when demolition of the building seemed at hand, CIV protested at the local urban renewal office.[51]

On the night of June 13, after a fire in the Ainslie Street building drove out forty-five CIV members, they held an emergency meeting and then went to an abandoned Nike missile base on the shores of Lake Michigan. No longer an active military site, it was guarded at night by a seventy-year-old, unarmed private watchman. The Indians approached him at 3:30 in the morning and told him they were "peacefully reclaiming land the white man has taken" and that he should leave. He complied. They then forced the padlock on the gate and went in. Just three days after the last occupiers had been taken off Alcatraz Island in San Francisco Bay, CIV had its own occupation site on the shores of Lake Michigan and also the beginnings of its own media event.[52]

The next day, the occupiers started to explore the base. One CIV member found the controls to the base equipment, and the Indians rode up and down on elevators once used to lift missiles into firing position. As they explored, they began to talk about converting the Nike site to a housing, cultural, and educational center for Indians and made rough sketches of how the barracks building, two garages, and five rocket pits could be converted to housing. Chosa, too, was still talking about the need for housing, but at times it was a housing project in Uptown and at times it was "eighty acres in the Fox River Valley." If CIV was not sure of its next move, then neither were the police. In part because the Nike site was in the process of being transferred from the army to the Chicago Park District and in part because of the recent history of Indian militancy nationwide, police remained inactive. As the days went on, donations of food, clothing, blankets, cooking utensils, and furniture flowed in from Chicagoans who read about the occupation daily in their newspapers. One day, two truckloads of furniture and clothing arrived from a suburban church.[53]

Problems and tensions remained within CIV, however, even as it briefly became a fashionable cause in Chicago. The most serious difficulty concerned alcohol. Sometimes Chosa and others who were not problem drinkers recognized that drunkenness had caused the group to suffer. While camped in the Ainslie Street building, CIV members for a time had managed to repair it to the point that it was habitable. After a few parties and episodes of binge drinking, however, the building deteriorated to a hopeless point. Chosa himself was ambivalent about alcohol and alcoholism, sometimes expressing sadness when drinking wreaked havoc on his group but other times calling CIV "a bunch of drunks," pride apparent in his voice. It seemed that to be a "street Indian"—and thus the opposite of "educated Indians" at the center—was to go through bouts of heavy drinking or at least not to shun those who did.

The problems associated with drinking, evident from CIV's earliest days, continued at the Nike missile site. Some Indians who were not in

CIV but who followed its activities were not surprised. After hearing about the Nike site takeover, Edward E. Goodvoice, who "tended to drink too much" at the time, decided to stay away for his own good. "I had some idea that there would be a lot of drinking down there," he recalls. "That creates problems, so I didn't want to have anything to do with it." Indeed, soon after occupying the Nike missile site, CIV split into drinking and nondrinking factions, each occupying a different section of the base. Others at the site also noticed the strong influence of alcohol. Clyde Belle- court and six other AIM members from Minneapolis who had come to the Nike base soon after the takeover left because of persistent drinking. "We won't participate when drinking like that is involved," Bellecourt said. "We want to change the stereotype of the drunken Indian." Later, Tusca- rora medicine man Mad Bear Anderson, who traveled throughout the United States during the early 1970s to lend support to Indian activists, visited with some of his supporters. Anderson, too, believed that drink- ing compromised the group and its mission. He handed Chosa a sign that read "no alcoholic beverages permitted," which he hoped Chosa would post at the camp entrance. Chosa consulted privately with CIV members, and some told him that they considered Anderson to have shown disre- spect in offering the sign and that he was "putting them down." Later, speaking of Anderson's group, a CIV leader observed that they "weren't ready for their medicine." CIV decided to continue having a separate area for drinkers in camp.[54]

The prominent media coverage of CIV at the Nike site and elsewhere not only created great interest early on but also came to pose a problem. Newspaper and television reporters appeared much more frequently at the Nike site than they had at the lot near Wrigley Field or at the Ains- lie Street building. Chosa charmed some of them. After he played the Indian mystic for a group of reporters, the *Chicago Tribune* ran an col- umn entitled "Mike Chosa: An Indian Moses." Other members of CIV shared Chosa's fascination with the media. The day after the occupation of the Nike site began, Carol Warrington speculated on media attention and coverage, asking, "I wonder what President Nixon will say about us with his forked tongue—and the mayor? I wonder if they will say any- thing about us?" At times, Chosa's power as a media magnet slowed CIV's negotiations with federal officials, who had stepped in to try to resolve the issue soon after the Nike site takeover. Courting the media also dis- affected some who had allied themselves with Chosa and caused them to claim he kept money for himself and reduced donations to other groups while taking advantage of his "self-appointed" status as leader. Susan K. Power, a Sioux who had been connected to many different organizations, including CIV, later said, "Chosa turned. He started believing the media. He started believing he was a chief and he was important."[55]

After almost three weeks under the steady gaze of the media, CIV's negotiations with various federal officials at the Nike base proved unproductive. Chosa had been asking for two hundred public housing units and an educational complex to be built for Indians by the federal government. Federal officials listened but were unsure about whom to deal with even if a program was agreed upon. One Nixon administration official later wrote that it was difficult to gauge the relationship between CIV and other Indians in Chicago. He and his colleagues had focused on "involving the broader Indian community while getting the militants within acceptable bounds."[56]

That approach was not producing a quick resolution at the Nike site, though, and at 5:30 on the morning of July 1, Chicago Park District workers arrived to remove the fence encircling it. CIV members were quickly awakened, and they rushed to the fence with buckets of water and iron bars to try and ward off the park workers, who said they had federal authorization to take down the fence. After the Indians began hitting workers' wire cutters—although not the workers themselves—with iron bars a large group from the Chicago Police Department, stationed nearby in riot gear, rushed to the scene to help the workers. During the melee some CIV members drained the gas tanks of cars in the compound to make Molotov cocktails. The first six thrown over the fence failed to explode after shattering. Only one, thrown off-target toward a nearby marina, successfully exploded and burned an empty boat docked there. The two-hour battle between roughly fifty Indians and police and park workers ended with twelve Indians being arrested for mob action.[57]

Still rejecting the city's offer of apartments for CIV members, Chosa and about forty others returned the next day to the Fourth Presbyterian Church. The few who managed to gain entry before the doors were locked helped the rest of the group, and some reporters, climb through a window. Church officials were not so receptive as they had been in March, and they ordered CIV to leave immediately or they would send for the police. While waiting, church members who were doctors treated the Indians' ailments, and church officials chartered two buses to transport CIV members from the church to the American Indian Center. Soon the Indians had filed into the buses and were headed to the Cook County Forest Preserve on Big Bend Lake near Des Plaines, Illinois, where park officials waived the rule requiring campers to leave by 11 P.M. Other Indian leaders from around the country soon joined CIV members.[58]

Shortly thereafter, however, CIV was on the move again. Charging that Cook County officials at the forest preserve had harassed them, on July 30 they went to yet another former Nike missile site near the Argonne National Laboratory in DuPage County. The eighty-acre site, like the first one, was also in the process of being handed over to the Cook County Forest Preserve District, and jurisdiction over it was unclear. CIV members eagerly moved into twelve recently abandoned army housing units and began to explore nearby forests and streams. Negotiations between Chosa and federal officials continued at Argonne. By now, a sympathetic group of local residents who called themselves the Concerned Citizens of DuPage County were writing frequent letters to the newspaper and lobbying officials to give CIV the housing and other facilities it wanted. The federal officials from Washington who were trying to untangle the collection of various local Indian organizations and interests grew frustrated with the Concerned Citizens. One believed the group was more persistent than popular, describing it as "two priests, some suburban housewives, and others in attendance, with a claimed membership of several thousand people." Two weeks after CIV had arrived at Argonne, negotiations began to break down, and CIV members grew angrier and more eager for a violent confrontation. But on August 19, as some CIV members talked of burning down Argonne and were rolling out oil drums to ignite, Chosa agreed on a deal. First, the Chicago Housing Authority would build 132 units and a cultural site in Uptown for CIV. Second, CIV members in the meantime would be permitted to move to Camp Seager, a Methodist youth camp near Naperville, Illinois. Third, further discussions between CIV and federal officials would continue. And, finally, CIV members would not be forcibly evicted from Argonne. Yet even this advantageous deal was put at risk when Chosa later demanded retention of some land at Argonne.[59]

By the end of 1971, CIV was still frequently on the move but having less success. The tone of newspaper accounts began to change and included more critical comments. Columnists began to poke fun at Chosa's desire to remain in the spotlight and questioned why the housing offered his group was unsatisfactory. Wendell Verduin of the Office of Equal Opportunity (OEO) was pressuring Chosa's supporters to break with him, using the promise of a possible $100,000 federal grant as an incentive.[60]

As winter arrived, Chosa and his supporters were evicted from Camp Seager. Although he said they had winterized the camp by installing oil heating in one building and setting up space heaters in the others, the Methodist camp's directors said it was not equipped for winter habitation. Warrington, whose housing protest had first given rise to CIV, began to hold her own protests with some of her friends and later formally split from Chosa. In January 1972 she and twenty supporters formed INDIAN (Indians Near Death in American Nations). She explained that she now recognized that Chosa had been a divisive force among Chicago Indians for a while and had prevented them from getting an OEO grant. Chosa's thirty supporters, half of whom were children, once more were evicted from Camp Seager after returning there, again rejected housing "even the Blacks don't want," and soon moved to Camp Logan north of Chicago near Zion, Illinois. Within a few months, in the summer of 1972, they were evicted from there and went to Milwaukee. Chosa periodically spent time in Chicago in 1972 and 1973 and tried to revive CIV, but the organization had effectively dissolved.[61]

By the summer of 1972, the energies that had created The Village and attracted Indian people to it were exhausted. CIV had certainly inspired some young Indian people for a time and given them the sense that they had power and could shape their destiny. Yet it failed to achieve anything enduring and was gone in only two years. Why was this so? For one thing, Chosa had difficulty finding a single effective target for his protests. He had come to Chicago influenced and energized by earlier labor organizing experiences in California, where he had used workers' control of ladders to put pressure on employers. He never found the equivalent tactic in Chicago, however. He never found the one weak point in the system on which he could effectively and continuously put pressure. That led CIV to be somewhat unfocused concerning the main culprit responsible for its troubles. Slumlords, politicians, "establishment Indians," the BIA, and churches all took their turn as the main target of CIV, but none played the role permanently. The attempts of Chosa and others to borrow from the Indian protest tradition produced mixed results. At times, CIV's use of the drum and teepee was successful. Yet complaints that parking lot owners had "broken a treaty" or that Richard Nixon—by then known to support Indian self-determination—had, like President Andrew Jackson, spoken with a "forked tongue" seemed to be strained and forced applications of the protest tradition.

Finally, the geographical context to CIV's protests also played a part in their limited success. In some ways, CIV resembled other Indian activist groups of the late 1960s and early 1970s—such as the Alcatraz occupiers—in the way it focused on the act of protest itself as much as on any particular goal or outcome.[62] Yet CIV did not share the same symbolic benefits enjoyed by those who occupied "the rock" in the middle of the San Francisco Bay between November 1969 and June 1971. The young Indian people at Alcatraz took advantage of their physical separation from the Bay Area by setting up their own distinct—and, to some onlookers, exotic—community. They established housing, government, courts, and a transportation system. When government officials, reporters, or curious onlookers arrived, they were often greeted with rituals usually reserved for meetings with heads of state. The Chicago Indian Village could practice a similar symbolic and media-friendly style of politics while briefly occupying the Nike missile site. At their other temporary homes (a parking lot, church basement, and county forest preserve), however, the group found it more difficult to shape its image. That, too, made it more difficult to appeal to both potential Indian participants and non-Indian observers.

The emphasis on self-determination and Indian pride—which the American Indian Center, St. Augustine's, American Indians–United, the Native American Committee, and the Chicago Indian Village had each in its own way fostered—lived on and found expression in education during the early 1970s. New Indian schools became the means by which old values and beliefs were disseminated.

The widespread desire on the part of Indian parents to have their children understand their heritage and identity led to the establishment of two schools in Chicago. In 1971 a branch of Senn High School, calling itself the Little Big Horn School, was established at the center. The new school offered classes for both preschool children and high school students. After a year at the center it moved to 919 Barry Street and later to Senn High School itself. Even before it opened its doors, members of the community had talked about the need for a new school, given the dropout rate among Indian schoolchildren and the problem of Indians being harassed and beaten by gangs. A $244,000 federal grant allowed for establishment of the school, and its five teachers taught eighty high school students and twenty preschool children in 1972. Throughout its early years the school contributed to continuing community development. As students wrote in a paper on their school's mission, "Pride is our greatest accomplishment, pride in ourselves, and in our community, in our culture and heritage." Marlene Strouse, a Papago mother whose son attended Little Big Horn School, was pleased that "the kids have something they can call their own."[63]

In 1973 Indian parents succeeded in establishing a branch of Goudy School, O-wai-ya-wa School ("place of learning"). Led by Louis Delgado, it served forty-five kindergarten and primary school students in the mornings and forty-five intermediate and junior high school students in the afternoons. Following what was by now a well-established tradition in

Chicago's Indian community, the school took a "multi-tribal approach," Delgado said. The school offered classes in the languages and customs of several different tribes, as well as in traditional academic subjects.[64]

Developments in Indian education in Chicago during the early 1970s extended to higher education as well. In 1971 the University of Illinois at Chicago started a Native American studies program led by Matthew War Bonnet, a Sioux and member of the American Indian Center. Thirty-five students enrolled in the program during its first year. In 1973 the Newberry Library opened the Center for the History of the American Indian, begun with a matching grant from the National Endowment for the Humanities. At the opening ceremony three medicine men from different tribes blessed the new center, and students from Little Big Horn School sang and danced. And, finally, Native American Educational Services (NAES) College opened in 1974, started by Faith Smith, the Chippewa who had earlier been at the center of controversy at the American Indian Center, and Robert V. Dumont, Jr., an Assiniboine-Sioux educator. Many NAES students were single parents, the first in their families to attend college, or G.E.D. holders wishing to advance their educations. After being accredited in 1984, NAES College began offering a degree in community studies and became the only private, Indian-controlled B.A.-granting college in the United States.[65]

---

The new Indian schools and the constituencies they served began the slow, unsteady process of unification in Chicago's American Indian community. There were new challenges to overcome in the process. Always crowded, Uptown, beginning in the 1970s, received a wave of new migrants: Cubans, Koreans, Hispanics, Arabs, blacks, and immigrants from Southeast Asia. Chicago's Indian population became more dispersed, especially after the 1970s, and Uptown no longer played the role it once had in the Indian community.[66] Furthermore, the center continued to be plagued by debt and frequent turnover in administration. Yet by the 1980s new community leadership again ushered in a period of successful adjustment as Chicago's Indians continued the process of reconciling urban life and Indian identity.

## Notes

1. *The Warrior* (Oct. 1965); *The Warrior* (Nov. 1968); Russell Means and Marvin J. Wolf, *Where White Men Fear to Tread: The Autobiography of Russell Means* (New York: St. Martin's Press, 1995), 144.

2. Program Report, Mar. 1966, American Indian Center [hereafter AIC], no. 0400, sec. 3, Urban Records Collection, Community Archives, Native American Educational Services College, Chicago [hereafter URC, CA, NAES]; Janusz Mucha, "From Prairie to the City: Transformation of Chicago's American Indian Community," *Urban Anthropology* 12 (Fall 1983): 360; *The Warrior* (Mar. 1965).

3. *The Warrior* (Mar. 1967); *The Warrior* (Jan. 1964).

4. *The Warrior* (Nov. 1967); *The Warrior* (Sept. 1968); American Indian Center service report, 1967, Church Federation of Greater Chicago [hereafter CFGC] Files, 33–5, Manuscript Collection, Chicago Historical Society [hereafter MC, CHS].

5. *The Warrior* (July 1967); "History of the St. Augustine's Center," undated unpublished ms., St. Augustine's Center, no. 1800, sec. 1, URC, CA, NAES; "Indian Center Gets First Indian Director," *Chicago Tribune*, 21 Jan. 1971, Clip File: "Ethnic Groups-Chicago-Indians, American," Harold Washington Public Library, Chicago [hereafter CF, HWPL]; "Survival Overshadows Militancy," *Uptown News*, 3 Dec. 1972, CF, HWPL.

6. *The Warrior* (special 1968 powwow edition); "We Don't Want to Jump into the Melting Pot," *Chicago Tribune*, 26 June 1966, CF, HWPL; *The Warrior* (May–June 1967).

7. *The Warrior* (July 1968); *The Warrior* (Nov. 1968) (first quotation); "City's American Indians Share Unique Problem," *Chicago Tribune*, 28 Jan. 1969, CF, HWPL (second quotation); *The Warrior* (Oct. 1969) (third quotation).

8. *The Warrior* (Sept. 1968); *The Warrior* (Apr. 1969).

9. Deborah Browning Leveen, "Hustlers and Heroes: Portrait and Analysis of the Chicago Indian Village," Ph.D. diss., University of Chicago, 1978, 75–76; *The Warrior* (Oct. 1965); Minutes of Chicago Indian Ministry Committee, 12 Mar. 1969, CFGC Files, 29–3, MC, CHS (quotation).

10. *The Warrior* (Dec. 1967); *The Warrior* (Mar. 1968); *The Warrior* (Sept. 1968).

11. *The Warrior* (Oct. 1969); Minutes of Chicago Indian Ministry Committee, 20 Aug. 1968 and 19 Sept. 1969, CFGC Files, 29–3, MC, CHS.

12. Merwyn S. Garbarino, "Indians in Chicago," in *Urban Indians: Proceedings of the Third Annual Conference on Problems and Issues Concerning American Indians Today* (Chicago: Newberry Library, 1981), 62.

13. Minutes of Chicago Indian Ministry Committee, 8 Oct. 1968, CFGC Files, 29–3, MC, CHS.

14. Report from American Indians–United 1969 national convention, CFGC Files, 34–2, MC, CHS.

15. Minutes of Chicago Indian Ministry Committee, 15 Feb. 1968 and 16 Apr. 1968, CFGC Files, 29–3, MC, CHS; Meeting list, box 89, Record Group 220: Records of the national Council on Indian Opportunity, National Archives II [hereafter RG 220, NA II]; American Indians–United membership brochure, folder "American Indians–United," Clip Files, Milwaukee Public Museum [hereafter CF, MPM].

16. *The Warrior* (Sept. 1968); *The Warrior* (Mar. 1968); "American Indians–

United, More Than a Concept," n.d., CFGC Files, 34–1, MC, CHS; "The Indian Movement Here," *Chicago Sun-Times,* 8 June 1970, CF, HWPL.

17. *The Warrior* (Sept. 1968); "Cherokee Cop Takes Year Off to Aid Indians," *Chicago American,* 18 Jan. 1969, CF, HWPL; "A New Kind of Indian Chief," *Chicago Daily News,* 1 Feb. 1969, CF, HWPL.

18. Minutes of Chicago Indian Ministry Committee, 12 Mar. 1969, CFGC Files, 29–3, MC, CHS; Report from American Indians–United 1969 National Convention, CFGC Files, 34–2, MC, CHS.

19. Report from American Indians–United 1969 National Convention, CFGC Files, 34–2, MC, CHS.

20. Ibld.; William Redcloud to American Indians–United Board, 7 Nov. 1969, folder "American Indian Center/Chicago," CF, MPM.

21. *The Warrior* (Oct. 1969).

22. *The Warrior* (Nov. 1969).

23. "The American Indian NOW," *Chicago Today,* 12 July 1970, CF, HWPL; Robert V. Dumont, "Notes from a Visit to the City," *Youth Magazine,* Nov. 24, 1973, 30–37; Mucha, "From Prairie to the City," 362; interview with Marlene Strouse (Papago), Chicago, 18 July 1983, Chicago American Indian Oral History Pilot Project, no. 011, Newberry Library, Chicago, and Native American Educational Services College, Chicago [hereafter CAIOHP, NL and NAES].

24. Interview with Marlene Strouse (Papago), Chicago, 18 July 1983, CAIOHP, no. 011, NL and NAES; Dumont, "Notes from a Visit to the City," 30–37.

25. Minutes of Chicago Indian Ministry Committee, 9 Jan., 22 Feb. 1970, CFGC Files, 29–3, MC, CHS; David McCreath to Richard Lupke, 8 Apr. 1970, CFGC Files, 29–5, MC, CHS.

26. Minutes of Chicago Indian Ministry Committee, 6 Apr. 1970, CFGC Files, 29–5, MC, CHS; *Chicago Tribune,* 24 Mar. 1970, CF, HWPL; "Indians vs. the City," *Chicago Magazine* (Apr. 1970), CF, HWPL; "Indians Renew Attacks on Agency's Programs," *Chicago Tribune,* 11 June 1970, CF, HWPL; "Indian Activists Freed in Sit-in," *Chicago Sun-Times,* 3 July 1970, CF, HWPL.

27. "Indians Disrupt Welfare Conference, Demand Funds," *Milwaukee Journal,* 3 June 1970, CF, MPM; "The Indian Movement Here," *Chicago Sun-Times,* 8 June 1970, CF, HWPL; Means and Wolf, *Where White Men Fear to Tread,* 158–59.

28. Leveen, "Hustlers and Heroes," 354–75; Mucha, "From Prairie to the City," 358.

29. Minutes of AIC Board of Directors Meeting, 20 Aug. 1971, AIC, no. 0400, sec. 4, URC, CA, NAES; Marvin Tahmahkera to American Indian Center Members, 30 Aug. 1971, AIC, no. 0400, sec. 4, URC, CA, NAES; "Court Drops Seven from Indian Center Board," *North Town,* 28 Nov. 1971, CF, HWPL; "City Indian Powwow Turns into Family Squabble," *Chicago Tribune,* 9 Jan. 1972, CF, HWPL.

30. Interview with Phyllis Fastwolf (Sioux-Oneida), Chicago, 8 May 1983, CAIOHP, no. 006, NL and NAES; author interview with Margaret Curtis (Sioux), Chicago, 26 Oct. 1993.

31. Minutes of Chicago Indian Ministry Committee, 26 May 1968, CFGC Files, 29–6, MC, CHS; Minutes of Chicago Indian Ministry Committee, 12 Mar. 1969, CFGC Files, 29–3, MC, CHS; "Indian Center Aides Charge Exploitation," *Chicago Daily News*, 15 Dec. 1972, CF, HWPL; "Local Indians Divided," *Chicago Tribune*, 3 Mar. 1973, CF, HWPL.

32. "Last Stand for Indian Center?" *Chicago Today*, 13 Mar. 1973, CF, HWPL; "Indian Center Pins Hopes on Survival March," *Chicago Sun-Times*, 1 Apr. 1973, CF, HWPL.

33. "Albert Cobe: 'I Must Step Up,'" *Chicago Tribune*, 30 May 1971, CF, HWPL; Leveen, "Hustlers and Heroes," 335–54; Mucha, "From Prairie to the City," 362; "Annual Report, 1972, Regional Council Task Force, Urban Committee," box 17, RG 220, NA II; "Indian Center Here Gets U.S. Jobs Grant," *Chicago Tribune*, 28 Nov. 1974, CF, HWPL; "Indians Get U.S. Grant," *Uptown News*, 19 Feb. 1975, CF, HWPL.

34. "Indian Dream Meets City Reality," *Uptown News*, 25 Nov. 1972, CF, HWPL.

35. *The Warrior* (Apr. 1972) (first quotation); "Indian Dream Meets City Reality," *Uptown News*, 25 Nov. 1972, CF, HWPL (second, third, and fourth quotations); Dumont, "Notes from a Visit to the City," 31–35.

36. Dumont, "Notes from a Visit to the City," 33; interview with Floria Forica (Chippewa), Chicago, 25 Mar. 1983, CAIOHP, no. 004, NL and NAES (quotation from Helen Whitehead); "NAC: Education Key to Indian Success," *Uptown News*, 18 Sept. 1976, CF, HWPL; "$42,000 OK'd for Indian Elderly," *Sunday Star*, 4 Dec. 1977, CF, HWPL.

37. Leveen, "Hustlers and Heroes," 107–12; Natalia Wilson, "The Chicago Indian Village, 1970," in *Native Chicago*, ed. Terry Straus and Grant P. Arndt (Chicago: Native Chicago, 1998), 155–62; "The Indian Movement Here," *Chicago Sun-Times*, 8 June 1970, CF, HWPL.

38. Leveen, "Hustlers and Heroes," 93–99; "Indians vs. the City," *Chicago Magazine* (Apr. 1970), CF, HWPL; "The Indian Movement Here," *Chicago Sun-Times*, 8 June 1970, CF, HWPL.

39. "Housing," 12 May 1970, CFGC Files, 29–6, MC, CHS (first quotation); "A Special Bulletin from the Chicago Indian Village," n.d., CFGC Files, 29–6, MC, CHS; "Protesting Indians Set Up a Squatters' Village on N. Side," *Chicago Sun-Times*, 1 June 1970, CF, HWPL (second quotation); "Indian Camp Raided Again," *Chicago Daily News*, 8 June 1970, CF, HWPL; "Whitemen on 'Warpath,'" *Chicago Today*, 9 June 1970, CF, HWPL; "Tents Back Up, Indians Dare Arrest," *Chicago Tribune*, 13 July 1970, CF, HWPL (third quotation).

40. Roger Biles, *Richard J. Daley: Politics, Race, and the Governing of Chicago* (DeKalb: Northern Illinois University Press, 1995), 171. On the effects of federal urban policy in Chicago during the 1960s and 1970s, see also Nicholas Lemann, *The Promised Land: The Great Black Migration and How It Changed America* (New York: Knopf, 1991).

41. Marilou Hedlund to Irene Hutchinson, 5 Oct. 1972, box 16, Marilou Hedlund Papers, MC, CHS; Jesse Escalente to Judith Walker, 4 May 1974, box

2, Marilou Hedlund Papers, MC, CHS; Jon C. Teaford, *The Rough Road to Renaissance: Urban Revitalization in America, 1940–1985* (Baltimore: Johns Hopkins University Press, 1990), 213.

42. "Petition of Indian Women Protests N. Side Village," *Chicago Sun-Times*, 11 June 1970, CF, HWPL.

43. Leveen, "Hustlers and Heroes," 86; "Indians Here Square Off on Wrigley Field Village," *Chicago Sun-Times*, 19 June 1970, CF, HWPL; "There's a Tempest in a Teepee," *Chicago Daily News*, 19 June 1970, CF, HWPL.

44. Merwyn S. Garbarino, "Life in the City: Chicago," in *The American Indian in Urban Society*, ed. Jack O. Waddell and O. Michael Watson (Boston: Little, Brown, 1971), 198–99; author interview with Edward E. Goodvoice (Sioux), Chicago, 14 June 1995; author interview with Daniel W. Battise (Alabama-Coushatta), Chicago, 15 June 1995.

45. Interview with Phyllis Fastwolf (Sioux-Oneida), Chicago, 8 May 1983, CAIOHP, no. 006, NL and NAES.

46. Biles, *Richard J. Daley*, 194–209; "City Promises Housing for Indian Villagers," *Chicago Sun-Times*, 14 July 1970, CF, HWPL.

47. Lemann, *The Promised Land*, 97–103; "Indians Will Test City Housing Offer," *Chicago Today*, 14 July 1970, CF, HWPL; "The Indians Push Back," *The Booster*, 5 Aug. 1970, CF, HWPL.

48. "Chippewas' Mike Chosa a Different Kind of Indian," *Chicago Sun-Times*, 15 Aug. 1971, CF, HWPL; Leveen, "Hustlers and Heroes," 120–21.

49. "Church Gets Indian Demands," *Chicago Tribune*, 11 Mar. 1971, CF, HWPL; Leveen, "Hustlers and Heroes," 122–47, quotation from 147.

50. Clayborne Carson, *In Struggle: SNCC and the Black Awakening of the 1960s* (Cambridge: Harvard University Press, 1981), 294–95; James F. Findlay, *Church People in the Struggle: The National Council of Churches and the Black Freedom Movement, 1950–1970* (New York: Oxford University Press, 1993), 199–225.

51. "Indians, Power Crew in Standoff," *Chicago Tribune*, 9 June 1971, CF, HWPL; "Uptown Indians Stage Sit-in at Urban Renewal Office," *Chicago Sun-Times*, 10 June 1971, CF, HWPL.

52. "Indians Take Old Nike Base," *Chicago Daily News*, 14 June 1971, CF, HWPL; Indians Seize Nike Site," *Chicago Sun-Times*, 15 June 1971, CF, HWPL.

53. "Indians Occupy Missile Base," *Chicago Tribune*, 15 June 1971, CF, HWPL; "Nike Site Indians Kid on Square," *Chicago Today*, 15 June 1971, CF, HWPL (quotation); Leveen, "Hustlers and Heroes," 203; "Indian Tent-in Now in Lap of Percy, Nixon," *Chicago Daily News*, 21 June 1971, CF, HWPL.

54. Author interview with Edward E. Goodvoice (Sioux), Chicago, 14 June 1995 (first quotation); "Chippewa Mike Chosa a Different Kind of Indian," *Chicago Sun-Times*, 15 Aug. 1971, CF, HWPL (second quotation); Leveen, "Hustlers and Heroes," esp. 215–27 (third and fourth quotations).

55. "Indians Take Old Nike Base," *Chicago Daily News*, 14 June 1971, CF, HWPL; "Mike Chosa: An Indian Moses," *Chicago Tribune*, 18 July 1971, CF, HWPL; Charles Leonard, Office of Management and Budget, to Working Group, 27 Sept. 1971, box 17, RG 220, NA II; "Chippewas' Mike Chosa a

Different Kind of Indian," *Chicago Sun-Times*, 15 Aug. 1971, CF, HWPL; "Indian Unit Raps Chosa as a Fraud," *Chicago Tribune*, 3 Sept. 1971, CF, HWPL; author interview with Susan K. Power (Sioux), Chicago, 19 June 1995. Garbarino also comments on the tremendous news coverage of Chosa and CIV in "Indians in Chicago," 63–64.

56. Charles Leonard, Office of Management and Budget, to Working Group, 27 Sept. 1971, box 17, RG 220, NA II.

57. "Indians Battle Cops," *Chicago Today*, 1 July 1971, CF, HWPL; "Indians Leave Base after Battling Cops," *Chicago Daily News*, 1 July 1971, CF, HWPL; Leveen, "Hustlers and Heroes," 217.

58. "Church Orders Indians: Get Out or Face Arrest," *Chicago Daily News*, 2 July 1971, CF, HWPL; "Forty Indians Lost Haven," *Chicago Daily News*, 3 July 1971, CF, HWPL; "Indians Here Go for Broke in Protest—End with Nothing," *Chicago Tribune*, 3 July 1971, CF, HWPL; "County Won't Oust Indians from Preserve, Dunne Says," *Chicago Daily News*, 6 July 1971, CF, HWPL.

59. Bruce Carroll, OEO, to Task Force on Urban Indians, 15 Aug. 1971, box 17, RG 220, NA II; Leveen, "Hustlers and Heroes," 310–11.

60. "Chosa Supporter Reports Job-Dismissal Threat by OEO," *Chicago Sun-Times*, 3 Dec. 1971, CF, HWPL; "Affidavit of Wayne Kennedy," 20 Dec. 1971, box 17, RG 220, NA II.

61. "Methodists Act to Oust Band of Indians," *Chicago Tribune*, 27 Nov. 1971, CF, HWPL; "Indians Vow Daily Sit-in at Lion House," *Chicago Tribune*, 1 Dec. 1971, CF, HWPL; "Fire Leaves Twenty Homeless after Split in Indian Ranks," *Chicago Sun-Times*, 9 Jan. 1972, CF, HWPL; "Chosa's Band Is Routed Again," *Chicago Tribune*, 12 Dec. 1971, CF, HWPL; "Chosa's Indians Go to Wisconsin," *Chicago Sun-Times*, 5 July 1972, CF, HWPL; "Chosa Indians Begin Moving Back into City," *Chicago Sun-Times*, 20 July 1972, CF, HWPL.

62. Paul Chatt Smith and Robert Allen Warrior, *Like a Hurricane: The Indian Movement from Alcatraz to Wounded Knee* (New York: Free Press, 1996), 79.

63. "On the Warpath?" *Uptown News*, 9 Nov. 1972, CF, HWPL; "Pride Runs High at Chicago's Native American High School," *Sunday Star*, 5 Aug. 1979, CF, HWPL; interview with Marlene Strouse (Papago), Chicago, 18 July 1983, CAIOHP, no. 011, NL and NAES.

64. "Viable O-wai-ya-wa Leads to Education with Special Plus," *Sunday Star*, 15 Jan. 1977, CF, HWPL.

65. "Sioux Leader Charts Attack on 'Red Man' Stereotypes," *Chicago Tribune*, 12 Dec. 1971, CF, HWPL; Mucha, "From Prairie to the City," 362–63; David R. M. Beck, "The Chicago American Indian Community," in *Native Chicago*, ed. Terry Straus and Grant P. Arndt (Chicago: Native Chicago, 1998), 177; David R. M. Beck, "Native American Education in Chicago: Teach Them Truth," *Education and Urban Society* 32 (Feb. 2000): 248–52.

66. Dominic A. Pacyga and Ellen Skerrett, *Chicago, City of Neighborhoods: Histories and Tours* (Chicago: Loyola University Press, 1986), 111–12; Beck, "Native American Education in Chicago," 245.

# CONCLUSION

American Indians in Chicago—and in other cities as well—saw their lives change in dramatic ways between 1945 and 1975. With some perspective one also sees that they participated in some of the most important events and trends in twentieth-century American history. The history of Native Americans and the history of the United States are not two permanently separate stories. Nor does the latter necessarily overwhelm the former when they do connect. One sees that urban Indians often responded to broader social, political, and economic forces in interesting and unique ways that shed new light on old narratives.

For example, Indians participated in World War II both overseas and at home and in doing so responded to a series of personal, family, tribal, and national obligations. The years following the war opened new opportunities for many Americans. Indians were among millions nationwide who moved from rural areas to large cities in the middle of the twentieth century. Their experience differed, however, from that of other Americans, most obviously in the federal government's partial subsidization of their journey. Indian people in this account lived through a time of unprecedented affluence and consumerism in the United States. Yet the temptation to draw a dramatic contrast between national wealth and Native American poverty does not fully bear out, at least when considering Indian people in Chicago during this time. Urban Indians were not, strictly speaking, "other Americans" cut off from all significant economic transformations. Some in Chicago experienced real economic gain that they used for personal, family, community, or tribal benefit. Yet the contrast with the non-Indian population of Chicago as a whole made it clear that Indians lagged behind other groups in economic power. It also spurred acts of protest.

In race relations in particular, urban Indians contributed a distinct voice to a national discussion that attracted increasing interest during the middle of the twentieth century. Even before leaders of other groups concluded that old shibboleths did not hold all the answers to political, social, and economic problems, Indians were making the case. Many declared that equality under the law was not their preeminent goal. Instead they combined notions of equality with calls for Indian pride and self-determination.

A similar ambivalence to national trends and values is seen in Chicago Indians' responses to widespread political activism in the 1960s and 1970s. Negotiating their place in a rapidly changing larger society was a difficult, sometimes painful process for Indian people in Chicago. Many Chicagoans expected the Indians they had only recently noticed among them to play the symbolic role they had in mind and join them in their latest cause. Indeed, some Indians did believe that selected expressions of activism could be reconciled with "Indianness" and even build on it. Yet many also believed that some styles and strategies of protest opposed the Indian way of life.

To recognize these connections forged in cities between American Indians and American society is to begin to reassess twentieth-century American Indian history as a whole. To note them—as well as the majority status of urban Indians among all tribesmen since the 1970s—provides a new set of mental images to add to those commonly held concerning American Indian life. To be sure, part of Indian history during the twentieth century was characterized by images of reservation life and all that life entailed. Yet it was also about finding a place in labor markets, searching for housing, and maintaining visibility for one's people in a sea of cosmopolitan diversity.

While Indian people in increasing numbers responded to trends often centered in American cities, they, too, were transformed by their experiences there. Most important, they developed an identity less tied to the reservation and tribe and more connected to the vast array of tribes in the city. Its orientation was both pan-Indian and urban. The transformation has been dramatic, for it strikes at the heart of the question of who is an Indian. The sometimes-complicated process of answering that basic question was changed profoundly and permanently by urbanization.

Pan-Indianism of the sort forged in cities such as Chicago had many causes. The daily struggles of urban life, Indians' small numbers compared with those of other groups living in the city, and the prospect of far-reaching and threatening policy changes made pan-Indianism seem necessary. Sticking together against stiff challenges was an understandable and reasonable adjustment strategy for Indian people in the city.

Even beyond pan-Indianism, urbanization reshaped Indian life in a number of other ways, and reservation and urban Indians both eventual-

ly had to come to terms with its effects. One example of this development may be seen in the more recent debates about casinos on reservations. Supporters of casinos have touted their economic benefits, whereas opponents have warned against trading short-term gains for long-term
social, cultural, and economic problems. Even on reservations where
casinos have been built, debates have continued over control of the business and dispersal of profits. One debate began in 1996 at the Keweenaw
Bay Indian Community on Michigan's Upper Peninsula. There, Chippewas supporting the tribal chair and his program for casino profits squared
off against a dissident group that called itself Fight for Justice. The protestors disparagingly referred to those in power as "apples," while the
chair and his allies called their opponents "Hollywood Indians."

The controversy, seemingly centered on the reservation, revealed
important aspects of urban life. The chair reported that those responsible for the turmoil and anger were "ignorant city Indians coming [back
to the reservation] and demanding a free paycheck from the profits." He
suggested that they were not truly Indian—in large part because of their
urban experiences—and only cashing in on their claimed Indian identity because there was money to be made from it. Although the protestors
disagreed with that characterization of urbanization, they, too, acknowledged its impact. Yet they saw it operating in different ways. One woman in the dissident group had lived in several cities in California before
returning to Michigan. She summarized her experiences with urbanization by saying, "People who come back here with a wider perspective on
things question the tribal government's little empire." She believed that
her urban experiences could benefit other Chippewas on the reservation
and used her new skills to challenge corrupt authorities and try to make
the reservation a more just and democratic place. Partisans in the dispute
held two diametrically opposed viewpoints, yet both hinged on urbanization and the ways it affected Indian people.[1]

Other Indian people, such as Margaret Curtis, a Sioux, have also seen
casinos bring reservation-urban differences to the forefront. After living
many years in Chicago, she laughs at the proud and respectful tone that
Sioux on the reservation use to speak of their casino. "Their only thing
is that casino. That's the only thing that's great there now," she says with
disgust, pointing out that the reservation does not fund education or
much of anything else other than the casino. Even Sioux in Chicago who
want to return to the reservation and work at the casino are out of luck,
Curtis observes. "They will hire people that are there first before they
hire you, even though you are from that reservation. Once you leave your

reservation and you become urbanized, they no longer consider you a part of that."[2]

Debates concerning casinos and economic development are just some of the ways in which urbanization has created new dynamics in relationships among American Indians. Moreover, urbanization brought Indian people into contact with other racial groups and led them to rethink their position in American society as a whole. They have borrowed some ideas, practices, and strategies from non-Indians while carefully keeping others at arm's length for fear that they might corrupt Indian identity (or at least confuse the general public about its meaning). Only in the city was this type of experiment possible.

The leaders of Chicago's philanthropic and social welfare agencies played a particularly significant role in the lives of American Indians. From the beginning of large-scale migration in the early 1950s this group, comprised primarily of upper-middle-class whites, established contact with the Indians who were arriving in Chicago. The relationship, however, became a double-edged sword for Indians. On the one hand, they often needed financial assistance to start organizations, buy real estate for headquarters, and start community programs. Indeed, Chicago philanthropists and foundations helped shape Chicago's Indian community in the 1950s. On the other hand, continuing ties to these same groups led to frustration when they appeared to compromise Indian self-determination. Long-time "friends of the Indian" were at the center of many battles during the 1960s and 1970s, when various factions claimed their opponents were compromised by connections to non-Indians and so unable to lead the community. In such cases, philanthropic and social welfare agencies played a role—albeit unwittingly—in the partial dissolution of Chicago's Indian community.

To be sure, the story of urban Indian communities forming and developing is not Chicago's alone. In some ways, this account is part of a national story; Los Angeles, San Francisco, Phoenix, Denver, and other cities shared the same plot. Yet there are differences among these cities and their Indian communities as well. In Chicago, Indians were clearly influenced by the early establishment of the federal government's relocation program. Early migration patterns to Chicago were markedly regional, and Indians from the Upper Midwest and Northern Plains led the way. One might expect western regional migration patterns among other contemporary urban Indian centers. When compared to other cities, Chicago never developed a purely Indian neighborhood. They even shared Uptown with other groups. Most Chicago Indians' experiences with race relations were limited to whites and blacks, with fairly little contact with Latinos. That also differentiated Chicago from other western urban Indian centers.

Particularly by the 1970s, Indians in Chicago were among those hurt most by deindustrialization and its accompanying structural economic changes. Chicagoans had touted their home as "the city that works" throughout its prominent industrial period. A strong investment in the industrial base, however, left Indians (and many other Chicagoans) at a disadvantage after service-sector jobs replaced factory jobs.

Compared with the early Chicago Indian community in the 1950s, the community in the 1970s was more characterized by pan-Indianism and in general by urban trends. It was also more committed to self-determination—even when the route to that destination was unclear. On the whole, it had more economic success although that change was sometimes obscured by the higher expectations that urbanization created among Indians because of their new and closer connection to mainstream political and economic structures.

Within Chicago's Indian community, some of the events of the 1970s brought disputes to the surface and weakened the group for a time. Yet after those problems had passed, the community again began work toward building a shared commitment to self-determination and Indian pride. To be sure, many people had spent a great deal of time and energy arguing over just what those terms meant and who had the right to use them. Yet Indians in Chicago demonstrated that such ideas could again be the tools for building meaningful and successful lives.

## Notes

1. "Casino Builds a Wall in Tribe," *Chicago Tribune*, 7 July 1996.
2. Author interview with Margaret Curtis (Sioux), Chicago, 26 Oct. 1993.

# BIBLIOGRAPHY

*Primary Sources*

MANUSCRIPT COLLECTIONS

Chicago. Chicago Historical Society, Manuscript Collections.
  Church Federation of Greater Chicago Records
  Indian Fellowship League Records
  Marilou Hedlund Papers
  Welfare Council of Metropolitan Chicago Records
Chicago. Harold Washington Public Library.
  Clip Files: "Ethnic Groups—Chicago—Indians, American, 1957–1970"
  Clip Files: "Ethnic Groups—Chicago—Indians, American, 1971"
  Clip Files: "Ethnic Groups—Chicago—Indians, American, 1972–1979"
Chicago. National Archives-Great Lakes Region.
  Record Group 75, Records of the Bureau of Indian Affairs
    Chicago Field Office Files
    Employment Assistance Case Files, 1952–1960
    Employment Assistance Case Files, 1967
    Reports on Employment Assistance, 1951–1958
Chicago. Native American Educational Services (NAES) College Library, Community Archives.
  Robert Rietz Collection
  Sol Tax Papers
  Urban Records Collection
    American Indian Center, no. 0400
    *American Indian Center News*, no. 5100
    American Indian Chicago Conference of 1961, no. 3150
    *Amerindian*, no. 5150
    BIA Relocation, no. 2000
    *The Cross and the Calumet*, no. 5250
    Indian Council Fire, no. 0800
    *Indian News*, no. 5375
    *Indian Voices*, no. 5415
    St. Augustine's Center for American Indians, no. 1800
    *Teepee Topics*, no. 5925
    *The Warrior*, no. 5965
    World's Columbian Exposition, no. 2100

Chicago. Newberry Library, D'arcy McNickle Center for the History of the American Indian, Special Collections.
Indian Council Fire Papers
Madison, Wisconsin. State Historical Society of Wisconsin.
Illinois–Wisconsin Friends Committee for American Indians Papers
Milwaukee, Wisconsin. Milwaukee Public Museum.
Clip Files
Robert E. Ritzenthaler Field Notes
New Haven, Connecticut. Yale University, Sterling Memorial Library, Archives and Manuscripts Division.
John Collier Papers
Salt Lake City, Utah. University of Utah, Marriott Library.
Stanley D. Lyman Papers
Washington, D.C. National Archives, Washington D.C.
Record Group 75, Records of the Bureau of Indian Affairs
Field Placement and Relocation Office Employment Assistance Records
Financial Program
Narrative Reports, 1952–54, 1958–60
Placement and Statistical Reports, 1948–54
M595, Indian Census Rolls, 1885–1940
Washington, D.C. National Archives II, Washington D.C.
Record Group 220, Records of the National Council on Indian Opportunity
Washington, D.C. Smithsonian Institution, National Anthropological Archives.
American Indian Chicago Conference Records

GOVERNMENT DOCUMENTS

*Annual Report of the Commissioner of Indian Affairs.* Washington, D.C.: Department of the Interior, 1948–51.
Department of Health, Education, and Welfare. *A Study of Selected Socio-Economic Characteristics of Ethnic Minorities Based on the 1970 Census,* vol. 3: *American Indians.* Washington, D.C.: Department of Health, Education, and Welfare, 1974.
Department of the Interior, Bureau of Indian Affairs. *Adult Vocational Training Approved Courses,* 30 Nov. 1968.
House Subcommittee on Indian Affairs. *Indian Relocation and Industrial Development Programs.* 85th Cong., 2d sess., Committee Print no. 14, Oct. 1957.
National Council on Indian Opportunity. *Public Forum before the Committee on Urban Indians in Dallas, Texas.* Washington, D.C.: National Council on Indian Opportunity, 1969.
———. *Public Forum before the Committee on Urban Indians in Los Angeles, California.* Washington, D.C.: National Council on Indian Opportunity, 1968.
———. *Public Forum before the Committee on Urban Indians in Phoenix, Arizona.* Washington, D.C.: National Council on Indian Opportunity, 1969.
———. *Public Forum before the Committee on Urban Indians in San Francisco, California.* Washington, D.C.: National Council on Indian Opportunity, 1969.
Senate Committee on Indian Affairs. *Survey of Conditions among the Indians of the United States.* Washington, D.C.: Government Printing Office, 1932–44.

U.S. Bureau of the Census. *Census of Population: 1940, Nonwhite Population by Race.* Washington, D.C.: Government Printing Office.
———. *Census of Population: 1950, Nonwhite Population by Race.* Washington, D.C.: Government Printing Office.
———. *Census of Population: 1960, Nonwhite Population by Race.* Washington, D.C.: Government Printing Office.
———. *Census of Population: 1970, Nonwhite Population by Race.* Washington, D.C.: Government Printing Office.
———. *U.S. Census of Population: 1940. Census Tract Statistics, Chicago, Ill. and Adjacent Area.* Washington, D.C.: Government Printing Office, 1942.
———. *U.S. Census of Population: 1950. Census Tract Statistics, Chicago, Ill. and Adjacent Area.* Washington, D.C.: Government Printing Office, 1952.
———. *U.S. Census of Population and Housing: 1960. Census Tracts, Chicago, Ill.* Washington, D.C.: Government Printing Office, 1962.
———. *1970 Census of Population and Housing: Census Tracts, Chicago, Ill. Standard Metropolitan Statistical Area.* Washington, D.C.: Government Printing Office, 1972.
U.S. Congress, American Indian Policy Review Commission, Task Force Eight. *Report on Urban and Rural Non-Reservation Indians: Final Report to the American Indian Policy Review Commission.* Washington, D.C.: Government Printing Office, 1976.
U.S. Congress, House. *Termination of Federal Supervision, Concurrent Resolution 108.* 83d Cong., 1st sess., 1 Aug. 1953. Washington, D.C.: Government Printing Office, 1953.

PUBLISHED PRIMARY SOURCES

Armstrong, O. K. "Set the American Indian Free." *Reader's Digest* (Aug. 1945): 47–51.
———, and Marjorie Armstrong. "The Indians Are Going to Town." *Reader's Digest* 66 (Jan. 1955): 39–43.
Baerreis, David A., ed. *The Indian in Modern America.* Madison: State Historical Society of Wisconsin, 1956.
Brophy, William A. et al., eds. *The Indian: America's Unfinished Business.* Norman: University of Oklahoma Press, 1966.
Bruner, Edward M. "Assimilation among Fort Berthold Indians." *The American Indian* 6 (Summer 1953): 21–29.
Bruno, Hal. "Chicago's Hillbilly Ghetto." *The Reporter*, 4 June 1964, 28–31.
Carter, E. Russell. "Rapid City, South Dakota." *The American Indian* 6 (Summer 1953): 29–38.
Cash, Joseph H., and Herbert T. Hoover, eds. *To Be an Indian: An Oral History.* Rev. ed. Minneapolis: Borealis, Minnesota Historical Society, 1995.
"Chicago's Indian Priest." *Newsweek*, 23 Jan. 1967, 91.
Clark, Blake. "Must We Buy America from the Indians All Over Again?" *Reader's Digest* 72 (Mar. 1958): 45–49.
Conly, Robert L. "The Mohawks Scrape the Sky." *National Geographic* 102 (1952): 133–42.
Department of Geography, DePaul University. *Chicago's People, Jobs and Homes:*

*A Human Geography of the City and Metropolitan Area.* Chicago: The Department, 1964.

*Directory of Large Employers in the Chicago Metropolitan Area.* Chicago: Chicago Association of Commerce and Industry, 1955.

Dumont, Robert V. "Notes from a Visit to the City." *Youth Magazine,* 24 Nov. 1973, 30–37.

Emmons, Glenn. "U.S. Aim: Give the Indians a Chance." *The Nation's Business* (July 1955): 42–44.

Engstrom, George, and Sister Providencia. "City and Reservation Indians." *Social Order* 5 (Feb. 1955): 66.

Gillan, John. "Acquired Drives in Culture Contact." *American Anthropologist* 44 (Oct.–Dec. 1942): 545–54.

Golden, Madelon, and Lucia Carter. "New Deal for America's Indians." *Coronet* 38 (Oct. 1953): 74–76.

Gridley, Marion. *Indians of Today.* 3d ed. Chicago: N.p., 1960.

Griggs, Anthony. "Alaskan Natives Face Urbanization." *Race Relations Reporter,* 20 Aug. 1973, 4–6.

Hamilton, Andrew. "Their Indian Guests." *Saturday Evening Post,* 17 Sept. 1960, 43, 84–86.

Harmer, Ruth Mulvey. "Uprooting the Indians." *Atlantic Monthly* 197 (Mar. 1956): 54–57.

Harris, Michael. "American Cities: The New Reservations." *City* 5 (Mar.–Apr. 1971): 44–48.

Hauser, Philip M., and Evelyn M. Kitagawa, eds. *Local Community Fact Book for Chicago, 1950.* Chicago: Chicago Community Inventory, University of Chicago, 1953.

Hoch, Irving. *Forecasting Economic Activity for the Chicago Region: Final Report.* Chicago: Chicago Area Transportation Study, 1959.

I.A.L. "The Changing Fate of the American Indian." *World Today* (Aug. 1957): 351–60.

Ickes, Harold L. "Go East Young Indian!" *New Republic,* 3 Sept. 1951, 29–33.

"Indian Reservations May Some Day Run Out of Indians." *Saturday Evening Post,* 27 Nov. 1957, 23–25.

Kitagawa, Evelyn M., and Donald J. Bogue. *Suburbanization of Manufacturing Activity within Standard Metropolitan Areas.* Oxford, Ohio: Scripps Foundation for Research in Population Problems, 1955.

Kitagawa, Evelyn M., Donald J. Bogue, and Karl E. Taeuber, eds. *Local Community Fact Book: Chicago Metropolitan Area, 1960.* Chicago: Chicago Community Inventory, University of Chicago, 1963.

LaFarge, Oliver. "They Were Good Enough for the Army." *Reader's Digest* 52 (Feb. 1948): 115–18.

———, ed. *The Changing Indian.* Norman: University of Oklahoma Press, 1942.

Leupp, Francis E. *The Indian and His Problem.* New York: Charles Scribner's Sons, 1910.

Lindquist, G. E. E. "The Church and the Indian in Urban Centers." In *Indians in Transition: A Study of Protestant Mission to Indians in the United States.* Ed. G. E. E. Lindquist. New York: Division of Home Missions, National Council of Churches of Christ in the United States, 1952.

*Local Community Fact Book: Chicago Metropolitan Area, Based on the 1970 and 1980 Censuses.* Chicago: Chicago Review Press, 1984.

Lohmann, Karl B. *Cities and Towns of Illinois: A Handbook of Community Facts.* Urbana: University of Illinois Press, 1951.

Madigan, LaVerne. *The American Indian Relocation Program.* New York: Association on American Indian Affairs, 1956.

*Major Employers in the Chicago Metropolitan Area.* Chicago: Chicago Association of Commerce and Industry, 1959.

*Major Employers, Metropolitan Chicago.* Chicago: Chicago Association of Commerce and Industry, 1963–64.

Mekeel, H. Scudder. *The Economy of a Modern Teton Dakota Community.* New Haven: Yale University Press, 1936.

Meriam, Lewis et al. *The Problem of Indian Administration.* Baltimore: Johns Hopkins University Press, 1928.

*Metropolitan Area Planning for Northeastern Illinois and Northwestern Indiana.* Chicago: Chicago Metropolitan Housing and Planning Council, 1956.

*Metropolitan Chicago Major Employers.* Chicago: Chicago Association of Commerce and Industry, 1968–69.

Mirrielees, Edith R. "The Cloud of Mistrust." *Atlantic Monthly* 199 (Feb. 1957): 55–59.

Myer, Dillon S. "Indian Administration: Problems and Goals." *Social Science Review* 27 (Winter 1953): 193–200.

———. "Program of the Bureau of Indian Affairs." *Journal of Negro Education* 25 (Summer 1951): 346–53.

Peters, Scott Henry. "Chippewa Favors Business Profession for the Indian." *The American Indian* (July 1927): 15.

Reifel, Ben. "Cultural Factors in Social Adjustment." *Indian Education,* 15 Apr. 1957.

Rietz, Robert. "The American Indian Center." *Illinois Journal of Education* 61 (Apr. 1970): 63–68.

Ritzenthaler, Robert E. "The Impact of War on an Indian Community." *American Anthropologist* 45 (Apr.–June 1943): 325–26.

———, and Mary Sellers. "Indians in an Urban Situation." *Wisconsin Anthropologist* 36 (Dec. 1955): 147–58.

"The Sioux Indians: Their Plight Is Our Worst Disgrace." *Look,* 19 Apr. 1955, 32–37.

*A Social Geography of Metropolitan Chicago.* Chicago: Northeastern Illinois Metropolitan Planning Commission, 1960.

Solomon, Ezra, and Zarko Bilbija. *Metropolitan Chicago: An Economic Analysis.* Glencoe: Free Press, 1959.

*Suburban Factbook, 1950–1960.* Chicago: Northeastern Illinois Metropolitan Planning Commission, 1960.

*A Survey of the Resources of the Chicago Industrial Area.* Chicago: Chicago Association of Commerce and Industry, 1950.

Terkel, Studs. *Division Street America.* New York: Pantheon Books, 1967.

Trillin, Calvin. "U.S. Journal: Gallup, New Mexico." *The New Yorker,* 25 Sept. 1971, 110–14.

————. "U.S. Journal: Los Angeles, New Group in Town." *The New Yorker*, 18 Apr. 1970, 95–104.

Useem, John, Gordon Macgregor, and Ruth Hill Useem. "Wartime Employment and Cultural Adjustments of the Rosebud Sioux." *Applied Anthropology* 2 (Jan.–Mar. 1943): 1–9.

VandeMark, Dorothy. "The Raid on the Reservations." *Harper's Magazine* 212 (Mar. 1956): 48–53.

Wagner, James R., and Richard Corrigan. "BIA Brings Indians to Cities but Has Few Urban Services." *National Journal*, 11 July 1970, 1493–502.

Weltfish, Gene. "When the Indian Comes to the City." *American Indian* 1 (Winter 1944): 6–10.

Wilbur, Ray Lyman. "Uncle Sam Has a New Indian Policy." *Saturday Evening Post*, 8 June 1929, 5–6.

Wirth, Louis, and Eleanor H. Bernert. *Local Community Fact Book of Chicago.* Chicago: University of Chicago Press, 1949.

INTERVIEWS

American Indian Oral History Research Project, Doris Duke Oral History Collection
  Curt Campbell (Sioux), 23 June 1970, pt. 1, no. 63, MS 504
  Dan Clark (Sioux), Summer 1968, pt. 1, no. 19, MS 7
  Lenora DeWitt (Sioux), 25 Aug. 1971, pt. 1, no. 39, MS 786
  William Isburg (Sioux), 26 July 1968, pt. 1, no. 22, MS 54
  Gordon Jones (Sioux), 2 June 1971, pt. 1, no. 34, MS 684
  Richard LaRoche (Sioux), 25 Aug. 1971, pt. 1, no. 41, MS 784
  Josephine Spotted Hawk (Sioux), 1 Sept. 1971, pt. 1, no. 43, MS 787
  Floyd Taylor (Sioux), 9 Aug. 1968, pt. 1, no. 25, MS 50
  Keith Wakeman (Sioux), Summer 1971, pt. 1, no. 32, MS 825
Chicago American Indian Oral History Pilot Project, Newberry Library and NAES College, Community Archives
  Daniel W. Battise (Alabama-Coushatta), Chicago, n.d., no. 020
  Phyllis Fastwolf (Sioux-Oneida), Chicago, 8 May 1983, no. 006
  Floria Forica (Chippewa), Chicago, 25 Mar. 1983, no. 004
  Willard LaMere (Winnebago), Chicago, 1 Feb. 1984, no. 009
  Ann Lim (Winnebago), Chicago, 7 Feb. 1984, no. 019
  Rose Maney (Winnebago), Chicago, 2 May 1984, no. 002
  Rosella Mars (Chippewa), Chicago, 18 Apr. 1984, no. 013
  Cornelia Penn (Sioux), Chicago, 3 Sept. 1983, no. 017
  Susan K. Power (Sioux), Chicago, 26 Sept. 1983, no. 016
  Ada Powers (Sioux), Chicago, 19 Apr. 1984, no. 012
  Margaret Redcloud (Chippewa), Chicago, 12 Feb. 1984, no. 021
  Amy Lester Skenandore (Stockbridge), Chicago, n.d., no. 003
  Marlene Strouse (Papago), Chicago, 18 July 1983, no. 011
  Joe White (Winnebago), Chicago, n.d., no. 022
Author's personal interviews
  Daniel W. Battise (Alabama-Coushatta), Chicago, 15 June 1995
  Ronald Bowan, Sr. (Menominee), Chicago, 15 June 1995

Margaret Curtis (Sioux), Chicago, 26 Oct. 1993
Edward E. Goodvoice (Sioux), Chicago, 14 June 1995
Samson Keahna (Mesquakie), Chicago, 27 Oct. 1993
Diane Maney (Winnebago), Chicago, 20 June 1995
Susan K. Power (Sioux), Chicago, 19 June 1995
Candace Ryan (Sioux), Chicago, 13 June 1995
Sharon Skolnick (Apache), Chicago, 15 June 1995
Lucille Spencer (Choctaw), Chicago, 22 June 1995
Josephine Willie (Choctaw), Chicago, 14 June 1995

## Secondary Sources

Ablon, Joan. "The American Indian Chicago Conference." *Journal of American Indian Education* 1 (Jan. 1962): 17–23.

———. "The American Indian Chicago Conference." In *Currents in Anthropology: Essays in Honor of Sol Tax.* Ed. Robert Hinshaw. New York: Mouton Publishers, 1979.

———. "American Indian Relocation: Problems of Dependency and Management in the City." *Phylon* 26 (Winter 1965): 362–71.

———. "Cultural Conflict in Urban Indians." *Mental Hygiene* 55 (Apr. 1971): 199–205.

———. "Relocated American Indians in the San Francisco Bay Area: Social Interactions and Indian Identity." *Human Organization* 23 (Winter 1964): 296–304.

Allswang, John M. *House for All Peoples: Chicago's Ethnic Groups and Their Politics, 1890–1936.* Lexington: University Press of Kentucky.

Anderson, Philip J., and Dag Blanck, eds. *Swedish-American Life in Chicago: Cultural and Urban Aspects of an Immigrant People, 1850–1930.* Urbana: University of Illinois Press, 1992.

Arends, Wade B., Jr. "A Socio-Cultural Study of the Relocated American Indians in Chicago." M.A. thesis, University of Chicago, 1958.

Arndt, Grant. "'Contrary to Our Way of Thinking': The Struggle for an American Indian Center in Chicago, 1946–1953." *American Indian Culture and Research Journal* 22, no. 4 (1998): 117–34.

———. "Relocation's Imagined Landscape and the Rise of Chicago's Native American Community." In *Native Chicago.* Ed. Terry Straus and Grant P. Arndt. Chicago: Native Chicago, 1998.

Bahr, Howard M., Bruce A. Chadwick, and Robert C. Day, eds. *Native Americans Today: Sociological Perspectives.* New York: Harper and Row, 1972.

Beck, David R. M. *The Chicago American Indian Community, 1893–1988: Annotated Bibliography and Guide to Sources in Chicago.* Chicago: NAES College Press, 1988.

———. "The Chicago American Indian Community." In *Native Chicago.* Ed. Terry Straus and Grant P. Arndt. Chicago: Native Chicago, 1998.

———. "Native American Education in Chicago: Teach Them Truth." *Education and Urban Society* 32 (Feb. 2000): 237–55.

———. "Relocation in Chicago." *RULE: Reservation Urban Learning Exchange* (Summer 1993): 5–7.

Bernardi, Adria. *Houses with Names: The Italian Immigrants of Highwood, Illinois.* Urbana: University of Illinois Press, 1990.

Bernstein, Alison R. *American Indians and World War II: Toward a New Era in Indian Affairs.* Norman: University of Oklahoma Press, 1991.

Bieder, Robert E. *Native American Communities in Wisconsin, 1600–1960: A Study of Tradition and Change.* Madison: University of Wisconsin Press, 1995.

Biles, Roger. *Richard J. Daley: Politics, Race, and the Governing of Chicago.* DeKalb: Northern Illinois University Press, 1995.

Biolsi, Thomas. *Organizing the Lakota: The Political Economy of the New Deal on the Pine Ridge and Rosebud Reservations.* Tucson: University of Arizona Press, 1992.

Boatman, John F. *Wisconsin American Indian History and Culture: A Survey of Selected Aspects.* Milwaukee: University of Wisconsin–Milwaukee, 1993.

Bodnar, John. *The Transplanted: A History of Immigrants in Urban America.* Bloomington: Indiana University Press, 1985.

——, Roger Simon, and Michael P. Weber. *Lives of Their Own: Blacks, Italians, and Poles in Pittsburgh, 1900–1960.* Urbana: University of Illinois Press, 1982.

Borman, Leonard D. "Action Anthropology and the Self-Help/Mutual-Aid Movement." In *Currents in Anthropology: Essays in Honor of Sol Tax.* Ed. Robert Hinshaw. New York: Mouton Publishers, 1979.

Bowly, Devereux, Jr. *The Poorhouse: Subsidized Housing in Chicago, 1895–1976.* Carbondale: Southern Illinois University Press, 1978.

Brody, Hugh. *Indians on Skid Row.* Ottawa: Department of Indian Affairs and Northern Development, 1971.

Burner, David. *Making Peace with the Sixties.* Princeton: Princeton University Press, 1996.

Burt, Larry W. "Roots of the Native American Urban Experience: Relocation Policy in the 1950s." *American Indian Quarterly* 10 (Spring 1986): 85–99.

——. *Tribalism in Crisis: Federal Indian Policy, 1953–1961.* Albuquerque: University of New Mexico Press, 1982.

Carmichael, Stokely. "What We Want." *New York Review of Books,* 22 Sept. 1966, 5–8.

Carson, Clayborne. *In Struggle: SNCC and the Black Awakening of the 1960s.* Cambridge: Harvard University Press, 1981.

Castile, George Pierre. *To Show Heart: Native American Self-Determination and Federal Indian Policy, 1960–1975.* Tucson: University of Arizona Press, 1998.

Chadwick, Bruce A., and Joseph H. Stauss. "The Assimilation of American Indians into Urban Society: The Seattle Case." *Human Organization* 34 (Winter 1975): 359–69.

Chadwick, Bruce A., and Lynn C. White. "Correlates of Length of Urban Residence among the Spokane Indians." *Human Organization* 32 (Spring 1973): 9–16.

*Chicago American Indian Community Service Directory.* Chicago: NAES College Press, 1980.

Clark, Blue. "Bury My Heart in Smog." In *The American Indian Experience: A Profile.* Ed. Philip Weeks. Arlington Heights: Forum Press, 1988.

——. "Bury My Lungs in Smog: Assessing Urban Indian Studies." In *Native Views of Indian-White Historical Relations.* Ed. Donald L. Fixico. Chicago: The Newberry Library, 1989.

Cobb, Daniel M. "Philosophy of an Indian War: Indian Community Action in the Johnson Administration's War on Poverty, 1964–1968." *American Indian Culture and Research Journal* 22, no. 2 (1998): 71–102.

Cohen, Fay G. "The Indian Patrol in Minneapolis: Social Control and Social Change in an Urban Context." *Law and Society Review* 7 (Summer 1973): 779–86.

Cohen, Lizabeth. "The Class Experience of Mass Consumption." In *The Power of Culture: Critical Essays in American History.* Ed. Richard W. Fox and Jackson Lears. Chicago: University of Chicago Press, 1993.

Colburn, David R., and George E. Pozzetta. "Race, Ethnicity, and the Evolution of Political Legitimacy." In *The Sixties: From Memory to History.* Ed. David Farber. Chapel Hill: University of North Carolina Press, 1994.

Conzen, Kathleen Neils, David A. Gerber, Ewa Morawska, George E. Pozzetta, and Rudolph J. Vecoli. "The Invention of Ethnicity: A Perspective from the U.S.A." *Journal of American Ethnic History* 12 (Fall 1992): 3–41.

Cornell, Stephen. *The Return of the Native: American Indian Political Resurgence.* New York: Oxford University Press, 1988.

Cowger, Thomas W. "'The Crossroads of Destiny': The NCAI's Landmark Struggle to Thwart Coercive Termination," *American Indian Culture and Research Journal* 20 (1996): 121–44.

———. *The National Congress of American Indians: The Founding Years.* Lincoln: University of Nebraska Press, 1999.

Danziger, Edmund Jefferson. *The Chippewas of Lake Superior.* Norman: University of Oklahoma Press, 1979.

———. *Survival and Regeneration: Detroit's American Indian Community.* Detroit: Wayne State University Press, 1991.

Deloria, Philip J. *Playing Indian: Making American Identities from the Boston Tea Party to the New Age.* New Haven: Yale University Press, 1998.

Deloria, Vine, Jr. "Identity and Culture." *Daedalus* 110 (1982): 13–28.

———. "The Twentieth Century." In *Red Men and Hat Wearers: Viewpoints in Indian History.* Ed. Daniel Tyler. Boulder: Pruett Publishing, 1976.

Dennehy, William J. "John Ralph Nichols (1949–50)." In *The Commissioners of Indian Affairs, 1824–1977,* 289–92. Lincoln: University of Nebraska Press, 1979.

Diner, Hasia R. *Erin's Daughters in America: Irish Immigrant Women in the Nineteenth Century.* Baltimore: Johns Hopkins University Press, 1983.

Dosman, Edgar J. *Indians: The Urban Dilemma.* Toronto: McClelland and Stewart, 1972.

Drake, St. Clair, and Horace R. Cayton. *Black Metropolis: A Study of Negro Life in a Northern City.* New York: Harcourt, Brace and Company, 1945.

Edmunds, R. David. "On Being Indian: Cultural Change in Historical Perspective." Unpublished paper in author's possession.

———. "Native Americans, New Voices: American Indian History, 1895–1995." *American Historical Review* 100 (June 1995): 717–40.

Fey, Harold E., and D'Arcy McNickle. *Indians and Other Americans.* New York: Harper and Brothers Publishers, 1959.

Findlay, James F. *Church People in the Struggle: The National Council of Churches and the Black Freedom Movement, 1950–1970.* New York: Oxford University Press, 1993.

Fixico, Donald L. *Termination and Relocation: Federal Indian Policy, 1945–1960.* Albuquerque: University of New Mexico Press, 1986.

———. *The Urban Indian Experience in America.* Albuquerque: University of New Mexico Press, 2000.

———. *Urban Indians.* New York: Chelsea House, 1991.

Forbes, Jack D., ed. *The Indian in America's Past.* Englewood Cliffs: Prentice-Hall, 1964.

Fowler, Loretta. *Arapahoe Politics, 1851–1978: Symbols in Crises of Authority.* Lincoln: University of Nebraska Press, 1982.

———. *Shared Symbols, Contested Meanings: Gros Ventre Culture and History, 1778–1984.* Ithaca: Cornell University Press, 1987.

Fremon, David K. *Chicago Politics: Ward By Ward.* Bloomington: Indiana University Press, 1988.

Fuchs, Estelle, and Robert J. Havighurst. *To Live on This Earth: American Indian Education.* Garden City: Doubleday, 1972.

Garbarino, Merwyn S. "The Chicago Amerian Indian Center: Two Decades." In *American Indian Urbanization.* Ed. Jack O. Waddell and O. Michael Watson. West Lafayette: Institute for the Study of Social Change, 1973.

———. "Indians in Chicago." In *Urban Indians: Proceedings of the Third Annual Conference on Problems and Issues Concerning American Indians Today.* Chicago: The Newberry Library, 1981.

———. "Life in the City: Chicago." In *The American Indian in Urban Society.* Ed. Jack O. Waddell and O. Michael Watson. Boston: Little, Brown, 1971.

Garcia, Anthony M. "'Home' Is Not a House: Urban Relocation among American Indians." Ph.D. diss., University of California at Berkeley, 1988.

Gitlin, Todd, and Nanci Hollander. *Uptown: Poor Whites in Chicago.* New York: Harper and Row, 1970.

Goodner, James. *Indian Americans in Dallas: Migrations, Missions and Style of Adaptation.* Minneapolis: Training Center for Community Programs, University of Minnesota, 1969.

Gouveia, Grace Mary. "'Uncle Sam's Priceless Daughters': American Indian Women during the Depression, World War II, and Post-War Era." Ph.D. diss., Purdue University, 1994.

———. "'We Also Serve': American Indian Women's Role in World War II." *Michigan Historical Review* 20 (Fall 1994): 153–82.

Graves, Theodore D., and Minor VanArsdale. "Values, Expectations and Relocation: The Navaho Migrant in Denver." *Human Organization* 25 (Winter 1966): 300–307.

Green, Michael D. *The Politics of Indian Removal: Creek Government and Society in Crisis.* Lincoln: University of Nebraska Press, 1982.

Gregory, James N. *American Exodus: The Dust Bowl Migration and Okie Culture in California.* New York: Oxford University Press, 1989.

Griffen, Joyce. "'Life Is Harder Here': The Case of the Urban Navajo Woman." *American Indian Quarterly* 6 (1982): 90–104.

Griffith, Robert. "Dwight D. Eisenhower and the Corporate Commonwealth." *American Historical Review* 87 (Feb. 1982): 87–122.

Grossman, James R. *Land of Hope: Chicago, Black Southerners and the Great Migration.* Chicago: University of Chicago Press, 1989.

Guillemin, Jeanne E. *Urban Renegades: The Cultural Strategy of American Indians.* New York: Columbia University Press, 1975.

Gundlach, James H., and Alden E. Roberts. "Native American Indian Migration and Relocation: Success or Failure." *Pacific Sociological Review* 21 (Jan. 1978): 117–28.

Gutman, Herbert G. *Work, Culture, and Society in Industrializing America: Essays in American Working-Class and Social History.* New York: Knopf, 1976.

Hagan, William T. "Full Blood, Mixed Blood, Generic, and Ersatz." *Arizona and the West* 27 (Winter 1985): 309–26.

Harkins, Arthur M., and Richard G. Woods. *Attitudes and Characteristics of Selected Wisconsin Indians.* Minneapolis: Training Center for Community Programs, University of Minnesota, 1969.

Harvey, Gretchen G. "Cherokee and American: Ruth Muskrat Bronson, 1897–1982." Ph.D. diss., Arizona State University, 1996.

Hasse, Larry J. "Termination and Assimilation: Federal Indian Policy, 1943 to 1961." Ph.D. diss., Washington State University, 1974.

Hauptman, Laurence M. *The Iroquois Struggle for Survival: World War II to Red Power.* Syracuse: Syracuse University Press, 1986.

———, and Jack Campisi. "The Voice of Eastern Indians: The American Indian Chicago Conference of 1961 and the Movement for Federal Recognition." *Proceedings of the American Philosophical Society* 132 (Dec. 1988): 316–29.

Hirabayashi, James, William Willard, and Luis Kemnitzer. "Pan-Indianism in the Urban Setting." In *The Anthropology of Urban Environments: Monograph Series No. 11.* Ed. Thomas Weaver and Douglas White. Washington, D.C.: Society for Applied Anthropology, 1972.

Hirsch, Arnold R. *Making the Second Ghetto: Race and Housing in Chicago, 1940–1960.* New York: Cambridge University Press, 1983.

Hodge, William H. *The Albuquerque Navajos.* Tucson: University of Arizona Press, 1969.

Hoikkala, Päivi. "Feminists or Reformers? American Indian Women and Community in Phoenix, 1965–1980." In *American Indians and the Urban Experience.* Ed. Susan Lobo and Kurt Peters. Lanham: Rowman and Littlefield, 2000.

Holli, Melvin G. and Peter d'A. Jones, eds. *The Ethnic Frontier: Essays in the History of Group Survival in Chicago and the Midwest.* Grand Rapids: Eerdmans, 1977.

Holm, Tom. "Fighting a White Man's War: The Extent and Legacy of American Indian Participation in World War II." *Journal of Ethnic Studies* 9 (Summer 1981): 69–81.

———. *Strong Hearts, Wounded Souls: The Native American Veterans of the Vietnam War.* Austin: University of Texas Press, 1996.

Hoover, Herbert T. "Yankton Sioux Experience in the 'Great Indian Depression,' 1900–1930." In *The American West: Essays in Honor of W. Eugene Hollon.* Ed. Ronald Lora. Toledo: University of Toledo, 1980.

Hosmer, Brian C. *American Indians in the Marketplace: Persistence and Innovation Among the Menominees and Metlakatlans, 1870–1920.* Lawrence: University Press of Kansas, 1999.

Hoxie, Frederick E. *A Final Promise: The Campaign to Assimilate the Indians, 1880–1920.* Lincoln: University of Nebraska Press, 1984.

―――. "From Prison to Homeland: The Cheyenne River Indian Reservation before World War I." *South Dakota History* 9 (Winter 1979): 1–24.

―――. *Parading through History: The Making of the Crow Nation in America, 1805–1935.* New York: Cambridge University Press, 1995.

―――, Richard A. Sattler, and Nancy Shoemaker. *Reports of the American Indian Family History Project.* Chicago: The Newberry Library, 1992.

Indians of All Tribes. "We Must Hold on to the Old Ways." In *Red Power: The American Indians' Fight for Freedom.* Ed. Alvin M. Josephy, Jr. New York: McGraw-Hill, 1971.

Iverson, Peter. "Building toward Self-Determination: Plains and Southwestern Indians in the 1940s and 1950s." *Western Historical Quarterly* 16 (Apr. 1985): 163–73.

―――. *Carlos Montezuma and the Changing World of American Indians.* Albuquerque: University of New Mexico Press, 1982.

―――. *"We Are Still Here": American Indians in the Twentieth Century.* Arlington Heights: Harlan Davidson, 1998.

―――. *When Indians Became Cowboys: Native Peoples and Cattle Ranching in the American West.* Norman: University of Oklahoma Press, 1994.

Jennings, Francis. *The Founders of America: How Indians Discovered the Land, Pioneered in It, and Created Great Classical Civilizations; How They Were Plunged into a Dark Age by Invasion and Conquest; and How They Are Reviving.* New York: Norton, 1993.

Johnson, Troy R. *The Occupation of Alcatraz Island: Indian Self-Determination and the Rise of Indian Activism.* Urbana: University of Illinois Press, 1996.

―――. "Roots of Contemporary Native American Activism." *American Indian Culture and Research Journal* 20, no. 2 (1996): 127–54.

―――, Joane Nagel, and Duane Champagne, eds. *American Indian Activism: Alcatraz to the Longest Walk.* Urbana: University of Illinois Press, 1997.

Jorgensen, Joseph G. "Indians and the Metropolis." In *The American Indian in Urban Society.* Ed. Jack O. Waddell and O. Michael Watson. Boston: Little, Brown, 1971.

Josephy, Alvin M., Jr. *Now That the Buffalo's Gone: A Study of Today's American Indians.* New York: Knopf, 1982.

―――, ed. *Red Power: The American Indians' Fight for Freedom.* New York: McGraw-Hill, 1971.

Kazal, Russell A. "Revisiting Assimilation: The Rise, Fall, and Reappraisal of a Concept in American Ethnic History." *American Historical Review* 100 (Apr. 1995): 437–71.

Keil, Hartmut, and John B. Jentz, eds. *German Workers in Industrial Chicago, 1850–1910: A Comparative Perspective.* DeKalb: Northern Illinois University Press, 1983.

Kelly, William H. "The Economic Basis of Indian Life." *Annals of the American Academy of Political and Social Sciences* 311 (May 1957): 71–79.

Koppes, Clayton R. "From New Deal to Termination: Liberalism and Indian Policy, 1933–1953." *Pacific Historical Review* 46 (Nov. 1977): 543–66.

Kvasnicka, Robert M., and Herbert J. Viola, eds. *The Commissioners of Indian Affairs, 1824–1977.* Lincoln: University of Nebraska Press, 1979.

LaGrand, James B. "Whose Voices Count? Oral Sources and Twentieth-Century

American Indian History." *American Indian Culture and Research Journal* 21 (Winter 1997): 73–105.

LaPier, Rosalyn R. "'We Are Not Savages, but a Civilized Race': American Indian Activism and the Development of Chicago's First American Indian Organizations, 1919–1934." M.A. thesis, DePaul University, 2000.

Laxson, Joan Dorothy. "Aspects of Acculturation among American Indians: Emphasis on Contemporary Pan-Indianism." Ph.D. diss., University of California, Berkeley, 1972.

Lazewski, Tony. "American Indian Migrant Spatial Behavior as an Indicator of Adjustment in Chicago." In *Geographical Perspectives on Native Americans: Topics and Resources.* Ed. Jerry N. McDonald and Tony Lazewski. Washington, D.C.: Association of American Geographers, 1976.

———. "American Indian Migration to and within Chicago, Illinois." Ph.D. diss., University of Illinois at Urbana-Champaign, 1976.

Lemann, Nicholas. *The Promised Land: The Great Black Migration and How It Changed America.* New York: Knopf, 1991.

Leveen, Deborah Browning. "Hustlers and Heroes: Portrait and Analysis of the Chicago Indian Village." Ph.D. diss., University of Chicago, 1978.

Levine, Stuart, and Nancy O. Lurie, eds. *The American Indian Today.* Deland: Everett, 1968.

Liebow, Edward D. "Urban Indian Institutions in Phoenix: Transformation from Headquarters City to Community." *Journal of Ethnic Studies* 18 (Winter 1991): 1–27.

Littlefield, Alice, and Martha C. Knack, eds. *Native Americans and Wage Labor: Ethnohistorical Perspectives.* Norman: University of Oklahoma Press, 1996.

Lobo, Susan. "Is Urban a Person or a Place? Characteristics of Urban Indian Country." In *American Indians and the Urban Experience.* Ed. Susan Lobo and Kurt Peters. Lanham: Rowman and Littlefield, 2000.

———, and Kurt Peters, eds. *American Indians and the Urban Experience.* Lanham: Rowman and Littlefield, 2000.

Loew, Patty. "The Back of the Homefront: Black and American Indian Women in Wisconsin during World War II," *Wisconsin Magazine of History* 82 (Winter 1998–99): 83–103.

Lomawaima, K. Tsianina. *They Called It Prairie Light: The Story of Chilocco Indian School.* Lincoln: University of Nebraska Press, 1994.

Lovoll, Odd S. *A Century of Urban Life: The Norwegians in Chicago before 1930.* Chicago: The Norwegian-American Historical Association, 1988.

Lurie, Nancy O. "The Voice of the American Indian: Report on the American Indian Chicago Conference." *Current Anthropology* 2 (Dec. 1961): 478–500.

———. "Winnebago." In *Handbook of North American Indians,* vol. 15: *Northeast.* Ed. Bruce G. Trigger. Washington, D.C.: Smithsonian Institution Press, 1978.

———. *Wisconsin Indians.* 2d ed. Madison: State Historical Society of Wisconsin, 1980.

Lyman, Stanley David, Floyd A. O'Neil, June K. Lyman, and Susan McKay. *Wounded Knee 1973: A Personal Account.* Lincoln: University of Nebraska Press, 1991.

MacKay, Kathryn L. "Warrior into Welder: A History of Federal Employment Programs for American Indians, 1878–1972." Ph.D. diss., University of Utah, 1987.

Marozas, Bryan. *Demographic Profile of Chicago's American Indian Community*. Chicago: NAES College Press, 1984.

Martin, Harry W. "Correlates of Adjustment among American Indians in an Urban Environment." *Human Organization* 23 (Winter 1964): 290–95.

Mattern, Mark. "The Powwow as a Public Arena for Negotiating Unity and Diversity in American Indian Life." *American Indian Culture and Research Journal* 20 (Fall 1996): 183–201.

Matusow, Allen J. *The Unraveling of America: A History of Liberalism in the 1960s*. New York: Harper and Row, 1984.

Mayer, Harold M., Richard C. Wade, and Glen E. Holt. *Chicago: Growth of a Metropolis*. Chicago: University of Chicago Press, 1969.

McCaffrey, Lawrence. *The Irish in Chicago*. Urbana: University of Illinois Press, 1987.

McDonnell, Janet A. *The Dispossession of the American Indian, 1887–1934*. Bloomington: Indiana University Press, 1991.

Means, Russell, and Marvin J. Wolf. *Where White Men Fear to Tread: The Autobiography of Russell Means*. New York: St. Martin's Press, 1995.

Metcalf, Ann. "Navajo Women in the City: Lessons from a Quarter Century of Relocation." *American Indian Quarterly* 6 (Spring–Summer 1982): 71–89.

Metcalf, R. Warren. "Arthur V. Watkins and the Indians of Utah: A Study of Federal Termination Policy." Ph.D. diss., Arizona State University, 1995.

Metzger, Lynn Rodeman. "Cleveland American Indian Center: Urban Survival and Adaptation." Ph.D. diss., Case Western Reserve University, 1989.

Meyer, Melissa L. "'We Can Not Get a Living as We Used To': Dispossession and the White Earth Anishinaabeg, 1889–1920." *American Historical Review* 96 (Apr. 1991): 368–94.

———. *The White Earth Tragedy: Ethnicity and Dispossession at a Minnesota Anishinaabeg Reservation, 1889–1920*. Lincoln: University of Nebraska Press, 1994.

Miles, George. "To Hear an Old Voice: Rediscovering Native Americans in American History." In *Under an Open Sky: Rethinking America's Western Past*. Ed. William Cronon, George Miles, and Jay Gitlin. New York: Norton, 1992.

Miller, Carol. "Native Sons and the Good War: Retelling the Myth of American Indian Assimilation." In *The War in American Culture: Society and Consciousness during World War II*. Ed. Lewis A. Erenberg and Susan E. Hirsch. Chicago: University of Chicago Press, 1996.

Mohl, Raymond A. "Shifting Patterns of American Urban Policy since 1900." In *Urban Policy in Twentieth-Century America*. Ed. Arnold R. Hirsch and Raymond A. Mohl. New Brunswick: Rutgers University Press, 1993.

Momaday, N. Scott. *House Made of Dawn*. New York: Harper and Row, 1968.

Monroe, Mark. *An Indian in White America*. Philadelphia: Temple University Press, 1994.

Mucha, Janusz. "American Indian Success in the Urban Setting." *Urban Anthropology* 13 (Winter 1984): 329–54.

———. "From Prairie to the City: Transformation of Chicago's American Indian Community." *Urban Anthropology* 12 (Fall 1983): 337–71.

NAES Religion and Philosophy Class. 1990. "Narrative Traditions of the Chicago American Indian Community." In *Indians of the Chicago Area*. Ed. Terry Straus. Chicago: NAES College.

Nagel, Joane. *American Indian Ethnic Renewal: Red Power and the Resurgence of Identity and Culture*. New York: Oxford University Press, 1996.

———. "Constructing Ethnicity: Creating and Recreating Ethnic Identity and Culture." *Social Problems* 41 (Feb. 1994): 152–76.

———, and C. Matthew Snipp. "Ethnic Reorganization: American Indian Social, Economic, Political, and Cultural Strategies For Survival." *Ethnic and Racial Studies* 16 (Apr. 1993): 203–35.

Nash, Gerald D. *The American West Transformed: The Impact of the Second World War*. Bloomington: Indiana University Press, 1985.

*Native Americans Information Directory*. Detroit: Gale Research, 1993.

Neils, Elaine M. *Reservation to City: Indian Migration and Federal Relocation*. Chicago: University of Chicago Department of Geography Research Paper no. 131, 1971.

Nelli, Humbert S. *Italians in Chicago, 1880–1930: A Study in Ethnic Mobility*. New York: Oxford University Press, 1970.

Nichols, Roger L. "Something Old, Something New: Indians since World War II." In *The American Indian Experience: A Profile*. Ed. Philip Weeks. Arlington Heights: Forum Press, 1988.

O'Neill, Colleen. "The 'Making' of the Navajo Worker: Navajo Households, the Bureau of Indian Affairs, and Off-Reservation Wage Work, 1948–1960." *New Mexico Historical Review* 74 (Oct. 1999): 375–405.

O'Neill, William L. *American High: The Years of Confidence, 1945–1960*. New York: Free Press, 1986.

Ourada, Patricia K. "Dillon Seymour Myer (1950–53)." In *The Commissioners of Indian Affairs, 1824–1977*. Ed. Robert K. Kvasnicka and Herbert J. Viola. Lincoln: University of Nebraska Press, 1979.

———. "Indians in the Work Force." *Journal of the West* 25 (Apr. 1986): 52–58.

Pacyga, Dominic A. *Polish Immigrants and Industrial Chicago: Workers on the South Side, 1880–1922*. Columbus: Ohio State University Press, 1991.

———, and Ellen Skerrett. *Chicago, City of Neighborhoods: Histories and Tours*. Chicago: Loyola University Press, 1986.

Padilla, Felix M. *Puerto Rican Chicago*. Notre Dame: University of Notre Dame Press, 1987.

Palmer, James O. "A Geographical Investigation of the Effects of the Bureau of Indian Affairs' Employment Assistance Program upon the Relocation of Oklahoma Indians, 1967–1971." Ph.D. diss., University of Oklahoma, 1975.

Parman, Donald L. "The Indian and the Civilian Conservation Corps." *Pacific Historical Review* 40 (Feb. 1971): 39–56.

———. *Indians and the American West in the Twentieth Century*. Bloomington: Indiana University Press, 1994.

———. "Indians of the Modern West." In *The Twentieth-Century West: Historical Interpretations*. Ed. Gerald D. Nash and Richard W. Etulain. Albuquerque: University of New Mexico Press, 1989.

———. "Lewis Meriam's Letters during the Survey of Indian Affairs, 1926–1927 (Part 2)." *Arizona and the West* 24 (Winter 1982): 341–70.

Patrick, Mary. "Indian Urbanization in Dallas: A Second Trail of Tears?" *Oral History Review* (1973): 48–65.

Patterson, James T. *Grand Expectations: The United States, 1945–1974.* New York: Oxford University Press, 1996.

Peroff, Nicholas C. *Menominee Drums: Tribal Termination and Restoration, 1954–1974.* Norman: University of Oklahoma Press, 1982.

Peters, Kurt. "Santa Fe Indian Camp, House 21, Richmond, California: Persistence of Identity among Laguna Pueblo Railroad Laborers, 1945–1982." *American Indian Culture and Research Journal* 19 (Summer 1995): 33–70.

Philp, Kenneth R. "Dillon S. Myer and the Advent of Termination: 1950–1953." *Western Historical Quarterly* 19 (Jan. 1988): 37–59.

———. *John Collier's Crusade for Indian Reform, 1920–1954.* Tucson: University of Arizona Press, 1977.

———. "Stride toward Freedom: The Relocation of Indians to Cities, 1952–1960." *Western Historical Quarterly* 16 (Apr. 1985): 175–90.

———. "Termination: A Legacy of the Indian New Deal." *Western Historical Quarterly* 14 (Apr. 1983): 165–80.

———. *Termination Revisited: American Indians on the Trail to Self-Determination, 1933–1953.* Lincoln: University of Nebraska Press, 1999.

Pommersheim, Frank. *Broken Ground and Flowing Waters: An Introductory Text with Materials on Rosebud Sioux Tribal Government.* Rosebud, S.D.: Sinte Gleska College Press, 1979.

Powers, William K. *War Dance: Plains Indian Musical Performance.* Tucson: University of Arizona Press, 1990.

Price, John A. "The Development of Urban Ethnic Institutions by U.S. and Canadian Indians." *Ethnic Groups* 1 (1976): 107–31.

———. "The Migration and Adaptation of American Indians to Los Angeles." *Human Organization* 27 (Summer 1968): 168–75.

———. "U.S. and Canadian Urban Ethnic Institutions." *Urban Anthropology* 4 (1975): 35–52.

Prucha, Francis Paul. "American Indian Policy in the Twentieth Century." *Western Historical Quarterly* 15 (Jan. 1984): 5–18.

———. *The Great Father: The United States Government and the American Indians.* Lincoln: University of Nebraska Press, 1984.

Rascher, Leonard Phillip. "Urban Indian Attitudes toward Education." Ph.D. diss., Northwestern University, 1977.

Rawls, James J. *Chief Red Fox Is Dead: A History of Native Americans since 1945.* Fort Worth: Harcourt Brace College Publishers, 1996.

Reddy, Marlita A., ed. *Statistical Record of Native North Americans.* Detroit: Gale Research, 1993.

Rhodes, Terrel. "The Urban American Indian." In *A Cultural Geography of North American Indians.* Ed. Thomas E. Ross and Tyrel G. Moore. Boulder: Westview Press, 1987.

Ritzenthaler, Robert E. "Southwestern Chippewa." In *Handbook of North American Indians*, vol. 15: *Northeast.* Ed. Bruce G. Trigger. Washington, D.C.: Smithsonian Institution Press, 1978.

———, and Pat Ritzenthaler. *The Woodland Indians of the Western Great Lakes.* Garden City: Natural History Press, 1970.

Sánchez, George J. *Becoming Mexican American: Ethnicity, Culture and Identity in Chicano Los Angeles, 1900–1945.* New York: Oxford University Press, 1993.

Sanford, Margaret. "Pan-Indianism, Acculturation, and the American Ideal." *Plains Anthropologist* 16 (Aug. 1971): 222–27.

Schlesinger, Arthur M., Jr. *Robert Kennedy and His Times.* Boston: Houghton Mifflin, 1978.

Scott, George D., John Kennardh White, and Estelle Fuchs. *Indians and Their Education in Chicago.* Washington, D.C.: Educational Resources Information Center, 1969.

Shifferd, Patricia A. "A Study in Economic Change: The Chippewa of Northern Wisconsin, 1854–1900." *Western Canadian Journal of Anthropology* 6, no. 4 (1976): 16–41.

Shoemaker, Nancy. *American Indian Population Recovery in the Twentieth Century.* Albuquerque: University of New Mexico Press, 1999.

———. "Urban Indians and Ethnic Choices: American Indian Organizations in Minneapolis, 1920–1950." *Western Historical Quarterly* 19 (Nov. 1988): 431–47.

Silko, Leslie Marmon. *Ceremony.* New York: New American Library, 1977.

Smith, Paul Chatt, and Robert Allen Warrior. *Like a Hurricane: The Indian Movement from Alcatraz to Wounded Knee.* New York: Free Press, 1996.

Sorkin, Alan L. "The Economic and Social Status of the American Indian, 1940–1970." *Journal of Negro Education* 45 (Fall 1976): 433–47.

———. *The Urban American Indian.* Lexington, Mass.: Lexington Books, 1978.

Spear, Allan H. *Black Chicago: The Making of a Negro Ghetto, 1880–1920.* Chicago: University of Chicago Press, 1967.

Spindler, Louise S. "Menominee." In *Handbook of North American Indians,* vol. 15: *Northeast.* Ed. Bruce G. Trigger. Washington, D.C.: Smithsonian Institution Press, 1978.

Stauss, Joseph H., and Bruce A. Chadwick. "Urban Indian Adjustment." *American Indian Culture and Research Journal* 3 (Spring 1979): 23–38.

Steigerwald, David. *The Sixties and the End of Modern America.* New York: St. Martin's Press, 1995.

Steiner, Stan. *The New Indians.* New York: Harper and Row, 1968.

Straus, Terry, ed. *Indians of the Chicago Area.* Chicago: NAES College, 1990.

———, and Grant P. Arndt, eds. *Native Chicago.* Chicago: Native Chicago, 1998.

Stuart, Paul. *Nations within a Nation: Historical Statistics of American Indians.* Westport: Greenwood Press, 1987.

Szasz, Margaret Connell. *Education and the American Indian: The Road to Self-Determination.* Albuquerque: University of New Mexico Press, 1974.

Tax, Sol. "Action Anthropology." *Current Anthropology* 16 (Dec. 1975): 514–17.

———. "The Impact of Urbanization on American Indians." *Annals of the American Academy of Political and Social Sciences* 436 (Mar. 1978): 121–36.

Teaford, Jon C. *The Rough Road to Renaissance: Urban Revitalization in America, 1940–1985.* Baltimore: Johns Hopkins University Press, 1990.

———. *The Twentieth-Century American City.* 2d ed. Baltimore: Johns Hopkins University Press, 1993.

Thornton, Russell. "Patterns and Processes of American Indians in Cities and

Towns: The National Scene." In *Urban Indians: Proceedings of the Third Annual Conference on Problems and Issues Concerning American Indians Today.* Chicago: The Newberry Library, 1981.

———, Gary D. Sandefur, and Harold G. Grasmick. *The Urbanization of American Indians.* Bloomington: Indiana University Press, 1982.

Tischauser, Leslie V. *The Burden of Ethnicity: The German Question in Chicago, 1914–1941.* New York: Garland, 1990.

Tjerandsen, Carl. *Education for Citizenship: A Foundation's Experience.* Santa Cruz: Emil Schwarzhaupt Foundation, 1980.

Trennert, Robert A. "Phoenix and the Indians: 1867–1930." In *Phoenix in the Twentieth Century: Essays in Community History.* Ed. G. Wesley Johnson. Norman: University of Oklahoma Press, 1993.

Tyler, S. Lyman. "William A. Brophy (1945–48)." In *The Commissioners of Indian Affairs, 1824–1977.* Ed. Robert M. Kvasnicka and Herbert J. Viola. Lincoln: University of Nebraska Press, 1979.

Tuttle, William M. *Race Riot: Chicago in the Red Summer of 1919.* New York: Atheneum, 1970.

*Urban Indians: Proceedings of the Third Annual Conference on Problems and Issues Concerning American Indians Today.* Chicago: The Newberry Library, 1981.

Usner, Daniel H., Jr. *Indians, Settlers, and Slave in a Frontier Exchange Economy: The Lower Mississippi Valley before 1783.* Chapel Hill: University of North Carolina Press, 1992.

VandeMark, Dorothy. "The Raid on the Reservations." *Harper's Magazine* 212 (March 1956): 45–55.

Vogel, Virgil J. "Chicago's Native Americans: Cheechakos, Old-Timers and Others in the City of the Wild Garlic." *City: A Journal of the City Colleges of Chicago* (Winter 1986): 44–46.

Waddell, Jack O., and O. Michael Watson, eds. *American Indian Urbanization.* West Lafayette: Institute for the Study of Social Change, Department of Sociology and Anthropology, Purdue University, 1973.

———. *The American Indian in Urban Society.* Boston: Little, Brown, 1971.

Watkins, Arthur V. "Termination of Federal Supervision: The Removal of Restrictions over Indian Property and Person." *Annals of the American Academy of Political and Social Sciences* 311 (May 1957): 47–55.

Weeks, Philip, and Lynn R. Metzger. "American Indians." In *The Encyclopedia of Cleveland History.* Ed. David D. Van Tassel and John J. Grabowski. Bloomington: Indiana University Press, 1996.

Weibel-Orlando, Joan. "And the Drumbeat Still Goes On . . . Urban Indian Institutional Survival into the New Millennium." In *American Indians and the Urban Experience.* Ed. Susan Lobo and Kurt Peters. Lanham: Rowman and Littlefield, 2000.

———. *Indian Country, L.A.: Maintaining Ethnic Community in Complex Society.* Urbana: University of Illinois Press, 1991.

White, John Kennardh. "The American Indian in Chicago: The Hidden People." M.A. thesis, University of Chicago, 1970.

———. *Patterns in American Indian Employment: A Study of the Work Habits of American Indians in Chicago, Illinois.* Chicago: St. Augustine's Center for American Indians, 1971.

White, Lynn C., and Bruce A. Chadwick. "Urban Residence, Assimilation, and Identity of the Spokane Indian." In *Native Americans Today: Sociological Perspectives.* Ed. Howard M. Bahr, Bruce A. Chadwick, and Robert C. Day. New York: Harper and Row, 1972.

White, Richard. *"It's Your Misfortune and None of My Own": A New History of the American West.* Norman: University of Oklahoma Press, 1991.

———. *The Middle Ground: Indians, Empires, and Republics in the Great Lakes Region, 1650–1815.* New York: Cambridge University Press, 1991.

———. *Roots of Dependency: Subsistence, Environment, and Social Change among the Choctaws, Pawnees, and Navajos.* Lincoln: University of Nebraska Press, 1983.

Woods, Richard G., and Arthur M. Harkins. *An Examination of the 1968–1969 Urban Indian Hearings Held by the National Council on Indian Opportunity.* Minneapolis: University of Minnesota, 1971.

———. *Indian Americans in Chicago.* Minneapolis: Training Center for Community Programs, University of Minnesota, 1968.

Wunder, John R. *"Retained by the People": A History of American Indians and the Bill of Rights.* New York: Oxford University Press, 1994.

Wyman, Mark. *Round-Trip to America: The Immigrants Return to Europe, 1880–1930.* Ithaca: Cornell University Press, 1993.

Yans-McLaughlin, Virginia. *Family and Community: Italian Immigrants in Buffalo, 1880–1930.* Ithaca: Cornell University Press, 1971.

Yaseen, David W. "Settlement Patterns of Relocated American Indians." M.A. thesis, University of Chicago, 1962.

Young, Gloria A. "Powwow Power: Perspectives on Historic and Contemporary Intertribalism." Ph.D. diss., Indiana University, 1981.

Zunz, Olivier. *The Changing Face of Inequality: Urbanization, Industrial Development, and Immigrants in Detroit, 1880–1920.* Chicago: University of Chicago Press, 1982.

# INDEX

JAMES B. LAGRAND is an assistant professor of history at Messiah College in Grantham, Pennsylvania.

The University of Illinois Press
is a founding member of the
Association of American University Presses.

---

Composed in 9.5/12.5 Trump Mediaeval
by Celia Shapland
for the University of Illinois Press
Manufactured by Thomson-Shore, Inc.

University of Illinois Press
1325 South Oak Street
Champaign, IL 61820-6903
www.press.uillinois.edu